Marketing Engineering

Marketing Engineering

Computer-Assisted Marketing Analysis and Planning

Gary L. Lilien
The Pennsylvania State University

Arvind Rangaswamy
The Pennsylvania State University

Joel Steckel, Series Editor
New York University

Co-sponsored by

ISBM

**Institute for
the Study of
Business Markets**

 **ADDISON-WESLEY**

An imprint of Addison Wesley Longman, Inc.

Reading, Massachusetts • Menlo Park, California • New York • Harlow, England
Don Mills, Ontario • Sydney • Mexico City • Madrid • Amsterdam

Acquisitions Editor: Michael Roche
Production Supervisor: Lou Bruno
Project Coordination: Electronic Publishing Services Inc., NYC
Text Designer: Electronic Publishing Services Inc., NYC
Compositor: Electronic Publishing Services Inc., NYC
Cover Designer: Regina Hagen

For permission to use copyrighted material, grateful acknowledgment is made to the copyright holders in source notes throughout the text, which are hereby made part of this copyright page.

Library of Congress Cataloging-in-Publication Data

Lilien, Gary L., 1946—
    Marketing engineering : computer-assisted marketing analysis and planning / Gary L. Lilien,
Arvind Rangaswamy.
       p.   cm.
    Includes bibliographical references and index.
    ISBN 0-321-00194-X (pbk.)
      1. Marketing—Data processing. 2. Marketing—Decision making—Mathematical models.
    3. Marketing—Decision making—Data processing. I. Rangaswamy, Arvind. II. Title.
    HF5415.125.L54   1997
    658.8'02'0285—dc21
                                                    97-21787
                                                   CIP

ISBN 0-321-00194-X
12345678910—CRW—0100999897

To my love and best friend,
Dorothy, for sharing her time
with one more book.

—Gary

To Ann for her love and support,
and Cara for providing the
needed distraction.

—Arvind

Contents

Preface

Several forces are transforming the structure and content of the marketing manager's job. As a profession, marketing is evolving. It is no longer based primarily on conceptual content. Marketing resembles design engineering—it consists of putting together data, models, analyses, and computer simulations to design effective marketing plans. While many view traditional marketing as art and some view it as science, the new marketing increasingly looks like engineering (that is, combining art and science to solve specific problems). Our purpose in writing this book is to help educate and train a new generation of marketing managers.

Several key forces are changing the marketer's job:

Pervasive high-powered personal computers on networks: During the 1980s marketing managers used personal computers mainly for such tasks as composing letters and presentations and doing simple spreadsheet analyses. Today many marketing managers have the equivalent of an early 1980s supercomputer on their desks. And that computer is networked to other PCs and to the company's mainframe on a local area network (LAN), and to external computers and databases all over the world through wide area networks (WANs). This means that a marketing manager can access current data, reports, and expert opinions, and he or she can also combine and process that information in new ways to enhance decision making. Today basing decisions on such information is a minimum requirement to be a player in many industries.

Exploding volumes of data: A brand manager in the packaged goods industry now sees perhaps a thousand times the volume of data (more frequently collected in finer detail) he or she saw five years ago. The growth of database marketing and direct marketing parallels data explosions in other industries as well. The human brain, however, has not become comparably more powerful in the same period. More data cannot lead to better decision making unless managers learn how to use that data in meaningful ways.

Reengineering marketing activities: All over the world organizations face increasingly well-informed customers who seek value. As a result they are carefully scrutinizing the productivity of all management processes. To reduce their costs and to improve productivity, they are reengineering many marketing functions, processes, and activities. They are reengineering such activities as segmentation and targeting, new product development, market measurement and analysis, and customer satisfaction management for the information age.

Flatter, right-sized organizations: Organizations could respond effectively to the afore-mentioned trends using traditional organizational mechanisms if they trained an army of specialists to harness computer hardware, software, networks, and data. They do not have that luxury. Global competition is driving organizations everywhere to do more with fewer employees. Managers are finding themselves empowered (i.e., without support staff): they have the hardware, software, and data at their desks and are expected to use them, operating independently.

Marketing managers must learn to function in the rapidly changing environment and to exploit evolving trends. Firms and business schools can help marketing managers to cope in two ways. They can offer traditional, concept-based education and training, with the hope that good people will figure out on their own how to cope with the changing environment. The education-as-usual approach will always have some success—well-motivated and intelligent marketers will figure out how to get reasonable value from the new resources. This approach is analogous to lecturing golf novices on the rules and giving them golf clubs and self-training books. Through study, networking, and observing successful golfers, some novices will become pretty good golfers. Others will become duffers. Still others will quit the game because it seems too hard. The lack of formal training limits development.

Those who want to excel need lessons, especially early on. Hence another way to help marketing managers respond to the changes is to provide information-age-specific education and training. There will always be a role for marketing concepts, and using the powerful information tools now available requires sound conceptual grounding. But marketers need much more than concepts to fully exploit the resources available to them. They need to move from conceptual marketing to marketing engineering: *using computer decision models in making marketing decisions.* In this book we integrate concepts, analytic marketing techniques, and operational software to train the new generation of marketers, helping them to become marketing engineers.

OBJECTIVES FOR THE STUDENT

We designed this book for you, the business school student or marketing manager who seeks the education you need to perform effectively in information-technology-intensive environments. Most traditional books focus on marketing from conceptual, empirical, or qualitative perspectives. With this book we aim to train marketing engineers to translate concepts into context-specific operational decisions and actions using analytical, quantitative, and computer modeling techniques. We link theory to practice and practice to theory.

Our specific objectives for the book are

- To help you understand how analytical techniques and computer models can enhance decision making by converting data and information into insights and decisions
- To help you learn to view marketing phenomena and processes in ways that are amenable to decision modeling
- To expose you to a number of examples of the successful use of marketing engineering
- To provide you with a software toolkit that will enable you to apply marketing engineering to real marketing decision problems

Our pedagogic philosophy embraces two main principles: *learning by doing and end-user modeling.* Each concept we describe has a software implementation and at least one problem or case you can resolve by using the software. You may make errors and struggle at times, attempting to apply the tools. That is part of the learning-by-doing process; you will learn what the tools and software can do as well as what they cannot do. Traditional methods of teaching in business schools (i.e., lectures and case analyses) do not go far enough in helping students to make decisions, assess risks, and solve problems. The learning-by-doing approach extends traditional marketing education. With model-based tools for decision making, you can learn to anticipate and deal with the potential consequences of your decisions—this will help you improve your strategic thinking, sensitize you to customer needs, and force you to anticipate competitive moves.

Decision models range from large-scale, enterprise-wide applications to those that can be quickly put together by an individual with an understanding of basic marketing and marketing engineering. We emphasize end-user modeling here. End-user modeling has the characteristics of good engineering: do as good a job as you can with the time and resources you have available.

Good end-user modeling provides direct benefits, permits rapid prototyping for more elaborate approaches, and makes the user a better customer (and critic) of larger, enterprise-wide applications. We are not trying to train you to be a technical specialist. Rather we hope to prepare you to put together technically simple but operationally useful decision models and to become astute users of those models and of the results of models that others have developed.

ORGANIZATION

The book has two volumes. We have organized volume 1 as follows:

In Part 1 (Chapters 1 and 2) we introduce and define marketing engineering and develop key marketing engineering building blocks—market response models.

In Part 2 (Chapters 3 through 6) we focus on strategic marketing issues such as segmentation, targeting, positioning, market selection, portfolio analysis, market measurement, and strategic planning.

In Part 3 (Chapters 7 through 10) we address tactical marketing issues such as product design, advertising and communications, salesforce deployment, outlet location, and price and promotion decisions.

In Part 4 (Chapter 11) we conclude, summarizing some key points and highlighting new developments that are driving the future of marketing engineering.

Volume 2 of the book contains software tutorials (step-by-step instructions on how to use the software) for the many software packages that accompany the book and the cases and problem sets that are keyed to each of the concepts. The organization of volume 2 parallels that of volume 1.

In addition, instructors who adopt the book receive videotapes that highlight award-winning marketing engineering applications and the impact that those applications have had at the following firms:

- ABB Electric (the profitable use of choice-based segmentation)
- Marriott Hotels (the use of conjoint analysis to design the Courtyard by Marriott hotel)
- ASSESSOR (the use of the ASSESSOR pretest market model and procedure at hundreds of firms)

- AT&T (the use of systematic copy testing to develop AT&T's cost-of-visit advertising campaign)
- Syntex Labs (the use of judgmental response functions to size and allocate a salesforce)
- American Airlines (the use of a yield management system to increase profits)

USES OF THE BOOK FOR INSTRUCTORS

We designed this book primarily as a text for a one-semester, capstone MBA course. Students need not have strong backgrounds in quantitative methods; however, they will find some quantitative and marketing background and some facility with microcomputers and related (Windows-based) software helpful. We have used the material successfully in executive programs and in undergraduate classes as well.

As there are more than 25 software modules (each with a different focus), the book includes twice as much material as can be covered in a normal one-semester course. The software and related problems should be viewed as a menu; students need not use all the software to gain benefit from the material. Indeed we find that students can readily absorb only 6 to 10 modules in a semester. For shorter courses and executive programs you should make a much more limited selection.

Many of the software modules are intended for general use (i.e., not just for the problem set provided); they can be used for term projects that can provide a very valuable learning experience.

The software empowers students to solve marketing problems. We find that classes work best when we keep lectures to a minimum and have one or two student groups present their problem analyses to the rest of the class, which acts as (skeptical) management. This follows the learning-by-doing philosophy and makes students responsible for their own learning. It also simulates how marketing engineering works in the real world.

While we think the book is a useful text, students should understand that they will really learn marketing engineering concepts only by using the software to do the problems and cases.

ACKNOWLEDGMENTS

This book includes a text, software modules, tutorials, help files, problem sets, cases, and supplementary material. The book was a large undertaking and could not have been accomplished without the support of many people and institutions.

We gratefully acknowledge the support of the companies that sponsor Penn State's Institute for the Study of Business Markets (the book's copublisher), whose contributions helped us to create the book. The vision of Anne Smith and Michael Roche at Addison Wesley and the series editor, Joel Steckel of NYU, helped us to turn our ideas into reality.

Marketing engineering is built on the intellectual contributions of a number of people. In particular we owe an intellectual debt to Robert Blattberg, Philip Kotler, and Andris Zoltners at Northwestern University, John Hauser, John Little, and Glen Urban at MIT, Paul Green, Leonard Lodish, and Jerry Wind at the University of Pennsylvania, Frank Bass at the University of Texas, Dallas, Seenu Srinivasan at Stanford, Robert Buzzell at George Mason University, Dennis Gensch at the University of Wisconsin, Milwaukee, and Alvin Silk at Harvard, whose pioneering ideas made this book possible.

A number of our colleagues provided suggestions and comments on earlier versions of the book and the software (dedicated beta-testers!), including Raymond Burke, Michel Claessens, Chris Dubelaar, Jehoshua Eliashberg, James Hess, John Little, and Vijay Mahajan. Students in several MBA classes at Penn State and the Australian Graduate School of Management and executive programs provided many useful suggestions as well.

While we wrote portions of the software, we were involved more in the design and testing than in the actual implementation of most of the codes. Software implementation was ably executed by Philippe Bertrand, Louis Jia, Animesh Karna, Jean-Francois Latour, John Lin, Katrin Starke, Andrew "Nuke" Stollak, Selva Vaidiyanathan, and Jianan Wu. These folks cheerfully put in untold hours under challenging circumstances. In addition, Vaman Kudpi Shenoy provided source code that he developed for his doctoral dissertation at Northwestern University. They are the original members of the Association of Marketing Engineers!

A number of our students (in addition to those above) provided very valuable support, including Lakshmi Anand, Steven Bellman, James Dietrich, Eric Hoffman, Bruce Semisch, and Inge van de Ven.

Katrin Starke put in uncounted hours piecing together volume two in a cell (also known as the "computer room") at the ISBM. We are pleased she did not charge us by the hour.

Mary Haight, our editor, eliminated as much jargon as we would allow and transformed the book from the passive to the active voice. What clumsy prose remains is here in spite of her efforts. She also designed and oversaw the execution of volume 2.

Our copy editor, Andrew Schwartz, not only cleaned up the manuscript, but pointed out errors in our math and explanations. We hereby grant him an honorary degree in Marketing Engineering.

The production of the manuscript was made possible by administrative support from Vickie Schlegel and Fiona Reay, and Steve Dahm produced the artwork.

Finally, we offer special thanks to Mary Wyckoff who supported and managed the whole process for us. She put in countless hours, always met our unreasonable deadlines, and did so with good humor that we did not deserve but gratefully accept and acknowledge.

This book is a highly collaborative work where our efforts are intertwined throughout. Our partnership continues to strengthen as we learn from each other and capitalize on our complementarities. We now know why this exhausting enterprise has not only been worthwhile but very enjoyable as well.

Part I: The Basics

CHAPTER **1**

Introduction

In this chapter, we

- Define marketing engineering
- Identify the trends that make it important to learn about the emerging field of marketing engineering
- Indicate how marketing engineering facilitates decision making
- Highlight the benefits and challenges associated with the marketing engineering approach to decision making
- Summarize the philosophy and structure of the book
- Introduce the software provided with this book to support the marketing engineering concept

MARKETING ENGINEERING: FROM MENTAL MODELS TO DECISION MODELS

Marketing and marketing management

Marketing is pervasive in market economies around the world. Many people associate marketing with its most manifest characteristics, namely, advertising and retailing, which represent only a small part of the functions and processes that make up marketing. Formally marketing is a *societal* and *managerial process* by which *exchanges* are brought about in an economy to satisfy the *needs and wants* of *individuals* and *organizations*. At the core of a market economy are the millions of voluntary exchanges that take place daily between consenting parties. An exchange occurs if two or more parties come together, each having something of value to offer to the other(s). We all engage in a number of exchanges every day. Whenever you go to a grocery store, make an airline reservation, order a book from a mail order company, visit a hairdresser, bid in an auction, or send out a résumé, you are participating in this exchange process.

In modern economies, both buyers and sellers take steps to initiate desirable exchanges and exchange relationships in the marketplace. Marketing facilitates this exchange process and can be viewed as a management philosophy with associated processes and activities that enable individuals and firms to proactively bring about desirable exchanges. As an example, let us consider how marketing management facilitates exchanges between a firm, Conglomerate, Inc., and its customers: Conglomerate uses marketing insights and techniques to choose who to sell to (to target a segment of the market), to design its physical product offerings, to set prices, to position its products relative to those of competitors, and to develop support services and the distribution mechanisms it needs to deliver its products to customers. The firm's goal is to maximize its returns, while at the same time providing value to customers through the exchange process. To effect the matching and exchange process, Conglomerate has to make targeted customers aware of its products (through advertising, promotion, and personal selling) and to ensure that its offerings provide more value than those of its competitors in the eyes of its current and potential customers. This entire marketing process is founded on an intimate knowledge of what customers value, what they know about Conglomerate's (and competitive) offerings, and the process those customers go through in gathering information and effecting exchange (e.g., visiting the store, ordering by phone, or through personal negotiation).

At the heart of marketing management is the ability to understand customers and markets and to translate this understanding into decisions and actions that produce desirable exchanges in the marketplace. While marketing management begins and ends with customers, it serves the goals of the marketer.

Marketing engineering

Marketing managers must make ongoing decisions about product features, prices, distribution options, sales compensation plans, and so forth. In making these decisions, managers choose from among alternative courses of action in a complex, uncertain world. Like all decisions involving people, marketing decision making involves judgment calls. A typical approach to systematic decision making is to develop a mental model of the decision situation that combines known facts with intuition, reasoning, and experience. For example, in deciding how much to spend on advertising, managers can use different approaches:

> *Rely on experience*: Marketing managers often say that experience is the best teacher. By trying different advertising programs over the course of their careers, managers develop mental models of the levels of advertising that are appropriate under different conditions. To set the advertising budget, they may rely on this mental model or they may tap into the experience and wisdom (mental models) of colleagues and consultants.

> *Use practice standards*: Companies that are successful often codify their decisions as practice standards, or rules of thumb. These are essentially the collective mental models for the organization. Typically these rules are in the form of ratios (e.g., "advertising expenses to sales ratio should be 0.05" or "30 percent of our advertising should be used for new products"). Using practice standards, managers might set the advertising budget as a fixed percentage of projected sales for the current year.

In many cases such mental models may be all that managers need to feel psychologically comfortable with their decisions. Yet mental models are prone to systematic errors. No one can deny the value of experience. But experience is unique to every person, and there is no objective way to choose between the best judgment based only on the experience of Mary versus Tom. Experience can also be confounded with a responsibility bias: sales managers might choose lower advertising budgets in favor of higher expenditures on personal selling, whereas advertising managers might prefer larger advertising budgets.

The use of practice standards can also lead to critical errors: they may be good on the average, but they ignore idiosyncratic elements of a decision context. Suppose that a new competitor enters the market with an aggressive advertising program, which results in a decrease in the firm's sales. A fixed advertising-to-sales ratio would then prescribe a *decrease* in advertising, while other reasonable mental models would suggest some form of retaliation based on increased advertising. Rarely do practice standards provide the flexibility to act in changing marketing environments, where sound decisions are in fact most needed.

As an alternative approach to deciding advertising expenditures, managers might choose to build a spreadsheet decision model of how the market would respond to various expenditure levels. They could then use this model to explore the sales and profit consequences of alternative expenditure levels before making a decision.

This book is about the use of decision models for making marketing decisions. We use the term *marketing engineering* (ME) to refer to this approach. In contrast, relying solely on mental models may be referred to as *conceptual marketing*. Marketing engineering is not a substitute for conceptual marketing; rather, ME complements it, with the combination being greater than the sum of its parts.

To illustrate the marketing engineering approach and its potential value, we summarize below some real-world examples that we expand on in later chapters. The book includes software implementations of simple versions of these models.

ABB Electric, a manufacturer and distributor of power generation equipment, wanted to increase its sales and market share in an industry that was facing a projected 50 percent drop in demand. By carefully analyzing and tracking customer preferences and actions, it determined which customers to focus its marketing efforts on and what features of its products were most important to those customers. Its managers used a marketing engineering tool called *choice modeling* to provide ongoing support for their segmentation and targeting decisions. The firm credits its modeling effort as being a major factor in its successful performance in a declining market.

Marriott Corporation was running out of good downtown locations for new full-service hotels. To maintain its growth, Marriott's management planned to locate hotels outside the downtown area that would appeal to both business travelers and weekend leisure travelers. The company designed and developed the highly successful Courtyard by Marriott chain using a marketing engineering tool called *conjoint analysis*.

American Airlines faces the ongoing problem of deciding what prices to charge for its various classes of service on its numerous routes and determining how many seats on each scheduled flight to allocate to each class of service. Too many seats sold at discount prices, overselling seats on a flight, or allowing too many seats to go empty leads to low revenues. Maximizing revenue in a competitive environment is crucial to the successful operation of the firm. It uses a marketing engineering tool called *yield management* to fill its planes with the right mix of passengers paying different fares.

Syntex Laboratories was concerned about the productivity of its salesforce. In particular, managers were unsure whether the size of the salesforce was right for the job it had to do and whether the firm was allocating its salesforce effort to the most profitable products and market segments. The company used a resource sizing and allocation tool that we call *Syngen* to evaluate the current performance of its salesforce and to develop salesforce deployment strategies that were in line with its long-term growth plans.

Johnson's Wax and many other firms in the packaged goods industry try to predict the likely success of their new products in a cost-effective manner and to use this information to decide how best to proceed in developing a new product. Traditionally these firms relied on test marketing to get a reading on the likely success of the new product. However, test marketing is expensive, and it is also transparent to competitors.

The company realized dramatic cost reductions in its new product testing program without harming decision effectiveness by implementing a marketing engineering tool called ASSESSOR, a pre-test market measurement and modeling system.

Exhibit 1.1 is an overview of the marketing engineering approach to decision making—using a computer model to help transform objective and subjective data about the marketing environment into insights, decisions, and implementation of decisions.

Data are facts, beliefs, or observations used in making decisions. Thus numbers representing dollar sales in the previous month in various sales territories are data. So is the belief that the brand name Coke evokes a positive emotion, or the observation that a competitor has introduced a new product. A common misconception is that decision models require objective data. This is not the case. As we will show with several models in this book, the marketing engineering approach is useful even when one uses only beliefs (subjective data) as inputs to models.

Information refers to summarized or categorized data. For example, the average or the standard deviation of sales across all territories or the classification of sales as low or high constitutes information.

Insights provide meaning to the data or information, and they help the manager gain a better understanding of the decision situation. For example, insights offer us plausible explanations for why sales vary a lot between territories, or why some territories have consistently low sales performance. Information is a derived property of the data. On the other hand, managers gain insight as they mull over and process data and information (using either mental models or decision models) and as they incorporate information with their own internal knowledge.

A *decision* is a judgment favoring a particular insight as offering the most plausible explanation or favoring a particular course of action. For example, choosing to devote more effort in subsequent periods to territories with low sales constitutes a decision. Thus decisions provide purpose to information.

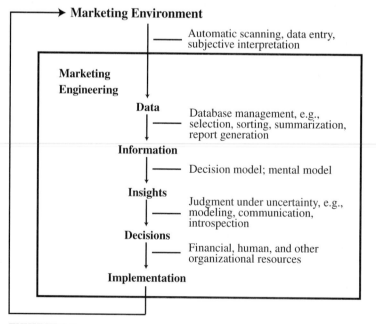

EXHIBIT 1.1
The marketing engineering approach to decision making helps transform objective and subjective data about the marketing environment into decisions and decision implementations.

Finally, *implementation* is the set of actions the manager or the organization takes to commit resources toward physically realizing a decision. For example, a decision may require hiring and training more salespeople to work in poorly performing territories.

Although marketing engineering encompasses all the elements shown in Exhibit 1.1, we will focus mostly on ways to transform information and insights into decisions. Several cases in the book highlight key issues that arise in implementing model-based decisions within organizations.

In many ways computer models are simply tools that managers can use to explore the potential consequences of their decisions. The idea of using computer models to enhance decisions is not new. Researchers and practitioners have long developed and implemented powerful models that facilitate decision making in real-world marketing settings. (For case studies and examples, see Lilien, Kotler, and Moorthy (1992), Little (1970), Rangaswamy (1993), and Wierenga and van Bruggen (1997).) Yet until recently much of the knowledge about marketing decision models resided in specialized academic journals or required considerable technical expertise to use. As a result, despite their potential value, these models have not seen the extent of managerial use indicated by their potential.

Recent advances in computer hardware and software now make it possible to put these models in the hands of every marketing manager. Several hundred commercially available canned software decision aids are of potential interest to marketers. At the same time, almost no associated teaching material is available to help marketing managers learn to be intelligent users and consumers of the available marketing models. We designed this book to serve this purpose.

Why marketing engineering?

Many marketing managers succeed without relying on computer models. Conceptual marketing based on deep insights and years of experience may often be sufficient for making good decisions. Such tasks as identifying the market segments that are likely to be most attractive to a firm, positioning a product in a competitive setting, or anticipating customer response to a proposed marketing program can all be based on conceptual marketing. However, is conceptual marketing sufficient for the marketing managers of the future? Should you bet your future on relying only on intuitive methods when the marketing environment is undergoing major changes? The following trends are fundamentally changing the marketing manager's job.

High-powered personal computers connected to networks are becoming ubiquitous: Like other professionals, marketing managers are increasingly depending on computers to perform their jobs. Even managers in small firms use PCs. According to Dataquest (http://www.dataquest.com), worldwide shipments of PCs are expected to exceed 70 million units in 1996 and to grow at nearly 20 percent per year over the next few years. Many marketing departments have more computing power today than entire firms did five years ago. A senior marketing executive told us recently, "Ten years ago in my department, we had lots of people and very little software. Today we have lots of software and very few people." These computers are being networked with other computers through local area networks (LANs) and, in some cases, connected to external computers and databases all over the world through wide area networks (WANs), such as the Internet.

Although many managers currently use their PCs mainly for word processing and e-mail, sophisticated managers have begun to use their computers to access, combine, and process different types of information to improve their decisions. The most common analysis tools available to managers are spreadsheet programs, like Excel from Microsoft, which had an installed base of over 30 million units by June 1996. With the wider availability and use of these tools, computer-assisted decision making is becoming important in many firms.

The volume of data is exploding: The automatic electronic capture of data related to transactions with consumers is generating massive amounts of potentially useful information about the preferences and behavior of customers. For example, the typical brand manager in the packaged goods industry is inundated with 1000 times the volume of data (more frequently collected in finer detail) than was available five years ago. The growth of direct marketing has led to similar data explosions in other industries as well. While available data has grown exponentially, the human brain has not advanced in a comparable manner to process and interpret these data. Managers need new concepts, methods, and technologies, such as marketing engineering, to make decisions in data-intensive environments.

Firms are reengineering marketing: The new corporate mantra seems to be "flatter organizations, ad hoc teams, outsourcing, and reduced cycle times." In this environment, firms are reengineering marketing functions, processes, and activities for the information age. In the reengineered firm, centralized decision making, characteristic of traditional hierarchical organizations, is giving way to decentralized decision making that is characteristic of entrepreneurial organizations. As a consequence marketing managers are increasingly dealing directly with market information and using computers to do tasks that were once done by staff support people.

These changes are forcing an evolution in the marketing manager's job from one based primarily on conceptual skills to one that is more akin to the way an engineer works— putting together data, models, analyses, and computer simulations to design an effective marketing program. As Peter Francese, president and founder of Marketing Tools puts it, "emerging corporations don't have any need for classical marketing education. What they have a need for is understanding customers. What they want to know is how to analyze databases—supplier databases, demographic and geographic databases. . . . If you presented one of your students to me and asked me to hire him or her, I'd give that student a diskette and say, 'Here are some of my customers. Tell me what I should do.' There are no right answers. You either fail to create greater value and you're out of a job, or you create more income for the company and you continue to be employed. It's that simple. That's the test, and it's being applied to middle managers all over the country" (quoted in *Selections*, Spring 1996, published by the American Management Admission Council).

Marketing engineering is a way to capitalize on these trends. It is not, however, a panacea for coping with complex and uncertain decision environments. Markets are not controlled settings where careful observation will permit clear and unambiguous understanding. But neither are they so complex as to defy understanding. They fall somewhere between these two extremes. Marketing engineering enables us to capture the essence of marketing phenomena in well-specified models, and it improves our ability to make decisions that influence market outcomes.

MARKETING DECISION MODELS

Definition

Decision models are a special category of models that provide the foundation for marketing engineering, in much the same way that a skeleton provides the structure for the human body. We first define a generic model and then articulate what we mean by a decision model.

A model is a *stylized representation* of reality that is easier to deal with and explore for a *specific purpose* than reality itself. Let us explore key terms in this definition:

Stylized: Models do not capture reality fully but focus only on some aspects. They are simplified depictions, or analogies, of real-world phenomena and systems. For example, as a model a road map contains only some geographical aspects of the landscape such as main roads, rivers, and towns and ignores many other aspects, such as hills and valleys, vegetation, and buildings in an area.

Representation: A model is only a convenient analogy that may bear little resemblance to the physical characteristics of the reality it is trying to capture. For example, a map printed on paper has little physically in common with the terrain it represents. Most marketing models use verbal, graphical, or mathematical representations. The marketing decision models we describe in this book are often presented as mathematical equations embedded within a set of logical relationships, bearing no obvious physical resemblance to a marketplace of customers. (Note that models can also represent artificial worlds, as in virtual reality simulations.)

Specific purpose: People develop models with a specific purpose in mind. Cartographers design road maps so that you can find a route from one location to another, estimate the time or distance between locations, or plan a long trip. They do not design them for settling property disputes or planning crop planting. Likewise, modelers design marketing decision models to highlight some aspects and ignore others. The purpose of a marketing model could be to understand or influence certain types of behavior in the marketplace (e.g., repeat purchase of the firm's products), to improve planning and prediction associated with a specific marketing issue (e.g., customer response to a new ad campaign), or to facilitate communication within the firm about a particular marketing problem.

This book is about a special category of models called *interactive decision models*. These are computer models (i.e., simplified representations of reality encoded as packaged software) that can be customized to a specific decision situation faced by a manager. They provide simulated learning environments where a manager can interactively explore the consequences of alternative actions while avoiding the expense, dangers, and irreversibility of the real world. Such models are tools for the mind, to help managers use objective and subjective data to support their decisions. In some situations, decision models do not lead directly to decisions but enable managers to test and update their mental models of market behavior, perhaps leading to changes in future decisions.

Characteristics of decision models

The decision models we describe in the book incorporate explicit statements of *purpose*, *assumptions*, *variables*, and *relationships* of interest.

A decision model has a well-defined *purpose*, which represents the reason for its construction and circumscribes its domain of applicability. For example, the ADBUDG model (Chapter 8) is designed primarily to help managers arrive at good advertising budgets. The clustering model (Chapter 3) is useful for identifying attractive market segments. A model could have several secondary purposes as well. For example, the ADBUDG model could be used to simulate the sales effect of different advertising spending levels, that is, as a forecasting tool.

Assumptions provide the context or framework for a model. For example, a model to evaluate the advertising budget for a product could include the following assumptions:

- Product sales are related to its advertising.
- Sales will go up if advertising is increased.
- There is a maximum level of sales for this product. No amount of advertising will make it possible for sales to exceed this maximum level.
- Increased advertising will decrease customers' sensitivity to the price of the product.

All models contain assumptions, either explicit or implicit, and unlike mental models, decision models require that these assumptions be made explicit. This explicitness also allows managers to more clearly evaluate the consequences of modifying their assumptions and provides them a means of communicating and sharing their assumptions with others in the organization.

Variables are those aspects of a marketing phenomenon that are not fixed. In a marketing system, many things can vary: the firm's sales, the likelihood that customers will purchase a new product, the calling patterns salespeople use, and the intensity of competition. We distinguish between three types of variables. *Controllable* variables are those that the firm controls, such as the level of advertising and the product features to be designed into a new product. *Noncontrollable* variables are those that are under the control of other players in the market, such as suppliers and competitors. Although a firm may try to influence a noncontrollable variable, it cannot manipulate it directly. *Environmental* variables are noncontrollable variables that are not under the control of any one player in the marketing system. These variables include general trends, such as the aging of the population, and variables whose values are determined by the actions of a number of different actors, such as new regulations or industry capacity. Together, controllable, noncontrollable, and environmental variables are referred to as *independent* or *input* variables. In contrast, *dependent* or *output* variables are those whose values are determined by a set of independent variables. For example, in many marketing models, product sales are driven by the level of advertising spending and the quality of the product. Although the distinction between independent and dependent variables may not always be precise, it is still a useful one.

Relationships between the variables, based on marketing theories and managerial insights, specify how changes in one variable affect another variable. For example, a change in *package design* can be hypothesized to increase *customer attention* at the point-of-purchase. Most marketing decision models use mathematical functions to represent how independent variables (e.g., advertising expenditures) affect dependent variables (e.g., sales). In Chapter 2 we provide details on the concepts, specification, calibration, and interpretation of the various types of relationships among marketing variables.

Verbal, graphical, and mathematical models

One way to distinguish between decision models is on the basis of their structural characteristics: verbal, graphical, or mathematical.

Verbal models are described in words. For example, Lavidge and Steiner (1961) state that advertising moves consumers' mental states along the following chain:

awareness *to* knowledge *to* liking *to* preference *to* conviction *to* purchase.

This model specifies the variables influenced by advertising and the sequence in which this influence will take place. The model also suggests that an increase in advertising will lead to an increase in awareness, which will lead to an increase in knowledge, eventually leading to an increase in purchase. However, it does not specify the magnitude of increase in these variables for a given increase in advertising. This lack of quantification is a fundamental limitation of verbal models, especially when they are used for decision making. On the other hand, verbal models are easy to explain, are intuitively understandable, and in many cases are sufficient for the purpose at hand.

Almost all models start out as verbal models and are then refined into the other types. Some of the most important models of individual, social, and societal behavior, such as those of Freud, Marx, and Darwin, are verbal models. We all use verbal models all the time, even without being aware of it.

EXAMPLE

Try this exercise. The next time you are feeling guilty about something (you were out later than you said you would be, and your spouse or parent seems upset and asks for an explanation), check to see if you use a verbal model to "pre-test" possible explanations before offering one. You consider saying, "I got a flat tire on the way home," and you expect a sympathetic reaction, or alternatively, "I was out drinking with friends and lost track of time," and you expect an angry reaction. If you go through this process, you are conducting a thought experiment, using a verbal model to forecast the reaction of your spouse or parent. You then choose an explanation (suppose you really *were* out drinking), balancing the goal of getting sympathy instead of a reprimand against the moral cost of stretching the truth. If the reaction you get is the one you had expected, your model is confirmed, and you become more confident of your mental model; if you get an unexpected reaction, you will update or abandon your verbal model.

Graphical models are represented in the form of pictures or charts. Examples include road maps, organizational charts, and flow diagrams. These models describe the overall nature of a phenomenon, stripped of nonessentials, so that the viewer can grasp the whole and select specific relationships for closer examination. We are all familiar with the notion that a picture is worth a thousand words. Graphical models are parsimonious compared with verbal models, and at the same time they are more explicit in representing relationships. To understand the power and parsimony of a graphical representation, look at Exhibit 1.2, which summarizes the weather records of New York City for an entire year.

Graphical models help illuminate and identify key issues relevant to a phenomenon, aid communication about the phenomenon, and guide analysis. In addition graphical models provide a bridge between verbal models and the more formal mathematical models.

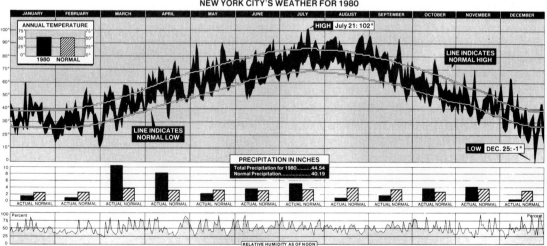

New York Times, January 11, 1981, p. 32

EXHIBIT 1.2
The graphical model of New York City weather for 1980 displays an amazing amount of information with great parsimony. *Source: New York Times*, January 11, 1981, p. 32.

Mathematical models specify the relationships embodied in a model in the form of equations. For example, the relationship between advertising expenditure and sales often incorporates two important properties (Chapter 2): saturation and diminishing returns. Saturation suggests that after some point, no amount of additional advertising will increase sales. Diminishing returns suggest that each incremental unit of advertising will lead to progressively decreasing increases in sales. These properties can be represented in the form of an equation:

$$\text{Sales} = a\left(1 - e^{-bx}\right) \tag{1.1}$$

where a is the market potential for the product (i.e., the maximum sales that would be achieved at infinite levels of advertising), e is the exponent, x is the proposed advertising expenditure, and b is a parameter that indicates that rate at which sales will approach the market potential as the level of advertising expenditure is increased. This equation can also be represented graphically as in Exhibit 1.3.

In a mathematical representation, both the nature and the magnitude of the relationships between variables must be specified. This quantification allows the manager to explore how variations in the level of an independent variable (e.g., advertising) influence both the direction and the level of the dependent variable of the model (e.g., sales). A disadvantage of mathematical models is that many managers are not comfortable dealing with mathematical representations. They think of them as mysterious "black boxes," because they do not see intuitively how the models work. However, advances in software and hardware are making it easier to provide graphical representations of equations and model outputs, as is the case with many of the software implementations of decision models in this book.

Widely available spreadsheet software, such as Excel and Lotus 1-2-3, has also made it easier to work with mathematical representations such as Eq. (1.1). For example, marketing spreadsheets typically include planned marketing expenditures and the associated gross and net revenues. However, in most cases the model developer does not

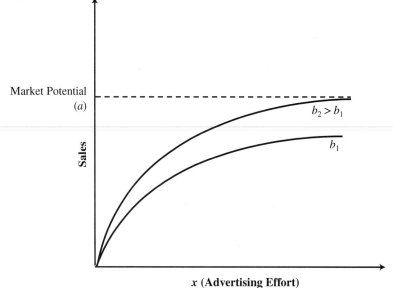

EXHIBIT 1.3
This is a graphical representation of a mathematical model (sales = a(1 − e⁻ᵇˣ)) showing the relationship between advertising effort and sales. This function incorporates the properties of saturation and diminishing returns.

establish a relationship, within the spreadsheet, between marketing inputs (e.g., advertising) and sales revenues. Thus marketing inputs only affect net revenue as a cost item. We refer to such spreadsheets as "dumb" models. They make little sense because they are silent about the nature of the relationship between marketing inputs and outputs. For the spreadsheet to make sense, the model developer must define objectives and variables explicitly and specify the relationships among variables. In a "smart" model, an equation such as Eq. (1.1) will be embedded in the spreadsheet. The manager can then look at the effect of advertising on both sales and revenues to see if increases or decreases in advertising can be justified. This is precisely how we will approach the advertising expenditure decision in Chapter 8.

Each of the three types of models has its particular strengths and weaknesses. The same marketing phenomenon can be represented in verbal, graphical, or mathematical forms, depending on the purpose of the model and the level of knowledge about that phenomenon. Exhibit 1.4 contains verbal, graphical, and mathematical models that describe the trajectory of sales of a new product. The verbal model provides a starting point for developing the more refined graphical and mathematical models. The graphical representation adds finer details about the model, and finally the formal mathematical representation adds precision. The sequence from verbal to graphical to mathematical representations is the path by which many models are actually developed. For this phenomenon the mathematical model can make more specific numerical predictions (not necessarily more accurate ones) of future sales of the new product than both the graphical and verbal models. In turn, the graphical model will have higher specificity of predictions than will the verbal model.

Computer technology enables managers to develop models that combine verbal, graphical, and mathematical representations. For example, the user interface may be based on a verbal model, computations may be based on a mathematical model, and the results may be displayed graphically.

Descriptive and normative decision models

Decision models can also be categorized according to the kinds of managerial question they address. We distinguish between two main types: those that are descriptive or predictive, and those that are normative. This book includes decision models of both types.

Descriptive (predictive) decision models: Descriptive models address the question, "What will happen if we do X?" For example, a manager's decision about whether or not to introduce a new product might depend on the likely total sales for the product line if the new product is introduced; a decision to go ahead with a two-for-one promotional offer might depend on the incremental profit that might be generated by that promotion. Using descriptive models the manager conducts "simulations" to evaluate the consequences of marketing actions. For example, the manager might use a descriptive model to compute the likely sales of the product line under various scenarios, taking into account both the sales of the new product and the cannibalization of other products in the product line.

Descriptive models are useful for (1) finding explanations (diagnostics) for a phenomenon by identifying the specific variables and relationships that form causal links (e.g., poor new product sales are due to low repeat purchase rates caused by poor product design) and (2) predicting possible outcome(s) when model inputs are extended to parameter regions other than those used for developing the model (e.g., what will sales be next month?). The ASSESSOR model (Chapter 7) is a successful descriptive and predictive model in marketing that helps managers decide whether to introduce a new product into the market.

Normative decision models: Normative decision models address the question, "What is our best course of action in a given situation?" For example, a manager might want to determine the best location for a new store or the best level of advertising for a particular

Verbal Model

Sales of a new product often start slowly as "innovators" in the population adopt the product. The innovators influence "imitators," leading to accelerated sales growth. As more people in the population purchase the product, total sales continue to increase but sales growth slows down.

Graphical model (a)

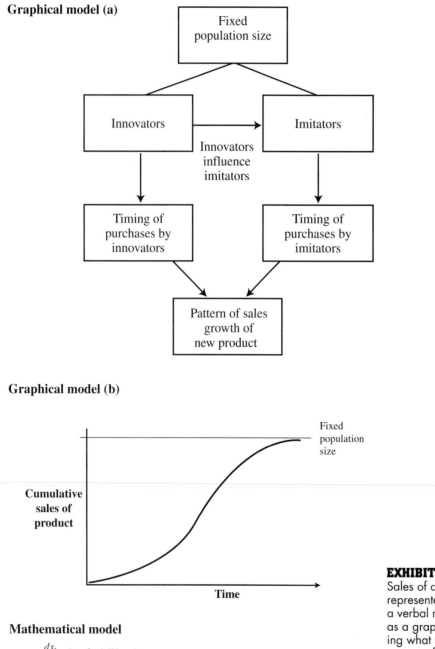

Graphical model (b)

Mathematical model

$$\frac{dx_t}{dt} = (a + bx_t)(N - x_t)$$

x_t = Total number of people who have adopted product by time t
N = Population size
a, b = Constants to be determined. The actual path of the curve in graphical model (b) will depend on these constants.

EXHIBIT 1.4
Sales of a new product can be represented in several ways: as a verbal model or description; as a graphical model (a) showing what factors influence the pattern of sales growth and (b) showing the pattern of cumulative sales; and as a mathematical model using a differential equation.

product. Normative models are designed to help managers to answer such questions by enabling them to explore the value of a decision option under different scenarios: The managerial question can be modeled as a *constrained optimization* problem where the *objective function* measures the value to the firm of a particular decision option and the constraints limit the range of allowed variation in the decision options. When the manager has only a few options, case studies or simulations using descriptive models may be adequate. When he or she is faced with many options to choose from, formal mathematical procedures are needed to identify good options (see the appendix to Chapter 2).

Firms have used normative decision models in marketing to resolve such problems as allocating salesforce resources to products and markets (see Chapter 9), media planning, designing retail shelf space, and locating stores. Normative models are often referred to as *prescriptive models* because such models can prescribe effective courses of action from among numerous options available without being driven by an explicit optimization of an objective function (see, for example, the ADCAD model in Chapter 8).

Hybrid models combine descriptive and normative elements. For example, conjoint analysis models (Chapter 7) contain descriptive models to represent the utility functions of a sample of customers and normative models to identify the best new product to satisfy a target segment of customers.

BENEFITS OF USING DECISION MODELS

The basic premise of marketing engineering is that the model-building process improves decisions. Let us look at some of the ways in which this comes about (Exhibit 1.5):

Improve consistency of decisions: One benefit of models is that they help managers to make more consistent decisions. Consistency is especially desirable in decisions that they make often. Several studies have shown the value of consistency in improving predictions (Exhibit 1.6).

Exhibit 1.7 lists variables experts often use to predict the academic performance of graduate business students (the first row of Exhibit 1.6). The formalized intuition of experts captured in a simple linear model outperforms the experts themselves! Accuracy here

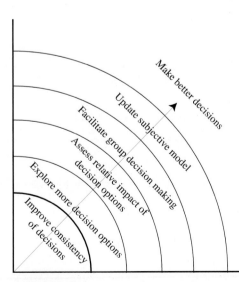

EXHIBIT 1.5
Managers derive a spectrum of benefits from using decision models, leading ultimately to better decisions.

Types of judgments experts had to make	Mental Model[*]	Subjective Decision Model[**]	Objective Decision Model[***]
Academic performance of graduate students	.19	.25	.54
Life expectancy of cancer patients	− .01	.13	.35
Changes in stock prices	.23	.29	.80
Mental illness using personality tests	.28	.31	.46
Grades and attitudes in psychology course	.48	.56	.62
Business failures using financial ratios	.50	.53	.67
Students' ratings of teaching effectiveness	.35	.56	.91
Performance of life insurance salesman	.13	.14	.43
IQ scores using Rorschach tests	.47	.51	.54
Mean (across many studies)	.33	.39	.64

[*] Outcomes directly predicted by experts.
[**] Subjective Decision Model: Outcomes predicted by subjective linear regression model, formalizing past predictions made by experts.
[***] Objective Decision Model: Linear model developed directly from data.

EXHIBIT 1.6
Degree of correlation with the true outcomes of three types of models, showing that even subjective decision models are superior to mental models, but that formal, objective models do far better. *Source*: Russo and Schoemaker 1989, p. 137.

Appli- cant	Personal Essay	Selectivity of Undergraduate Institution	Undergrad- uate Major	College Grade Average	Work Exper- ience	GMAT Verbal	GMAT Quanti- tative
1	Poor	Highest	Science	2.50	10	98%	60%
2	Excellent	Above avg	Business	3.82	0	70%	80%
3	Average	Below avg	Other	2.96	15	90%	80%
⋮	⋮	⋮	⋮	⋮	⋮	⋮	⋮
117	Weak	Least	Business	3.10	100	98%	99%
118	Strong	Above avg	Other	3.44	60	68%	67%
119	Excellent	Highest	Science	2.16	5	85%	25%
120	Strong	Not very	Business	3.98	12	30%	58%

EXHIBIT 1.7
Input data for all three models, namely, mental model, subjective decision model, and objective decision model, used for predicting the performance of graduate students. See first row of Exhibit 1.6. *Source*: Russo and Schoemaker 1989, p. 132.

improved from 19 percent correlation with the actual student performance to 25 percent correlation. An explanation for this improvement is that the decision model more consistently applies the expertise of the experts to new cases.

The third column in Exhibit 1.6 lists the accuracy of an "objective" linear regression model. For the academic performance study the independent variables for the regression model were the same factors used by the experts, but the dependent variable was a known measure of the academic performance of the graduate students. The predictions in this case were based on a hold-out sample of data to which the objective model was applied. For this model the correlation of the predictions with the true outcomes was 54 percent. Exhibit 1.6 also shows the average correlations between predictions and true outcomes across several studies. We see that subjective decision models had an average correlation of 39 percent with true outcomes as compared with 33 percent for the intuitive mental models. For more details about these studies, see Camerer (1981), Goldberg (1970), and Russo and Schoemaker (1989).

In sum these results point to a few interesting conclusions: (1) When you can build an objective model based on actual data, you will generally make the best predictions. However, in many decision situations we do not have data that show the accuracy or the consequences of past decisions made in the same context. In such cases the next best option is to codify the mental model decision makers use into a formal decision model. The calibrating of response models using the decision calculus method (Chapter 2) is a way to formalize the mental models of decision makers. (2) Among these three types of models, the least accurate is the mental model. However, on average all three types of models had a positive correlation with the truth, whereas a model with random predictions would have zero correlation with the truth. (3) Managers should focus their attention on finding variables useful for prediction but should use decision models to combine the variables in a consistent fashion.

Explore more decision options: In some situations the number of options available to the decision makers is so large that it would be physically impossible for them to apply mental models to evaluate each option. For example, in allocating a firm's sales effort across products and market segments, in deciding which media vehicles to use for an advertising campaign, or in pricing the various travel classes and routes of an airline, thousands of possible options are available to managers. The manager may develop decision heuristics that help cut down the number of options to be evaluated. The use of heuristics helps refine the mental model to incorporate additional considerations that narrow the number of decision options. But such pruning of decision options may lead to worse decisions than considering each of the available options more carefully. An alternative approach is to develop a computer decision model that facilitates the exploration of more options. A number of decision models of this type are available to marketing managers, and these have been shown to improve decisions. For example, several salesforce-allocation models have resulted in a 5 to 10 percent improvement in profitability with no additional investments (Fudge and Lodish 1977; Rangaswamy, Sinha, and Zoltners 1990).

Assess the relative impact of variables: In some situations, the decision options may be few, but the variables that might affect the decision may be numerous. For example, in test marketing a new product a manager may be considering only two decision options—withdraw the product or introduce it in selected markets—but many variables may influence this decision. Such variables as competitor and dealer reactions, consumer trial rates, competitive promotions, the brand equity associated with the brand name, and the availability of the product on the shelf influence product sales. A decision model provides the manager with a framework to more fully explore each decision option and to understand the impact of each of the variables on product sales. The model also serves as a diagnostic tool in helping the manager assess the relative importance of the variables in influencing test market sales of the product. Models such as ASSESSOR (discussed in Chapter 7) have been successfully used in test marketing. Urban and Katz (1983) report that, on the average, the use of the ASSESSOR model offers a 6:1 benefit:cost ratio.

Facilitate group decision making: Modeling provides focus and objectivity to group decision making by externalizing ideas and relationships that reside inside the minds of decision makers. In the same way that an explicit agenda helps direct meetings, the model or the results from a modeling effort can help a group deliberate and converge on a decision. For example, discussions on allocating resources tend to degenerate into turf battles, like congressional budget debates. However, if the entire group participates in a decision modeling exercise, then group discussions can be directed toward *why* someone prefers a particular allocation, rather than focusing simply on *what* allocation that person prefers.

Likewise, if the members of a group agree on a modeling approach, then they may view the model results as unbiased and coming from an external source and therefore favor more rational (less emotional) decision options.

Update subjective mental models: Marketing managers have mental models of how their markets operate. They develop these models through trial and error over years of experience, and these mental models serve as valuable guides in decision making. Yet in forming these mental models they may not take advantage of how managers in other industries have approached similar problems, or they may not incorporate academic research that addresses such problems. When managers are exposed to decision models, they update their own internal mental models in subtle but significant ways. Formal models require that key assumptions be made explicit, or their structure may require new ways of thinking about a familiar problem, resulting in learning that may affect future decisions. Although new learning is an indirect benefit of using models, in many cases it is the most important benefit. As a rough analogy, recall your first view of the sky through a telescope. It not only provided a clearer picture of familiar celestial objects but perhaps also altered your conception of the universe by revealing many new objects and providing more detail about the familiar objects.

Using decision models can produce all of these benefits. While managers can potentially realize one or more of these benefits in any decision situation, we must remember that the mere use of a decision model does not guarantee better decisions or the realization of increased value for the firm.

Although models can produce significant benefits, many managers are reluctant to use models. This reluctance arises partly from the lack of simple-to-use computer software implementations of many marketing models. However, some managers may choose not to use a model even if they are familiar with it and the model is inexpensive, readily available, and provides quick results. Here are some of these reasons:

> *Mental models are often good enough*: Evolution has provided us with a brain that is an efficient processor of all kinds of information, particularly information that is visual in nature. However, managers mistakenly believe that because mental models do well most of the time, they will also suffice when decisions concern complex and dynamic market behavior. To understand this, look at the sketchy visual information in Exhibit 1.8 and the table of data from a marketing report in Exhibit 1.9. In the case of the picture the brain sorts out the pattern quickly even though the picture is fuzzy, whereas in the other case the pattern represented by the numbers is unclear, even though the numbers themselves are very precise. If you look at the picture in Exhibit 1.8 carefully, you may even be able to tell what kind of dog is shown in the picture. On the other hand, you will find it difficult to immediately see any "big picture" in the data of Exhibit 1.9.

> Mental models, however, are not always effective, especially when the information does not form a familiar pattern. The pattern-matching ability of the human brain is helpful for making decisions when a new situation has a pattern similar to past situations, but not otherwise. Indeed, in an experimental study involving forecasting, Hoch and Schkade (1996) find that mental models perform much better in predictable decision environments than in unpredictable environments, where an overreliance on familiar patterns can lead to misleading insights.

> *Models are incomplete*: Managers recognize that models are incomplete, and therefore they correctly believe that model results cannot be implemented without being modified by judgments. If model results are to be tempered by intuitive judgments, why not rely on judgments in the first place? The latter conclusion, however, does not follow from the former. As Hogarth (1987, p. 199) notes, "When driving at night with

EXHIBIT 1.8
Visual pattern of information, showing how you can "get the picture" even with sketchy visual information. *Source*: Morton Hunt 1982, p. 72.

your headlights on you do not necessarily see too well. However, turning your head-lights off will not improve the situation." Or as W. Edwards Deming puts it, "All models are wrong; some are useful."

Decision models and mental models should be used in conjunction, so that each works to strengthen the areas where the other is weak. Mental models can incorporate idiosyncratic aspects of a decision situation, but they also overfit new cases to old patterns. On the other hand, decision models are consistent and unbiased, but they under-weight idiosyncratic aspects. In a forecasting task, Blattberg and Hoch (1990) find that predictive accuracy can be improved by combining the forecasts generated by decision models with forecasts from mental models. Furthermore, they report that a 50-50 (equal weighting) combination of these two forecasts provides high predictive accuracy.

Opportunity costs of decisions are not observed: Managers observe only the consequences of decisions they have actually made and not the consequences of those they didn't. Therefore they are often unable to judge for themselves whether they could have made better decisions by using decision models. Without this ability to observe the value of systematic decision making, many managers continue to do what is intuitively comfortable for them. In some industries, such as mutual funds, managers are rewarded based on their performance compared with that of managers of funds with similar risk portfolios. Here managers can observe indirectly the consequences of decisions they did not make. It is not surprising then that the mutual fund industry is one of the heaviest users of computer modeling to support decisions.

With the automatic capture of customer transaction data, marketing managers can now establish stronger links between their decisions and market outcomes. For example, in the packaged goods industry weekly data are available that include measures of in-store environment (e.g., special displays, price discounts) and consumer purchases for all brands in a product category. With these data we can track the performance of competing brands and the promotional strategies used by each of them. This ability to

Category: Frozen Dinner Volume is expressed in pounds Quarter ending Sept 1987 Including only brands purchased by 0.5% or more of all households	Data Reflect Grocery Store Purchases Only						Percent Volume with the Specified Deal							Avg. % off on price deals
	Category volume share	Type volume share %	% of hshlds buying %	Volume per purch	Purch. per buyer	Share category reqmts %	Price per volume	Any trade deal %	Print ad feature %	In store display %	Shelf price reduc %	Store coupon %	Mfr coupon %	
Category: **Frozen Dinners** **Type:** **Frozen Dinner**	927.5+	100.0	26.7	1.5	2.3	100	2.80	26	12	5	23	0	8	21
All American Gourmet	10.1	10.1	5.3	1.1	1.6	45	2.71	34	15	8	30	0	3	18
The Budget Gourmet	10.1	10.1	5.3	1.1	1.6	45	2.71	34	15	8	30	0	3	18
Campbell Soup Co.	34.9	34.9	11.4	1.4	2.0	61	3.22	8	3	1	7	0	6	18
Le Menu Light Style	2.4	2.4	1.7	0.9	1.5	24	4.44	18	8	3	15	0	27	20
Swanson	17.4	17.4	6.3	1.3	2.0	48	2.58	9	4	1	9	0	3	18
Swanson Hungryman	8.0	8.0	2.8	1.7	1.6	43	2.68	3	0	0	3	0	3	13
Swanson Le Menu	6.5	6.5	3.1	1.1	1.8	36	5.05	6	1	0	6	0	10	15
Conagra	38.7	38.7	13.6	1.5	1.8	59	2.32	39	19	7	36	0	7	22
Banquet	18.4	18.4	6.2	1.7	1.7	56	1.73	47	25	10	43	0	1	20
Banquet Manpleaser	2.2	2.2	0.9	1.8	1.3	38	1.75	29	12	9	24	0	1	13
Classic Lite	2.6	2.6	1.9	0.9	1.4	24	4.65	24	7	1	21	0	21	25
Dinner Classics	7.4	7.4	4.0	1.1	1.6	32	3.99	27	15	6	24	0	25	27
Morton	6.4	6.4	2.5	1.5	1.6	50	1.44	31	15	3	41	0	1	16
Patio	1.0	1.0	0.6	1.1	1.5	29	1.88	51	15	0	48	0	8	22
General Foods	2.2	2.2	1.1	1.2	1.6	42	3.68	24	8	2	24	0	54	38
Birds Eye Fresh Creat.	2.2	2.2	1.1	1.2	1.6	42	3.68	24	8	2	24	0	54	38
Nestle Company	1.9	1.9	1.3	1.1	1.3	26	4.68	26	10	5	16	0	35	23
Stouffer Dinner Supreme	1.8	1.8	1.2	1.1	1.3	26	4.69	27	10	6	16	0	36	23
O'Donnel-USEN	0.7	0.7	0.6	0.8	1.3	26	2.87	31	17	7	18	1	5	28
Taste O Sea	0.7	0.7	0.6	0.8	1.3	26	2.87	31	17	7	18	1	5	28
Aggregated Vendors	8.2	8.2	4.3	1.1	1.6	37	3.01	24	11	4	20	0	15	24
Private Label	1.8	1.8	0.5	1.9	1.7	47	1.62	39	16	13	39	0	0	14

EXHIBIT 1.9

In this table from a marketing report, we are given a great deal of numerical information but may have difficulty seeing a pattern (do you see one?). In general we have far less ability to see a pattern in numerical information than we do in visual information (see Exhibit 1.8).
Source: The Marketing Fact Book, Information Resources, Inc., Chicago.

link managerial decisions with market performance has led to increased use of decision models in this industry.

Models require precision: Models require that assumptions be made explicit, that data sources be clearly specified, and so forth. Some managers perceive all this concreteness as a threat to their power base and a devaluation of their positions, particularly middle managers in hierarchical organizations. A traditional role of middle managers in such organizations has been to gather information from the front lines and structure that information to facilitate top management decision making. However, as information management becomes more computerized and decentralized, middle managers need to focus more on the decision consequences of information. Rarely does information by itself lead to better decisions. Only when decision makers draw insights from information and use those insights as a basis for action does information translate into value for an organization.

Models emphasize analysis: Managers prefer action. Little (1970) noted this many years ago. In the past, managers could call on corporate support staff whenever they needed help with analysis, so that they could concentrate on what they liked to do best. In today's flatter organizations, support staff is increasingly a luxury that few firms can afford.

PHILOSOPHY AND STRUCTURE OF THE BOOK

Philosophy

We designed this book for business school students and managers who wish to train themselves to function in marketing organizations in the information age. We hope to impart knowledge of the concepts and tools underlying decision models and of the skills needed to apply the models we describe for real-world marketing decision making. This is an advanced book that requires you to be familiar with the basic concepts of marketing, as covered in an introductory course. You should also be familiar (though not necessarily proficient!) with basic business mathematics (algebra, statistics, and elementary calculus). The most important requirement is a *willingness* to approach problems in a systematic and logical manner.

The book straddles theory and practice, and we try to demonstrate how they reinforce each other. It will not take you long to learn how to run the software implementations of the various decision models we describe. However, you will need patience and diligence to learn and internalize the underlying principles of the modeling approaches in a way that will allow you to use them effectively in decision situations you will encounter in the future.

We based this book on two fundamental principles: learning by doing and end-user modeling.

Learning by doing: We believe that the best way to learn about marketing engineering is to put yourself in situations that require you to make decisions. Instead of focusing on modeling theory, we challenge you with practical exercises in marketing decision making. We hope that in making these decisions you will develop the ability to recognize a broad range of marketing decision problems, to structure problems to facilitate decision making, to carry out logical analyses, and to present the results of the modeling effort in a nontechnical manner to interested audiences.

As you use the models described in this book, you will have questions about their adequacy, their advantages, and their limitations, and you may want to know how to adapt the models to related problem areas. It is when you try to answer these questions in actual decision contexts that real learning takes place. To learn to ride a bike, you need to get on and try it. Merely learning about the laws of mechanics or watching other people ride bikes will not make you a bike rider. Learning by doing in the real world is expensive and error prone. This book and software simulate a safe and structured environment in which to explore and experiment with alternative courses of action.

End-user modeling: Decision models in marketing range from very sophisticated models that are developed by a team of experts (e.g., the Marriott conjoint study and the American Airlines yield management system mentioned earlier) to those that can be quickly put together by an individual (end user) with a basic knowledge of marketing and marketing engineering. In this book, we emphasize end-user models, which have the following key characteristics (Powell 1996):

- The modeling process is initiated and completed by an individual who has to deal with a business problem. The user is rarely a technical analyst or a modeling specialist. The objective of the modeling effort is to gain a better understanding of the specific decision problem and the alternative courses of action available to the user.
- The modeling effort is nonmathematical in nature, although the underlying models themselves may be mathematical. The user relies on graphics, spreadsheets, and canned software to put together a model to reflect his or her understanding of the business problem.
- The user develops the model under budget and time constraints, and it has the characteristics of a good engineering solution—do as good a job as you can, cheaply, and with what you can obtain easily. The modeler uses whatever information is readily available along with a healthy dose of creativity. The model itself may be less thorough and scientific than models developed by academic researchers or by professional management scientists. Judgment plays a big role in generating inputs to the model and in interpreting the results.
- The models are often used for generating directional insights rather than for providing specific numerical guidelines. In contrast to full-blown decision support systems (e.g., a yield management system), end-user models produce outputs that are useful for the general patterns they reveal (e.g., the feasible range of prices) and not for their own sake.

Exhibit 1.10 summarizes these and other differences between end-user models and high-end models. Success with end-user models may provide the impetus for managers to develop organization-wide implementations of the models in the form of decision support systems that are linked to corporate databases.

Objectives and structure of the book

Our primary objective is to get you to personally experience the value of the marketing engineering approach. We have been involved in conceptualizing and implementing many decision models, and we have experienced the opportunities, the challenges and frustrations, the excitement, and the "aha" moments associated with making models work in organizational settings. In many instances we have also seen that models offer considerable value to modern enterprises. We want to share with you our insights and experiences and those of others in academia and industry with similar experiences.

Although you will work hands-on with models, our objective here is *not* to train you to be an analyst or a modeler. Rather, our main goal is to help you to become an astute user of models and a knowledgeable consumer of modeling results generated by others. In particular, we hope that this book will enable you to recognize decision situations that could ben-

	End-user models	**High-end models**
Scale of problem	Small to medium	Small to large
Time availability (for setting up model)	Short	Long
Costs/benefits	Low to medium	High
User training	Moderate to high	Low to moderate
Technical skills for setting up model	Low to moderate	High
Recurrence of problem	Low	Low or high*

*Low for one-time studies (e.g., Marriott Conjoint Study) and high for models in continuous use (e.g., American Airlines Yield Management System).

EXHIBIT 1.10
Two extremes of marketing decision models: end-user versus high-end models. Although the marketing engineering approach applies to both types of models, we focus on end-user models in this book. Source: Stephen G. Powell 1996.

efit from the marketing engineering approach and that it will help you focus the modeling effort and interpretation of results to facilitate the decision making process. Specifically we hope to accomplish the following objectives:

- Show how and why the marketing engineering approach *can* enhance marketing decisions
- Provide a basic understanding of the most successful marketing decision models, and offer examples showing why they are successful
- Help you improve your skills in understanding and formulating marketing processes and relationships analytically
- Give you hands-on experience applying decision models

There are mathematical descriptions of many models here. We recommend that if you have difficulty with mathematics, you skip over math as you read, do the case problems with the software and use the mathematics to help deepen your understanding.

We chose the models in the book to be both theoretically sound and practically useful. The models are based on academic research that provides some justification for them, or the models have been widely used in industry. Thus the models are robust and have been tested in field settings.

In Chapter 2 we focus on how to build models. In Chapters 3 through 6 we focus on strategic marketing issues, such as segmentation, positioning, portfolio analysis, and market measurement and strategic planning. In Chapters 7 through 10 we explore many tactical issues, such as product design, setting advertising budgets, salesforce deployment, store location, and yield management. Finally, in Chapter 11 we summarize the key points for you to take from the book and speculate on the future of marketing engineering. For each chapter we include examples, cases, and exercises to illustrate the concepts covered in the chapter and to gradually ease you into the underlying structure of the models.

There are mathematical descriptions of many models here. We recommend that if you have difficulty with mathematics, skip over the math as you read, do the case problems with the software and use the mathematics to help deepen your understanding.

Design criteria for the software

This book comes packaged with an extensive set of software tools. The book contains the conceptual material that you will need to understand the decision models embedded in the software. The software helps you learn to apply these concepts and models for making decisions in managerial settings. We used several criteria in designing the software to ensure that it is compatible with our objectives for the book:

It runs under the Windows Operating System: The software will run on IBM-compatible machines running Windows 3.X, Windows 95, or Windows NT operating systems. This means you cannot run this software as a native application on Apple/Macintosh computers. We recommend that the software be installed only on PCs with the Intel 80486 chip, or higher, with 16 MB of RAM. It will run much slower on PCs with the 80386 chip, and some of the spreadsheet programs will be extremely slow unless you have more than 8 MB of RAM.

While this software will run under Windows 95 and Windows NT operating systems, some of the programs do not take full advantage of the features of these 32-bit operating systems.

It links to Microsoft Excel: In addition to the Windows operating system, you should have the Microsoft Excel spreadsheet program, version 5.0c or higher, to take full advantage of the software. Excel is required for running all the spreadsheet models included in the book. In addition Excel may be used to set up the data for other models, such as cluster analysis (Chapter 3) and promotional analysis using the multinomial logit model (Chapter 10).

It provides access to all packages from a single menu: A major benefit of this software package is that it allows you to access all the programs from a common window. However, all the programs may not work in the same way or have the same menu options. This is because each program is designed to address a specific problem area and, therefore, may contain idiosyncratic menu options. At the same time, we have tried to make similar programs have similar menu structures and look and feel the same. Thus, for example, all the spreadsheets are similar in many ways, although submenu options may be different.

It covers the major areas of marketing decision making: We have tried to include representative decision models from all major areas of marketing decision making. Naturally some areas are stronger than others, given our own interests and the availability of software that is compatible with the goals of this book.

It runs on local area networks (LANs): The software supplied with this book will run only on stand-alone PCs. But another version of the software will run on local area networks. However, the network version of the software is available only to instructors who adopt the book, and it must be installed by a network professional to customize the software to run on the specific network program used at that LAN.

It restricts commercial use: All the software tools we provide are educational versions that have some built-in restrictions that limit their value in commercial applications. All the basic features however, remain intact. However, we have imposed such restrictions as limits on data size or the inability to save large-scale problems for later use, to ensure that most commercial-size applications cannot be executed with this version of the software. You will always be able to use a part of your data to evaluate whether it would be beneficial to attempt a full-scale application of the decision model to a particular problem you are facing.

Like other newly developed products, this software is subject to continuous improvement. Writing a book is quite different from putting together a complex piece of software, where even small errors can turn out to be critical. Please visit our World Wide Web site *http://hepg.awl.com/lilien-rangaswamy/mktgeng* to obtain the latest updates and tips for using this software or to give us suggestions for improving the software.

A TOUR OF THE SOFTWARE

In this section we assume that you are familiar with personal computers. We also assume that you have some working knowledge of IBM-compatible PCs, the Windows operating system, and Microsoft Excel software. If you have no experience with them, we recommend that you spend a few hours getting some basic knowledge of these topics before proceeding further.

Installation guidelines: The software is distributed on a CD and can be installed on personal computers that use the Windows 3.X, Windows 95, or Windows NT operating systems.

- Start Windows. If Windows is already running, exit any other currently active programs.
- Insert the CD in the CD-ROM drive.
- **Run D:\install.exe** (if your CD-ROM is not the D: drive, substitute the correct drive letter).

Installation is straightforward. You may be prompted to provide information that the installation program requires. We recommend that you install the software in the default directory **c:\mktgeng**. If you wish to alter the program setup after installation, see the customization instructions that follow.

When installation is complete, you will see a new icon for Marketing Engineering. Double-clicking on the icon starts the program, **mktgeng.exe.** If the program is correctly installed, you will then see the following screen:

Customization: After you install the software, you may have to fine tune the setup parameters to ensure that the program runs smoothly on your PC.

Setting up an automatic link between Excel and Marketing Engineering: The installation procedure establishes this link to make it possible for you to access all the Excel-based models from the same main menus you use for starting the other models, but in some cases, you will need to establish this link manually. To do this, first run the Marketing Engineering program. From the **H**elp menu, select the **P**references option. For the "Path to Microsoft excel.exe" entry, indicate the directory (e.g., c:\msoffice\excel) where the Excel executable file (i.e., excel.exe) is located. If you do not set up an automatic link, you have to separately open the Marketing Engineering and Excel applications. You can also disable the automatic link by not checking the Auto Start Excel option.

Preferences		☒
Path to Microsoft excel.exe	c:\msoffice\excel	
Path to Excel Spreadsheets	c:\mktgeng\excel	
Path to Data Files	c:\mktgeng\data	
Path to Temporary Files	c:\mktgeng\temp	
Path to Conjoint Data Files	c:\mktgeng\conjoint\data	
☑ Installed on Network? ☑ Auto Start Excel?	Browse	
OK	Cancel	Help

Installing Solver module in Excel: Several marketing engineering applications (e.g., the Syntex resource-allocation model and the ADBUDG model) require the installation of the Solver optimization module to function properly. If you have not installed Solver on your system, run the Excel or MSOffice setup program and add the Solver module.

Changing the default directories used by the Marketing Engineering program: You can customize the directories where Marketing Engineering looks for data files and where it writes out temporary files. Select the **H**elp menu and click on the **P**references option. Indicate your preferred locations for Path to Data Files, Path to Temporary Files, and Path to Conjoint Data Files.

In each of the boxes presented, indicate where the appropriate files are located: the directory containing Excel spreadsheets (this should be one level below the directory where the marketing engineering software is installed), the directory containing data files for the program, and a directory location for storing temporary files generated by the program.

Running a model: From the main menu, select the **M**odel option. You will see 27 different model options listed in this menu as shown in the screen on page 26. Highlighting a model and clicking will either execute the model or bring up a submenu with additional model options, which can then be executed by highlighting on the model of interest and clicking.

The models vary in their underlying structures. Many of the models are in the form of Excel spreadsheets. Some of the spreadsheet models (e.g., the GE planning matrix and the Syntex sales resource-allocation model) accept data sets provided by the user. Other spreadsheet models (e.g., the ADBUDG advertising budgeting model and the ASSESSOR pre-test market model) come with built-in data specific to a case and cannot easily be modified to accept new data sets. The book also contains several non-Excel models, all of which accept new data sets provided by the user. Most of these models (except ADCAD and AHP) offer links to Excel and in addition contain a built-in Excel-compatible spreadsheet facility. Exhibit 1.11 lists all the software components available with the book and the case or exercise that goes with each software.

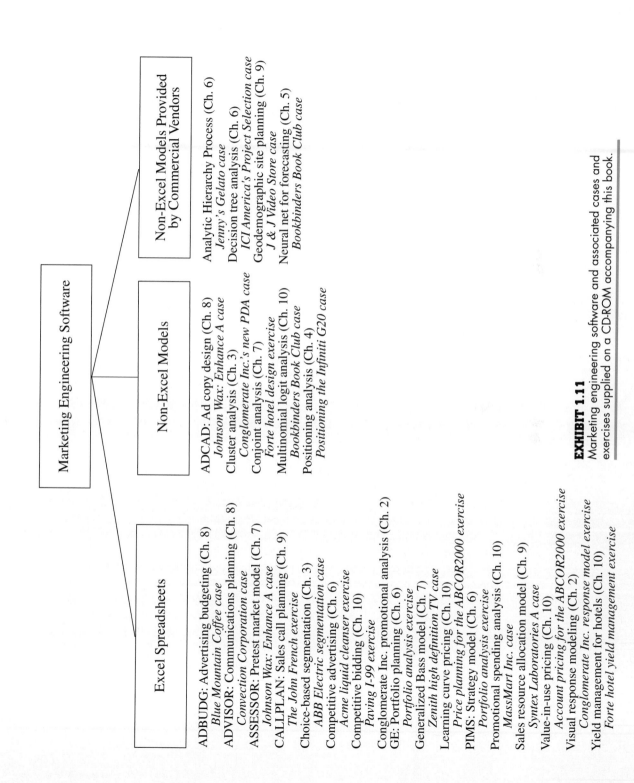

```
                                    Marketing Engineering Software
                    ┌──────────────────────┬────────────────────────┐
          Excel Spreadsheets        Non-Excel Models      Non-Excel Models Provided
                                                            by Commercial Vendors
```

Excel Spreadsheets

ADBUDG: Advertising budgeting (Ch. 8)
 Blue Mountain Coffee case
ADVISOR: Communications planning (Ch. 8)
 Convection Corporation case
ASSESSOR: Pretest market model (Ch. 7)
 Johnson Wax: Enhance A case
CALLPLAN: Sales call planning (Ch. 9)
 The John French exercise
Choice-based segmentation (Ch. 3)
 ABB Electric segmentation case
Competitive advertising (Ch. 6)
 Acme liquid cleanser exercise
Competitive bidding (Ch. 10)
 Paving I-99 exercise
Conglomerate Inc. promotional analysis (Ch. 2)
GE: Portfolio planning (Ch. 6)
 Portfolio analysis exercise
Generalized Bass model (Ch. 7)
 Zenith high definition TV case
Learning curve pricing (Ch. 10)
 Price planning for the ABCOR2000 exercise
PIMS: Strategy model (Ch. 6)
 Portfolio analysis exercise
Promotional spending analysis (Ch. 10)
 MassMart Inc. case
Sales resource allocation model (Ch. 9)
 Syntex Laboratories A case
Value-in-use pricing (Ch. 10)
 Account pricing for the ABCOR2000 exercise
Visual response modeling (Ch. 2)
 Conglomerate Inc. response model exercise
Yield management for hotels (Ch. 10)
 Forte hotel yield management exercise

Non-Excel Models

ADCAD: Ad copy design (Ch. 8)
 Johnson Wax: Enhance A case
Cluster analysis (Ch. 3)
 Conglomerate Inc.'s new PDA case
Conjoint analysis (Ch. 7)
 Forte hotel design exercise
Multinomial logit analysis (Ch. 10)
 Bookbinders Book Club case
Positioning analysis (Ch. 4)
 Positioning the Infiniti G20 case

Non-Excel Models Provided by Commercial Vendors

Analytic Hierarchy Process (Ch. 6)
 Jenny's Gelato case
Decision tree analysis (Ch. 6)
 ICI America's Project Selection case
Geodemographic site planning (Ch. 9)
 J & J Video Store case
Neural net for forecasting (Ch. 5)
 Bookbinders Book Club case

EXHIBIT 1.11
Marketing engineering software and associated cases and exercises supplied on a CD-ROM accompanying this book.

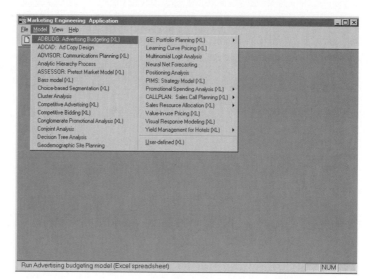

SUMMARY

In this chapter our primary objective was to introduce the emerging field of marketing engineering—the use of interactive computer decision models to facilitate marketing decisions. More and more marketing managers are functioning in decision environments characterized by increasing amounts of data, information (summarized data), and computing resources. Yet few business schools currently offer courses to train marketing managers in the tools and concepts of marketing decision models, which we believe will help you succeed in such environments. We developed this book to provide in one package both the concepts and software tools that we hope will be a part of the marketing curricula at business schools.

The marketing engineering approach is centered around interactive decision models, which are customizable computerized representations of marketing phenomena that enhance managerial decision making. We described the many potential benefits of using decision models, including improving the consistency of decisions, gaining the ability to evaluate more decision options, assessing the relative impact of different factors in influencing a decision, and updating one's own mental model of market behavior. We also summarized several reasons that many managers do not currently use decision models in spite of their potential benefits.

We emphasize learning by doing. The more you apply the concepts and tools to real decision problems, the more you will learn about marketing engineering and its value. We also emphasize end-user models, that is, models that you can either develop or use directly without having to bring in technical experts. As a result we hope that you will use the software provided in the book to deal with problems you encounter in your jobs, at least as a starting point, before undertaking or authorizing more extensive modeling efforts.

Finally, we also provided an overview of the software that accompanies the book, focusing on the software design criteria and tips for installation and use. *So get ready for marketing engineering!*

2

Tools for Marketing Engineering: Market Response Models

As we discussed in Chapter 1, decision models form the core of the marketing engineering approach to addressing marketing problems. The building blocks for decision models are market response models.

Our goals for this chapter are to

- Define and classify market response models, the key components of the marketing engineering approach to decision making
- Provide details of some of the types of market response models that will concern us here:
  - Aggregate market response models, to represent response behavior in the market as a whole
  - Individual response models (which can be "added up") to represent the market
  - Other market response models (shared experience models, qualitative response models)
- Develop criteria for calibrating and selecting response models
- Describe some alternative ways to specify decision model objectives
- Outline criteria for selecting response models

Software linked to this chapter includes a tool called Visual response modeling, which gives you hands-on experience with building simple response models. In the appendix to this chapter we discuss Excel's Solver tool and how it can help you to find good values of parameters for response functions and to determine cost-effective marketing strategies.

WHY RESPONSE MODELS?

Marketing systems present a number of challenges—the market is not a simple laboratory where you can carefully observe processes to understand them clearly and unambiguously. The following example of possible response effects of a marketing effort illustrates some of these challenges.

Suppose a soft drink manufacturer has developed an ad campaign and wants to determine how effective it is so that it can determine how to introduce the campaign into the market. The campaign could have an immediate effect on customer awareness, attitudes, or preference for the brand, on sales of the brand this week, or on these variables sometime in the future. Let us focus only on the current sales effects for the moment; those effects may be influenced by the current advertising campaigns of other soft drink manufacturers, by the prices of that brand and of competitive brands, and by the promotions the firm is currently running in the marketplace. Some of these effects are controllable (such as trade promotions to retailers), while others are not, such as the price the consumer sees. (The price to the consumer is set by retailers, some of whom may decide to run their own promotions or to not pass on the trade discounts to consumers.) The firm's advertising campaign may have a message that differentially appeals to certain demographic or age groups, and different markets around the country have different proportions of these groups. The advertised soft drink can be purchased through supermarkets, through giant retailers (like Wal-Mart), through convenience stores (like 7 Eleven), through vending machines, through fast food outlets, and the like. Each of these channels is likely to produce a different level or type of sales response. The response may differ by package size (12 pack vs. individual 12 oz vs. 64 oz), package type (aluminum can vs. plastic), and the like. And what if there are diet and nondiet versions of the product? Caffeinated and decaffeinated versions? And what if the manufacturer has an entire line of soft drinks and is interested in determining possible synergies (helping other company brands) and cannibalization (stealing sales from some of its other products)?

We could complicate this example even more (we did not really indicate what the firm's goals were or whether nonsales objectives, such as building awareness or brand preference, were to be considered), but we hope the point is clear—marketing decisions take place in an environment that is difficult to analyze or control.

Because of the complexities of marketing problems and the limitations of mental models for decision making, the marketing engineering (ME) approach is of increasing interest to managers. This approach requires that the following be made explicit:

Inputs: The marketing actions that the marketer can control, such as price, advertising, selling effort, and the like—the so-called marketing mix—as well as noncontrollable variables, such as the market size, competitive environment, and the like

Response model: The linkage from those inputs to the measurable outputs of concern to the firm (customer awareness levels, product perceptions, sales levels, and profits)

Objectives: The measure that the firm uses for monitoring and evaluating those actions (e.g., their level of sales in response to a promotion, the percent of a target audience that recalls an ad)

Response models function within the framework of marketing decision models (Exhibit 2.1). A firm's marketing actions (arrow 1) along with the actions of competitors (arrow 2) and environmental conditions (arrow 3) combine to drive the market response, leading to key outputs (arrow 4). Those outputs are evaluated relative to the objectives of the firm (arrow 5),

EXHIBIT 2.1
Market response models translate marketing inputs, competitive actions, and environmental variables into observed market outputs within the framework of a marketing decision model—arrow 6, the decision-modeling link.

and the firm then adapts or changes its marketing actions depending on how well it is doing (arrow 6)—the decision-modeling link.

The ME approach enables managers to be more systematic about how they make decisions in partially structured decision situations. Without ME, we see such statements as: ". . . sales in Minneapolis are down 2.3 percent relative to forecast [Goal: meet or exceed forecast?]; I suggest that we increase our promotional spending there by 10 percent over the previous plan [Assumption: an increase in current promotional spending (input) will lead to a (short-term?) sales response of at least +2.3 percent, and this will be cost-effective]. . . ."

With ME we might get: "Sales are down 2.3 percent in Minneapolis. After including that information in our database and recalibrating our Minneapolis response model, it looks as if a promotional spending increase of 12.2 percent will maximize our profit in that market this quarter."

The response models that are used in the ME approach are usually mathematical models, although some formalized verbal models are used as well.

TYPES OF RESPONSE MODELS

To the craftsman with a hammer, the entire world looks like a nail, but the availability of a screwdriver introduces a host of opportunities! So it is with marketing models. One of our goals is to expose you to a range of models, both conceptually (through this book) and operationally (through the associated software).

Response models can be characterized in a number of ways:

1. By the number of marketing variables; do we consider the relationship between advertising and sales alone (a one-variable model) or do we include price as well (a two-variable model)?
2. By whether they include competition or not; does our model explicitly incorporate the actions and reactions of competitors or is competition considered simply part of the environment?
3. By the nature of the relationship between input variables—such as advertising—and output (dependent) variables—such as sales; does every dollar of advertising provide the same effect on sales (a linear response) or are there ranges of spending where that additional dollar gives larger or smaller returns (an S-shaped response)?
4. By whether the situation is static or dynamic; do we want to analyze the flow of actions and market response over time or simply to consider a snapshot at one point in time?
5. By whether the models reflect individual or aggregate response; do we want to model the responses of individuals (for direct marketing or targeting specific sales efforts) or overall response (the sum of the responses of individuals)?
6. By the level of demand analyzed (sales versus market share); to determine the sales of a brand one can try to analyze brand sales directly (the most common approach) or one can analyze market share and total market demand separately (the product of the two is sales).

In this chapter we will focus first on the simplest of the model types: aggregate response to a single marketing instrument in a static, noncompetitive environment. Then we will introduce additional marketing instruments, dynamics, and competition.

Before we proceed, we need vocabulary:

We use several terms to denote the equation or sets of equations that relate *dependent variables* to *independent variables* in a model (described in Chapter 1), such as *relationship*, *specification*, and *mathematical form*.

Parameters are the constants (usually the *a*'s and *b*'s) in the mathematical representation of models. To make a model form apply to a specific situation, we must estimate or guess what these values are; in this way we infuse life into the abstract model. Parameters often have direct marketing interpretations (e.g., market potential or price elasticity).

Calibration is the process of determining appropriate values of the parameters. You might use statistical methods (i.e., estimation), some sort of judgmental process, or a combination of approaches.

For example, a simple model is

$$Y = a + bX. \tag{2.1}$$

In Eq. (2.1), X is an *independent variable* (advertising, say), Y is a *dependent variable* (sales), the model form is linear, and a and b are *parameters*. Note that a in Eq. (2.1) is the level of sales (Y) when X equals 0 (*zero advertising*), or the *base* sales level. For every dollar increase in advertising, Eq. (2.1) says that we should expect to see a change in sales of b units. Here b is the slope of the sales/advertising response model. When we (somehow) determine that the right value of a and b are 23,000 and 4, respectively, and place those values in Eq. (2.1) to get

$$Y = 23,000 + 4X, \tag{2.2}$$

then we say we have *calibrated* the model (given values to its parameters) (Exhibit 2.2).

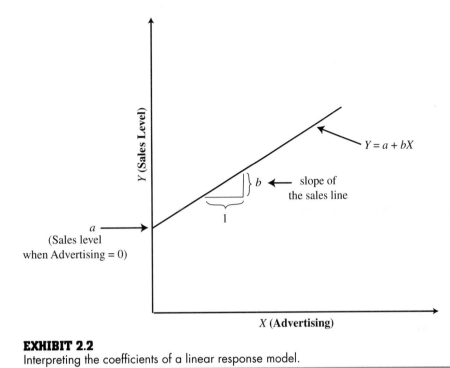

EXHIBIT 2.2
Interpreting the coefficients of a linear response model.

SOME SIMPLE MARKET RESPONSE MODELS

This book is *not* about building complex and complete market response models. Applying even simple, disciplined analysis to marketing problems can yield great benefits as compared with relying on mental models. And using complex models is not necessarily better; indeed their very complexity may hinder people's understanding and using them. It is best to start with simple tools and gradually add complexity if it is useful.

In this section, we will provide a foundation of simple but widely used models of market response that relate one dependent variable to one independent variable in the absence of competition. The linear model shown in Exhibit 2.2 is used frequently, but it is far from consistent with the ways markets appear to behave.

Saunders (1987) summarizes the simple phenomena that have been reported in marketing studies and that we should be able to handle using our toolkit of models (Exhibit 2.3). In describing these eight phenomena here, we use the term *input* to refer to the level of marketing effort (the X or independent variable) and *output* to refer to the result (the Y or dependent variable):

P1. Output is zero when input is zero.
P2. The relationship between input and output is linear.
P3. Returns decrease as the scale of input increases (every additional unit of input gives *less* output than the previous unit gave).
P4. Output cannot exceed some level (saturation).
P5. Returns increase as scale of input increases (every additional unit of input gives *more* output than the previous unit).
P6. Returns first increase and then decrease as input increases (S-shaped return).
P7. Input must exceed some level before it produces any output (threshold).
P8. Beyond some level of input, output declines (supersaturation point).

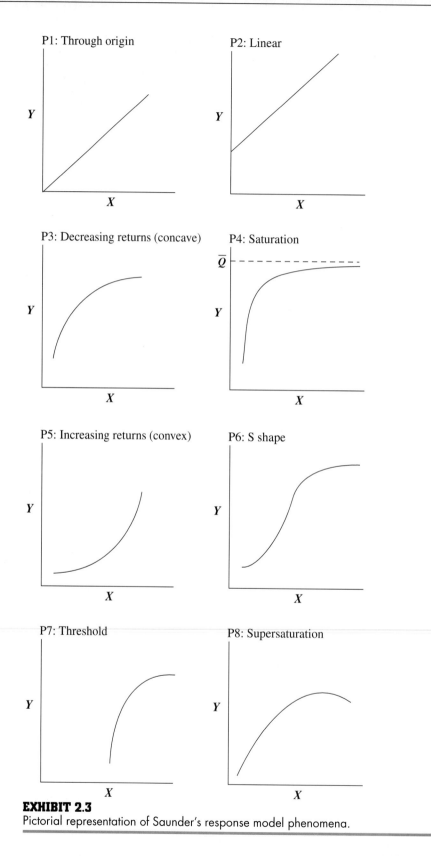

EXHIBIT 2.3
Pictorial representation of Saunder's response model phenomena.

What phenomena we wish to incorporate in our model of the marketplace depend on many things, including what we have observed about the market (data), what we know about the market (judgment or experience), and existing theory about how markets react. We now outline some of the common model forms that incorporate these phenomena.

The linear model: The simplest and most widely used model is the linear model:

$$Y = a + bX. \tag{2.3}$$

The linear model has several appealing characteristics:

- Given market data, one can use standard regression methods to estimate the parameters.
- The model is easy to visualize and understand.
- Within specific ranges of inputs, the model can approximate many more complicated functions quite well—a straight line can come fairly close to approximating most curves in a limited region.

It has the following problems:

- It assumes constant returns to scale everywhere, i.e., it cannot accommodate P3, P5, or P6.
- It has no upper bound on Y.
- It often gives managers unreasonable guidance on decisions.

On this last point, note that the sales slope ($\Delta Y/\Delta X$) is constant everywhere and equal to b. Thus if the contribution margin (assumed to be constant, for the moment) is m for the product, then the marginal profit from an additional unit of spending is bm. If $bm > 1$, more should be spent on that marketing activity, without limit—that is, every dollar spent immediately generates more than a dollar in profit! If $bm < 1$, nothing should be spent. Clearly this model is of limited use for global decision making (it says: Spend limitless amounts or nothing at all!), but locally the model suggests whether a spending increase or decrease might be recommended.

Linear models have seen wide use in marketing, and they readily handle phenomena P1 and P2. If X is constrained to lie within a range ($\underline{B} \leq X \leq \bar{B}$), the model can accommodate P4 and P7 as well.

The power series model: If we are uncertain what the relationship is between X and Y, we can use a power series model. Here the response model is

$$Y = a + bX + cX^2 + dX^3 + \cdots \tag{2.4}$$

which can take many shapes.

The power series model may fit well within the range of the data but will normally behave badly (becoming unbounded) outside the data range. By selecting parameter values appropriately the model may be designed to handle phenomena P1, P2, P3, P5, P6, and P8.

The fractional root model: The fractional root model,

$$Y = a + bX^c \text{ (with } c \text{ prespecified)}, \tag{2.5}$$

has a simple but flexible form. There are combinations of parameters that give increasing, decreasing, and (with $c = 1$) constant returns to scale. When $c = 1/2$ the model is called the *square root model*. When $c = -1$ it is called the *reciprocal model*; here Y approaches the value a when X gets large. If $a = 0$, the parameter c has the economic interpretation of elasticity (the percent change in sales, Y, when there is a 1 percent change in marketing effort X). When X is price, c is normally negative, whereas it is positive for most other marketing variables. This model handles P1, P2, P3, P4, and P5, depending on what parameter values you select.

The semilog model: With the functional form

$$Y = a + b \ln X, \tag{2.6}$$

the semilog model handles situations in which constant percentage increases in marketing effort result in constant absolute increases in sales. It handles P3 and P7 and can be used to represent a response to advertising spending where after some threshold of awareness, additional spending may have diminishing returns.

The exponential model: The exponential model,

$$Y = ae^{bX} \text{ where } X > 0, \tag{2.7}$$

characterizes situations where there are increasing returns to scale (for $b > 0$); however, it is most widely used as a price-response function for $b < 0$ (i.e., increasing returns to decreases in price) when Y approaches 0 as X becomes large. It handles phenomena P5 and, if b is negative, P4 (Y approaches 0, a lower bound here).

The modified exponential model: The modified exponential model has the following form:

$$Y = a(1 - e^{-bx}) + c. \tag{2.8}$$

It has an upper bound or saturation level at $a + c$ and a lower bound of c, and it shows decreasing returns to scale. The model handles phenomena P3 and P4 and is used as a response function to selling effort; it can accommodate P1 when $c = 0$.

The logistic model: Of the S-shaped models used in marketing, the logistic model is perhaps the most common. It has the form

$$Y = \frac{a}{1 + e^{-(b+cX)}} + d. \tag{2.9}$$

This model has a saturation level at $a + d$ and has a region of increasing returns followed by decreasing return to scale; it is symmetric around $d + a/2$. It handles phenomena P4 and P6, is easy to estimate, and is widely used.

The Gompertz model: A less widely used S-shaped function is the following Gompertz model:

$$Y = ab^{cX} + d, \ a > 0, \ 1 > b > 0, \ c < 1. \tag{2.10}$$

Both the Gompertz and logistic curves lie between a lower bound and an upper bound; the Gompertz curve involves a constant ratio of successive first differences of log Y, whereas the logistic curve involves a constant ratio of successive first differences of $1/Y$. This model handles phenomena P1, P4, and P6. (The better known logistic function is used more often than the Gompertz because it is easy to estimate.)

The ADBUDG Model: The ADBUDG model, popularized by Little (1970), has the form

$$Y = b + (a - b) \frac{X^c}{d + X^c} . \tag{2.11}$$

The model is S-shaped for $c > 1$ and concave for $0 < c < 1$. It is bounded between b (lower bound) and a (upper bound). The model handles phenomena P1, P3, P4, and P6, and it is used widely to model response to advertising and selling effort.

Even readers with good mathematical backgrounds may not be able to appreciate the uses, limitations, and flexibility of these model forms. A software tool called visual response modeling, included with the book, allows you to "see" these models. The software also enables you to develop your own models. More importantly, the tool allows you to calibrate the models (either statistically or judgmentally) and see how they change in shape and behavior when the parameters change. Some experience with the visual response modeler software should help make the abstract mathematical equations more transparent.

CALIBRATION

Calibration means assigning good values to the parameters of the model. Consider the simple linear model (Eq. 2.3). If we wanted to use that model, we have to assign values to a and b. We would want those values to be good ones. But what do we mean by good? A vast statistical and econometric literature addresses this question, but we will try to address it simply and intuitively:

Calibration goal: We want estimates of a and b that make the relationship $Y = a + bX$ a good approximation of how Y varies with values of X, which we know something about from data or intuition.

People often use least squares regression to calibrate a model. In effect, if we have a number of observations of X (call them x_1, x_2, etc.) and associated observations of Y (called y_1, y_2, etc.), regression estimates of a and b are those values that minimize the sum of the squared differences between each of the observed Y values and the associated "estimate" provided by the model. For example, $a + bx_7$ would be our estimate of y_7, and we would want y_7 and $a + bx_7$ to be close to each another. We may have actual data about these pairs of X's and Y's or we may use our best judgment to generate them ("What level of sales would we get if our advertising were 10 times what it is now? What if it were half of what it is now?").

When the data that we use for calibration are actual experimental or market data, we call the calibration task "objective calibration" (or objective parameter estimation). When the data are subjective judgments, we call the task "subjective calibration."

In either case we need an idea of how well the model represents the data. One frequently used index is R^2, or R-square. If each of the estimated values of Y equals the actual value of Y, then R-square has a maximum value of 1; if the estimates of Y do only as well as the average of the Y values, then R-square has a value of 0. If R-square is less than 0, then we are doing worse than we would by simply assigning the average value of Y to every value of X. In that case we have a very poor model indeed!

Formally R-square is defined as

$$R^2 = 1 - \frac{\text{(Sum of squared differences between actual } Y\text{'s and estimated } Y\text{'s)}}{\text{(Sum of squared differences between } Y\text{'s and the average value of } Y\text{)}}$$

EXAMPLE

Suppose we have run an advertising experiment across a number of regions with the following results:

Region	Annual Advertising (per capita)	Annual Sales Units (per capita)
A	$ 0	5
B	2	7
C	4	13
D	6	22
E	8	25
F	10	27
G	12	31
H	14	33

Let us take the ADBUDG function (Eq. 2.11). If we try to estimate the parameters of the ADBUDG function (a, b, c, d) for these data, to maximize the R-square criterion, we get

$$\hat{a} = 39.7, \ \hat{b} = 4.6, \ \hat{c} = 2.0, \ \hat{d} = 43.4, \ \text{with } R^2 = 0.99.$$

Exhibit 2.4 plots the results, showing how well we fit these data. (Try using the visual response modeling software to duplicate this analysis.)

In many cases managers do not have historical data that are relevant for calibrating the model for one of several reasons. If the firm always spends about the same amount for advertising (say 4 percent of sales in all market areas), then it has no objective information about what would happen if it changed the advertising-to-sales ratio to 8 percent. Alternatively, the firm may have some historical data, but that data may not be relevant because of changes in the marketplace such as new competitive entries, changes in brand-price structures, changes in customer preferences, and the like. (Consider the problem of using year-old data in the personal computer market to predict future market behavior.)

As we pointed out in Chapter 1, formal models based on subjective data outperform intuition. To formally incorporate managerial judgment in a response function format, Little (1970) developed a procedure called "decision calculus." In essence decision calculus asks the manager to run a mental version of the previous market experiment.

Q1: What is our current level of advertising and sales? Ans.: Advertising = $8/capita; sales = 25 units/capita.

Q2: What would sales be if we spent $0 in advertising? ($A$ = $0/capita)

Q3: What would sales be if we cut 50 percent from our current advertising budget (A = $4/capita)?

Q4: What would sales be if we increased our advertising budget by 50 percent (A = $12/capita)?

Q5: What would sales be if advertising were made arbitrarily large? (A = $∞/capita)

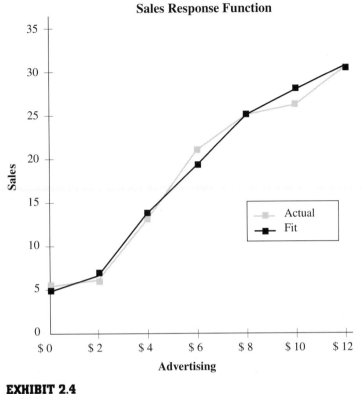

EXHIBIT 2.4
Calibration example using ADBUDG function, with $R^2 = 0.99$.

Suppose that the manager answered Questions 2 through 5 by 5, 13, 31, and 40, respectively; we would get essentially the same sales response function as in the previous example.

The Conglomerate Inc. promotional analysis case at the end of this chapter and the John French exercise and the Syntex Labs case (Chapter 9) employ this judgmental response modeling approach.

OBJECTIVES

Consider the role of the objectives in Exhibit 2.1. To evaluate marketing actions and to improve the performance of the firm in the marketplace, the manager must specify objectives. Those objectives may have different components (profit, market share, sales goals, etc.), and they must specify the time horizon, deal with future uncertainty, and address the issue of "whose objectives to pursue."

EXAMPLE

You have just constructed an advertising response model for Blue Mountain Coffee (see Blue Mountain Coffee case). It gives three outputs: short-term profit (after one year), long-term profit (after three years), and long-term market share (after three years). Suppose that the advertising level that maximizes short-term (annual) profit is $1 million per quarter, the advertising level that maximizes long-term (three year) profit is $2 million per quarter, and that our market share will be maximized at the end of three years if we spend $3 million per quarter. What should we do?

As this example suggests, there is no single (or natural) objective. We will introduce here some of the key issues to consider in setting objectives and develop them through the exercises in the rest of the book.

Short-run profit: The simplest and most common objective (in line with our focus on a single marketing element in a static environment) is to maximize short-run profit. The equation focusing on that single marketing element in a static environment is

$$\text{Profit} = (\text{Unit price} - \text{Unit variable cost}) \times \text{Sales volume} - \text{Relevant costs} \tag{2.12a}$$

$$= \text{Unit margin} \times \text{Quantity} - \text{Relevant costs.} \tag{2.12b}$$

We can use response models to see how the sales volume in Eq. (2.12a) is affected by our marketing actions. If our focus is on price, then (assuming costs are fixed) as price increases, unit margin goes up and quantity sold generally goes down. If we focus on another marketing instrument, such as advertising, then margin is fixed, quantity goes up, but costs go up as well.

Relevant costs generally consist of two components: fixed and discretionary. Discretionary costs are those associated with the marketing activity under study and should always be considered. Fixed costs include those plant and overhead expenditures that should be appropriately allocated to the marketing activity. Allocating fixed costs is thorny and difficult; it keeps accountants employed and frequently frustrates managers of profit centers. For our purposes only two questions are relevant concerning fixed costs:

Are the fixed costs really fixed? Suppose that tripling advertising spending leads to a 50 percent sales increase, leading in turn to the need to increase plant size. These costs of capacity expansion must be taken into account. Normally fixed costs are locally fixed; that is, they are fixed within the limits of certain levels of demand and shift to different levels outside those regions. As with our response models, as long as we focus locally most fixed costs are indeed fixed.

Are profits greater than fixed costs? If the allocated fixed costs are high enough, absolute profitability may be negative. In this case the decision maker may want to consider dropping the product, not entering the market, or some other action.

Long-run profit: If a marketing action or set of actions causes sales that are realized over time, we may want to consider profit over a longer time horizon. If we look at the profit stream over time, then an appropriate way to deal with long-run profits is to take the present value of that profit stream:

$$PV = Z_0 + Z_1 r + Z_2 r^2 + Z_3 r^3 + \cdots \tag{2.13}$$

where Z_1 is the profit for period i, and $r = 1/(1 + d)$, with d being the discount rate. The discount rate d is often a critical variable; the closer d is to 0, the more oriented to the long term the firm is, whereas a high value of d (over .25 or so) reflects a focus on more immediate returns. In practice the more certain the earnings flow, the lower the discount rate that firms use.

Dealing with uncertainty: Managers know few outcomes of marketing actions with certainty. Consider the following:

EXAMPLE

Conglomerate, Inc., is considering two possible courses of action: continuing with its current laser pointer, whose profit of $100,000 for the next year is known (almost for sure); or bringing out a replacement that would yield a profit of $400,000 if it is successful (likelihood = 50 percent) or a loss of $100,000 if it is unsuccessful (likelihood = 50 percent). What should it do?

If the firm had lots of money and the ability to make many decisions of this type, on average it would make 50% × $400,000 + 50% × $100,000 or $150,000 with the new product, and so it seems clear that this is the better decision. But if the firm (like capital markets) values more certain returns over less certain ones, then the decision is not that clear. What about a $310,000 gain vs. the $100,000 loss for an average gain of $105,000, but a 50 percent chance of losing $100,000? Is it worth the risk?

In Chapter 6 we discuss decision-tree analysis, which formalizes a preference for more rather than less certainty—a concept known as *risk aversion*. For the moment we introduce two useful, closely related concepts: certainty monetary equivalent and risk premium.

Consider Conglomerate, Inc.'s, risky investment. And suppose that Conglomerate's managers would be just indifferent between the 50-50 chance of a $400,000 profit or a $100,000 loss and a $125,000 gain for sure. We call the $125,000 in this case the *certainty monetary equivalent* for the risky investment. The difference between the average gain ($150,000) and the certainty monetary equivalent ($125,000) is called the *risk premium*.

Either formally through utility theory (Lilien, Kotler, and Moorthy 1992) or informally by applying some combination of high discount rates or risk premiums, Conglomerate's managers should incorporate their attitude toward risk in evaluating potential actions when the outcomes are uncertain.

Multiple goals: Although profit of some sort is an overriding goal of many organizations, it is not the only factor managers consider in trying to decide among possible courses of action. Managers may say, "We want to maximize our market share and our profitability in this market!" or "We want to bring out the best product in the shortest possible time." Such statements are attractive rhetoric but faulty logic. For example, one can almost always increase market share by lowering price; after some point, however, profit will be decreasing while market share continues to increase. And when price becomes lower than cost, profit becomes negative even though market share is still increasing!

If a firm has two or more objectives that possibly conflict, how can the decision maker weight those goals to rank them unambiguously? A sophisticated branch of analysis called multicriteria decision making deals with this problem. The simplest and most common approach is to choose one (the most important) objective and to make all the others constraints; then management optimizes one (e.g., a profit criterion) while considering others to be constraints (e.g., market share must be at least 14 percent).

A second approach is *goal programming*, in which managers set targets for each objective, specify a loss associated with the difference between the target and actual performance, and try to minimize that loss. *Trade-off analysis* (Keeney and Raiffa 1976) and the analytic hierarchy process (Chapter 6) are further procedures for handling multiple objectives and trade-offs among objectives. Ragsdale (1995) provides a nice discussion of how to implement multiobjective optimization in a spreadsheet framework. The software associated with the Blue Mountain Coffee case implements a multicriteria approach.

Whether you use a simple formal method, such as the approach employing a single goal plus constraints, or a more sophisticated method of dealing with trade-offs among goals, it is critical that you neither ignore nor poorly assess important goals.

After you have specified goals or objectives, the ME approach facilitates the process of decision making—suggesting those values of the independent variables (such as level of advertising, selling effort, or promotional spending) that will best achieve these goals(s) (such as maximize profit, meet target levels of sales, or maximize market share). Throughout this book we will be exploring ways of finding those values.

We will use optimization procedures often in our search for good marketing policies (good values for our independent variables). The Excel-based software in the book relies on an add-in module called Solver for optimization problems that require model calibration (searching for the best values for the parameters of response models) or model optimization (looking for the best values for independent variables). In the appendix to this chapter, we describe how Solver works.

MULTIPLE MARKETING-MIX ELEMENTS: INTERACTIONS

In the section on calibration we dealt with market response models of one variable. When we consider multiple marketing-mix variables, we should account for their interactions. As Saunders (1987) points out, interactions are usually treated in one of three ways: (1) by assuming they do not exist, (2) by assuming that they are multiplicative, or (3) by assuming they are multiplicative and additive. For example, if we have two marketing-mix variables X_1 and X_2 with individual response functions $f(X_1)$ and $g(X_2)$, then assumption (1) gives us

$$Y = af(X_1) + bg(X_2); \tag{2.14}$$

assumption (2) gives us

$$Y = af(X_1)g(X_2); \tag{2.15}$$

and assumption (3) gives us

$$Y = af(X_1) + bg(X_2) + cf(X_1)g(X_2). \tag{2.16}$$

In practice when multiple marketing-mix elements are involved, we can resort to one of two forms: the (full) linear interactive form or the multiplicative form. The full linear interactive model (for two variables) takes the following form:

$$Y = a + bX_1 + cX_2 + dX_1X_2. \tag{2.17}$$

Note here that $\Delta Y/\Delta X_1 = b + dX_2$, so that sales response to changes in marketing-mix element X_1 is affected by the level of the second variable, X_2.

The multiplicative form is as follows:

$$Y = aX_1^b X_2^c. \tag{2.18}$$

Here $\Delta Y/\Delta X_1 = abX_1^{b-1}X_2^c$, so that the change in the response at any point is a function of the levels of both independent variables. Note here that b and c are the *constant* elasticities of the first and second marketing-mix variables, respectively, at all effort levels X_1 and X_2.

DYNAMIC EFFECTS

Response to marketing actions does not often take place instantly. The effect of an ad campaign does not end when that campaign is over; the effect, or part of it, will continue in a diminished way for some time. Many customers purchase more than they can consume of a product during a short-term price promotion. This action leads to inventory buildup in customers' homes and lower sales in subsequent periods. Furthermore, the effect of that sales promotion will depend on how much inventory buildup occurred in past periods (i.e., how much potential buildup is left). If customers stocked up on brand A cola last week, a new promotion this week is likely to be less effective than one a long period after the last such promotion.

Carryover effects is the general term used to describe the influence of a current marketing expenditure on sales in future periods (Exhibit 2.5). We can distinguish several types of carryover effects. One type, the *delayed-response effect*, arises from delays between when marketing dollars are spent and their impact. Delayed response is especially evident in industrial markets, where the delay, especially for capital equipment, can be a year or more. Another type of effect, the *customer-holdover effect*, arises when new customers created by the marketing expenditures remain customers for many subsequent periods. Their later purchases should be credited to some extent to the earlier marketing expenditures. Some percentage of such new customers will be retained in each subsequent period; this phenomenon gives rise to the notion of the *customer retention rate* and its converse, the *customer decay rate* (also called the attrition or erosion rate).

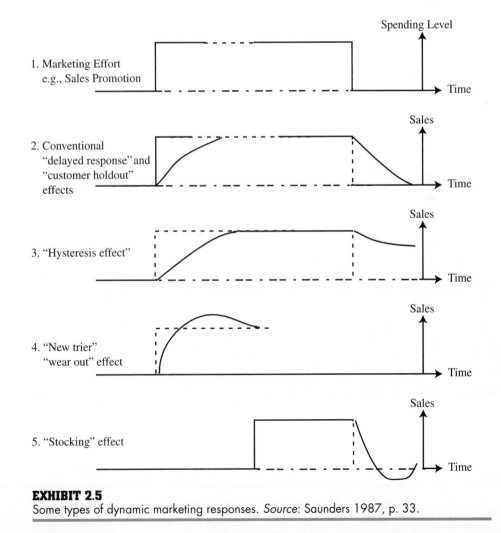

EXHIBIT 2.5
Some types of dynamic marketing responses. *Source*: Saunders 1987, p. 33.

A third form of delayed response is *hysteresis*, the asymmetry in sales buildup compared with sales decline. For example, sales may rise quickly when an advertising program begins and then remain the same or decline slowly after the program ends.

New trier effects, in which sales reach a peak before settling down to steady state, are common for frequently purchased products, for which many customers try a new brand but only a few become regular users.

Stocking effects occur when a sales promotion not only attracts new customers but encourages existing customers to stock up or buy ahead. The stocking effect often leads to a sales trough in the period following the promotion (Exhibit 2.5).

The most common dynamic or carryover effect model used in marketing is

$$Y_t = a_0 + a_1 X_t + \lambda Y_{t-1}. \tag{2.19}$$

Equation (2.19) says that sales at time t (Y_t) are made up of a constant minimum base (a_0), an effect of current activity $a_1 X_t$, and a proportion of last period's sales (λ) that carries over to this period. Note that Y_t is influenced to some extent by all previous effort levels $X_{t-1}, X_{t-2}, \ldots, X_0$, because Y_{t-1} depends on X_{t-1} and Y_{t-2}, and in turn Y_{t-2} depends on X_{t-2} and Y_{t-3}, and so on. The simple form of Eq. (2.19) makes calibration easy—managers can either guess λ directly as the proportion of sales that carries over from one period to the next or estimate it by using linear regression.

MARKET-SHARE MODELS AND COMPETITIVE EFFECTS

Thus far we have ignored the effect of competition in our models, assuming that product sales result directly from marketing activities. Yet, if the set of product choices characterizing a market are well defined, we can specify three types of models that might be appropriate:

- Brand sales models (Y)
- Product class sales models (V)
- Market-share models (M)

Note that by definition

$$Y = M \times V. \tag{2.20}$$

Equation (2.20) is a powerful reminder that we obtain our sales (Y) by extracting our share (M) from the market in which we are operating (V). Thus an action we take may influence our sales by affecting the size of the market (V), our share of the market (M), or both. It is possible that an action of ours may result in zero incremental sales in at least two ways. First, it might have no effect at all. But second, it might entice a competitive response, leading to a gain in total product class sales (V goes up) while we lose our share of that market (M goes down). Equation (2.20) allows us to disentangle such effects.

Models of product class sales (V) have generally used many of the analytic forms we have introduced earlier, using time-series or judgmental data and explaining demand through environmental variables (population sizes, growth, past sales levels, etc.) and by aggregate values of marketing variables (total advertising spending, average price, etc.). Market-share models are a different story. To be logically consistent, regardless of what any competitor does in the marketplace, each firm's market share must be between 0 and 100 percent (range restriction) and market shares, summed over brands, must equal 100 percent (sum restriction).

A class of models that satisfy both the range and the sum restrictions are attraction models, where the attraction of a brand depends on its marketing mix. Essentially these models say our share = us/(us + them), where "us" refers to the attractiveness of our brand and (us + them) refers to the attractiveness of all brands in the market, including our brand.

Thus the general attraction model can be written as

$$M_i = \frac{A_i}{A_1 + A_2 + \cdots + A_n} \tag{2.21}$$

where

A_i = attractiveness of brand i, and $A_i \geq 0$, and

M_i = firm i's market share.

Attraction models suggest that the market share of a brand is equal to the brand's share of the total marketing effort (attractiveness).

While many model forms of A's are used in practice, two of the most common are the linear interactive form and the multiplicative form outlined in the section on interactions of marketing-mix elements. Both of these models suffer from what is called the "proportional draw" property. We can see this best via an example:

EXAMPLE

Suppose $A_1 = 10$, $A_2 = 5$, and $A_3 = 5$.
In a market with A_1 and A_2 only,

$$m_1 = \frac{10}{10 + 5} = 66\,\tfrac{2}{3}\,\% \text{ and } m_2 = \frac{5}{10 + 5} = 33\,\tfrac{1}{3}\,\%.$$

Suppose A_3 enters. Then after entry,

$$\overline{m}_1 = \frac{10}{10 + 5 + 5} = 50\%, \; \overline{m}_2 = 25\%, \text{ and } \overline{m}_3 = 25\%.$$

Note that brand 3 draws its 25 percent market share from the other two brands, $16\tfrac{2}{3}$ percent from brand 1 and $8\tfrac{1}{3}$ percent from brand 2—that is, proportional to those brands' market shares. But suppose that brand 3 is a product aimed at attacking brand 1; one would expect it to compete more than proportionally with brand 1 and less than proportionally with brand 2.

Thus when using simple market-share models, be sure that all the brands you are considering are competing for essentially the same market. Otherwise you will need to use extensions of these basic models that admit different levels of competition between brands (Cooper 1993).

RESPONSE AT THE INDIVIDUAL CUSTOMER LEVEL*

Thus far we have looked at market response at the level of the entire marketplace. However, markets are composed of individuals, and we can analyze the response behaviors of those individuals and either use them directly (at the segment or segment-of-one level) or aggregate them to form total market response.

Because information at the individual level is now widely available, researchers are increasingly interested in response models specified at the individual level. The information comes from scanner panels, where a panel of consumers uses specially issued cards for their supermarket shopping, allowing all purchase information—captured by bar-code scanners—by that consumer to be stored and tracked; database marketing activities, which capture purchase information at the individual level; and other sources.

Whereas aggregate market response models focus, appropriately, either on brand sales or market share, models at the individual level focus on purchase probability. Purchase probability at the individual level is equivalent to market share at the market level; indeed, by summing purchase probabilities across individuals (suitably weighted for individual differences in purchase quantities, purchase timing, and the like), one gets an estimate of market share. Hence it should not be surprising that the most commonly used individual response models have forms that are like Eq. (2.21), our general market-share response model. At the individual level, the denominator represents all those brands that an individual is willing to consider before making a purchase.

The specific functional form most commonly used to characterize individual choice behavior is the multinomial logit model. A simple form of the multinomial logit model is

$$P_{i1} = \frac{e^{A_1}}{\sum_j e^{A_j}} . \tag{2.22}$$

where

$$A_j = \sum_k w_k b_{ijk} \tag{2.23}$$

b_{ijk} = individual i's evaluation of product j on product attribute k (product quality, for example), where the summation is over all brands that individual i is considering purchasing; and

w_k = importance weight associated with attribute k in forming product preferences.

Equation (2.22) gives the probability of individual i choosing brand 1. Analogous equations may be specified for the probabilities of individual i choosing the other brands. We can estimate the importance weights w_k in a number of different ways, depending on whether we have information on *likelihood-of-purchase* measures or whether we have observations of actual recent purchase events. In either case the weights are often called "revealed importance weights," because they are revealed by an analysis of the past behavior (e.g., choice) of consumers rather than by directly asking consumers. They are interpreted in much the same way as regression coefficients.

What is the value of using the logit form (Eq. 2.22)? The answer, briefly, is that the structure of logit mirrors the differential sensitivities we expect in actual choice behavior. To see how this works, consider the properties of logit. It assumes that each choice alter-

---

*This section draws on material from Huber (1993).

native has an intervally scaled measure of attractiveness. The predicted probability that an individual chooses an alternative is simply the exponent of its utility over the sum of the exponents of all alternatives in the set.

The exponentiation in (2.22) ensures that the probabilities are always positive, since the exponentiation of any real number is always positive. Exponentiation also ensures that the probabilities do not change if all the measures of attractiveness are increased by a constant. Thus the measures of attractiveness need only form interval scales, something quite useful since most customer-based measures only achieve interval quality.

A major value of logit is that it produces an S-shaped curve, tracking the expected relationship between attractiveness and choice. Graphing Eq. (2.22) as a function of A_i produces an S-shaped curve that asymptotes to zero for very unattractive brands and to one for very attractive ones.

In most applications of the logit model, the attractiveness of the brand is assumed to be a function of the characteristics of the object. This function is typically linear as in Eq. (2.23).

With this specification the marginal impact of a change in an attribute of an alternative b_{ilk} takes a particularly simple form. The derivative of P_i as a function of b_{ilk} is

$$\frac{dP_{il}}{db_{ilk}} = w_k P_{il}^* \left(1 - P_{il}^*\right), \tag{2.24}$$

where P_{il}^* is the predicted probability of choosing product i in the current choice set given the model. Thus the marginal value of a change in one variable is a function of the predicted probability of choosing the alternative. A graph of Eq. (2.24) is given in Exhibit 2.6. The marginal impact of a given marketing effort is maximized when the probability of choosing the brand is .5, but the marginal impact approaches zero when the probability of choosing that brand is near zero or close to one. Thus the logit model has a nice behavioral property: it assumes the incremental impact of marketing effort is at its peak when the consumer is "on the fence" about choosing it.

Thus a good reason to use logit is that it mimics the way we expect choice behavior to occur. Another choice model, probit (Daganzo 1979), also has this property, and indeed it is empirically indistinguishable from logit, except for very extreme probabilities. Probit, however, is far more difficult to estimate. Thus logit is generally preferred over probit simply because the available computer programs are easier to run.

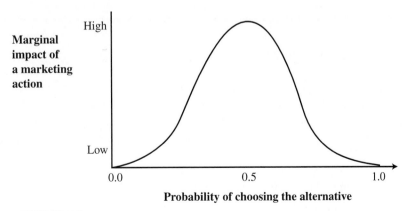

EXHIBIT 2.6
The marginal impact of marketing effort depends on the probability of choice.

The important point is that both logit and probit are better than a linear probability model, which simply predicts P_{il} as a function of a linear combination of the b_{ilk}'s. The linear probability model assumes a constant probabilistic impact of any change in the b_{ilk}'s. That is counter to our ideas of what the impact of external factors on choice ought to be and can result in predicted probabilities that are less than zero or greater than one!

Consider the following example:

EXAMPLE

Suppose that someone performed a survey of shoppers in an area to understand their shopping habits and to determine the share of shoppers that a new store might attract. The respondents rated three existing stores and one proposed store (described by a written concept statement) on a number of dimensions: (1) variety, (2) quality, (3) parking, and (4) value for the money (Exhibit 2.7). By fitting shoppers' choices of existing stores to their ratings through the logit model, we can estimate the coefficients $[w_k]$:

$$A_j = w_1 b_{j1} + \cdots + w_k b_{jk} + \cdots + w_K b_{jK}, \tag{2.25}$$

where

A_j = attractiveness of store j;

b_{jk} = rating for store j on dimension k, $k = 1, \ldots, K$; and

w_k = importance weight for dimension k.

The data in Exhibit 2.7 come from a group of similar customers. Exhibit 2.8 gives the share of the old stores with and without the new store, the potential share of the new store, and the draw estimated from this group.

The multinomial logit model has seen wide application, but it includes several assumptions that may limit its applicability. The assumption that invites the most criticism is the "proportional draw" assumption that we discussed in the section on market-share models. In column e of Exhibit 2.8, the draw is proportional to market share. In other words, this model assumes that all individuals consider all brands in their choice process, that they do not go through any prescreening or eliminate some brands. (This prescreening is often referred to as a consideration process.)

Attribute ratings by store

Store	Variety	Quality	Parking	Value for Money
1	0.7	0.5	0.7	0.7
2	0.3	0.4	0.2	0.8
3	0.6	0.8	0.7	0.4
4 (new)	0.6	0.4	0.8	0.5
Importance weight	2.0	1.7	1.3	2.2

EXHIBIT 2.7
Ratings and importance data for the store-selection example.

Store	(a) $A_i = w_k b_{jk}$	(b) e^{A_i}	(c) Share estimate without new store	(d) Share estimate with new store	(e) Draw [(c) – (d)]
1	4.70	109.9	0.512	0.407	0.105
2	3.30	27.1	0.126	0.100	0.026
3	4.35	77.5	0.362	0.287	0.075
4	4.02	55.7		0.206	

EXHIBIT 2.8
Logit model analysis of new store share example.

Researchers have developed several ways to deal with the proportional draw problem. One way is a priori segmentation; the researcher segments the market into groups that *do* consider (different) sets of brands differently. Another alternative is to group products (rather than customers) into groups that more directly compete with one another. If we view the choice process as a hierarchy, we can then assume that consumers select among branches of a tree at each level of the hierarchy (Exhibit 2.9). The consumer might first choose the form of the deodorant and then, conditional on that choice, choose the brand. The form of the logit model that applies here is called the nested logit, and it incorporates an equation like (2.22) for the selection of product form (the upper level of the hierarchy) and a separate logit model for brand (conditional on the selection of form) at the lowest level of the hierarchy. (See Roberts and Lilien (1993) for a more complete discussion.)

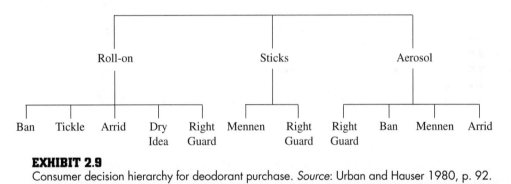

EXHIBIT 2.9
Consumer decision hierarchy for deodorant purchase. *Source*: Urban and Hauser 1980, p. 92.

Individual choice models of all sorts are difficult to estimate. If we measure only choices (yes-no or 0-1 responses) (and not market shares), then we cannot use regression-based methods (which assume that the dependent variable is continuous) and must use other procedures. These other procedures (maximum likelihood estimation is the most common) give outputs that can generally be interpreted like regression coefficients.

We illustrate the use of logit response models with the ASSESSOR model (Chapter 7), the gravity model (Chapter 9), and the promotion spending analysis model (Chapter 10).

SHARED EXPERIENCE AND QUALITATIVE MODELS

So far in this chapter we have focused on quantitative response models—equations that develop a formal analytic structure of the marketplace. We will now introduce two other forms of modeling that have proved valuable: shared-experience and qualitative models. We will discuss both in more depth in later chapters.

Shared experience models: If we do not have data about the way a market responds (or even if we do), it may be valuable to pool the experience of a wide range of businesses and develop norms or guidelines for response behavior from the pooled data. There are many ways that such pooling takes place. One example is benchmarking (comparing one's operations against acknowledged good alternatives).

In marketing there are a number of shared experience models. Two that we will explore are PIMS and ADVISOR. The PIMS model is based on the idea that by pooling the information on experiences of a sample of successful and unsuccessful businesses, one can gain useful insights and guidance for developing successful business strategies. ADVISOR relates the determinants of spending levels for business product advertising and selling to product, market, and environmental characteristics, providing norms for those spending levels. Neither model has a causal basis, although both provide clues about what might lead markets to respond in certain ways. Both are based on regression models, where the regressive weight inferred from a sample of practice might be applied to new situations to develop guidelines for action. We cover PIMS in Chapter 6 and ADVISOR in Chapter 8.

Qualitative response models: Some decision situations call for qualitative insights (the development of new copy for an advertising campaign, the structure of a negotiation between a buyer and a seller from different cultures, etc.). The experience of knowledgeable practitioners and guidelines generated by academic research can be useful in these situations. Qualitative response models help us to represent qualitative knowledge and insights.

In the physical sciences, mathematical models can often provide parsimonious and fairly accurate descriptions of phenomena. A well-known example is the equation $E = mc^2$, where an extraordinary range of physical phenomena are reduced to four symbols. In marketing, however, analytic functions are mostly a convenience, not necessarily accurate representations of phenomena. If a particular phenomenon can at best be described in a qualitative fashion, then a precise numerical model may be inappropriate for representing what is known. For example, if we can characterize consumer response to an ad only as positive, neutral, or negative, then a precise numerical model is inappropriate. Such a model would require managers to come up with an exact numerical value rather than allowing them to express exactly what they know. Here are two examples of qualitative response functions:

Example 1: The likely response to a price reduction by a competitor might be (1) match the new price, (2) maintain the current price, (3) change TV advertising, (4) increase trade promotion, or (5) fire the brand manager. These options do not fall along a continuum that can be succinctly represented by smooth analytic functions.

Example 2: The following response function might specify how a retailer might react to a trade promotion (McCann and Gallagher 1990): "This retailer always accepts a deal, but what he does with it is based on coop (shared) advertising dollars. If the deal includes coop money, the retailer will accept the deal and pass on all of the discount to the consumer. If the discount is greater than 30 percent, he will put up a big display. Otherwise, the retailer leaves the item at regular price and does not use an ad feature or a display."

We can use qualitative response functions in decision models by adopting nonmathematical representation schemes. Perhaps the most widely used approach is a rule-based representation. The response model is stated in the form of rules, which are statements joined by the connectives AND, OR, and NOT and properly specified by qualifiers FOR

ALL and THERE EXISTS. Using this representation, we can state Example 2 as a set of rules in computer representation form:

> If the deal includes coop money,
> Then the retailer will accept the deal.

> If the deal includes coop money,
> Then the retailer will pass on all the discount to the consumer.

> If the deal discount is greater than 30 percent,
> Then the retailer will put up a big display.

> If NOT(the deal includes coop money) AND
> NOT(discount is greater than 30 percent),
> Then the retailer will sell the item at regular price.

> If NOT(the deal includes coop money) AND
> NOT(discount is greater than 30 percent),
> Then retailer will use ad feature = No.

> If NOT(the deal includes coop money) AND
> NOT(discount is greater than 30 percent),
> Then retailer will use display = No.

When a response model consists of a set of rules, we can use artificial intelligence techniques, particularly logical inference, to derive recommendations in specific decision situations. Such rule sets are used for developing expert systems. In Chapter 8 we describe such an expert system called ADCAD for designing TV commercials.

CHOOSING AND EVALUATING A MARKETING RESPONSE MODEL

The model forms we have described in this chapter present a number of trade-offs. One model form is not better than another. Each is good in some situations and for some purposes. We need to consider the model's use. Although a number of criteria are useful in selecting a model, here are four we suggest that apply specifically to response models:

Model specification
- Does the model include the right variables to represent the decision situation?
- Are the variables, as represented, managerially actionable?
- Does the model incorporate the expected behavior of individual variables? (e.g., diminishing returns, carryover effects, or threshold effects).
- Does the model incorporate the expected relationships between variables? (e.g., patterns of substitutability and complementarity).

Model calibration
- Can the model be calibrated by using data from managerial judgment or historical data, or through experimentation?

Model validity
- Does the level of detail in the model match that in the available data?
- Does the model reproduce the current market environment reasonably accurately?
- Does the model provide value-in-use to the user?
- Does the model represent the phenomenon of interest accurately and completely?

Model usability

■ Is the model easy to use? (E.g., is it simple, does it convey results in an under-standable manner, and does it permit users to control its operation?)
■ Is the model as implemented easy to understand?
■ Does the model give managers guidance that makes sense?

When we select a model, we can summarize these criteria in one question: "Does this model make sense for this situation?" That is, does the model have the right form, can it be calibrated, is it valid, and is it useful? If the answers are all yes, then the model is appropriate.

SUMMARY

In this chapter we have given a very brief overview of market response models—the toolkit for marketing engineering. We have also introduced many concepts and the re-lated vocabulary.

We have defined, classified, and provided details of some simple, commonly used re-sponse models. We also have outlined how you can calibrate them, what criteria are most appropriate to use as model objectives, and how you can best select a model.

But you cannot learn to ride a bicycle by reading a book about it—you have to get on and try it out. That is what we want you to do now. We strongly recommend that you try the Conglomerate Inc. promotional exercise and visual response modeling exercises now. The former will give you some experience with judgmental calibration, with building models in Excel, and with using Excel's Solver tool to develop guidelines for marketing action. The visual response modeling exercise is linked to the Conglomerate Inc. promotional analysis exercise and shows you how to build a response model.

There is enormous potential value in learning to ride the ME bicycle—jump aboard and try it out!

Chapter 2 Appendix
ABOUT EXCEL'S SOLVER

We have used the Excel spreadsheet program as a platform to implement many of the mar-keting models in this book, because spreadsheets are excellent tools for viewing data and for building models. Moreover, spreadsheets provide utilities—such as graphing capabili-ties—that facilitate analysis. And finally, and important to us, they offer links to other util-ities that greatly expand the domain of an application. Excel's Solver add-in function (be sure your installation of Excel has this add-in feature before working with the Marketing Engineering software) is such a utility, and it is used in many of the Excel software tools.

Solver is a program that solves linear and nonlinear optimization problems, with or without constraints. In English this means that

■ If you can specify sales as a function of advertising spending, then Solver will tell you what level of advertising will maximize your profits. It will optimize the mar-keting mix.
■ If you are looking for some model parameters that will make a function represent data best, Solver will determine which parameters minimize squared differences between actual values and predicted values (model calibration—via least squares regression).

- If you want to determine what level of marketing effort will help you meet a sales target, Solver will help you determine the value that will do it (market-mix target setting).

All of these problems (and optimization problems in general) have three basic components: decision variables, constraints, and an objective function.

Decision variables are mathematical representations of the marketing-mix variables that we wish to set. An example variable is "Promotional spending (X) in Albuquerque (i) in July (t)," which we will represent below by X_{it}.

Constraints: All marketing problems have constraints. Promotional spending cannot be less than 0 (nonnegativity constraint). The number of sales calls in a period must be both nonnegative and an integer (integer constraint). The total promotional budget may be set at a fixed amount (equality constraint) or as a ceiling (inequality constraint).

Objectives: In the text of Chapter 2, we discussed objectives. We must specify the objective as the (single) criterion that we wish to maximize (profit), minimize (sum of squared deviations), or set equal to a target (a specific target ROI, for example).

We can characterize an optimization problem mathematically as follows:

(Decision Variables)

Find

$$\{X_{it}\};\ X_{it} \geq 0 \text{ for } i = 1, \ldots, \text{ number of markets and } t = 1, \ldots \text{ end of}$$
planning period.

(Objective)

To

$$\text{Max (or Min) } Z\big(\{X_{it}\}\big)$$

(Constraints)

Subject to

$$f_j\{X_{it}\} \geq b_j \text{ (or } \leq b_j, \text{ or } = b_j) \text{ for } j = 1, \cdots \text{ number of constraints.}$$

EXAMPLE

Find

X (the level of advertising spending—the decision variable)   (2A.1a)

To

$$\text{Max } \$0.70 \times \left(5 + 30 \times \left(\frac{X^2}{15 + X^2} \right) - X \right) \text{—the objective}$$ (2A.1b)

(i.e., margin TIMES sales response to advertising LESS advertising expenditures)

Subject to

$X \geq 0$ (advertising must be nonnegative—constraint).   (2A.1c)

This problem can be set up in a spreadsheet using Solver quite simply; the following spreadsheet implements the model:

	D6	▼		=0.7*(5+30*(D4^2/(D4^2+15)))-D4		
	A	B	C	D	E	F	G
1							
2							
3							
4		Advertising Level (X) =		$7.25			
5							
6		Profit =		$12.59			
7							
8							
9							
10				Advertising	Profit		
11				$0.00	$3.50		
12				$0.25	$3.34		
13				$0.50	$3.34		
14				$0.75	$3.51		

By selecting solver from the **T**ools menu, we set up the optimization as

Solver Parameters

Set Target Cell: D6
Equal to: ⦿ Max ○ Min ○ Value of: 0
By Changing Cells: D4 Guess
Subject to the Constraints: D4 >= 0 Add... Change... Delete Options... Reset All Help
Solve Close

Note that in this structure we

Set Cell: D6 (our profit objective)

Equal to Max

By Changing Cells: D4 (advertising spending)

Subject to the Constraints:

D4 $\geq$ 0.

Solver then finds the optimal value of advertising ($7.25 in this case). See your Excel User's Guide or select Excel **H**elp to obtain more details on setting up optimization problems using Solver.

HOW SOLVER WORKS

The Solver implemented in Excel (produced by a software firm called Frontline Systems) uses numerical methods to solve equations and to optimize linear and nonlinear functions with either continuous variables (as in advertising spending) or integer variables (number of account-visits in a quarter). The methods used are iterative; generally Solver calculates how small changes in the decision variables affect the value of the objective function. If the objective function improves (profit increases in our case), Solver moves the decision variables in that direction. If the objective function gets worse, Solver moves in the other direction. If the objective function cannot be improved by either an increase or a decrease in any of the decision variables, Solver stops, reporting at least a local solution.

The field of nonlinear, constrained optimization (especially with integer variables) is quite complex and beyond the scope of this book. (See Lilien, Kotler, and Moorthy (1992, Appendix A) for more discussion or Nemhauser, Kan, and Todd (1989) for a more thorough review of optimization theory. Ragsdale (1995) provides a practical introduction to analyses and optimization with spreadsheets.) However, you should be aware of some situations that can occur with nonlinear optimizers.

1. *Local optima*: While Solver may have found the top of a hill (the highest point in the region), there may be a higher peak elsewhere. Solver would have to go DOWN from the local peak and begin searching elsewhere to find it. In other words, Solver would need a new starting value (values in the "By Changing Variable" cells in the "Solver Parameter" box) to find the optimum.

EXAMPLE

Note the graph that follows of the advertising spending function that we optimized. Suppose that we started Solver with the level of advertising = 0. Note that advertising spending cannot be negative and that profit initially decreases with increases in advertising spending because we have an advertising response model with a threshold. (The form of Eq. (2A.1b) has us subtracting advertising spending from the sales/profit response function. If the latter is flat, the profit function will be decreasing.) Hence Solver cannot decrease advertising spending to less than zero (because of the constraint) and it does not want to go up (as, locally, at least, that would decrease profitability), and so we are at a local maximum. However, if we start the problem with advertising at 1.0 or greater, Solver will correctly find the optimum value at $7.25.

What this example illustrates is that when you are using market response functions that have threshold effects, you may need to try different starting values to be

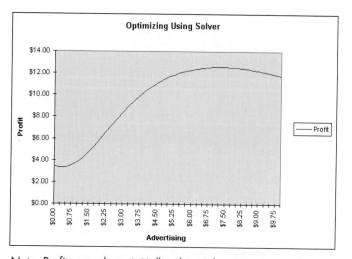

Note: Profit goes down initially when Advertising is near 0.

sure that you have reached a global optimal solution. Several of the software programs, like Syngen, have built-in options that permit you to, in effect, try a different starting value if Solver fails to converge or gives you a local solution.

2. *No feasible solution*: Suppose that we set two constraints: $X > 6$ and $X < 3$. Clearly both of these constraints cannot be satisfied at the same time, and Solver will fail to provide any solution. While the example here makes the lack of any feasible solution obvious, in larger problems this is often quite subtle.

3. *Other problems*: General nonlinear optimizers like Excel's Solver are remarkable technical additions to the analyst's toolkit. With their power and flexibility come a variety of other problems, however. The user who wants to use Solver directly in market analyses or who wants to adapt or adjust the operation of some of the software that uses Solver may run into a number of other questions or problems, many of which are addressed in Excel's User's Guide.

Some of those problems are caused by the way the user formulates the specific problem and employs Solver's options. Other problems may be caused by bugs in your version of Excel and in Excel's link to your operating system (your version of Windows). If the results you are getting do not make sense, it may help to quit Windows or even to reboot your computer before trying to solve the problem again.

CHAPTER **3**

Segmentation and Targeting

Segmentation, the process of dividing the market into consumer groups with similar needs and developing marketing programs that meet those needs, is essential for marketing success: the most successful firms drive their businesses based on segmentation. Targeting is the process of selecting that segment or those segments in a market to serve. In this chapter we discuss

■ Segmentation, the process of dividing customers into groups whose valuations of products are similar within groups and who differ across those groups
■ Defining a market: the set of products that are substitutes for one another within a usage segment
■ Segmentation research, the design of segmentation studies and associated data collection procedures to support a segmentation strategy
■ Segmentation methods, the models and procedures available to segment the market and to profile the segments, based on the data collected from segmentation research
■ Behavior-based segmentation, an approach to segmentation grounded not on direct measurement of customer values but on inference of those values based on customer purchase behavior
   Associated with this chapter are two key pieces of software: one that performs clustering and discriminant analysis and another that implements choice-based segmentation.

THE SEGMENTATION PROCESS

Defining segmentation

Markets are heterogeneous. Customers differ in their values, needs, wants, constraints, beliefs, and incentives to act in a particular way. Products compete with one another in attempting to satisfy the needs and wants of those customers. By segmenting the market, firms can better understand their customers and target their marketing efforts efficiently and effectively. Through segmentation an organization strives to attain a happy middle ground where it does not rely on a common marketing program for all customers, nor does it incur the high costs of developing a unique program for each customer.

Three definitions are critical to the concept of segmentation:

A *market segment* is a group of actual or potential customers who can be expected to respond in a similar way to a product or service offer. That is, they want the same types of benefits or solutions to problems from the product or service, or they respond in a similar way to a company's marketing communications.

Market segmentation is the process of dividing customers whose valuations of a product or service vary greatly into groups or segments containing customers whose valuations vary very little within the group but vary greatly among groups.

A *target market* is a market that a company chooses to serve effectively and profitably.

Three fundamental factors provide the conditions that create an opportunity for a firm to successfully segment a market. First and most necessary is heterogeneity of customer needs and wants. In these circumstances customers actively seek and pay a premium for products and services that better meet their needs and wants. Second, although customers may be heterogeneous, they do cluster into specific groups whose members' needs are more similar to those of other customers in that group than they are to the needs of customers in other groups. Finally, the costs of serving customers in a segment must be no more than they are willing to pay, although they may be higher than the costs of serving an average customer. When customer needs differ or when the costs of serving different types of customers vary substantially, a firm that does not segment a market presents its competitors with an opportunity to enter the market.

At one extreme, a firm could think of each customer as a unique market segment: a segment of one. The business and production processes of most companies make it too costly to serve such small segments, and so they must strike a balance between the cost of serving a segment and the value customers get from their products—products designed to fit the needs of particular customers provide more customer utility than products that fit the average need. Because it provides this extra customer utility, the manufacturer may be able to charge a higher price for the more customized products, and it may reduce competitive pressure by making it more difficult for other manufacturers to tailor better products to meet the segment's needs.

Segmentation theory and practice

Firms use segmentation research to answer a wide variety of questions about the varying responses of market segments to marketing strategies (price changes, new product offerings, promotional plans, etc.), and about selecting and defining target segments for planned offerings. Some typical management problems addressed by segmentation studies are the following:

Which new-product concepts evoke the highest respondent interest, and how do the evaluations of these concepts differ by respondent group—heavy versus light users of the product and users versus nonusers of the company's brand?

In terms of target markets for a new-product concept, how do potential heavy and light users differ by demographic and socioeconomic characteristics, attitudes, and product-use characteristics?

Can the market for potential new products be segmented in terms of customers' price sensitivity (or other benefits sought)? What are the concept evaluations, attitudes, product use, demographic, and other background characteristics of the various price-sensitive segments (Wind 1978, p. 318)?

However, such questions have little to do with the basic theory of segmentation, which focuses on the relationship between customer characteristics, varying responses to potential products, and the optimal development of a marketing strategy. We try to bridge the gap between theory and real-world problems here.

To answer the management questions we have raised, we develop a segmentation model. The market segments identified in the model should satisfy three conditions: homogeneity/heterogeneity, parsimony, and accessibility. *Homogeneity* is the measure of the degree to which the potential customers in a segment (a) have similar responses to some marketing variable of interest, and (b) are different from other groups of customers. Unfortunately, no segmentation is perfect; members of different segments frequently show considerable overlap in their responses to marketing variables. *Parsimony* is a measure of the degree to which the segmentation would make every potential customer a unique target. If a study is to be useful to managers, it should identify a small set (often between three and eight) of groupings of substantial size. Finally, *accessibility* is the degree to which marketers can reach segments separately using observable characteristics of the segments (descriptor variables).

A segmentation model requires a dependent variable, usually called a segmentation *basis*, and independent variables, or segment *descriptors*. The segmentation basis should describe why customers will respond differently (why they value offerings differently, i.e., their needs and wants) while segment *descriptors* (like age, income, use of media) help marketers deliver different product or service offerings to various customer segments. In practice the distinction between bases and descriptors is contingent on the reasons for conducting the segmentation study. Analytical methods such as regression or discriminant analysis can be used to relate segment membership to descriptors. Analysts use the resulting model to predict whether a potential customer belongs to a specific segment.

Given a measure of managerial interest, such as purchase likelihood, we can use relevant segment variables (descriptors) to discriminate among segments of the population along the criterion (basis) of interest. A relevant segmentation descriptor for responsiveness to solar water-heating systems might be different climates—solar regions—in which individuals live (Exhibit 3.1a). An irrelevant segmentation descriptor for the same product would be the educational level of the potential buyer (Exhibit 3.1b).

In practice segmentation approaches focus either on descriptions of customers or on their observed or likely values or actions, although some approaches blend the two. Many articles tout one approach over another. Most of these arguments are moot, partly because no method exists for determining how similar two customers are who differ on a number of needs and behavioral dimensions. The management problem at hand, combined with cost and information on availability, should point to the best approach to use. Also, the best approach depends on the reason for undertaking the segmentation study. Wind's (1978) recommendations about appropriate bases for different types of marketing problems (Exhibit 3.2) underscore this point.

There is no single segmentation approach. The marketing problem, the timing, the availability of relevant data, and similar considerations should dictate the appropriate approach.

Segmentation is best viewed as the first step in a three-step process of segmentation, targeting, and positioning (STP). Segmentation groups customers with similar wants, needs, and responses. Targeting determines which groups a firm should try to serve (and how). Positioning addresses how the firm's product will compete with others in the market. We address the first two steps in this chapter and describe positioning in the next.

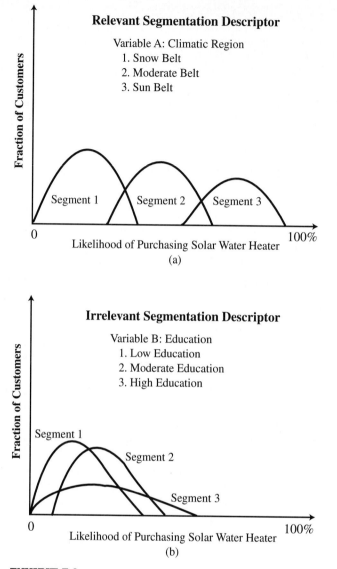

EXHIBIT 3.1
Relevant and irrelevant segment descriptors: relevant descriptors separate segments (a) while irrelevant ones do not (b).

The STP approach

Segmentation has two phases:

Phase 1 Segment the market using demand variables (e.g., customer needs, wants, benefits sought, problem solutions desired, and usage situations).

Phase 2 Describe the market segments identified using variables that help the firm understand how to serve these customers (e.g., shopping patterns, geographic locations, clothing size, spending power, and price sensitivity), how to talk to these customers (e.g., media preference and use, attitudes, activities, interests,

For General Understanding of a Market
   Benefits sought (in industrial markets the criterion used is purchase decision)
   Product-purchase and product-use patterns
   Needs
   Brand-loyalty and brand-switching patterns
   A hybrid of the variables above

For Positioning Studies
   Product use
   Product preference
   Benefits sought
   A hybrid of the variables above

For New-Product Concepts (and New-Product Introduction)
   Reaction to new concepts (intention to buy, preference over current brand, etc.)
   Benefits sought

For Pricing Decisions
   Price sensitivity
   Deal proneness
   Price sensitivity by purchase/use patterns

For Advertising Decisions
   Benefits sought
   Media use
   Psychographic/lifestyle
   A hybrid (of the variables above and/or purchase/use patterns)

For Distribution Decisions
   Store loyalty and patronage
   Benefits sought in store selection

EXHIBIT 3.2
The most appropriate segmentation bases depend on the managerial use of the segmentation—
there is no single, best segmentation. *Source*: Wind 1978, p. 320.

and opinions), and buyer switching costs (the costs associated with changing products or suppliers).

Targeting has two phases:

Phase 3   Evaluate the attractiveness of each segment using variables that quantify the demand possibilities of each segment (e.g., its growth rate), the costs of serving each segment (e.g., distribution costs), the costs to the firm of producing the products and services the customers want (e.g., production and product differentiation costs), and the fit between the firm's core competencies and the target market opportunity.

Phase 4   Select one or more target segments to serve based on the profit potential of the segments and their fit with the firm's corporate strategy.

Positioning is the final phase:

Phase 5   Identify a positioning concept for the firm's products and services that attracts target customers and that enhances the firm's desired corporate image.

We elaborate on the first four phases next (segmentation and targeting) and address Phase 5 (positioning) in Chapter 4.

Segmenting markets (Phase 1)

Of the many possible ways to segment markets, we recommend segmenting based on customers' needs and the situations in which they use the product. Given this perspective, we can segment markets in two ways. We can start with characteristics of customers that are easy to identify and see if the resulting customer groups have different needs. For example, do people in New York have different entertainment needs than those in Fort Lauderdale? Alternatively, we can group customers based on their needs and then search for discriminating characteristics that enable us to identify groups that differ in their need. For example, are customers who frequent live entertainment venues price sensitive, heavy users, and so forth? The first approach is often called *convenience-group* or *backward* segmentation. That is, we form market segments based on how convenient they are to serve. Companies serving industrial markets often use convenience-group or backward segmentation; it is a reactive form of market segmentation.

Whenever possible, firms should be proactive in segmenting the market. They should identify differences in customers' needs, wants, and preferences and then see if they can design products and strategies to profitably serve these different needs. We suggest a five-step approach.

Step 1 is to explicitly outline the role of market segmentation in the company's strategy. How will it help the firm to establish a competitive advantage, and what other actions might the firm take to achieve its objectives? For example, the firm's abilities to develop truly new products or business processes are two strategic factors that may influence the way it segments its markets. The underlying cost (dis)advantage arising from the firm's position on its experience curve is another factor to consider. A firm should not segment the market without first considering its overall strategic intent and its core competencies.

Step 2 is to select a set of segmentation variables. These variables should be based on some aspect of a potential customer's needs or wants and should reflect differences between customers. To do this the firm needs intimate knowledge of the factors that drive demand for its products and services. Geodemographic segmentation (often used in direct marketing) focuses on the location, income, sex, marital status, and other such characteristics of target customers. In many consumer markets, the segmentation variables reflect customer differences on perceptual dimensions (see Chapter 4) and often concern geodemographic and socioeconomic characteristics. In industrial markets, the benefits the customers seek depend less on the psychological and socioeconomic characteristics of the individual making the purchase decision and more on the end use of the product and the profitability it generates (see Chapter 10 and the value-in-use concept). In the end, the segmentation variables one chooses should isolate groups of customers whose needs show within-group homogeneity and between-group heterogeneity.

Step 3 is to choose the mathematical and statistical procedures one can use to aggregate individual customers into homogeneous groups or segments; this entails an implicit strategic decision: Are customer segments to be discrete (each customer in only one segment), overlapping (a customer can be in two or more groups), or fuzzy (each customer is assigned a proportional membership in each segment). Assigning each customer to a single segment is easier to understand and to apply, but we may be sacrificing information. Overlapping or fuzzy segments are intuitively more appealing, more realistic, and theoretically more accurate. However, under these fuzzy circumstances developing a segmentation strategy is much more complex, since the firm needs to position identical products differently to the different overlapping segments.

In steps 4 and 5, the firm must make two crucial decisions: *step 4* is to specify the maximum number of segments to construct based on the segmentation variables; *step 5* is to search across those segments to determine how many of those segments to target. We have no theory to guide us in deciding on the correct number of segments; this is more art than science.

Firms decide on the number of segments to target using both statistical criteria and managerial judgment. What usually happens is that firms split the (potential) market into two groups, then three groups, four groups, and so on, up to the maximum number of segments they have decided to consider. They examine each of these segment structures using various managerial and statistical criteria to eliminate any groups that are statistically or managerially unsuitable. This process invariably leads to conflict. Middle managers and salespeople naturally focus on a large number of narrowly defined market segments, while upper managers tend to view the market as comprised of a small number of broadly defined segments (Exhibit 3.3).

EXAMPLE

Dowling and Midgley (1988) found that they could use two market structures to reflect needs in the Australian women's clothing market. Splitting the market into three segments was appropriate for making broad strategic decisions, while six segments were more appropriate for tactical marketing decisions. The narrow tactical segments are related to the broad strategic segments (Exhibit 3.3). The six tactical segments rank weakly from low fashion to high fashion. These tactical segments aggregate up into three broader strategic segments, again ranging roughly from low to high fashion. With both coarse and fine structures of segments, top managers can develop strategy at the broad level, while middle managers and salespeople can—and really must—implement it at the narrow level. The only complication is that the small segments have no one-to-one relationship with the large segments. For example, in Exhibit 3.3 the innovative communicators include higher status leaders but overlap with two other segments at the tactical level (low status leaders and professional singles). The segmentation strategy must account for this so that managers can determine how to implement the strategy (e.g., which distribution channels to use and which advertising message to use).

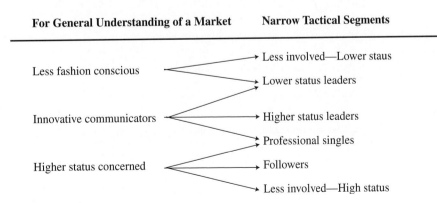

For General Understanding of a Market	Narrow Tactical Segments
Less fashion conscious	Less involved—Lower staus
	Lower status leaders
Innovative communicators	Higher status leaders
	Professional singles
Higher status concerned	Followers
	Less involved—High status

EXHIBIT 3.3
Resolving the conflict between needs for segmentation at different levels in the Australian women's clothing market. Top management usually focuses on the broad strategic segments while middle management is concerned with narrower segments.

In the case of industrial markets, Robertson and Barich (1992) found that, at the broad strategic level, they could break customers down into three groups: first-time prospects, novices, and sophisticates. First-time prospects are new to the market and have just begun to evaluate vendors. Novices have purchased the product but are still uncertain about its use and appropriateness. Sophisticates have purchased and used the product and are knowledgeable about it (Exhibit 3.4). Although Robertson and Barich's approach is limited, it illustrates a basic form of segmentation, one that is based on knowledge-based needs that are independent of the idiosyncratic nature of the individual market. According to them, industrial markets generally exhibit these knowledge-based segments.

Describing market segments (Phase 2)

After isolating a number of segments in a market, one must describe these segments. The variables you choose to describe the various market segments should highlight the profit potential (price sensitivity and size) of each segment and how the company might serve these segments. You can use two general types of variables for this purpose: those that outline broad market characteristics and those that provide insight into serving one or more of the market segments.

For consumer and industrial markets, you can use broadly similar variables to describe the various segments (Exhibit 3.5). Using these variables you can profile the segments in the market to find actual and potential customers, to understand their purchase motivations, and to understand how to communicate with them.

Many combinations of variables can be used to describe a market (Exhibit 3.5). In determining strategy, you should select variables that help you to

- Measure the size and purchasing power of the segments
- Determine the degree to which you can effectively reach and serve the segments
- Develop effective programs to attract customers

Properly implemented, this approach normally leads to readily distinguishable segments.

First-Time Prospects	**Novices**	**Sophisticates**
Dominant Theme: "Take care of me"	**Dominant Theme:** "Help me make it work"	**Dominant Theme:** "Talk technology to me"
Benefits Sought: Knowledge of my business Honest sales representative Vendor who has experience Sales representative who can communicate in an understandable manner	**Benefits Sought:** Easy-to-read manuals Technical support hotlines A high level of training Sales representative knowledgable about products and services	**Benefits Sought:** Compatibility with systems Customization Track record of vendor Sales support and technical assistance
What's Less Important: Sales representative's knowledge about products and services	**What's Less Important:** Honest sales representative Knowledge of my business	**What's Less Important:** Sales representative who can communicate in an understandable manner Training Trial Easy-to-read manuals

EXHIBIT 3.4
Robertson and Barich's classification of three generic segments in industrial markets and what they value. *Source:* Robertson and Barich 1992.

	Consumer	Industrial
Segmentation Bases	Needs, wants, benefits, solutions to problems, usage situation, usage rate.	Needs, wants, benefits, solutions to problems, usage situation, usage rate, size*, industry*
Descriptors		
• Demographics/ Firmographics	Age, income, marital status, family type and size, gender, social class, etc.	Industry, size, location, current supplier(s), technology utilization, etc.
• Psychographics	Lifestyle, values, and personality characteristics.	Personality characteristics of decision makers.
• Behavior	Use occasions, usage level, complementary and substitute products used, brand loyalty, etc.	Use occasions, usage level, complementary and substitute products used, brand loyalty, order size, applications, etc.
• Decision making	Individual or group (family) choice, low or high involvement purchase, attitudes and knowledge about product class, price sensitivity, etc.	Formalization of purchasing procedures, size and characteristics of decision making group, use of outside consultants, purchasing criteria, (de)centralized buying, price sensitivity, switching costs, budget cycle, etc.
• Media patterns	Level of use, types of media used, times of use, etc.	Level of use, types of media used, times of use, patronage at trade shows, receptivity to salespeople, etc.

*These are "macro-segmentation"— or first stage—bases.

EXHIBIT 3.5
A list of common bases and descriptors that can be used to segment and describe markets, noting the differences between consumer and industrial variables.

Evaluating segment attractiveness (Phase 3)

In the next phase you choose one or more markets to serve. We suggest that you use nine measures, grouped into three broad factors, to evaluate the attractiveness of a segment of customers (Exhibit 3.6). One factor (criteria 1 and 2) concerns the size of the group and its growth potential. Although bigger, faster growing segments seem intuitively appealing, what constitutes the right size and growth potential for a company will depend on its resources and capabilities.

The second factor concerns the structural characteristics of the segment and includes four criteria (criteria 3, 4, 5, and 6): competition, segment saturation, protectability, and environmental risk. Porter (1980) identified a set of competitive factors (criterion 3) that is widely used to assess competitive rivalry in a market segment. That set includes such items as barriers to entry, barriers to exit, the threat of new entrants, pressure from substitute products, customer bargaining power, and supplier bargaining power. A company should also assess whether the existing competitors in the market are serving all the obvious segments or if they have left gaps in the market.

The third factor, product-market fit, includes criteria 7, 8, and 9. A company should ask at least three types of screening questions. First, does serving a segment fit the company's strengths and its desired corporate image? Second, can the company gain any synergy from serving this segment? Third, can the company sustain the costs of entering this segment, and can it price its products and services to achieve the desired margins and returns

Criterion	Examples of Considerations
I. Size and Growth	
1. Size	• Market potential, current market penetration
2. Growth	• Past growth forecasts of technology change
II. Structural Characteristics	
3. Competition	• Barriers to entry, barriers to exit, position of competitors, ability to retaliate
4. Segment saturation	• Gaps in the market
5. Protectability	• Patentability of products, barriers to entry
6. Environmental risk	• Economic, political, and technological change
III. Product–Market Fit	
7. Fit	• Coherence with company's strengths and image
8. Relationships with other segments	• Synergy, cost interactions, image transfers, cannibalization
9. Profitability	• Entry costs, margin levels, return on investment

EXHIBIT 3.6
Some suggested criteria to use when evaluating segment attractiveness: use the ones that are most appropriate in your industry and for your business problem.

on investment? Many companies have tried to grow and failed by pursuing a market segment that offers a high return on investment but a poor fit with the firm's current capabilities. This strategy is sometimes referred to as the "unrelated diversification trap."

Selecting target segments (Phase 4)

After developing the criteria to evaluate the attractiveness of various market segments, the firm must select which segments to serve. It has five basic options (Kotler 1997, p. 284):

- To concentrate on a single segment
- To select segments in which to specialize
- To provide a range of products to a specific segment
- To provide a single product to many segments
- To cover the full market

Which option should the firm choose? A small company with limited resources probably cannot serve the full market. Despite their being able to serve the entire market, big companies should make a strategic choice. Most often firms use a simple heuristic; for example, they select those segments that rate highest for the attractiveness criteria described in the previous section. Sometimes managers use a matrix (Exhibit 3.7) to help them evaluate the opportunities facing the firm. For segments (such as E and A) that are very attractive and match the firm's competencies very well or the opposite, they can make clear decisions; serve segment E and keep out of segment A. They must make true strategic decisions for segments whose attractiveness or in which the firm's competencies are not so extreme (B, C, and D), trading off segment attractiveness against the core strengths and competencies of the company.

This type of analysis was originally developed by General Electric, and it relies on a fairly common form of portfolio matrix.

When a company targets only its most attractive segment, it concentrates all its resources on serving a single group of customers. This focus should enable the firm to understand and

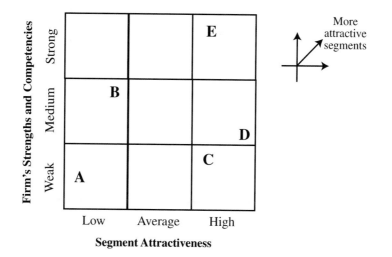

EXHIBIT 3.7
Selecting segments to serve: We plot five segments—A through E—along segment attractiveness and firm competence dimensions and note that segments are more attractive as we move in a northeasterly direction.

serve the needs of this segment. Such concentration in a single segment, however, comes at a price; the company has exposed itself to high risk: it has put all its eggs in one basket.

> ### EXAMPLE
>
> McDonald's originally focused on lunchtime and dinnertime hamburger customers. But how could it make its existing business grow? It targeted the fast food breakfast-eater, opening earlier and adding such items as Egg McMuffins to the menu. It also targeted other tastes (beyond hamburgers), adding chicken products (McNuggets) to the menu. It tested pizza varieties in a number of locations with mixed results. The firm continues to balance the benefits of targeting multiple segments against the costs of serving those new segments and of possibly becoming less attractive to their traditional loyal (hamburger) customers.

> ### EXAMPLE
>
> Lotus Corporation's product, Lotus 1-2-3, targeted spreadsheet users. It lost market share to Microsoft's Excel product, especially after Microsoft included Excel as part of the Microsoft Office suite of software, running under a Microsoft operating system. It appeared that the spreadsheet segment was so narrow that Lotus could not defend its spreadsheet from competition from office suites. Lotus developed Lotus Notes (among other products) to address different but related needs and is busily defending that broader segment from competition.

To reduce the risk associated with choosing a single segment, a company may instead decide to serve two or more segments. The selection of these segments can be analyzed in two steps. First, which segments pass the attractiveness criteria we have outlined? Second, which of these acceptable segments offers the best combination of risk and return to the company, given its risk tolerance?

A variant of the single-segment strategy is market specialization. Here the company identifies a particular segment and offers a broad range of products and services to meet its needs. For example, the explosives divisions of both DuPont and ICI target open-cut and underground mines with a range of different explosives, for example, wet hole and dry hole, and blasting control systems.

A variant of this market specialization strategy is product-line specialization. Here the company makes one product or a limited range of products for sale to any customer who can pay. For example, Boeing makes aircraft, Kodak makes film, Intel makes computer chips, and MGM makes movies. When you think of a particular product category, such as cola or rental cars, it is often a product specialist (Coke or Pepsi, or Hertz or Avis) that comes to mind.

Finally, a firm such as IBM may choose to provide something for everyone. But trying to serve multiple types of customers simultaneously can be costly, since most companies alter their product offerings for different market segments. They do this by varying the physical product or by varying such nonproduct attributes as price, packaging, warranty, distribution, and image-based advertising. Most changes combine product and nonproduct attributes. However, if they can achieve substantial economies of scale, they may change only the brand name, packaging, advertising, and price.

Differentiated products targeted to different market segments typically create higher sales than a single product targeted to the average customer. However, differentiated marketing almost always increases the costs of doing business (e.g., product modification costs, production costs, administrative costs, inventory costs, and promotion costs).

Finally, as the following example shows, the STP approach can be applied successfully to almost any market.

EXAMPLE

Funk and Phillips (1990) used the STP approach to study the consumer market for eggs! They used attitudinal variables to come up with four segments:

> Disinterested consumers
>
> Casual egg users
>
> Health conscious egg users
>
> Enthusiastic users

They profiled the users using the following variables:

> Beliefs
>
> Attitudes
>
> Lifestyles
>
> Health/nutrition consciousness
>
> Media habits
>
> Consumption habits
>
> Demographics

They recommended targeting three of the four segments—all except the disinterested consumers (Exhibit 3.8).

Strategy	Casual Users	Health Conscious Consumers	Enthusiastic Users
Positioning	Convenient and useful in many situations	Ideal and natural food Good for family	Traditional food with many applications Very convenient Good for the family
Copy visuals	Informal settings	Health-oriented personality or situation	Larger family setting Major meal, possibly with guests
Copy tonality	Easy pace, relaxed atmosphere	Fresh, clean setting Very natural	Reinforcing Emphasis on benefits and wide use
Promotions	Reminders at checkout, egg display, or dairy	Matter-of-fact information on the nutritional value and health attributes of in recipes and leaflets	Simple reminders to buy eggs

EXHIBIT 3.8
The egg study yielded four segments, three of which could be targeted. This exhibit outlines a possible positioning and marketing strategy for each of the three segments. *Source*: Funk and Phillips 1990.

DEFINING A MARKET

We have been using the word *market* but have not defined it yet. To segment a market, one must first define that market. While the term *market* is often used loosely, the traditional approach to describing markets has been to use both a generic title and physical properties. For example, we use "auto market" (a generic title) and the size of the car—subcompact, compact, midsize, or full size (a physical property). The idea behind this traditional approach is that more (actual or perceived) competition exists within markets than across markets. It is most useful to define markets to reflect the way consumers view them.

Kotler (1997, p. 13) defines a product market as follows:

> A market consists of all the potential customers sharing a particular need or want who might be willing and able to engage in exchange to satisfy that need or want.

By this definition the physical product alone does not define a market; the same physical product may compete in different markets, and different physical products may compete in the same market. For example, the same (physical) automobile may be sold to a consumer or to a taxi company (fleet sales); the needs and buying behaviors of the manager of fleet operations and the individual customer are quite different. And both a PC and a mechanical typewriter, very dissimilar physical products, can provide "word processing solutions" (see the following example).

EXAMPLE

A classical example from the 1980s demonstrates two ways to define the word processor market. In Exhibit 3.9 we define the market as electric typewriters or electromechanical equipment to solve word processing needs. Firm A sees its market share increase but both its sale and total market sale decline in this market.

Shipments

	1980	1981	1982	1983	1984	1985
A (Us)	403,027	495,192	548,905	550,351	541,388	515,000
B	369,916	388,520	349,396	323,005	342,197	297,000
Other	367,057	324,010	343,885	370,374	202, 495	129,070
Total	1,140,000	1,207,722	1,242,186	1,243,730	1,086,080	941,070

Market Shares (%)

	1980	1981	1982	1983	1984	1985
A (Us)	35.4	41.0	44.2	44.2	49.8	54.7
B	32.4	32.2	28.1	26.0	31.5	31.6
Other	32.2	26.8	27.7	29.8	18.6	13.7

EXHIBIT 3.9
(Fictitious) Electric typewriter shipment data. If firm A defines itself as a typewriter manufacturer, it sees declining sales but increasing market share in a declining market.

If we broaden the market definition to include electronic solutions (Exhibit 3.10), we get a different picture: Firm A's share of a growing market is declining along with its sales.

How do we know which definition of a market is right? It depends on the strategic orientation of the firm, and what marketing actions (milk the business, invest in new technology, or divest, for example) are appropriate depend on what definition the firm chooses.

Shipments

	1980	1981	1982	1983	1984	1985
A (Us)	403,027	495,192	548,905	550,351	541,387	515,000
B	369,916	388,520	349,396	323,005	342,197	297,000
Other electric	367,057	324,010	343,885	370,374	202,495	129,070
Electronic word processors	60,040	112,220	209,800	392,352	733,699	1,372,016
Total	1,200,040	1,319,942	1,451,986	1,636,082	1,819,778	2,313,086

Market Shares (%)

	1980	1981	1982	1983	1984	1985
A (Us)	33.6	37.5	38.7	33.6	29.8	22.3
B	30.8	29.4	24.1	19.7	18.8	12.8
Other electric	30.6	24.5	23.7	22.6	11.1	5.6
Electronic word processors	5.0	8.5	14.4	24.0	40.3	59.3

EXHIBIT 3.10
Word processor shipments data. If firm A is in the word processing market, its market share is eroding in a rapidly growing market.

Day, Shocker, and Srivastava (1979) classify methods for identifying product markets by whether they rely on behavioral or judgmental data. Exhibit 3.11 presents their basic classification.

Purchase or Use-Behavior Approaches	Customer-Perception or Judgmental Approaches
Cross-elasticity of demand Similarities in behavior Brand switching	Decision-sequence analysis Perceptual mapping Technology-substitution analysis Customer judgments of substitutability

EXHIBIT 3.11
Analytic methods for defining product markets are based either on what customers do or what customers say. *Source*: Day, Shocker, and Srivastava 1979, p. 11.

Economists consider *cross-elasticity of demand* to be the standard criterion against which other criteria should be judged. Essentially, if the price of product *i* goes up and that *causes* demand for product *j* to go up, *i* and *j* are said to be in the same market. This approach, despite its logic, may be limited because (1) it assumes a firm has no response to another's price changes, (2) it is static and cannot accommodate changes in the composition of the market for the product, and (3) it is difficult to estimate cross elasticity in relatively stable markets, where data vary very little. (Most cross-elasticity studies rely on some form of regression analysis, using methods like Excel's regression tool.)

We can also define a market by looking at *similarities in use behavior*, that is, what customers buy. Cocks and Virts (1975) addressed the question of the substitutability of drugs with different chemical makeups but of similar therapeutic value. A panel of 3000 physicians provided data on the need for the drug (the diagnosis) as well as the drugs they prescribed to treat the problem. As more detailed data on consumption behavior become available, we expect that use of this approach will increase. (Tools like our cluster analysis program can segment based on use behavior.)

We can look at *brand switching* to discover markets. A matrix of brand-switching proportions breaks down into competitive markets, with high switching rates between brands in the same market, but with low switching rates across markets. The approach is applicable in relatively stable markets with high repeat-purchase rates, such as the soft drink market (Exhibit 3.12).

Current Purchase Occasion

		Coke	Diet Coke	Pepsi	Diet Pepsi	Sprite	Diet Sprite	Total
	Coke	53%	9%	27%	4%	5%	2%	100%
Last	Diet Coke	12%	61%	4%	15%	2%	5%	100%
Purchase	Pepsi	24%	3%	58%	9%	5%	1%	100%
Occasion	Diet Pepsi	4%	14%	11%	63%	2%	6%	100%
	Sprite	21%	2%	17%	3%	52%	6%	100%
	Diet Sprite	2%	15%	2%	12%	7%	61%	100%

EXHIBIT 3.12
Segmentation by brand switching: a brand-switching matrix suggesting a cola/noncola segment and a diet/nondiet segment: i.e., highest switching levels are Coke → Pepsi; Pepsi → Coke; Diet Coke → Diet Pepsi and Coke; Diet Pepsi → Diet Coke and Pepsi; Sprite → Coke/Pepsi; and Diet Sprite → Diet Coke/Diet Pepsi.

All the methods that rely on behavioral data to define a market suffer from analyzing *what was* rather than focusing on *what might be*. For instance, problems such as lack of availability may prevent substitution of one brand for another when they might otherwise be substitutes. Unless researchers gather data in a laboratory-based setting, using behavioral methods may bias the definition of a market. To complement behavioral data, consumer perceptions and judgments are useful.

In analyzing consumers' *decision-sequence,* researchers consider protocols or descriptions of the consumer decision-making process that indicate the sequence in which people use decision criteria to choose products (Bettman 1971). For example, they might ask a potential customer "When choosing a margarine, do you chose a form first (stick versus tub), a raw material first (corn oil, safflower oil, etc.), or a brand first?" Because respondents are not used to this type of introspection, there is a danger that the stated responses may not truly reflect reality.

Perceptual mapping represents in a geometric space the way customers think about products (Chapter 4). Those brands that are close together on the map form a market and are substitutes. The approach is flexible and has seen wide use in market-definition studies.

Another way of determining how products (industrial products, generally) are likely to compete is to look at *technology substitution*. The rate at which one material is substituted for another (e.g., polyvinyl for glass in bottles) indicates its relative utility in each use situation. One can calculate an economic measure of relative utility that can be used to estimate substitutability among competing products or technologies in certain situations.

Consumer judgments of substitutability can be gathered in various ways, ranging from simply asking customers to methods with more diagnostic power. (Day, Shocker, and Srivastava (1979) give a critical review of these methods.)

While we have a wide range of methods for defining markets, in choosing a method we must take into account both management's needs and the cost and availability of data. We have yet to resolve Day, Shocker, and Srivastava's concern: "The most persistent problem is the lack of defensible criteria for recognizing [market] boundaries" (1979, p. 18), and we must blend judgment with one or more of the methods outlined in this section.

SEGMENTATION RESEARCH: DESIGNING AND COLLECTING DATA

While there are many ways to segment markets and many data sources, both internal and external to the firm, we will focus here on a typical formal segmentation research study, based on the collection of primary source data.

Such a study consists of four key steps:

1. Developing the measurement instrument (survey form, for example): what information do we want to collect and how should we collect it?
2. Selecting a sample: who (what respondents? where? in what households or organizations?) are we studying?
3. Selecting and aggregating respondents: how can we take different responses from several individuals in a household or an organization and use them to predict how the household or organization will behave?
4. Analyzing the data and segmenting the market: what statistical procedures can we use to segment (potential) customers and to describe aspects of their behavior that are crucial to serving their needs?

These topics are covered in much more detail in market research texts; what we try to do here is to outline the key issues and illustrate the important points. (Note that when you are dealing with data from a secondary source—data already collected—steps 1 and 2 have been bypassed, but you still must follow steps 3 and 4.)

Developing the measurement instrument

Measurement instruments for segmentation studies are usually designed to collect several types of data:

- Demographic descriptors, such as age, income, marital status, and education, on the consumer side, and industry classification, size (number of employees or sales), and job responsibilities on the industrial side
- Psychological descriptors, such as activities, interests, and lifestyle, for consumer and service markets
- Demand, including historical purchases or consumption and anticipated future purchases
- Needs, which could be stated needs or needs inferred through such methods as conjoint analysis (Chapter 7) or value-in-use analysis (Chapter 10)
- Attitudes, which could be about products, suppliers, risk of purchase, or the adoption process in general
- Media and distribution channel use, such as the types and amount of media used and where products and services are typically bought

Usually the data collected in a segmentation study are structured into a *data matrix*; the columns in the matrix correspond to the variables measured and each row contains the responses of one respondent. Exhibit 3.13 shows part of a data matrix from a study of needs for organizational use of PCs. Even when a particular study does not organize data in this way, it is a useful way to think about segmentation data.

In collecting data, and constructing a data matrix, you should address a number of issues:

Q1: Who is the respondent? Different respondents in the same household or, more critically, in the same organization may give quite different responses. (A husband, a wife, and their children may have quite diverse opinions about what constitutes an ideal vacation; design engineers and purchasing agents have different views about key purchasing criteria.)

Q2: What kind of data are you gathering? Nominal data, such as yes-no, or industry classification data, are not easy to compare with data obtained from rating scales.

Q3: Are the measurement scales the same? If the scales are different (agree-disagree on a 1 to 7 scale vs. estimated demand on a 1- to 10,000-unit scale), you need some form of data standardization.

Q4: Are the variables correlated? Often several variables measure different aspects of the same thing: For example, if "quality of service" and "on-time arrival" mean the same thing to airline customers, perceptions and importance ratings for those items should be combined in some way to avoid double counting.

Q5: How should you handle outliers, that is, unusual respondents? Some outliers represent incorrect data, while others may represent unique situations that are better discarded. But some outliers represent new, emerging segments!

Selecting the sample

For any market research study, the analyst must define the population to be studied (the *universe*) and the means for gaining access to a representative sample of that universe (the *sampling frame*). The sample universe might be all U.S. firms, the sample frame might be the list

Company	Job title	SIC code	# PCs	# employees	Office use	LAN	Color	Mem. needs	Speed needs	Storage needs	Wide connect	Periph.	Budget
#1	design eng.	361	6	8	3	4	5	6	6	6	1	3	$5,000
	purch. agent	361	6	8	3	4	4	4	4	5	1	2	$2,500
#2	design eng.	363	4	5	3	4	6	5	5	5	2	4	$5,500
	purch. agent	363	4	5	3	4	4	3	3	4	1	1	$3,000
#3	design eng.	871	75	82	2	5	5	6	6	5	2	3	$6,500
	purch. agent	871	75	82	2	4	4	5	5	3	1	2	$4,000
#4	design eng.	871	52	57	2	5	5	6	6	5	1	3	$4,500
	purch. agent	871	52	57	2	5	3	4	4	4	1	2	$2,500
#5		602	90	100	6	4	2	3	3	5	7	2	$2,500
#6		621	8	9	7	5	1	4	4	4	7	2	$3,200
#7		731	61	68	4	3	7	5	5	7	2	5	$5,500
#8		733	4	5	3	4	7	7	7	6	1	6	$3,250
#9		731	3	3	4	5	7	7	7	7	2	6	$5,700
#10		653	7	8	7	7	3	1	1	4	3	1	$2,500
#11		654	54	60	6	6	2	2	2	5	2	2	$2,000
#12		672	18	20	5	5	1	2	2	4	3	2	$2,750
#13		811	225	250	7	6	2	2	2	4	4	1	$2,200
#14		451	32	36	6	7	1	1	1	5	2	1	$2,400
#15		801	3	3	6	6	1	1	1	4	2	2	$1,999
Means		661.73	42.80	47.60	4.73	5.07	3.67	3.87	3.87	5.07	2.73	2.87	$3,700
std. dev.		163.33	58.41	64.74	1.83	1.16	2.41	2.26	2.26	1.03	1.91	1.68	$1,572

Demographic Variables (# PCs, # employees)

Needs (Office use, LAN, Color, Mem. needs, Speed needs, Storage needs, Wide connect, Periph.)

EXHIBIT 3.13
This abbreviated data matrix for industrial PC purchases shows demographic data, stated needs, respondent attitudes, and conjoint part worths (inferred needs).

of those firms that are furnished by Dun and Bradstreet, and the sample might be the actual firms selected for study from the Dun and Bradstreet list. For exploratory research or for small-sample studies, using a convenience sample or judgmental approach is appropriate.

For quantitative research, analysts usually use some form of probability sample, such as

- Simple, random sampling, where every member of the sample frame has an equal chance of being chosen to be a member of the sample
- Cluster sampling, where the unit of selection is a group (say, all households on a street) and each group has an equal chance of being selected as a member of the sample
- Stratified sampling, where the sampling frame is broken into strata that the user believes are different from one another but whose members are relatively homogeneous, and where simple random sampling within each strata is used to generate the sample

Where possible, we recommend some form of stratified sampling, with larger samples taken from more "important" strata (e.g., heavy users, likely brand switchers, larger organizations, or target demographic segments).

Selecting and aggregating respondents

Even in households, people make many purchases for the household as a whole (vacation spot, entertainment event, etc.), basing the purchase on the preferences of several parties.

Leading edge	Cen-tralized	Slack	Price			Memory		Tasks			
			1000	1500	2000	640K	2MB	4	8	12	16
4	4	6	0.6	0.4	0.2	0.1	0.9	0.2	0.3	0.4	0.6
3	5	4	0.9	0.8	0.6	0.2	0.9	0.4	0.5	0.5	0.6
7	6	5	0.3	0.3	0.3	0.1	0.8	0.3	0.5	0.8	0.9
5	5	6	0.8	0.7	0.5	0.3	0.7	0.2	0.4	0.7	0.8
6	6	5	0.6	0.6	0.4	0.2	0.8	0.3	0.4	0.7	0.8
4	7	6	0.8	0.7	0.5	0.3	0.6	0.4	0.5	0.5	0.7
6	5	5	0.4	0.3	0.2	0.3	0.7	0.1	0.6	0.8	0.9
4	5	5	0.9	0.7	0.5	0.3	0.7	0.4	0.7	0.8	0.7
6	6	6	0.5	0.3	0.3	0.4	0.6	0.4	0.5	0.6	0.7
6	6	7	0.6	0.6	0.4	0.3	0.7	0.1	0.5	0.6	0.7
7	7	6	0.7	0.5	0.4	0.1	0.8	0.3	0.5	0.6	0.8
7	7	2	0.4	0.8	0.6	0.2	0.9	0.2	0.7	0.8	0.9
6	6	2	0.5	0.4	0.1	0.1	0.9	0.1	0.5	0.7	0.9
3	3	3	0.8	0.5	0.5	0.3	0.7	0.5	0.4	0.4	0.4
2	2	7	0.8	0.7	0.5	0.5	0.5	0.4	0.6	0.7	0.8
1	3	3	0.9	0.7	0.4	0.4	0.7	0.5	0.5	0.5	0.5
3	1	4	0.7	0.6	0.5	0.3	0.8	0.6	0.5	0.4	0.3
2	2	5	0.8	0.4	0.3	0.4	0.7	0.4	0.5	0.5	0.4
1	2	2	0.7	0.4	0.4	0.5	0.6	0.2	0.4	0.5	0.5
4.47	4.40	4.53	62	50	37	38	74	31	49	60	67
2.26	2.06	1.77	17	16	13	14	12	16	10	15	21

Attitude Measures

Conjoint Part Worths

In organizations, a number of individuals representing different points of view may be involved in purchase decisions, including a purchasing agent (frequently most interested in price, service, and on-time delivery), a user (interested in certain specific features), a gatekeeper (involved heavily in managing and maintaining supplier relationships), the financial analysts (interested in the impact on finances—perhaps willing to trade off higher initial costs for savings elsewhere). Exhibit 3.14 illustrates that the purchasing agents from the data set shown in Exhibit 3.13 have less need for features than the design engineers (who would be the users).

In choosing a sample you must consider two key issues:

- How many respondents per unit should you survey?
- If there is more than one respondent per unit, how should you aggregate their responses?

Common sense tells us that if everyone in a household or an organization agrees about their needs, then we need only a single respondent. However, Wilson, Lilien, and Wilson (1991) found that when a firm has little prior experience with the purchase and when the purchase is critically important to the firm, the responses of a single respondent can be misleading.

When the needs of those within the group differ, Wilson, Lilien, and Wilson (1991) show that it is important to study the two or three people who have the most influence in the decision and to aggregate their responses in such a way that the aggregated preference scores are higher for those alternatives that require the least compromise for the individuals involved in the decision process.

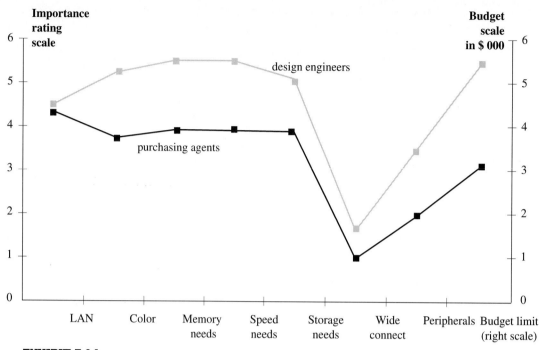

EXHIBIT 3.14
Needs assessment for PCs of engineers vs. purchasing agents from data in Exhibit 3.13, showing that design engineers are generally more concerned about product features than are purchasing agents, who try to adhere to a tighter budget.

EXAMPLE

In a study of the market for industrial cooling equipment, Choffray and Lilien (1978) found that a number of types of people often participated in making the decision. They developed an instrument called a decision matrix to assess the likelihood of a person participating in the decision (Exhibit 3.15).

Three types of individuals who *were not firm employees* influenced the decision—HVAC (heating, ventilation, and air conditioning) consultants, architects and contractors, and air conditioning (A/C) manufacturers. (Note how this observation expands the definition of the sample universe and the sampling frame.)

After a macrosegmentation phase, in which they segmented the market by industry type and location, Choffray and Lilien (1978) further (micro)segmented the market according to the decision structure in the organization (as reflected in the decision matrix)—that is, they grouped firms together who reported similar decision matrices. Interestingly, another part of their research showed more differences in attitudes and preferences by job category than by firm. The responses of purchasing agents in one firm (A) were more like those of purchasing agents in another firm (B) than responses of design engineers in firm A.

They found four major microsegments (Exhibit 3.16). We will focus on segment 4 here, primarily consisting of top managers and HVAC consultants.

Top managers and HVAC consultants are almost exactly opposite in what they consider important (Exhibit 3.17). Top managers value modernity, energy savings, and low operating costs most highly, while HVAC consultants think these issues are of little importance. These and other results of this study showed that to target a marketing strategy to this segment, a firm should focus on the value compromises participants in a purchase decision would need to make.

| | **Decision Phases** | | | | |
| | **1** | **2** | **3** | **4** | **5** |
Decision Participants	Evaluation of A/C needs, specifications of system requirements	Preliminary A/C budget approval	Search for alternatives, preparations of a bid list	Equipment and manufacturer evaluation*	Equipment and manufacturer selection
Company personnel					
• Production and maintenance engineers	5%	0%	10%	25%	10%
• Plant or factory managers	20%	20%	10%	15%	20%
• Financial controller or accountant	0%	30%	5%	10%	5%
• Procurement or purchasing department personnel	0%	0%	40%	10%	5%
• Top management	10%	50%	0%	0%	40%
External personnel					
• HVAC/engineering firm	20%	0%	20%	25%	10%
• Architects and building contractors	25%	0%	15%	15%	10%
• A/C equipment manufacturers	20%	0%	0%	0%	0%
Column total	100%	100%	100%	100%	100%

*Decision phase 4 generally involves evaluation of all alternative A/C systems that meet company needs, whereas decision phase 5 involves only the alternatives (generally 2-3) retained for final selection.

EXHIBIT 3.15
Decision matrix for the industrial air conditioning study, showing that the purchase process has several phases and that individuals both inside and outside the firm (such as heating, ventilation, and air conditioning—HVAC—engineers) influence the purchase decision.

	Segment 1	**Segment 2**	**Segment 3**	**Segment 4**
Microsegment size in potential market	12%	31%	32%	25%
Major decision participant categories in equipment selection decision (frequencies of involvement)	Plant Managers (1.00)	Production Engineers (.94)	Production Engineers (.97)	Top Managers (.85)
	HVAC Consultants (.38)	Plant Managers (.70)	HVAC Consultants (.60)	HVAC Consultants (.67)

EXHIBIT 3.16
Major microsegments of organizations in the industrial air conditioning study, showing those categories of decision makers who are most influential in equipment selection (1.00 = maximum influence).

	More Important	**Less Important**
Production Engineers	Operating cost Energy savings Reliability Complexity	First cost Field proven Substitutability of components
Plant Managers	Operating cost Use of unproductive areas Modernness Power failure protection	First cost Complexity Substitutability of components
Top Managers	Modernness Energy savings Operating cost Fuel rationing protection	Noise level in plant Reliability
HVAC Consultants	Previous system experience Ease of installation Modularity/accessibility Reliability	Modernness Energy savings Operating cost

EXHIBIT 3.17
Issues of importance for each category of decision participant, showing clear conflict between HVAC consultants and top managers.

SEGMENTATION METHODS

After you have administered the measurement instrument to the people in your sample, you should be able to assemble the resulting data into a sound data matrix. You are now ready to do the segmentation analysis, which consists of data reduction, segment formation, and interpretation of results.

Using factor analysis to reduce the data

In many segmentation studies, researchers collect data on a wide battery of attitude- and needs-based items. If many of those items measure similar or interrelated constructs, then subsequent analyses may lead to misleading conclusions because some data are over-weighted and other data underweighted. Analysts also should drop irrelevant variables (i.e., those on which customers do not differ) from the study. Research has shown that including even a couple of irrelevant variables can damage the detection of the segment structure in the data (Milligan and Cooper 1987).

In factor analysis, we use several methods to reduce a large set of data to a smaller set. Specifically, we analyze the interrelationships among a large number of variables (attitudes, questionnaire responses) and then represent them in terms of common, underlying dimensions (factors). As these methods are central to constructing perceptual maps and conducting positioning studies, we will develop them in more detail in Chapter 4 and in the appendix to that chapter.

Forming segments by cluster analysis: Measures of association

To form segments or clusters, you must

- Define a measure of similarity (or dissimilarity—distance) between all pairs of elements (individuals, families, Decision Making Units, etc.)
- Develop a method for assigning elements to clusters or groups

Exhibit 3.18 illustrates the issue: to form the (three) clusters there, we need to know the distances between all pairs of respondents or clusters of respondents. While this exhibit covers only two dimensions, it actually exists in multidimensional space: the number of dimensions equals the number of factors you retained in the previous, data-reduction step.

The most common method of grouping elements is the cluster analysis method. Cluster analysis is a set of techniques for discovering structure (groupings) within a complex body of data, such as the data matrix used in segmentation analysis. We can explain the concept by considering a deck of cards. Each card varies from the other cards along three dimensions (variables): suit, color, and number. If you are asked to partition a pack of cards into two distinct groups, you might sort them into red and black, or into numbered cards and picture cards. While you can partition a pack of cards intuitively, partitioning a large number of items into groups can be very complex, especially if those items vary along a number of different dimensions.

To understand the complexity, consider partitioning 25 items (or respondents in our case) into two groups, with at least one item in a group. There are $2^{24} - 1$ (= 16,777,215) possible partitions. In partitioning 25 items into five groups, the number of possibilities is an astounding 2,436,684,974,110,751 (2.44×10^{15}). Clearly we need a systematic and feasible method of finding a good partition. We can use cluster analysis to address this problem. (It is also called numerical taxonomy by biologists, unsupervised pattern recognition by computer scientists, regionalization or clumping by geographers, partitioning by graph theorists, seriation by anthropologists, and segmentation by marketers.) To perform a cluster analysis, you must select variables and construct a measure of association between all pairs of items.

Choosing variables: Variables that have similar values for all your respondents do not provide a good basis for distinguishing between respondents. On the other hand, including variables that strongly differentiate between respondents but that are not

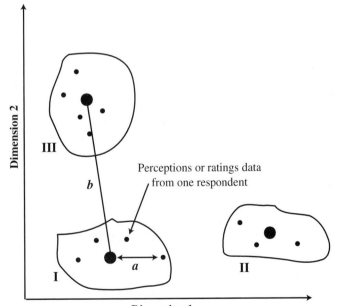

EXHIBIT 3.18
This exhibit illustrates how distance is measured in cluster analysis. Here there are three clusters (I, II, and III); distance "*b*" is the distance from the center of cluster I to the center of cluster III, and "*a*" is the distance from the center of cluster I to one of its member respondents.

relevant for the purposes at hand will give misleading results. We suggest including a number of variables, so that adding or deleting any one variable will not appreciably affect the results.

Defining measures of similarity between individuals: Most cluster analyses require you to define a measure of similarity for every pair of respondents. Similarity measures fall into two categories, depending on the type of data that are available. For scaled data you use distance-type measures. For nominal data (male/female, for example) you use matching-type measures. When the data type is mixed, other segmentation methods, for example, automatic interaction detection (AID)—described in the next subsection—may be most appropriate.

The following example illustrates the use of *matching coefficients*:

EXAMPLE

We ask respondents from four organizations that will purchase a copier to state which of its eight features (F) are essential, (F1 = sorting, F2 = color, etc.) with the following result:

	Essential Features? (Yes or No)							
	F1	*F2*	*F3*	*F4*	*F5*	*F6*	*F7*	*F8*
Organization A	Y	Y	N	N	Y	Y	Y	Y
Organization B	N	Y	N	N	N	Y	Y	Y
Organization C	Y	N	Y	Y	Y	N	N	N
Organization D	Y	N	N	N	Y	Y	Y	Y

We can define one similarity measure (among the organizations across these eight features)—a similarity coefficient—as

Similarity coefficient = number of matches/total possible matches (= 8).

The resulting associations are shown in Exhibit 3.19.

Researchers develop other types of matching coefficients in a similar fashion, often weighting differences between positive and negative matches differently. For

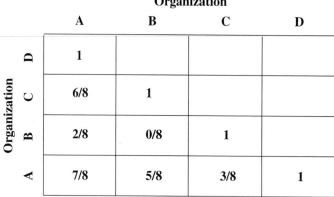

Organization

		A	B	C	D
Organization	**D**	1			
	C	6/8	1		
	B	2/8	0/8	1	
	A	7/8	5/8	3/8	1

EXHIBIT 3.19
Similarity/association data for "essential features" data: firms A and B match on 6 of their essential features needs (Y-Y or N-N) out of 8 possible matches.

example, suppose we counted only the number of positive (Yes-Yes) matches; in that case there would still be a possibility of eight matches, but organizations A and B would have only four of those possible eight matches (4/8) instead of the six (6/8) shown in Exhibit 3.19.

Distance-type measures fall into two categories: measures of similarity or measures of dissimilarity, where the most common measure of similarity is the correlation coefficient and the most common measure of dissimilarity is the (Euclidean) distance.

Two common distance measures are defined as follows:

- Euclidean distance = $\sqrt{\left(x_{1i} - x_{1j}\right)^2 + \cdots + \left(x_{ni} - x_{nj}\right)^2}$,   (3.1)

where i and j represent a pair of observations, x_{ki} = value of observation i on the kth variable, and 1 to n are the variables.

- Absolute distance (city-block metric) = $\left|x_{1i} - x_{1j}\right| + \cdots + \left|x_{ni} - x_{nj}\right|$,   (3.2)

where | | means absolute distance.

All distance measures are problematic if the scales are not comparable, as the following example shows.

EXAMPLE

Consider three individuals with the following characteristics:

	Income ($ thousands)	Age (years)
Individual A	34	27
Individual B	23	34
Individual C	55	38

Straightforward calculation of Euclidean distances across these two characteristics gives

$d_{AB} = 13.0$, $d_{AC} = 23.7$, and $d_{BC} = 32$.

However, if age is measured in months, rather than years, we get

$d_{AB} = 84.7$, $d_{AC} = 133.6$, and $d_{BC} = 57$.

In other words, when we use months individuals B and C are closest together; when we use years they are farthest apart!

To avoid this scaling problem, many users standardize their data (divide it by its standard deviation) before doing the distance calculation. This allows them to weight all variables equally in computing the distance in Eq. (3.1). In some cases, however, it is important not to standardize the data; for example, if the segmentation is being done on needs data obtained by such procedures as conjoint analysis (Chapter 7), the values of all the variables are already being measured on a common metric.

A frequently used measure of association is the correlation coefficient, calculated as follows:

$X_1, \cdots, X_n$ = Data from organization x,

$Y_1, \cdots, Y_n$ = Data from organization y;

$$x_i = X_i - \overline{X}, \quad y_i = Y_i - \overline{Y} \text{ (difference from mean values } \overline{X} \text{ and } \overline{Y}); \tag{3.3}$$

then r_{xy} = $\dfrac{x_1 y_1 + \cdots + x_n y_n}{\sqrt{\left(x_1^2 + x_2^2 + \cdots + x_n^2\right)\left(y_1^2 + y_2^2 + \cdots + y_n^2\right)}}$

Warning: The correlation coefficient incorporates normalization in its formula. However, it also removes the scale effect. So an individual who gives uniformly high ratings (7's on a 1 to 7 scale) on all items would be perfectly correlated ($r = 1$) with two other individuals, one who also gave all high ratings and another who gave all low ratings (all 1's on a 1 to 7 scale)! For this reason, we feel that, while correlation coefficients are commonly used in segmentation studies, the results of such studies should be carefully scrutinized.

We recommend that if you have scaled data, you standardize that data first (subtract its mean and divide by its standard deviation) and use a Euclidean distance measure.

Clustering methods

After developing a matrix of associations between the individuals in every pair, you are ready to cluster. There are two basic classes of methods:

- Hierarchical methods, in which you build up or break down the data row by row
- Partitioning methods, in which you break the data into a prespecified number of groups and then reallocate or swap data to improve some measure of effectiveness

Our software includes one method of each type—Ward's (1963) (hierarchial) and *K*-means (partitioning).

Hierarchical methods produce "trees," formally called dendograms. Hierarchical methods themselves fall into two categories: build-up (agglomerative) methods and split-down (divisive) methods.

Agglomerative methods generally follow this procedure:

1. At the beginning you consider each item to be its own cluster.
2. You join the two items that are closest on some chosen measure of distance.
3. You then join the next two closest objects (individual items or clusters), either joining two items to form a group or attaching an item to the existing cluster.
4. Return to step 3 until all items are clustered.

Agglomerative methods differ in how they join clusters to one another:

In *single linkage clustering* (also called the nearest neighbor method), you consider the distance between clusters to be the distance between the two closest items in those clusters.

In *complete linkage clustering* (also called the farthest neighbor method), you consider the distance between two clusters to be the distance between the pair of items in those clusters that are farthest apart; thus all items in the new cluster formed by joining these two clusters are no farther than some maximal distance apart (Exhibit 3.20).

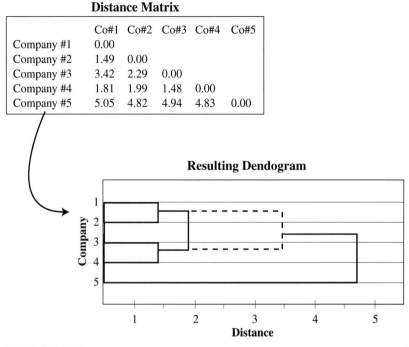

Distance Matrix

	Co#1	Co#2	Co#3	Co#4	Co#5
Company #1	0.00				
Company #2	1.49	0.00			
Company #3	3.42	2.29	0.00		
Company #4	1.81	1.99	1.48	0.00	
Company #5	5.05	4.82	4.94	4.83	0.00

Resulting Dendogram

EXHIBIT 3.20
This distance matrix yields one dendogram for single linkage clustering (solid line) and another for complete linkage clustering (dotted line). The cluster or segments formed by companies 1 and 2 join with the segment formed by companies 3 and 4 at a much higher level in complete linkage (3.42) than in single linkage (1.81). In both cases company 5 appears to be different from the other companies—an outlier. A two-cluster solution will have A = 5, B = {1, 2, 3, 4}, while a three-cluster solution will have A = 5, B = (1, 2), and C = (3, 4).

In *average linkage clustering*, you consider the distance between two clusters *A* and *B* to be the average distance between all pairs of items in the clusters, where one of the items in the pair is from cluster *A* and the other is from cluster *B*.

In *Ward's method*, one of the two methods included in the software, you form clusters based on the change in the error sum of squares associated with joining any pair of clusters (see the following example).

EXAMPLE

Drawn from Dillon and Goldstein (1984). Suppose that we have five customers and we have measurements on only one characteristic, intention to purchase on a 1 to 15 scale:

Customer	Intention to purchase
A	2
B	5
C	9
D	10
E	15

Using Ward's (1963) procedure, you form clusters based on minimizing the loss of information associated with grouping individuals into clusters. You measure loss of information by summing the squared deviations of every observation from the mean of the cluster to which it is assigned. Using Ward's method you assign clusters in an order that minimizes the error sum of squares (ESS) from among all possible assignments, where ESS is defined as

$$ESS = \sum_{j=1}^{k} \left(\sum_{i=1}^{n_j} X_{ij}^2 - \frac{1}{n_j} \left(\sum_{i=1}^{n_j} X_{ij} \right)^2 \right), \tag{3.4}$$

where X_{ij} is the intent to purchase score for the ith individual in the jth cluster, k is the number of clusters at each stage, and n_j is the number of individuals in the jth cluster. Exhibit 3.21(a) shows the calculations, and Exhibit 3.21(b) is the related dendogram. The ESS is zero at the first stage. At stage 2, the procedure considers all possible clusters of two items; C and D are fused. At the next stage, you con-

First Stage:	**A** = 2	**B** = 5	**C** = 9	**D** = 10	**E** = 15
Second Stage:		**AB** = 4.5	**BD** = 12.5		
		AC = 24.5	**BE** = 50.0		
		AD = 32.0	**CD** = 0.5		
		AE = 84.5	**CE** = 18.0		
		BC = 8.0	**DE** = 12.5		
Third Stage:	**CDA** = 38.0	**CDB** = 14	**CDE** = 20.66	**AB** = 5.0	
	AE = 85.0	**BE** = 50.5			
Fourth Stage:		**ABCD** = 41.0	**ABE** = 93.17	**CDE** = 25.18	
Fifth Stage:			**ABCDE** = 98.8		

EXHIBIT 3.21(a)
Summary calculations for Ward's ESS (Error Sum of Square) method. *Source:* Dillon and Goldstein 1984, p. 174.

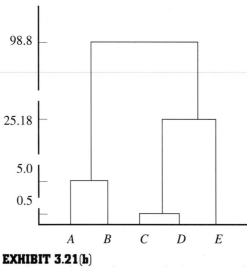

EXHIBIT 3.21(b)
Dendrogram for Ward's ESS method. *Source:* Dillon and Goldstein 1984, p. 174.

sider both adding each of the three remaining individuals to the *CD* cluster and forming each possible pair of the three remaining unclustered individuals; *A* and *B* are clustered. At the fourth stage, *CDE* form a cluster. At the final (fifth) stage, all individuals are ultimately clustered.

In using divisive methods, you successively divide a sample of respondents. One popular method is automatic interaction detection (AID). It can be used with both categorical and scaled data. It works as follows: you determine group means on the dependent variable—brand usage, for example—for each classification of the independent variables and examine all dichotomous groupings of each independent variable. Suppose that there are four categories of job classification: professional, clerical, blue-collar, and other. You examine the group means on the dependent variable for all *dichotomous* groupings: blue-collar versus the other three categories, blue-collar plus professional versus the other two categories, and so on.

Then you split each independent variable into two nonoverlapping subgroups providing the largest reduction in unexplained variance. You choose the split to maximize the between sum of squares (BSS) for the *i*th group (the group to be split).

You then split the sample on the variable yielding the largest BSS, and the new groups formed become candidates for further splitting. The output can take the shape of a tree diagram, each branch splitting until terminated by one of three stopping rules: (1) a group becomes too small to be of further interest, (2) a group becomes so homogeneous that further division is unnecessary, or (3) no further possible division would significantly reduce BSS.

EXAMPLE

Assael and Roscoe (1976) reported on a market-segmentation study for AT&T to identify heavy and light long-distance callers. They studied a sample of 1750 individuals, all from the southern region. Exhibit 3.22 shows the output of the AID analysis, and Exhibit 3.23 shows the tree and intermediate splits.

Segment Profile	Average Long-Distance Bill	Percent of Sample	Percent of Total Long-Distance Billing Accounted for by Segment
1. Income $15,000 and over	$11.10	15.4	29.0
2. Income less than $15,000, one or more phones, higher socioeconomic status based on education and occupation	7.56	15.6	20.1
3. Same as 2 but medium to low socioeconomic status	5.16	18.6	16.2
4. Income under $15,000, one phone, and family has teenage children	7.38	5.1	6.4
5. Same as 4 but no teenage children	3.69	45.3	28.3

EXHIBIT 3.22
Final output of AID analysis of the long-distance-telephone market. *Source:* Assael and Roscoe 1976, p. 70.

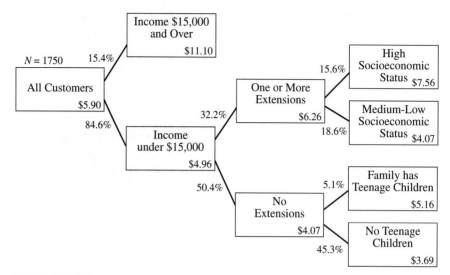

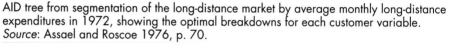

EXHIBIT 3.23

AID tree from segmentation of the long-distance market by average monthly long-distance expenditures in 1972, showing the optimal breakdowns for each customer variable. *Source:* Assael and Roscoe 1976, p. 70.

This analysis shows that one can segment the long-distance market based on demographic and telephone-equipment characteristics. Exhibit 3.22 shows that the segment with the most concentrated use, those with incomes over $15,000, represents 29 percent of long-distance billing but accounts for only 15.4 percent of the sample. In addition, the most- and the least-concentrated-use segments differ in expenditures three to one.

In terms of marketing strategy, this study suggests that income alone is one criterion for reaching the heavy-use segment. It also identifies a relatively heavy-use segment (Exhibit 3.23) among those who have low incomes but have high socioeconomic status and have one or more extension phones.

Partitioning methods, unlike hierarchical methods, do not require you to allocate an item to a cluster irrevocably—that is, you can reallocate it if you can improve some criterion by doing so. These methods do not develop a treelike structure; rather they start with cluster centers and assign those individuals closest to each cluster center to that cluster.

The most commonly used partitioning method is *K-means clustering*. The procedure works as follows:

1. You begin with two starting points and allocate every item to its nearest cluster center.
2. Reallocate items one at a time to reduce the sum of internal cluster variability until you have minimized the criterion (the sum of the within-cluster-sums of squares) for two clusters.
3. Repeat steps 1 and 2 for three, four, or more clusters.

4. After completing step 3, return to step 1 and repeat the procedure with different starting points until the process converges—you no longer see decreases in the within-cluster sum of squares.

While there are many ways to determine starting points, we recommend using the output of Ward's procedure to give good starting points (this is the procedure we use in our software).

The number of clusters (K) to use is usually based on managerial judgment, but certain indices can also help you to determine an appropriate number of clusters. In hierarchical clustering, you can use the distances at which clusters are combined as a criterion—for example, in the dendogram output from our software (Exhibit 3.20). In using partitioning methods, you can study the ratio of total within-group variance to between-group variance and use the number of clusters at which this ratio stabilizes. In either case you are looking for a big improvement in your criterion followed by a smaller improvement as an indication that there is little benefit in producing finer clusters.

Interpreting segmentation study results

After forming your segments by following one of the foregoing methods, you need to interpret the results and link them to managerial actions. You can base targeting and positioning decisions on the results of a segmentation analysis. Technically, you need to address such issues as how many clusters you should retain, how good your clusters are, the possibility that there are really no clusters, and how you should profile the clusters.

How many clusters should you retain? There is no unambiguous statistical answer to this question. You should determine the number of clusters by viewing the results of your cluster analysis in light of the managerial purpose of the analysis.

How good are your clusters? How well would the clusters obtained from this particular sample of individuals generalize to the sampling frame? No one statistical or numerical scheme helps you to judge the goodness of clusters. You need knowledge of the context to make sense of the results. You should also ask: Do the means of basis variables in each cluster make intuitive sense (have face validity)? Can I think of an intuitively appealing name, for example, techno-savvy or mobile bloomers, for each of the resulting clusters?

Are there really no clusters? Do not overlook this possibility. If only a few basis variables show meaningful differences between individuals, it is possible that no really distinct segments exist in the market.

You can describe clusters informally by profiling them or more formally by using a method such as discriminant analysis. In *cluster profiling*, you prepare a picture of the clusters you found based on the variables of interest—both those variables you used for the clustering (the bases) and those variables withheld from the clustering but that you will use to identify and target the segments (the descriptors). Typically you report the average value of both the basis and the descriptor variables in each cluster in the profile.

Exhibit 3.24 is a snake chart, based on the data in Exhibit 3.14 where we only look at responses from design engineers. One segment concerned with buying PCs has a high relative need for power, color, storage, and peripherals and is not price sensitive (basis). We have labeled this the design segment. The other (business) segment is more interested in office use, local area networks (LAN), and wide area connectivity and is quite price sensitive.

Profiling of the other (descriptor) variables in Exhibit 3.14 will show that the "design" segment is made up primarily of design engineers from smaller firms.

Using *discriminant analysis*, you look for linear combinations of variables that best separate the clusters or segments; in cluster profiling, you separate a group one item at a time. Specifically, in using discriminant analysis you look for linear combinations of *descriptors* that maximize between-group variance relative to within-group variance.

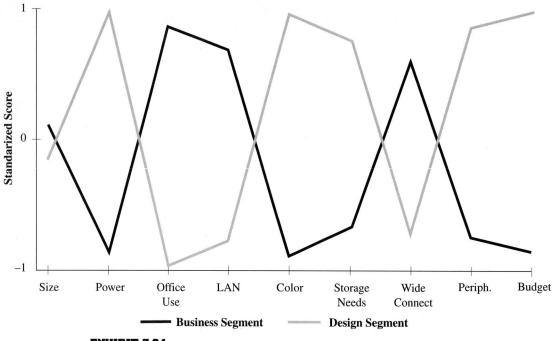

EXHIBIT 3.24
Segment profiles (snake chart) for two segments based on the data from Exhibit 3.14.

EXAMPLE

Exhibit 3.25 shows the results of a segmentation study on the need for Internet access, where one segment (X) is the high-need segment and other segment (O) is the low-need segment.

In the exhibit two segments or clusters determined from cluster analysis are plotted on two descriptor variable axes: number of employees and firm profitability. Segment X apparently comprises firms with fewer employees and higher profitability than segment O. Firm size appears to discriminate better than firm profitability. (While the output of discriminant analysis provides formal ways to see this, our picture shows that there is more of a split between X's and O's from east to west—number of employees—than from north to south—profitability).

Discriminant analysis ties us intimately to the targeting decision. As the discriminant function in Exhibit 3.25 moves toward the northwest, the likelihood of segment X membership increases. Indeed, if such descriptor variables as number of employees and firm profitability are readily available, you can assign a likelihood of segment membership to any organization in the target market, even if that organization was not in the original segmentation study sample!

How can you determine how good the results of a discriminant analysis are? We suggest the following:

To determine the *predictive validity of discriminant analysis* (how well the discriminant functions, taken as a whole, predict the group membership of each individual included in the analysis) you do this: Form a *classification matrix* that shows the actual cluster to which

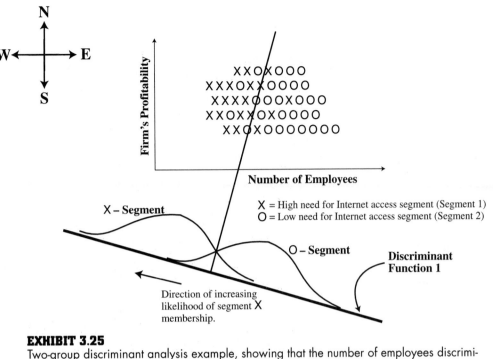

EXHIBIT 3.25
Two-group discriminant analysis example, showing that the number of employees discriminates well between the clusters while the firm's profitability does not.

an individual in the sample belongs and the group to which that individual is predicted to belong. (You determine predicted group membership by computing the distance between an individual and each group centroid along the discriminant function(s). You assign each individual to the group with the closest centroid.) The *hit rate* gives the proportion of all the individuals that are correctly assigned. The higher the hit rate, the higher the validity of the discriminant functions in finding meaningful differences among the descriptor variables between the clusters. (In our software, we compute the hit rate on the same sample on which we develop the discriminant functions. This is a weaker method for predictive validation than using a *hold-out sample* for validation.)

The statistical significance of each discriminant function indicates whether that discriminant function provides a statistically significant separation between the individuals in different clusters. (Note: If there are *n* clusters and *m* descriptor variables, then the maximum number of discriminant functions is equal to the smaller of $n - 1$ and m.)

The variance explained by each discriminant function is a measure of the operational significance of a discriminant function. Sometimes, especially if you have a large sample, a discriminant function that is statistically significant may actually explain only a small percentage of the variation among the individuals. Discriminant functions that explain less than about 10 percent of the variance may not provide sufficient separation to warrant consideration.

The correlations between your variables and the discriminant functions are also called *structure correlations* and *discriminant loadings*. If a variable has high correlation with a statistically and operationally significant discriminant function, then that variable is an important descriptor variable that discriminates among the clusters. The square of the correlation coefficient is a measure of the relative contribution of a variable to a discriminant function. To facilitate interpretation in the output of our software, we report the correlations between variables and discriminant functions in the order of absolute size of correlation within each discriminant function, putting the most important variable first. If correlations are small for a variable, it means either that the variable does not offer much discrimination between clusters, or that it is correlated with other variables that overshadow its effects.

You can *use relevant descriptors to profile a cluster*. Discriminant analysis provides information that is useful in profiling clusters. You should first examine the mean values of descriptor variables that are highly correlated (say, absolute correlations greater than 0.6) with the most important discriminant function. If these means are sufficiently different and managerially meaningful, you can use these variables as the basis on which to develop marketing programs for the selected segments. You should then look at the mean values of the descriptor variables that are associated with the next most important discriminant function, and so on, repeating the procedure for each discriminant function.

BEHAVIOR-BASED SEGMENTATION: CROSS-CLASSIFICATION, REGRESSION, AND CHOICE MODELS

The approach we described in the previous section assumes that there is a set of variables (bases) that we want to use to develop market segments.

If the goal of the segmentation study is simply to identify individuals or groups with a high propensity to buy, researchers often use other methods: (1) cross-tabulation, (2) regression analysis, and (3) choice models. In each case, the goal is to relate some descriptor variables to a measure of propensity to buy (susceptibility to our marketing effort). According to Peppers and Rogers (1993), an industry's best customers outspend its average customers by a factor of 16:1 in the retail industry, 12:1 for airlines, and 5:1 in hotels.

Cross-classification analysis

Cross-classification, or contingency table analysis, classifies data in two or more categories or dimensions. In spite of the proliferation of more sophisticated techniques, cross-classification is still a widely used segmentation technique. However, cross-classification becomes unwieldy if you have more than two or three classification variables. In addition, if segmentation bases are continuous, the breakpoints you select for cross-classification may obscure some important relationships. Cross-tabulation is also not appropriate if significant interactions exist among the variables. (Note: Excel offers an add-in called Cross-tab Sheet Function that can be used to execute cross-classification analysis.)

> **EXAMPLE**
>
> A cross-classification of product usage against a preference scale, split at the 50 percent point, shows little predictive ability (Exhibit 3.26a). Splitting the same sample at both the 50 percent and the 90 percent points, however, reveals an important relationship (Exhibit 3.26b).

Regression analysis

Multiple-regression-based procedures overcome many of the problems found in cross-classification. In a typical multiple-regression study, the dependent variable is usually some

Preference Score

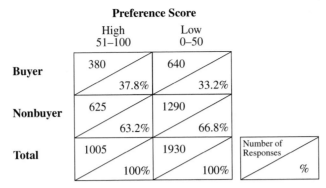

	High 51–100	Low 0–50
Buyer	380 / 37.8%	640 / 33.2%
Nonbuyer	625 / 63.2%	1290 / 66.8%
Total	1005 / 100%	1930 / 100%

Number of Responses / %

EXHIBIT 3.26(a)
With a 50-50 split on preference score in this cross-classification, high preference score shows a weak (37.8 vs. 33.2 percent) relationship to purchase behavior.

Preference Score

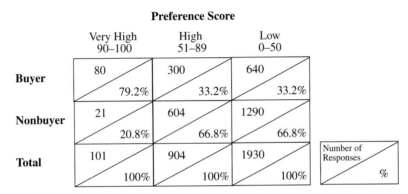

	Very High 90–100	High 51–89	Low 0–50
Buyer	80 / 79.2%	300 / 33.2%	640 / 33.2%
Nonbuyer	21 / 20.8%	604 / 66.8%	1290 / 66.8%
Total	101 / 100%	904 / 100%	1930 / 100%

Number of Responses / %

EXHIBIT 3.26(b)
Splitting the "High" category from (a) into "Very High" and "Medium" reveals a strong relationship between "Very High" preference and purchase.

measure of consumption, and the independent variables are socioeconomic and demographic variables postulated to vary with consumption. (Excel's add-in Analysis Tools include an easy-to-use regression package.)

EXAMPLE

McCann (1974) used regression analysis to determine differences in response rates (advertising, price, and promotion sensitivity) for different market segments. He studied the purchasing behavior for 29 brands of a frequently purchased consumer product by a panel of 7500 consumers over a period of over four years.

He found that such descriptors as usage rate, household income, homemaker's age, area population, household size, and employment status were significant in explaining differences in market response. He used that information to develop "segmentation coefficients" (the products of the relative size, level of demand, and response rate of the segments) and used them to rank segments for attractiveness and to decide which to target.

Choice-based segmentation

An increasingly common approach to segmentation, especially in direct marketing (also called database marketing), is choice-based segmentation. In choice-based segmentation we perform the analysis at the level of the individual, relating that individual's likelihood of purchase (or response to a proposed marketing program) to variables that the firm has in its database, such as geodemographics, past purchase behavior for similar products, and attitudes or psychographics. Individual choice models—such as the logit model described in Chapter 2—relate these variables to likelihood of choice.

With a new product offering, a direct marketer chooses a sample from a large database and sends out the offer. It then observes who purchases (and how much) and uses that information to estimate the parameters of the response function:

$$\text{Probability of purchase } = f(\text{geodemographics,}$$
$$\text{past purchase, psychographics, etc.)} \tag{3.5a}$$

or

$$\text{Probability of Purchase } = \frac{1}{1 + \exp\left(b_0 + \sum b_i x_i\right)}, \tag{3.5b}$$

where

b_i = importance of the ith basis variable, geodemographics, past purchase, etc.; and

x_i = value of the ith variable.

The firm then applies Eq. (3.5) to its database, plugging in the variables on the right-hand side of the equation to get *a predicted probability of purchase*. Equation (3.5b) is called a binary logit model and is closely related to Eq. (2.22).

The firm then uses that probability of purchase information to calculate an expected customer profitability. The firm directs the marketing campaign to those customer segments whose expected profitability in Eq. (3.6) exceeds the cost of reaching the segment:

$$\text{Expected (gross) customer profitability } = \text{ Probability of purchase}$$
$$\times \text{ Likely purchase volume if a purchase is made}$$
$$\times \text{ Profit margin (for this customer).} \tag{3.6}$$

EXAMPLE

Exhibit 3.27 shows part of a direct marketing database after the firm has completed the choice modeling step just discussed. Choice modeling provided the data in column *A*—purchase probability. The question, then, is which customers should the firm target?

Suppose that the total cost of reaching one of these customers is $3.50. What should the firm do? Firms commonly use several approaches to answer this question. First, if the firm looks at the average expected profit, it may decide to target all 10 groups and make a small profit (10 × ($3.72 − $3.50) = $2.20).

Customer	A Purchase Probability	B Average Purchase Volume	C Margin	D Customer Profitability = A×B×C
1	30%	$ 31.00	0.70	$6.51
2	2%	$143.00	0.60	$1.72
3	10%	$ 54.00	0.67	$3.62
4	5%	$ 88.00	0.62	$2.73
5	60%	$ 20.00	0.58	$6.96
6	22%	$ 60.00	0.47	$6.20
7	11%	$ 77.00	0.38	$3.22
8	13%	$ 39.00	0.66	$3.35
9	1%	$184.00	0.56	$1.03
10	4%	$ 72.00	0.65	$1.87

Average Expected Profit = $3.72

EXHIBIT 3.27
Choice-based segmentation example for database marketing: target those customers whose (expected) profitability exceeds the cost of reaching them by comparing column *D* with the cost to reach that customer.

Or it may target customers 1, 3, 5, and 6 and make

$6.51 + $3.62 + $6.96 + $6.20 − (4 × $3.50) = $9.29.

Notice that by using choice-based modeling the firm can target customers to improve profitability by over 400 percent.

Finally, using a more traditional segmentation by average purchase volume, the firm would target, say 30 percent, or the three largest customers in this case—2, 4, and 9—and lose $5.02!

In practice firms may do analysis at the level of a group or an a priori segment and then determine which of those segments to target. However, it is increasingly common for firms to do the analysis at the individual level and then sort the customer database in decreasing order of expected customer profitability (Exhibit 3.27, column *D*). The firm then targets customers who exceed some threshold (a profitability measure) or fall into the most profitable percentage of the database.

Choice-based segmentation can be used in a number of ways. We describe one creative and profitable use of choice models in the next example.

EXAMPLE

ABB Electric—achieving the fruits of segmentation: In its third year of existence, ABB Electric of Wisconsin faced a 50 percent drop in total industry sales. The company sold medium-sized power transformers, breakers, switchgear, relays, and the like, to electric utilities in the North American market. As a new firm in an industry dominated by General Electric, Westinghouse, and McGraw-Edison, ABB had to find a way to win customers from these major competitors or it would go out of business.

In 1974 ABB engaged a consultant, Dennis Gensch, to upgrade its information and to help it to gain insight about its customers. Gensch used customer research and consumer-choice models to better understand the preferences and the decision-making process of ABB's customers. He then helped ABB to use choice-based segmentation to segment its market and to design new products and a service program to better fit the needs of the customers it targeted.

At the heart of ABB's success was the insight it gained into its customers and how to segment the market to target its products and services. First, Gensch and ABB isolated the 8 to 10 attributes that customers used to select among alternative suppliers. They then used these characteristics to predict choice behavior and to form segments of customers who valued different combinations of these attributes differently.

Specifically, what Gensch did was to estimate the choice probability for every customer for every major brand in the market (using a logit model like Eq. (2.22)). He then tested for significant differences in those choice probabilities and used those differences to assign customers to one of four segments:

1. ABB loyal: Customers for whom the probability of choosing ABB was significantly higher than it was for choosing any other competitor

2. Competitive: Customers whose probability of choosing ABB was the highest, but *not* highest by a statistically significant amount relative to the next best alternative

3. Switchable: Customers who preferred a competitor to ABB, but for whom ABB was a close (not statistically significantly different) second

4. Competitor loyal: Customers who preferred a competitor to ABB by a statistically significant amount

Customer Attitude and Choice Data (Basis)

Brand	Cust. ID	Purch. Vol.	District	Choice	Price	Energy Loss	Maint.	Warranty	Spare Parts	Ease Install	Prob. Solv.	Quality
A	1	$761	1	0	6	6	7	6	6	5	7	5
B				1	6	6	6	7	9	9	7	5
C				0	6	5	7	5	3	4	7	6
D				0	5	5	6	7	8	2	6	5
A	2	$627	1	0	3	4	5	4	4	5	6	4
B				0	3	4	5	4	7	3	5	5
C				0	4	5	5	5	5	7	6	4
D				1	4	5	6	5	4	5	5	6
A	3	$643	2	1	6	6	7	7	6	7	7	6
B				0	5	6	7	7	5	6	8	6
C				0	5	6	7	5	5	8	6	5
D				0	6	5	5	4	2	8	6	5
A	4	$562	3	0	6	6	5	5	4	5	5	5
B				0	5	5	6	5	4	6	7	5
C				0	4	4	5	4	6	7	5	3
D				1	4	4	6	7	7	8	7	5

EXHIBIT 3.28(a)
Choice-based segmentation data for ABB-type analysis. Read as follows: customer 1 has annual purchase volume of $761,000, is in district 1, bought brand B last, rates price level as 6, 6, 6, 5 (on a seven-point scale) for brands A, B, C, D, respectively, and so forth.

				Estimated Purchase Probabilities				
Customer	Annual Purchase Volume ($K)	District	Firm Chosen	A(BB)	Firm B	Firm C	Firm D	Type
1	$761	1	B	13.9%	83.8%	2.3%	0.0%	4 lost
2	$625	1	D	0.0%	0.0%	2.2%	97.8%	4 lost
3	$643	2	A	54.3%	45.7%	0.0%	0.0%	2 competitive
4	$562	3	D	39.4%	49.2%	0.0%	11.4%	1 switchable

EXHIBIT 3.28(b)
Output of choice model—giving both probability of purchase and "switchability" indicators for each customer. ABB targeted switchable and competitive customers.

ABB targeted the Competitive and Switchable segments, while keeping its marketing efforts aimed at the other segments at a maintenance level. The result: in a one-year, three-territory test, sales went up by 18 percent and 12 percent in the two major sales regions that followed the recommendations, while they were down by 10 percent in the third region, which had followed the "old" procedure. In the same year, total industry sales decreased by 15 percent! (Gensch, Aversa, and Moore 1990). (Exhibits 3.28(a) and (b) show the type of input data and some of the resulting output one gets from this type of choice modeling. Our ABB Electric segmentation case uses these data.)

We can use a number of other tools, including discriminant analysis described in the last section, for choice modeling and choice-based segmentation (Roberts and Lilien 1993).

SUMMARY

In segmenting a market we divide it into distinct subsets of customers, where each subset (which could be as small as an individual customer) reacts to messages and product offerings differently—that is, has different needs. Marketing opportunities increase when a firm recognizes these differences and measures them. Market segmentation as a theory helps you to understand and explain these differences; as a strategy, our focus here, it helps you to exploit the differences. You can exploit the differences by using the STP approach.

Segmentation requires us to define a market, which we believe should be defined on the basis of shared customer needs, not on the basis of product similarities. To do a sound segmentation, you must specify the objectives for the study, define a sample, collect relevant data, analyze them, and interpret the results. People use a number of techniques to address segmentation problems, including cluster analysis, discriminant analysis, cross-classification analysis, AID, regression, and choice models.

Once a firm completes a segmentation analysis and targets one or more segments, it has to implement a segmentation scheme. Implementing segmentation consists of two related tasks:

1. You must develop a specific marketing program for each target segment: developing product features, price, distribution channels, and ad messages that are appropriate to that segment.

2. You must also identify current or potential customers and determine their segment membership. If you describe potential customers along the same descriptor variables that you used in developing the targeting scheme, then you can use the discriminant function(s) to predict the segment membership of any potential new customer.

By following these two steps, the firm can identify the target segment to which any current or potential customer belongs and direct the appropriate marketing program to that customer.

CHAPTER **4**

Positioning

In this chapter, we

- Highlight the importance of positioning
- Describe how positioning analyses can be used in developing new products, in positioning products, and in analyzing market structures
- Discuss techniques for positioning a firm and its products

DIFFERENTIATION AND POSITIONING

Definition

When you think of safe cars, the one that likely comes to mind is the Volvo. When you want a cold medicine at night, you probably think of Nyquil. If you are looking for healthy frozen food, you probably reach for Healthy Choice. These are products (more generally, offerings) that have a well-defined position in the minds of customers. They are differentiated from the other offerings in the market on one or more dimensions of importance to customers. "Positioning" in the minds of customers typically results from firms following deliberate strategies to design products with particular characteristics and to communicate with the targeted customers about those products. A common way to convey a product's positioning is through its advertising. One of the best known positioning statements is Avis's: "We're number two. We try harder." Reis and Trout (1981) document many other examples in which a firm's positioning strategies were instrumental to its long-term success.

Differentiation is the creation of tangible or intangible differences on one or two key dimensions between a focal product and its main competitors. *Positioning* refers to the set of strategies that firms develop and implement to ensure that these differences occupy a distinct and important position in the minds of customers. Thus Kentucky Fried Chicken differentiates its chicken meal by using its unique blend of spices, cooking vessels, and cooking processes. It conveys these differences to the market through its communications programs, which emphasize that its chicken is "finger-lickin' good."

Positioning using perceptual maps

To position an offering, the firm designs and develops it in such a way that members of the target segment both perceive it to be distinct and value it more than competitive offerings. Three common ways to position are the following:

Our product is unique ("The only product or service in the market that has a particular attribute" as in Polaroid is the only one capable of making instant photos).

Our product is different ("More than twice the [feature] than competitors" as in Listerine kills more germs than competing brands).

Our product is similar ("Same functionality as [competitor] at lower price" as in Meisterbrau tastes like Budweiser at a fraction of its price).

To position products in increasingly crowded markets, marketing managers must understand the dimensions along which target customers perceive products in a category and how those customers view the firm's offer relative to the competitive offers. In other words, the managers have to first understand the competitive structure of their markets as perceived by their customers: How do our customers (current or potential) view our brand? Which brands do those customers perceive to be our closest competitors? What product and company attributes seem to be most responsible for these perceived differences?

Once managers have answers to these questions, they can assess how well or poorly their offerings are positioned in the market. They can then identify the critical elements of a marketing plan that differentiate their offerings from those of competitive offerings: What should we do to get our target customer segments to perceive our offering as different? Based on customer perceptions, which target segments are most attractive? How should we position our new product with respect to our existing products? What product name is most closely associated with attributes our target segment perceives to be desirable?

There are many intuitive approaches that managers use to develop an understanding of the competitive structure of their markets. The perceptual mapping methods described in this chapter provide formal mechanisms to depict the competitive structure of markets in a manner that facilitates differentiation and positioning decisions. Before considering such mapping models, let us look at an example of a perceptual map and see how it facilitates managerial decisions.

A *perceptual map* is a spatial representation in which competing alternatives are plotted in a Euclidean space. The map has the following characteristics: (1) The pairwise distances between product alternatives directly indicate the "perceived similarities" between any pair of products, that is, how close or far apart the products are in the minds of customers. (2) A vector on the map (shown by a line segment with an arrow) indicates both magnitude and direction in the Euclidean space. Vectors are usually used to geometrically denote attributes of the perceptual maps. (3) The axes of the map are a special set of vectors suggesting the underlying dimensions that best characterize how customers differentiate between alternatives. Most frequently, orthogonal axes (straight lines at right angles) are used to represent the dimensions of the map, although nonorthogonal axes can also be used. In either case the axes can be rigidly rotated to aid interpretation. For example, in a two-dimensional map the horizontal and vertical axes are often used to characterize the two dimensions of the map. However, the axes can be rotated so that the southwest to northeast becomes one axis, and southeast to northwest becomes the other axis.

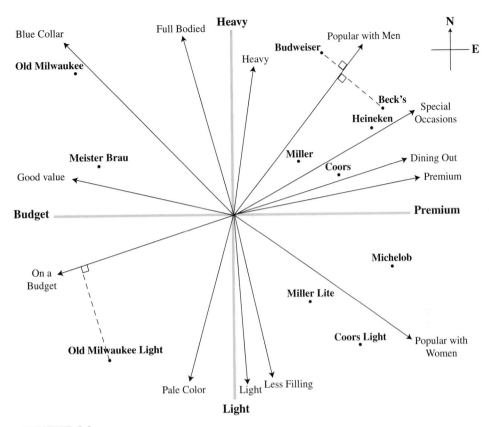

EXHIBIT 4.1
A perceptual map of the beer market, showing (among other things) that Budweiser is the most popular beer with men while Old Milwaukee Light is the least popular with men. The map summarizes customer evaluations of beer on 13 attributes into two dimensions: (1) budget–premium and (2) light–heavy. *Source*: Moore and Pessemier 1993, p. 145.

EXAMPLE

To understand the foregoing points, consider the perceptual map in Exhibit 4.1, which summarizes how a group of customers views the beer market (Moore and Pessemier 1993). In this map the perceived distance (dissimilarity) between Budweiser and Miller is about the same as that between Coors and Michelob. Furthermore, Beck's and Heineken are perceived to be the closest pair among this set of brands. In looking at the vectors, note that as you move in a northeast direction from the origin, the beers increase in their popularity with men. Budweiser is the most popular with men (Beck's is nearly as popular with men), and Old Milwaukee Light is the least popular with men. Budweiser is the farthest along the northeast direction. To see this most clearly, drop a perpendicular line from the point denoted as Budweiser to the vector denoted "popular with men." Likewise, if you drop a perpendicular line from Old Milwaukee Light to this vector extended in the southwest direction, you will see that this is the least popular beer with men. Customer perceptions of these beers along each of the attributes can be interpreted in the same manner. Note also that the horizontal axis (in the east direction) is most closely associated with attributes "premium," "dining out," and "special occasions." In the west direction, the horizontal axis is most closely associated with the attributes "on a budget" and "good value." Thus the horizontal axis (the west to east direction) indicates an underlying dimension of "budget–premium," along which customers seem to characterize their perceptions of the differences between these beers. This map captures many of the significant factors defining the competitive structure of the beer market. We can draw several other conclusions from this map:

- Michelob is located between the "heavy" beers and the "light" beers, competing in both markets.
- Old Milwaukee Light has very little direct competition (no other brand is near its location), indicating potential opportunity for a new beer positioned in this quadrant (if there is a large enough segment of customers in this location). To be positioned in this quadrant, a beer needs to be pale in color and to be viewed as appropriate for someone on a budget.
- Whether or not a beer is popular with women does not indicate anything about whether it will be popular with men (these two attributes are perpendicular to each other). Thus, although Beck's and Budweiser are equally popular with men, among women Beck's is much more popular than Budweiser.

In spite of its potential value in offering these insights, the map in Exhibit 4.1 does not say much about the brand locations that are most attractive to customers, except in broad terms such as "popular with men." For example, the map does not indicate whether more customers prefer heavy premium beers or light budget beers. Without such insights, firms risk investing in differentiating products along dimensions that are not aligned with increased customer preference. An example of such ineffective differentiation is the Westin Stamford Hotel in Singapore, which advertises that it is the world's tallest hotel, an attribute that is not important to any customer segment (Kotler 1991). To identify meaningful dimensions for differentiation, a perceptual map should incorporate the preferences of customers. Later in this chapter we describe "joint-space" techniques to incorporate both perceptions and preferences within the same map.

Perceptual maps facilitate decision making by enabling managers to *summarize* and *visualize* key elements of the market structure for their products. By summarizing a large amount of information, such maps help managers to think strategically about product positioning. For example, the underlying dimensions of *budget–premium* and *light–heavy* capture the combined essence of several attributes on which beers differ. By thinking about competitors in the beer market along these underlying dimensions, instead of along individual product attributes, managers gain a strategic focus to use in product positioning decisions. The use of underlying dimensions to summarize information parallels the process that people use to simplify cognitive tasks. We use such terms as brilliant or arrogant as summary descriptors of people, basing these descriptions on many different things they do, and we place political candidates on a liberal–conservative dimension to characterize their combined stands on a number of issues such as abortion, economic policies, aid to foreign countries, and military affairs. We *observe* other people's actions, but we *infer* the underlying characteristics of brilliance, arrogance, or liberalism. Likewise, we measure how people perceive products in the market, but we infer the underlying dimensions that determine these perceptions.

EXAMPLE

(Adapted from Grapentine 1995.) Two automobile manufacturers want to identify the physical features of a car that customers find attractive. Both manufacturers have a sample of target customers evaluate their vehicles on a series of attributes that describe the perceived attractiveness of these cars' physical features.

Manufacturer A conducts its study without developing a perceptual map showing how the various physical features of a vehicle are interrelated to influence perceived attractiveness. That is, it examines only the direct impact of each attribute on physical attractiveness. It finds that (1) its vehicle receives a relatively low rating on the grill design attribute, and (2) this attribute is highly correlated with the vehicle's overall attractiveness rating. Manufacturer A tells its engineers to redesign the grill to make the car more attractive.

Manufacturer B develops a perceptual map that helps it to determine the underlying dimensions that summarize the attributes used in the study, and it develops a framework to articulate how these dimensions influence perceived vehicle attractiveness. Manufacturer B finds that ratings of the grill are highly correlated with ratings of other attributes, such as those for the design of the outdoor mirrors, the slope of the hood, the design of the windshield, and the impact rating of front bumpers. Guided by this analysis manufacturer B recognizes that the attributes, as a group, reflect consumers' perceptions of the vehicle's aerodynamics. Instead of telling its engineers to change the design of the grill, it instructs them to change the car's aerodynamic styling.

In addition to summarization, maps offer managers a pictorial view of the competitive structure of their markets, helping them to sharpen their thinking about how their market works. People are better at processing visual than numerical information. Although managers may be able to describe verbally how their customers perceive the structure of a market, a data-derived map provides finer details. The details in a perceptual map are especially helpful to those making decisions in new contexts, such as when the firm is developing a positioning strategy for a new product. Other options, such as bar charts and snake plots (Exhibit 4.2), are also available to pictorially summarize customer perceptions. However, plots of this type are difficult to interpret if they include more than three or four alternatives. In addition, snake plots suggest that managers pay equal attention to all attributes, thereby implicitly assigning the same weight to each attribute.

APPLICATIONS OF PERCEPTUAL MAPS

The value of a perceptual map stems from the notion that perception is reality; that is, customer perceptions, in part, determine customer behavior. A primary use of perceptual mapping is to provide insights into the market structure for a defined set of competing alternatives. Because any location on a map results from the combined effects of a number of beliefs and perceptions, the map suggests which attributes of a product the firm should modify to effect a desired change in the position of the product. For example, the map in Exhibit 4.1 could help identify what attributes management must change to position Michelob clearly either as a light premium beer or as a heavy premium beer, instead of occupying an intermediate position. By making assumptions about how changes in the physical characteristics of a product influence customer perceptions, managers can tentatively predict the sales or market shares that would be associated with alternative positions on a map. Green (1975) urges caution here, pointing out that the primary use of perceptual maps should be providing diagnostic insights, rather than making specific predictions about sales.

In addition to their use in general positioning decisions, perceptual maps are particularly useful in several specific areas of marketing. We list four such areas:

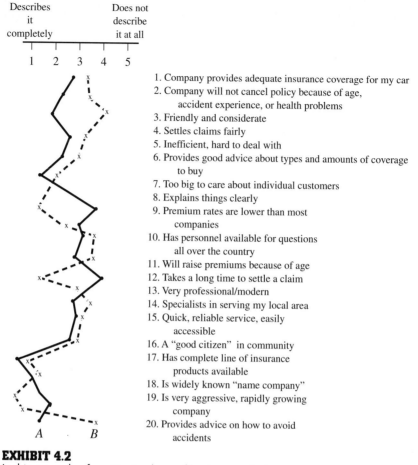

Describes it completely — Does not describe it at all

1   2   3   4   5

1. Company provides adequate insurance coverage for my car
2. Company will not cancel policy because of age, accident experience, or health problems
3. Friendly and considerate
4. Settles claims fairly
5. Inefficient, hard to deal with
6. Provides good advice about types and amounts of coverage to buy
7. Too big to care about individual customers
8. Explains things clearly
9. Premium rates are lower than most companies
10. Has personnel available for questions all over the country
11. Will raise premiums because of age
12. Takes a long time to settle a claim
13. Very professional/modern
14. Specialists in serving my local area
15. Quick, reliable service, easily accessible
16. A "good citizen" in community
17. Has complete line of insurance products available
18. Is widely known "name company"
19. Is very aggressive, rapidly growing company
20. Provides advice on how to avoid accidents

A   B

EXHIBIT 4.2
In this example of positioning by profile chart analysis, insurance company A is compared with its leading competitor B using customer evaluation on 20 attributes. *Source:* Wind 1982, p. 82.

1. *New product decisions:* Perceptual mapping is used to support new product decisions (Dolan 1993). It is useful in the opportunity-identification stage of new product development to locate gaps in the market, as a way to provide focus for new product development efforts. It is also useful in the concept-testing stage to evaluate the potential for the new concept in the context of other existing products and to identify segments who would find the product most appealing. GM used such a map (Exhibit 4.3) to evaluate the Buick Reatta, both as a concept and after a test drive (Urban and Star 1991, p. 280). This map helped reassure GM management that the Reatta had a distinct new upscale image compared with the other models of Buick. (It turned out that there was actually no market in this gap. Buick Reatta sold only a few thousand cars before GM started discounting it to reduce inventory.)

    We can also use perceptual maps to evaluate candidate names for a new product on a defined set of criteria. For example, when this book was at the concept stage, we evaluated potential titles using the following adjectives: boring, complicated, leading-edge, pretentious, relevant, and unique. Several faculty members in business schools in the United States responded to a structured questionnaire after going through a packet of information that contained the book outline and a demonstration version of

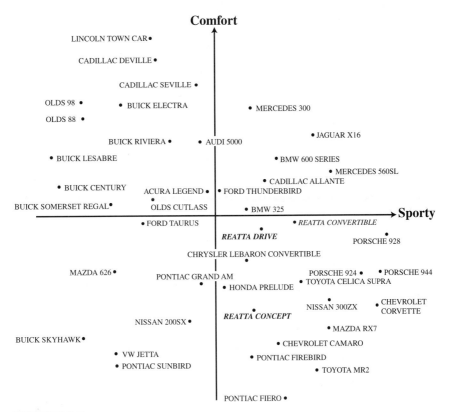

Comfort

LINCOLN TOWN CAR ●

CADILLAC DEVILLE ●

CADILLAC SEVILLE ●

OLDS 98 ●   ● BUICK ELECTRA   ● MERCEDES 300

OLDS 88 ●

BUICK RIVIERA ●   ● AUDI 5000   ● JAGUAR X16

● BUICK LESABRE   ● BMW 600 SERIES
                                        ● MERCEDES 560SL
                                ● CADILLAC ALLANTE
● BUICK CENTURY   ACURA LEGEND ●   ● FORD THUNDERBIRD
                        ●
BUICK SOMERSET REGAL ●   OLDS CUTLASS   ● BMW 325   **Sporty**

● FORD TAURUS   ● *REATTA CONVERTIBLE*
                              ●
                    REATTA DRIVE   PORSCHE 928 ●

              CHRYSLER LEBARON CONVERTIBLE
                              ●
MAZDA 626 ●   PONTIAC GRAND AM   PORSCHE 924 ● ● PORSCHE 944
                        ●   ● TOYOTA CELICA SUPRA
                    ● HONDA PRELUDE
                                        ●   ● CHEVROLET
                                NISSAN 300ZX   CORVETTE
NISSAN 200SX ●   *REATTA CONCEPT*
                                        ● MAZDA RX7
BUICK SKYHAWK ●
                                ● CHEVROLET CAMARO
        ● VW JETTA
        ● PONTIAC SUNBIRD   ● PONTIAC FIREBIRD
                                        ● TOYOTA MR2

                    PONTIAC FIERO ●

EXHIBIT 4.3
A perceptual map showing that the Reatta is perceived differently from other Buick cars, and after driving it (Reatta Drive), the Reatta is perceived better in comfort than before driving (Reatta Concept). *Source*: Urban and Star 1991, p. 280.

the software. Another way to obtain data for naming a product is to ask potential customers to state all the things that come to mind when they hear a particular title. Then you can use the number of mentions of each attribute as data for developing a perceptual map.

2. *As a check on managers' views of competitive structure and positioning*: Marketing managers have their own perceptions of how their customers and noncustomers perceive the different brands. These perceptions may or may not be consistent with how various customer segments actually view the different brands. Perceptual maps can provide managers with important insights on whether, how, and why their perceptions coincide with customer perceptions. For example, a manager noting the contributions of a perceptual mapping study said:

> Some of the facts we learned from this study shocked us. We had focused on physical product benefits as a basis for competitive advantage. Instead we found a market more interested in service issues. (Siemer 1989)

Wind (1982, p. 90) compared customer perceptions of food products to the "objective" perceptions of food technicians (Exhibit 4.4). That study included 40 different products and new-product concepts evaluated along 12 attributes. The study showed little relationship between objective characteristics and subjective perceptions concerning attributes such as fillingness, carbohydrates, proteins, and vitamins. On the other hand, there was a stronger relationship between subjective perceptions and such objective attributes as caloric content, sugar, fat, cholesterol, and convenience of preparation. These insights helped the firm to position the new products in a way that would not lead customers to overestimate undesirable attributes such as fattening. In many product categories, objective data are available through such sources as *Consumer Reports* and *PC Magazine*. In some cases these sources also publish maps of these objective data; Exhibit 4.5, for example, summarizes the price-performance characteristics of several brands of modems.

3. *Identifying who to compete against*: Many marketers try to differentiate their products from those of competitors. However, in some highly competitive markets, there are few gaps or opportunities to find distinct positions. In such cases it may be useful to select specific competitors to target, based on an understanding of their weakest points. Perceptual maps can highlight what attributes are associated with close substitutes and what points of difference among the substitutes are least relevant in influencing customer preferences (Wyner and Owen 1994). Thus perceptual maps can provide insights about differences between competitive products that customers do not notice (i.e., the company or its competitor has not successfully communicated these differences to customers) and insights about differences that customers notice but do not care about (i.e., products are differentiated, but the differences do

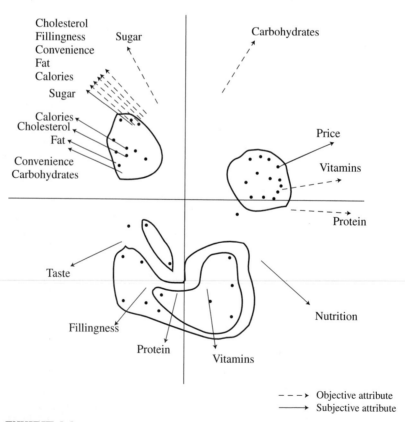

EXHIBIT 4.4
Two-dimensional perceptual configuration of 40 food products and their "perceived" and objective attributes, showing that characteristics like taste, fillingness, and perceived nutrition are not closely related to objective measures. Each dot represents a product. *Source*: Wind 1982, p. 90.

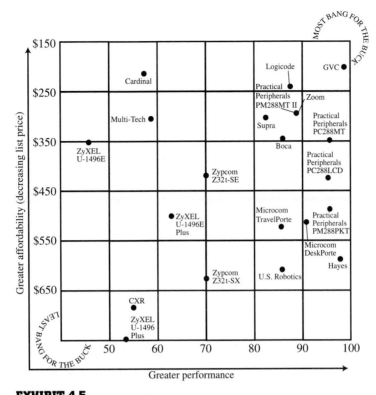

EXHIBIT 4.5
A map positioning high-speed modems in a "price-performance" space. *Source*: *PC Magazine*, September 13, 1994, p. 282.

not significantly influence customer preferences, such as Jolt Cola, which has twice the caffeine of other colas.)

4. *Image or reputation studies*: Image is a multidimensional concept that serves as a summary of what a firm stands for, as perceived by its various stakeholders. The objective of image or reputation studies is both to understand how stakeholders perceive a firm and to design an image that is consistent with the firm's strategic objectives. Perceptual maps offer a good way to summarize the key results of such studies.

Exhibit 4.6 shows a perceptual map comparing various retailers (e.g., regional chains, discount chains, and independent hardware stores) who compete for the do-it-yourself segment of the home improvement market in Chicago (Johnson 1994). This study was undertaken by independent retailers who were losing their markets all across the United States to discount chains such as Wal-Mart and mega home-centers such as Lowe's and Home Depot. The perceptual map is based on customer ratings of various retailers on 18 attributes. The map indicates that customers perceive Wal-Mart to be the most convenient, the two regional chains (Menards and Handy Andy) to stock hard-to-find items and preferred brands, and the independent store to offer the best customer service. The three types of retailers have occupied distinct positions on the map, and the regional chains are viewed as similar stores (they are located near each other on the map). One way for the independent store to remain viable in this market is by maintaining and strengthening its superior customer service. About 40 percent of the customers had shopped there in the previous 12 months. The map also suggests that there is a potential opportunity for a new retailer

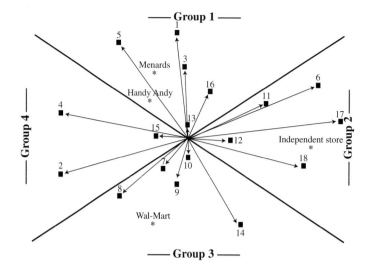

Attributes included in this study

1. Has hard-to-find items
2. Has good prices
3. Stocks preferred brands
4. Offers many price levels
5. Stocks unique products
6. Offers assistance and information
7. Place doesn't feel intimidating
8. Has convenient hours
9. Provides quick checkouts
10. Has easy-to-find departments
11. Will special order
12. Has convenient location
13. Keeps products in stock
14. Has good customer service
15. Has displays which highlight specials
16. Provides installation
17. Offers special services
18. Has sufficient number of employees

EXHIBIT 4.6
Image study of retailers in the do-it-yourself segment in Chicago, using a perceptual map. The map shows that customers perceive Wal-Mart to be convenient, the independent store to provide good customer service, and the regional chain to offer a good assortment of products. *Source*: Johnson 1994, p. 57.

to differentiate itself by offering lower prices (with possibly lower levels of service), an area of the map with no existing retailers.

PERCEPTUAL MAPPING TECHNIQUES

Psychometricians first developed perceptual mapping techniques to map psychological measurements of how people perceive things that vary on multiple dimensions. Marketers have adapted these multidimensional scaling (MDS) methods to represent customer perceptions and preferences for a set of entities (brands, geometric shapes, department stores, presidential candidates, etc.) on a map in Euclidean space.

Customer behavior is influenced by both perceptions and preferences. Two products may be perceived to be different, although physically they may essentially be the same.

For example, Toyota Corolla and Chevy Prizm are physically nearly identical cars with different names. However, customers perceive the Corolla to be superior to the Prizm. In other cases customers may not be able to perceive any differences even when the products are different. For example, in blind taste tests most customers cannot identify different brands of beer or cola. Customers are also unable to identify different brands of wine even when their prices differ by several hundred percent (experts, however, can distinguish different wines).

MDS methods vary depending on the nature of input data (e.g., similarities data, perceptions data, or preference data) and how these data are manipulated to derive the map (Exhibits 4.7 and 4.8). We will describe three major approaches in greater detail: (1) perceptual maps from attribute-based data, (2) perceptual maps from similarity-based data, and (3) joint-space maps that include both customer perceptions and their preferences. (Cooper (1983) and Green, Carmone, and Smith (1989) describe these methods in detail.)

Attribute-based methods

Managers can use attribute-based methods to derive perceptual maps from data consisting of customer evaluations of products (more generally, competing alternatives) along pre-specified dimensions. There are four major steps to this method.

Step 1: Identify the set of products and the attributes on which those products will be evaluated. The attributes you choose to include in the analysis depend on the objectives of the study. For strategic positioning studies you should select a broad set of competing alternatives and attributes. For example, the alternatives can be product class (e.g., mutual funds, bonds, and stocks in the financial services industry) or product forms (e.g., subcompact, compact, and intermediate in the automobile industry). For tactical positioning studies the alternatives can be close competitive offerings (e.g., different brands of shampoo, or different fragrances in shampoo, such as floral and herbal), and the attributes can be more operational in nature (e.g., color and miles per gallon.) The alternatives you choose should vary along all the chosen attributes. Kotler (1991) has summarized a number of generic attributes that can provide a useful starting point in selecting attributes for the study (Exhibit 4.9).

Step 2: Obtain perceptions data. The data for perceptual mapping typically come from questionnaires administered to a sample of customers in defined target segments. You should

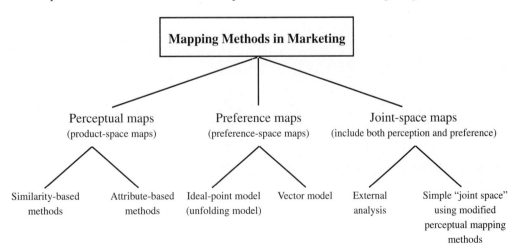

EXHIBIT 4.7
Mapping methods used in marketing fall into three categories: (1) perceptual maps,
(2) preference maps, and (3) joint-space maps.

Model	Input	Output	Computer programs	Comments
Perceptual map from similarity-based methods	Data matrix (or submatrix) consists of perceived pairwise similarities or other distance measures (e.g., correlations) between alternatives. The data may come from a single individual or be averaged across members of a target segment.	Spatial map showing the locations of the product alternatives.	KYST MDSCAL INDSCAL	Particularly useful when market structure is primarily based on intangible attributes such as image, aesthetics, smell, or taste.
Perceptual map from attribute-based methods	Data matrix consists of ratings of alternatives on a prespecified set of attributes. The data may either be from a single individual, or be averaged across members of a target segment.	Spatial map showing both the location of alternatives and the directional vectors associated with the attributes.	Factor Analysis (MDPREF) Discriminant Analysis	Particularly useful when market structure is driven primarily by tangible attributes, such as physical features of the product, its performance, and its service characteristics.
Preference map from ideal-point methods (Unfolding model)	Data matrix consists of the stated or derived preferences of individuals over a set of alternatives. Preferences may be rank-orders (nonmetric unfolding model) or ratings (metric unfolding model).	Spatial map showing the locations of the alternatives and the ideal points of the individuals. An ideal point refers to an individual's most preferred combination of the underlying dimensions defining the product space and will vary from individual to individual.	KYST GENFOLD ALSCAL	Particularly useful in categories where segment preferences are not unidirectional but exhibit an inverted U-shape. For example, preference for coffee brands may decline as the available options become either "stronger" or "weaker" in flavor as compared with an individual's ideal brand.
Preference map from vector method	Data matrix consists of the stated or derived preferences of individuals over a set of alternatives, where preferences are measured on a rating scale.	Spatial map showing the locations of the alternatives and the directional vectors associated with the preferences of each individual.	MDPREF	Useful in categories where segment preferences are unidirectional along the underlying attributes. For example, if competition is driven by factors such as quality, value, or speed of response, preferences are likely to be increasing in a unidirectional manner.
Joint-space map from external analysis	Data matrix consists of the stated or derived preferences of individuals over a set of alternatives, supplemented with data giving locations of the alternatives from a perceptual map.	Spatial map showing the locations of the alternatives, the directions of the attributes, and the ideal points or the preference vectors of individuals.	PREFMAP-3 GENFOLD	These are full-fledged systems with a number of processing options.
Simple joint-space map obtained from modified perceptual mapping methods	Data matrix may consist of (1) data like that in the similarity-based method where one of the alternatives is a hypothetical ideal-point of the individuals, or (2) data like that in the attribute-based method where one of the alternatives is the hypothetical ideal-point of the individuals, or all alternatives are rated on a "preference" attribute.	For data in (1), the spatial map provides the location of the alternatives, including the ideal alternative, and for data in (2), the spatial map provides the locations of all the alternatives, including the ideal alternative, and a directional vector for each attribute.	MDSCAL KYST INDSCAL MDPREF	These methods are fairly simple to implement, and they are often insightful.

EXHIBIT 4.8

A summary of the major perceptual and preference modeling methods, their required inputs and outputs, and computer programs that implement each method.

first organize the data into a matrix representing customer perceptions of each alternative on each of the prespecified attributes. Customers can either rank or rate all alternatives on one attribute at a time, or customers can rank or rate one alternative at a time along all the attributes. For example, airlines differ along many perceptual attributes, such as convenience, punctuality, overall service, and comfort. The following data matrix *from one customer* illustrates the nature of the data collected, where the customer ratings ranged from 1 to 9 for each attribute.

	American	United	USAir	Continental	Southwest
Convenience	5	8	3	3	8
Punctuality	6	5	5	4	8
Overall Service	8	7	5	4	6
Comfort	6	6	4	4	3

Attribute data for airlines: 1 = worst to 9 = best

FEATURES are characteristics that supplement a product's basic function (e.g., stereo system in a car).

PERFORMANCE refers to levels at which the product's primary characteristics operate.

DURABILITY is a measure of the product's expected operating life.

RELIABILITY is a measure of the probability that a product will malfunction or fail within a specified time period.

SERVICEABILITY is a measure of the ease of fixing a product that malfunctions or fails.

STYLE describes how well the product looks and feels to the customer.

PRODUCT IMAGE refers to attributes that convey the emotional aspects of the product - attributes that stir the heart as well as the mind of the customer. These include attributes such as the prestige or reputation associated with a product/company, the perceived lifestyle of the people who use the product, etc.

DELIVERY refers to all aspects of how the product or service is delivered to the customer. It includes the speed, accuracy, and the care attending the delivery process.

INSTALLATION refers to activities needed to be completed before the product becomes operational in its planned location.

TRAINING AND CONSULTING refer to the support services provided by the company to train the customer and its personnel in the use and maintenance of the product, and to help derive the maximum value from the use of the product.

REPAIR AND MAINTENANCE refers to convenience and quality of services provided by the company to prevent product failures, and to repair the product in the event it fails to conform to expected performance.

OTHER SERVICES include warranty, availability of "loaners," and services that add value to the customer's purchase or use of the product.

SERVICE IMAGE refers to a number of attributes that contribute to the overall perception of the service. It includes such attributes as competence, friendliness, and courteousness of service employees, the perception of being pampered with personalized attention, etc.

PERCEIVED QUALITY refers to the degree to which the product meets customers' expectations of what the product/service should be. It is closely associated with the other attributes such as features, performance, reliability, durability, etc., that are listed above (Garvin 1987).

EXHIBIT 4.9
Illustrative list of attributes relevant for positioning analysis using attribute-based perceptual mapping methods. *Source*: Adapted from Kotler 1991.

A key assumption in perceptual mapping is that all customers whose data are used in the study share roughly the same perceptions about the alternatives. Therefore it is important that you obtain data from a homogeneous sample of customers. If you believe that customers are from several different segments, it is better to group them first into separate segments using, for example, cluster analysis (Chapter 3). By averaging responses within each segment, you can generate an "average" data matrix for every segment and then develop a separate perceptual map for each segment.

Step 3: Select a perceptual mapping method. In positioning studies it is not unusual to obtain customer evaluations on 10 or more attributes relevant to the set of alternatives under consideration. However, it is unlikely that all these attributes extract unique information about the perceptions that customers have about these alternatives. It is more likely that subsets of attributes tap the same underlying construct (also referred to as factor, axis, or dimension). Thus perceived overall service and comfort might both be attributes that tap the more fundamental dimension of perceived quality.

Perceptual mapping techniques offer a systematic method for extracting information about the underlying construct(s) from a data matrix consisting of customer perceptions on observable attributes. While there are several methods for doing this with attribute-based data, Hauser and Koppelman (1979) recommend factor analysis. We will describe the factor analysis procedure. The model used in the software accompanying this book is called MDPREF, which contains options for a factor-analytic derivation of perceptual maps (Carroll 1972, and Green and Wind 1973).

Outline of the factor analysis procedure: Factor analysis is a technique for systematically finding underlying patterns and interrelationships among variables (here, attributes), based on a data matrix consisting of the values of the attributes for a number of different alternatives (brands, product classes, or other objects). In particular it enables us to determine from the data whether the attributes can be grouped or condensed into a smaller set of underlying constructs without sacrificing much of the information contained in the data matrix. Factor analysis is also useful in preprocessing data before undertaking segmentation studies, as described in the appendix to this chapter.

Let X be a matrix with m rows and n columns, in which the column headings are attributes and the rows are alternatives, with the data in the matrix consisting of the average ratings of each alternative on each attribute by a sample of customers. Note that X is the transpose of the example data matrix for perceptual mapping shown in the previous subsection. Let X_s represent a standardized matrix in which each column of X has been standardized. (To standardize a column, for each value we subtract the mean of all values on that attribute and divide by the standard deviation of the values. By standardizing we remove the effect of the measurement scale and ensure that all variables are treated equally in the analysis—i.e., it would not matter whether income is measured in dollars or pesos.) We denote the columns of X_s as $x_1, x_2, \ldots, x_n$.

In the principal-components approach to factor analysis (the most commonly used method in marketing), we express each of the original attributes as a linear combination of a common set of factors, and in turn we express each factor also as a linear combination of attributes, where the jth factor can be represented as

$$F_j = a_{j1}x_1 + a_{j2}x_2 + \cdots + a_{jn}x_n, \tag{4.1}$$

where the a's are weights derived by the procedure in such a way that the resulting factors F_j's are optimal. The optimality criterion is that the first factor should capture as much of the information in X_s as possible, the second factor should be orthogonal to the first factor and contain as much of the remaining information in X_s as possible, the third factor should be orthogonal to both the first and the second factors and contain as much as possible of the information in X_s that is not accounted for by the first two factors, and so forth.

Each value of the original data can also be approximated as a linear combination of the factors:

$$x_{kj} \approx z_{k1}f_{1j} + z_{k2}f_{2j} + \cdots + z_{kr}f_{rj}, \tag{4.2}$$

where the z_{kl}'s and f_{ij}'s are also outputs of the factor analysis procedure.

The relationships characterized by Eqs. (4.1) and (4.2) can be seen more clearly when represented as matrices (Exhibit 4.10). In Exhibit 4.10, the z's are called (standardized) factor scores and the f's are the factor loadings. Then Z_s is the matrix of standardized factor scores, and F is the factor loading matrix, with columns denoted as F_j, and represents the correlation matrix of attributes with factors. (Note that the factors by attributes matrix in Exhibit 4.10 is actually the transpose of the F matrix.) If $r = n$, that is, if the number of factors is equal to the number of attributes, there is no data reduction. In that case, (4.2) becomes an exact equation (i.e., the approximation symbol in Exhibit 4.10, $\approx$, can be replaced by the equality symbol, $=$) that shows that the standardized data values (x_{kj}'s) can be exactly recovered from the derived factors. All that we would accomplish in that case is to redefine the original n attributes as n different factors, where each factor is a linear function of all the attributes. However, in perceptual mapping we seek r factors (r typically being 2 or 3) that retain as much of the information contained in the original data matrix as is possible. Variance (the dispersion of values around a mean) is a measure of the information content of an attribute. The larger the variance, the higher the information content. Once we

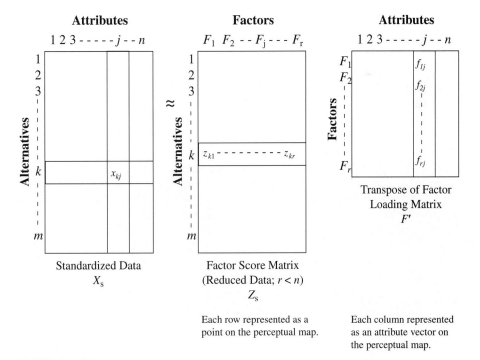

Each row represented as a point on the perceptual map.

Each column represented as an attribute vector on the perceptual map.

EXHIBIT 4.10
A pictorial depiction of attribute-based perceptual mapping. The model decomposes the (standardized) original data matrix (X_s) into two matrices: (1) the standardized factor score (Z_s) matrix and (2) the factor loading matrix (F); r is the number of factors (dimensions of the perceptual map) and is usually set to be equal to 2 or 3.

standardize the attributes, each attribute contains one unit of variance (except for attributes for which all values are identical, in which case the information content of that attribute is equal to 0). If there are n attributes in the analysis, then the total variance to be explained (information content) is equal to n.

The output of a factor analysis procedure is illustrated graphically in Exhibit 4.11 for the case of two attributes, elegance and distinctiveness, in a study of notebook computers. The procedure first finds a factor along which the points are maximally dispersed (i.e., this factor has the maximal variance when we project the points onto it). In this example the locations of the notebook computers are dispersed much more along factor 1 than factor 2. If factor 1 has a variance equal to 1.7, this factor alone accounts for 85 percent of the information content in the two attributes $((1.7 / 2.0) \times 100)$, suggesting that "elegance" and "distinctiveness" are correlated and possibly refer to a common underlying dimension called "design." The procedure then finds a second factor, orthogonal (perpendicular) to the first, that maximally recovers the remaining variance. In this case the remaining factor will recover 15 percent of the variance; together the two factors explain all the variance in the data. If there are n attributes, the procedure continues in this fashion until it extracts as many factors (up to n), all orthogonal to each other, as are needed to explain the variance in the original data.

Step 4: Interpreting factor analysis output. An important objective of factor analysis is to provide an interpretation of the underlying factors in terms of the original attributes. The key to interpretation is the factor loading matrix F. By looking at the pattern of the loadings, we should

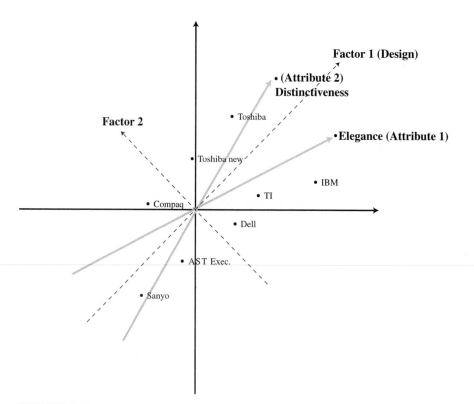

EXHIBIT 4.11
A two-attribute example of factor analysis for notebook computers. "Distinctiveness" and "elegance" are correlated with each other, and they are represented by an underlying factor (dimension) called "design." For this example a one-dimensional map captures most of the variation among the notebook computers.

be able to identify and name the factor. Loadings that have high absolute value (high absolute values of correlations) make interpretation easy. In a perceptual map the factor loading matrix is represented visually as attribute vectors, where correlation between any attribute and a factor is equal to the cosine of the angle between that attribute vector and the corresponding factor.

The factors may be rigidly rotated (i.e., F is transformed by an orthogonal matrix, while at the same time making the corresponding transformation to Z_s) to aid interpretation, forcing attributes to have either big or small cosines with the transformed factors (the transformation is called Varimax rotation). The result is that a set of attributes tends to line up closely with each factor. In this way, attributes tend to be closely aligned with a single factor. We can then better identify the attributes most closely associated with the transformed factors. Although rotation changes the variance explained by each factor, it does not affect the total variance explained by the set of retained factors. *To further aid interpretation, we can draw each attribute vector on the map with a length that is proportional to the variance of that attribute explained by the retained factors.* Exhibit 4.12 is a perceptual map derived from factor analysis, where the length of each attribute vector indicates the proportion of the variance of that attribute recovered by the map.

Variance explained by a factor: Each factor explains a proportion of the total variance in the data as follows:

$$\text{Variance explained by factor } i = f_{i1}^2 + f_{i2}^2 + \cdots + f_{in}^2. \tag{4.3}$$

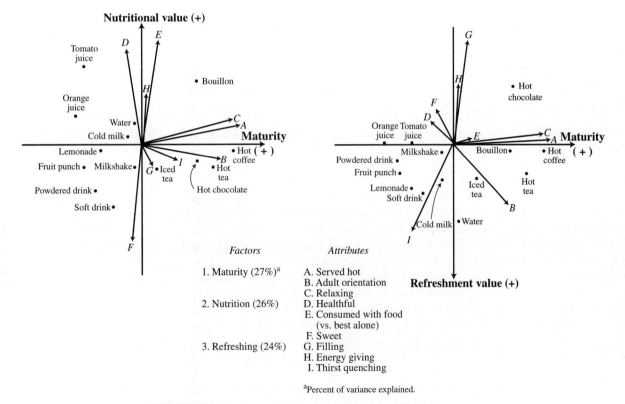

Factors	Attributes
1. Maturity (27%)[a]	A. Served hot
	B. Adult orientation
	C. Relaxing
2. Nutrition (26%)	D. Healthful
	E. Consumed with food (vs. best alone)
	F. Sweet
3. Refreshing (24%)	G. Filling
	H. Energy giving
	I. Thirst quenching

[a]Percent of variance explained.

EXHIBIT 4.12
An example of a three-dimensional attribute-based perceptual map of beverages, where the length of each attribute vector is proportional to the amount of its variance explained by the map. The three dimensions are (1) maturity of target segment, (2) refreshment value, and (3) nutritional value. *Source:* Aaker and Day 1990, p. 574.

The proportion of the variance explained by a single factor equals the variance explained by that factor divided by n, the total variance in the data. In Exhibit 4.12 the proportion of variance explained by the horizontal axis (factor 1) is equal to 0.27, and the variance explained by the vertical axis (factor 2) is equal to 0.26, giving a combined variance explained by the two axes of 0.53. If all n factors are retained, these proportions will sum to one.

Proportion of an attribute's variance explained by the retained factors: A good factor analysis solution explains a significant proportion of the variance associated with each original attribute as follows:

$$\text{Proportion of variance explained for attribute } j = f_{1j}^2 + f_{2j}^2 + \cdots + f_{rj}^2. \tag{4.4}$$

Number of factors retained: If the variance of any attribute is poorly recovered by the retained factors, that attribute is unique and would require additional factor(s) for it to be explained. In that case we might consider going to a higher-dimensional map, say from a two- to a three-dimensional map. This raises the broader question of how many factors we should retain in a factor analysis study. Unfortunately there is no simple answer to this question, although there are several useful guidelines. In the context of perceptual maps, it rarely makes sense to go beyond three dimensions, especially if a three-dimensional map recovers more than 60 to 70 percent of the variance in the original data. Another useful guideline is that every retained factor should individually account for *at least* one unit of variance (equivalent to the variance in a single attribute) and typically should account for substantially more than one unit of variance.

EXAMPLE

In a study of the market for both conventional and solar-powered cooling products for industrial buildings, Choffray and Lilien (1980) found that several different types of individuals participated in the purchase decision process for such equipment. Decision makers included production engineers (those who would be working with and maintaining the equipment), corporate engineers (those designing the systems), plant managers, and senior executives. Using the preceding guidelines (along with additional statistical methods), they determined that even the *number* of dimensions that these groups of individuals used in thinking about cooling systems differed—top managers and production engineers had perceptual spaces that could best be represented in three dimensions, while plant managers and corporate engineers had two-dimensional spaces.

Choffray and Lilien then studied whether it was appropriate to combine the perceptions of these groups. (Roughly this amounts to determining whether the data matrices in Exhibit 4.10 would be the same when they analyzed each group separately and when they combined the perceptions of all groups.) The answer was no, even when they used the same number of dimensions for the different groups. Exhibit 4.13 summarizes the qualitative results for plant managers and corporate engineers. Plant managers group operating costs, the system's use of currently unproductive areas, and the protection the system offers against irregularities in the supply of traditional energy sources as their first dimension (factor). Corporate engineers, however, include the system's initial costs, its vulnerability to weather damage, and its complexity.

This example underscores the importance of ensuring that the respondents who provide data for perceptual mapping form a homogeneous group. Alternatively we could perform some prior segmentation, because the groups may differ both in the number and the makeup of their perceptual dimensions.

	Factor 1	Factor 2
Plant Managers (PM)	(+) Energy savings (+) *Low cost a/c* (+) Fuel rationing protection (+) *Use unproductive areas* (+) Reduce pollution (+) *State of the art solution* (+) Modern image (+) *Power failure protection*	(−) Field proven (−) Reliability (+) Not fully tested (−) *Substitutability of components* (−) Climate sensitivity
Corporate Engineers (CE)	(+) Not fully tested (−) *System's cost* (−) Field proven (−) Reliability (+) *Vulnerability to weather* (+) *Complexity*	(+) Reduce pollution (+) Fuel rationing protection (+) Energy savings (+) Modern image

Notes:
- The factors listed have loadings greater than .50 and are listed in decreasing order of importance.
- Items in italics are important to the corresponding group, but not to the other group.
- The sign to the left of each factor is the sign of the correlation between an attribute and a factor. When the sign is positive (negative), then the factor and the attribute are positively (negatively) related to each other.

EXHIBIT 4.13
Source: Choffray and Lilien 1980, p. 125.

Location of the products (alternatives) in the perceptual map: An important element of the factor analysis output is the factor score matrix, which gives the location of each product on each factor. If we retain only two factors, then the location of the first product in a two-dimensional perceptual map is given by the first two elements in the first row of the factor loading matrix, the location of the second product is given by the first two elements of the second row of the factor loading matrix, and so on.

In summary, attribute-based methods provide a powerful set of tools for perceptual mapping. They are particularly useful when the product alternatives are differentiated along tangible attributes that are well understood and evaluated by customers. Compared with similarity-based methods, attribute-based methods identify the underlying dimensions more clearly. A further advantage is that you can develop the maps even when the respondents evaluate only a few alternatives.

Similarity-based methods for perceptual mapping

Similarity-based methods rely on the idea that perceived similarity (or dissimilarity) between alternatives may be conceptualized in terms of psychological distances. With this mapping method we try to produce a spatial map in which the *Euclidean distances* between any two alternatives closely correspond to the degree of similarity that customers perceive between the same pair of alternatives. The techniques for producing such a map differ in their assumptions regarding the nature of the input data and in the algorithms used to translate similarities into distances on the map. In the most common technique any two alternatives, C and D, that respondents perceive to be less similar to each other than another set of alternatives, A and C, are placed on the map at least as far apart as C is from D (to the extent feasible). Similarity-based methods usually require five steps to implement:

Step 1: Identify the alternatives of interest. Usually these alternatives will be competing products or services. The specific set of alternatives we choose depends on the objectives for the study. For strategic positioning studies, it is best to select a broad set of competing alternatives. For tactical positioning studies, we can choose a set of alternatives from among the firm's closest competitors. In either case we should choose alternatives familiar to the customers whose perceptions we are measuring, or we should brief the customers to make them familiar with the alternatives before eliciting their perceptions of these alternatives.

Step 2: Develop a matrix of similarities (also called proximities) between pairs of alternatives. The input data for generating similarity-based perceptual maps is a symmetric matrix consisting of the interproduct similarities (or dissimilarities) perceived by the target segment. The matrix is symmetric because we assume the similarity (psychological distance) between alternatives A and B is the same as that between alternatives B and A. In the following similarity matrix, we measure similarity on a scale ranging from 1 to 9, with 1 representing "most similar" and 9 representing "most dissimilar."

	Aqua-Fresh	Colgate	Crest	Gleem
Aqua-Fresh	1			
Colgate	2	1		
Crest	4	4	1	
Gleem	7	6	5	1

In this similarity matrix for a few toothpastes, 1 is most similar and 9 is least similar.

Another way to obtain the input data is to ask customers to *rank each pair* directly from the most similar pair to the least similar pair, with the rank 1 being assigned to the most similar pair. Although we can derive a perceptual map separately for each customer from a similarity matrix, typically one first computes average similarities data by averaging the responses of several customers. (Again, it is critical that the group of customers included in the study have reasonably homogeneous perceptions.) Averaging individual responses in this way is an acceptable approximation only if we can reasonably assume that all the customers in the target segment use the same underlying dimensions in comparing the alternatives.

Step 3: Develop the perceptual map. We can generate a perceptual map using one of several computer programs (Exhibit 4.8). The computer mapping program transforms the input data of the similarity between alternatives i and j (δ_{ij}) into distance on a map (d_{ij}). This is the critical step in this analysis, in which we transform "psychological distances" between the alternatives into distances in Euclidean space. The reason for making this transformation is that we can use more powerful analytical methods to interpret a map in Euclidean space. The similarity-based perceptual map in Exhibit 4.14 shows that customers perceive Close-up to be *three times* as far from Dentagard (i.e., three times as dissimilar) as Colgate is from Aqua-Fresh. The ability to quantify judgments is important in the next step: numerically evaluating the *relative* effects of alternative positioning strategies on market shares or on the sales of each alternative.

In general, to satisfy all the constraints (e.g., customers perceive A as most similar to B and least similar to F, which implies that A should be closest to B on the resulting map and farthest away from F) will require a map of $n - 1$ dimensions, where n is the number of product alternatives being evaluated. But maps with more than three dimensions have little managerial value, and so we balance interpretability with the goal of adhering to the constraints. The ideal way to resolve this trade-off is to produce a map in two- or three-dimensional space that summarizes the market structure with visual clarity.

Step 4: Determine the number of dimensions for the map. To make an intelligent decision on the appropriate number of dimensions, we use the notion of (weak) monotonicity, namely, that the rank order of product similarities should be the same (or close to same) as the rank order of distances on the associated perceptual map. Monotonicity requires that if $\delta_{ij} > \delta_{kl}$ then $d_{ij} \geq d_{kl}$, where i, j, k, l are alternatives, the δ's are similarities, and the d's distances on the perceptual map. The monotonicity constraint is always satisfied if the resulting map is in $n - 1$ dimensions. For fewer dimensions, the greater the departure from monotonicity, the less perfect the resulting map. We use the notion of "stress" to measure

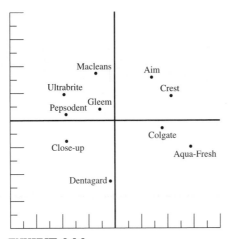

EXHIBIT 4.14
A similarity-based map of toothpastes. The map shows that Ultrabrite and Pepsodent are the closest substitutes in this market; Aqua-Fresh and Close-up, and Aim and Dentagard are least likely to be substituted for each other. *Source*: Malhotra 1993, p. 703.

departures from monotonicity. A stress value of 0 implies a perfect fit, a measure similar to $1 - R^2$ in regression. Stress values less than 0.05 are considered to be good, whereas maps with stress values greater than 0.20 are not generally meaningful. Computer program output typically includes the stress values associated with a map in any given number of dimensions. These programs use one of several formulae for computing stress. A frequently used formula is

$$\text{Stress} = \sqrt{\frac{\sum_{i<j}\left(d_{ij} - \hat{d}_{ij}\right)^2}{\sum_{i<j}\left(d_{ij} - \bar{d}\right)^2}}, \tag{4.5}$$

where

d_{ij} = the distance between alternatives i and j in the resulting Euclidean spatial map;

$\bar{d}$ = the average of all d_{ij}'s; and

$\hat{d}_{ij}$ = a set of numerical values that are as close as possible to d_{ij}, but that also represents a monotonic function of δ_{ij}.

To determine the appropriate number of dimensions, we trade off between monotonicity and the number of dimensions. The general idea is to start with one dimension, and increase the number of dimensions until the stress value decreases very little with the addition of each incremental dimension.

The foregoing approach uses "nonmetric analysis" to recover the rank orders in the similarity data. Other approaches based on "metric analysis" attempt to recover either the absolute magnitudes or differences in magnitudes in the similarity data.

Step 5: Interpret the dimensions in the map. As output, the computer program produces points (representing alternatives) in a perceptual map of the dimensionality we choose, along with a set of associated axes. Next we must interpret the axes. One simple way to interpret the map is to look for alternatives in extreme locations on each dimension and then try to determine the differentiating features between these alternatives. We can also shift the origin or rotate the axes to improve interpretation. Usually, however, we will need additional data from the study participants regarding their perceptions of the alternatives to help us interpret the map. (For example, if the study includes measures of product attributes as well, we can correlate the perceptual map positions with the attribute data.)

In summary, similarity-based methods are particularly useful in categories in which it is difficult to articulate the specific attributes on which various alternatives are differentiated (e.g., different fragrances). The maps can help a firm to identify new product opportunities and the competitive structure (e.g., closest competing brands) of the market. However, similarity-based methods do not provide a clear mechanism for interpreting the underlying dimensions of the map, and they generally require at least eight alternatives for the algorithms to produce a reliable map.

JOINT-SPACE MAPS

Overview

A major limitation of perceptual maps is that they do not indicate which areas (positions) of the map are desirable to the target segments of customers and which ones are not. In other words, the maps do not incorporate information about customer preferences or choices. We need to use a *joint-space mapping method* to incorporate both perceptions and preferences in the same map.

Perceptions are fundamentally different from preferences: customers may see Volvo as the safest car, but they may also have a low preference for it. In addition, unlike perceptions preferences do not necessarily increase or decrease monotonically with increases in the magnitude of an attribute. In some cases (e.g., sweetness of soft drink) each customer has an ideal level of the attribute above or below which a product becomes less preferred. In other cases customers always prefer more of the attribute (e.g., quality of a TV set) or always prefer less of an attribute (e.g., waiting time before a car is repaired). Exhibit 4.15 illustrates these different types of preferences. Preference maps that incorporate inverted U-shaped preferences are referred to as ideal-point (or unfolding) models. Maps that incorporate linear preference functions are referred to as vector models. (In a third kind of preference modeling, part-worths allow for arbitrary piecewise linear functions that can approximate both ideal-point and vector preference functions. In Chapter 7, we describe conjoint analysis, which allows for part-worth functions.)

Simple joint-space maps

The simplest way to incorporate preferences in a map is to introduce a hypothetical ideal brand into the set of alternatives that customers evaluate in the attribute-based mapping model. For each respondent, an ideal brand has that individual's most preferred combination of attributes. Assuming that both the perceptions and the preferences of customers in a target segment are fairly homogeneous, we can find the location of the "average" ideal brand using either similarity-based or attribute-based methods. The ideal brand thus becomes simply another alternative that customers evaluate. In the resulting map, locations that are farther away from the ideal point (location of the ideal brand) are less desirable to customers than locations closer to the ideal point. Using this approach in Exhibit 4.16(a), we can view alternative A, which is twice as far from the ideal point as alternative B, as being preferred half as much as B.

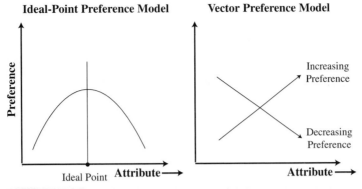

EXHIBIT 4.15
Different types of preference functions. Ideal-point models have an intermediate "best level," e.g., sweetness, whereas for vector models more (or less) is always more (less) preferred, e.g., waiting time, reliability.

Another way to include preferences in attribute-based models is to add an attribute called "preference" on which customers rate all the alternatives to indicate their preferences for these alternatives. When we aggregate and average these preference ratings, we can treat the average ratings as an additional row in the input data matrix to represent an attribute called "preference." The map we generate from this modified data set then includes a preference vector to indicate the direction of increasing preference. An alternative positioned farther along this vector is one for which customers have greater preference. Suppose that alternative A is farthest along the preference vector. Then if B is half as far from A as C is from A along the preference vector, customers prefer B twice as much as C (Exhibit 4.16b).

Exhibit 4.17 shows this approach in evaluating notebook computers. The preference vector shows that customer preference increases with improvements in screen quality and perceived value of the product and decreases with lower levels of battery life. In this example the two-dimensional map recovered over 80 percent of the variance in the preference "attribute." However, if it had recovered a low percentage, say less than 50 percent, then it would be unwise to use the map to interpret preference structure, even though the map could

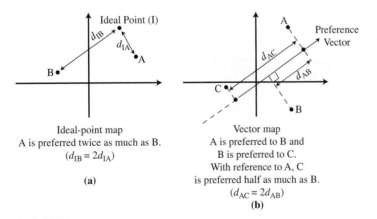

Ideal-point map
A is preferred twice as much as B.
$(d_{IB} = 2d_{IA})$

(a)

Vector map
A is preferred to B and
B is preferred to C.
With reference to A, C
is preferred half as much as B.
$(d_{AC} = 2d_{AB})$

(b)

EXHIBIT 4.16
Interpreting simple joint-space maps. In ideal-point maps distances directly indicate preference: the larger the distance from the ideal point, the less preferred the brand. In vector maps the product locations are projected onto a preference vector (dashed lines in b), and distances are measured along the preference vector.

still be useful for interpreting the perceptual dimensions. When variance recovery for the preference vector is poor, it may be worthwhile to drop some attributes from the analysis to see if we can produce a joint-space map that is easier to interpret.

External analysis using PREFMAP3

Overview: PREFMAP3 is a mapping model based on the assumption that respondents who have common perceptions of a set of alternatives may have widely differing preferences for these alternatives. The model superimposes the preferences of each respondent in a group onto a common perceptual map, developed external to the PREFMAP3 model. The perceptual map can be derived from the same set of respondents using the similarity- or attribute-based approaches described in the previous section.

PREFMAP3 starts with a perceptual map giving the locations of the product alternatives. In the second step it introduces for each respondent either an ideal brand or a preference vector into the map in a manner that ensures maximal correspondence between the input preference ratings (or rankings) for the alternatives and the preference relationships among the alternatives in the resulting joint-space map. Note that each respondent included in the study has a unique ideal point or a preference vector as the case may be.

EXHIBIT 4.17
In this example of a simple attribute-based joint-space map with a preference vector, the direction of increasing preference is indicated by the attribute "preference." Overall preference for notebook computers increases with screen quality, value, and long battery life but is unaffected by expandability, keyboard, and ease of use.

Description of the PREFMAP3 model: The input data for the model is the $N \times m$ preference matrix consisting of the preference ratings of the m alternatives by N respondents as shown in the following table. Here we show preference ratings for five airlines from five customers using a 1 to 9 scale, with 1 indicating most preferred and 9 indicating least preferred.

	Airlines				
	American	United	USAir	Continental	Southwest
Customer 1	1	7	2	5	8
Customer 2	7	7	4	2	1
Customer 3	4	6	6	6	7
Customer 4	3	1	8	6	2
Customer 5	2	2	3	7	8

Matrix of preference values, s_{ij} where i refers to customer and j refers to product alternatives (airlines).

(If the rating scale is reversed, i.e., if larger numbers indicate increased preference, then multiply every number in the data matrix by -1 to reverse the scale.)

Let s_{ij} denote the value of the preference rating of the jth alternative by the ith customer. The ideal-point version of PREFMAP3 attempts to optimally locate the ideal point of each respondent i on the perceptual map. Define

$$\hat{s}_{ij} = b + ad_{ij}^2, \tag{4.6}$$

where

$\hat{s}_{ij}$ = the estimated rating of alternative j by respondent i, as determined by the procedure for each i and j; $i = 1, 2, \ldots, I$ (# of respondents) and $j = 1, 2, \ldots, J$ (# of alternatives); and

d_{ij} = the squared distance of ideal point i from the fixed location of alternative j on the perceptual map.

The model tries to determine the constants a and b (which may be negative) in Eq. (4.6) such that $(\hat{s}_{ij})$ is as close as possible (i.e., in the sense of minimizing squared distance) to the ratings s_{ij} for all respondents i and all alternatives j given in the preference data matrix. Exhibit 4.18 shows a map produced from a preference mapping model.

In the vector version of PREFMAP3, the model attempts to find a preference vector (i.e., the direction in which preference increases) for each respondent by using the following equation to compute estimated ratings:

$$\hat{s}_{ij} = a_i \sum_{k=1}^{r} x_{ik} y_{jk} + b_i, \tag{4.7}$$

where

a_i = slope of the preference vector;

b_i = intercept term for preference vector;

y_{jk} = coordinate location of alternative j on dimension k, determined from a perceptual map;

x_{ik} = preference vector coordinate on dimension k; and

r = number of dimensions in the perceptual map.

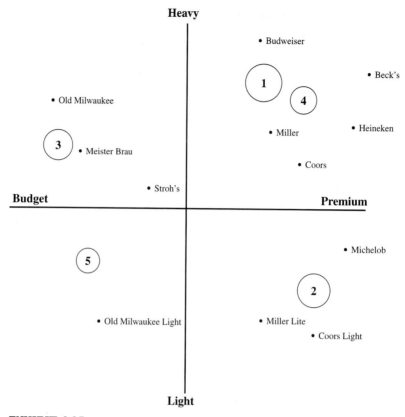

EXHIBIT 4.18
A joint-space map derived from external analysis with groupings of customer ideal points in circles. The size of the circle indicates relative size of the customer segment at that location. *Source*: Moore and Pessemier 1993, p. 146.

Given r and y_{jk} (for all j and k), the model attempts to find a_i, b_i, and x_{ik} such that $\hat{s}_{ij}$ is as close as possible (in the sense of minimizing squared distance) to the ratings s_{ij}. (To draw the map, we relocate the computed preference vectors by parallely shifting them so that they pass through the origin.) The product term, $x_{ik} y_{jk}$, in Eq. (4.7) ensures that the preference vector direction on the map will maximally recover the preference ratings s_{ij} for respondent i for all j, for the given positions of the product alternatives (y_{jk}, $j = 1, 2, \ldots, J$ and $k = 1, \ldots, r$).

There are several other options in the PREFMAP3 model, including the use of rank-order preference data and options that allow distances to be differentially weighted so that each dimension is accorded a different level of importance, which can vary by customer. The model can also be structured to use both the ideal-point and vector models on the same map, with the ideal-point mode used for respondents for whom it best recovers the original preference ratings and the vector mode used for the remaining respondents (for whom it best recovers their preferences). A full discussion of these topics will take us well beyond the scope of this book. Further details are available in Carroll (1972), and Green and Wind (1973), and Meulman, Heiser, and Carroll (1986). For this book we implemented the vector model version of PREFMAP3 (Meulman, Heiser, and Carroll 1986).

Interpreting PREFMAP3 results: An advantage of PREFMAP3 is that typically we can visually identify segments of customers on the map. For example, in Exhibit 4.18 the largest grouping of respondents (ideal points) is in the circle marked 1. These customers prefer Budweiser the most (i.e., their ideal points are located closest to Budweiser), Miller the next most, and so forth. The next largest segment is marked as a circle with the number 2. This segment prefers Coors Light and Michelob most. The model also shows that Stroh's is not the most preferred brand in any segment—it is a "compromise brand" that some respondents may choose (e.g., those in segments 5 and 3) when their most preferred brand is unavailable. To interpret a vector model, follow the suggestions we gave for interpreting attributes in Exhibit 4.1, that is, project each product alternative onto the preference vectors.

The preference map allows us to not only visually identify segments, but to also compute an index of predicted market share for any product at any location on the map. The latter requires us to first transform preferences into indices of market shares. We can consider two "choice rules" for doing this (see also Chapter 7): (1) first choice and (2) share of preference. Under the first choice rule, we assume that each customer only purchases the most preferred product (that is, the one closest to the ideal point or the one farthest along a preference vector). Under the share of preference rule, we assume that each customer purchases every product in proportion to its measured preference value (relative to the sum of the preference values for all other products included in the model). The first choice rule is appropriate for infrequently purchased products (e.g., cars), whereas the share of preference rule is appropriate for frequently purchased products (e.g., shampoo or soft drinks). The software automatically does these computations and enables us to explore the potential market performance that can be achieved by repositioning any one product assuming that all other products remain at their original locations on the map.

For some data sets, parameter a in Eq. (4.6) can turn out to be negative for some respondents. These respondents have "anti-ideal-points" such that the closer a product is to such points, the less it is preferred. Anti-ideal-points can cause difficulties in interpretation. This is the primary reason that we have only implemented the vector model in the software. It is also possible that the preference map poorly recovers the preferences of some respondents. This can be detected by checking the proportion of variance (of preferences) that the map explains for each respondent. If there are many such respondents, it may be worthwhile to redo the whole analysis after increasing the number of dimensions of the externally derived perceptual map.

INCORPORATING PRICE IN PERCEPTUAL MAPS

We can represent price in several ways in perceptual maps (Urban and Star 1991). In attribute-based methods we can include price as another attribute along which customers evaluate the products. Or we can include objective prices as an additional attribute in developing the map.

A completely different way to approach this issue is to divide the coordinates of each alternative by its price along each of the dimensions of the map. We can use this approach with any of the methods described in this chapter. Exhibit 4.19 shows a map of the mouthwash category with and without price included. When the coordinates of each alternative are transformed by its price, the underlying dimension becomes "per-dollar coordinates." Without this transformation it is difficult to see why Signal should survive in the market. Other brands dominate it along both dimensions (Exhibit 4.19a). Listerine is perceived to taste better and to have the same ability to fight bad breath. However, the price-transformed coordinates (Exhibit 4.19b) show that its price-adjusted position makes it an attractive alternative that is not dominated by other alternatives on both dimensions.

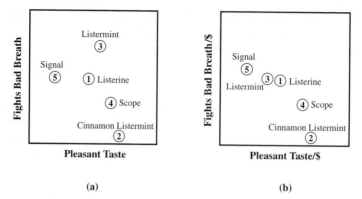

EXHIBIT 4.19
An example of a perceptual map with and without "dollar-metric" modification, showing that
Signal is dominated by the other brands on both attributes (a) unless price is considered (b).
Source: Urban and Star 1991, pp. 138–139.

SUMMARY

In this chapter we described methods to produce perceptual and preference maps that help
us to position products and services in the minds of our customers. Although many of our
examples were for consumer products, we can also apply these methods to technical and industrial products and services aimed at business markets.

These mapping techniques enable managers to understand the competitive structure
of their markets. Based on this understanding, they can then position their offerings to
gain a favorable response from their target segments. Although these techniques are powerful, it is important to understand their limitations so that they we can apply them where
they are most useful.

- Perceptual mapping methods provide only a partial explanation of customer perceptions and preferences. They provide insights that are limited by the particular
  set of alternatives and attributes included in the study—that is, they support positioning efforts within an existing framework. In similarity-based methods the set of
  alternatives selected for study will limit the set of underlying dimensions that are
  developed as a basis for positioning. In attribute-based methods the set of attributes
  chosen limit the dimensions along which new positioning options will be considered. Thus these methods may not encourage managers to think "outside the box"
  to develop positioning strategies along new attributes.

  We should also remember that the mapping techniques only serve to *represent* perceptions and preferences in a manner that aids decision making. They do not tell us
  much about *why* customers form certain perceptions or preferences.
- Several technical limitations (e.g., data size restrictions in attribute-based methods,
  minimum number of alternatives required for similarity-based methods, solutions
  that yield degenerate maps in joint-space methods, and so forth) make these methods less than perfect in applications.
- There are no "probability models" to provide us statistical guidance in selecting
  the most appropriate map (for the methods presented here). Thus we cannot statistically estimate whether a map based on data from a particular set of respondents
  will generalize to the target population of interest. The plausibility of a map is not
  an indicator of its validity (truth) or even of its reliability (whether we will obtain a

similar map when we use data from a new sample of respondents). Some newer mapping techniques, such as PROSCAL (MacKay and Zinnes 1996), incorporate an error model and offer statistical guidance in interpreting maps. However, these models are not yet in wide use.

In spite of these limitations, perceptual and preference maps offer two major benefits: they help managers to (1) view the competitive structure of their markets through the eyes of their customers and (2) communicate with each other about how the market is structured and what they might do to take advantage of that structure. These maps are particularly useful for strategic decision making, especially if the mapping exercise is part of a larger audit of the competitive position of the organization.

Finally, perceptual maps are useful even when there are no data available from customers. Subjective managerial data often provide useful insights. For example, managers developing a new product can each generate individual maps based just on their own perceptions of how the new product stacks up against existing competitors. These maps can stimulate good discussions that will help them develop a positioning strategy for the new product.

Chapter 4 Appendix
FACTOR ANALYSIS FOR PREPROCESSING SEGMENTATION DATA

Segmentation studies often rely on measurements (observations) about individuals on a number of attributes (variables). However, as mentioned in Chapter 3 correlated variables may mask the true segment structure. To address this problem we can use factor analysis to preprocess segmentation data before using cluster analysis. The objective is to reduce the data from a large number of correlated variables to a much smaller set of independent underlying factors, this reduced set retaining most of the information contained in the original data. The derived factors not only represent the original data parsimoniously, they often result in more reliable segments when used in cluster analysis procedures.

The form of factor analysis that is useful for segmentation studies is slightly different from the approach described in this chapter. Let X be a $m \times n$ data matrix consisting of needs (or attitudinal) data from m respondents on n variables. As before, the input data are standardized. Let X_s represent the standardized data matrix. However, here we work with unstandardized factor scores (we denote the factor score matrix as P to distinguish it from the standardized factor score matrix represented as Z_s in Exhibit 4.10). Thus we need a different set of variables to distinguish these factor analysis results from the ones we get in Eqs. (4.1) and (4.2):

$$P_j = u_{j1}x_1 + u_{j2}x_2 + \cdots + u_{jn}x_n, \tag{4A.1}$$

$$x_{kj} \approx p_{k1}u_{1j} + p_{k2}u_{2j} + \cdots + p_{kr}u_{rj}, \tag{4A.2}$$

where

x_i = ith column from the standardized data matrix X_s; x_{ki} is the element in the kth row and ith column of this matrix;

P_j = the jth column of the factor score matrix representing the scores of each respondent on factor j; $P = [P_1, P_2, \ldots, P_r]$ is the factor score matrix with r retained factors; and

u = "loadings" that characterize how the original variables are related to the factors.

As before, we seek r factors to represent the original data, where r is smaller than n, the number of variables we started with. If we can pick an r that is less than 1/3 of n, but where the retained factors account for more than 2/3 of the variance in the data, we can then consider the preprocessing of the data to be successful. There is, however, always a danger that some important information is lost by preprocessing sample data in a way that masks the true cluster structure. Thus, it is often a good idea to run the model with and without preprocessing of the data through factor analysis, to see which set of results make the most sense. To aid interpretability of the factors, we can orthogonally rotate the initial factor solution (Varimax rotation) so that each original variable is correlated most closely with just a few factors, preferably with just one factor. A full discussion of this topic is beyond the scope of this book.

We can then use the factor score matrix with r factors as the set of input variables for identifying segments through cluster analysis. By using unstandardized factor scores at this stage, we can determine during cluster analysis whether to standardize the factor scores, an option that we can select within the cluster analysis software provided with this book.

CHAPTER **5**

Strategic Market Analysis:
Conceptual Framework and Tools

In this chapter (and the next) we develop concepts and tools that we can apply when deploying marketing effort in the long term to different markets and for different products. The topics we cover in this chapter are

- Strategic marketing decision making, the process and steps that firms use to develop marketing programs
- Market demand and trend analysis, the methods and tools firms use to assess the current and future size of a market
- The product life cycle, the long-term evolution of a market
- Cost dynamics, how costs vary with scale of production and production experience

While we will discuss the use of these concepts and tools in more detail in the next chapter, we discuss the conceptual foundations here.

STRATEGIC MARKETING DECISION MAKING

In a large organization with several business divisions and several product lines within each division, marketing plays a role at each level. At the organizational level, marketing contributes perspectives and demand estimates to help top management decide on the corporation's mission, opportunities, growth strategy, and product portfolio. Corporate strategies provide the context in which division managers formulate strategy in each of the business divisions. Finally, the managers of each product or market within each division develop their marketing strategies within the context of the policies and constraints developed at the divisional and corporate levels.

Most firms have a corporate mission statement, and a related set of objectives, and they define their corporate strategies and related marketing strategies with respect to that mission statement and set of objectives:

The *corporate mission* is the firm's statement of the scope of its activities. For example, Xerox Corporation's mission statement defines whether Xerox is in the business of manufacturing copiers, improving business productivity for its customers, or providing automated office systems. The firm must translate that mission into a set of directly measurable objectives to make that mission operational. Those objectives normally concern all the firm's divisions. The firm's financial objectives may stress profitability, its accounting objectives may stress cost, its marketing objectives may focus on sales and creativity, and its engineering objectives may stress efficiency. To be useful guidelines for action, these objectives must be stated precisely and they must be easy to understand.

Some examples of objectives are

- To achieve a 15 percent average growth in sales over the next five years (marketing)
- To achieve a growth in after-tax return on investment of 8 percent for the next three years (finance)
- To reduce the costs of manufacturing and allocated overhead per unit of output by 3 percent per year over the next three years (accounting/manufacturing)
- To reduce the rate of product returns by 20 percent within the next three years (engineering/manufacturing)
- To increase customer satisfaction ratings by 30 percent within two years (marketing, service, manufacturing, operations)

As these examples show, achieving objectives requires the close cooperation of several areas of the firm.

In its *corporate strategy*, then, the firm sets forth the actions it intends to undertake to secure a sustainable (long-term) advantage while meeting its corporate objectives. Firms usually state their strategies in terms of what products they plan to offer to what markets or market segments using what technologies. In formulating its strategy the firm defines the areas it is targeting for growth, the level and focus of its R&D effort, and how it intends to commit its resources over the long term to meet its corporate objectives. The firm's strategy will include the details about product innovation, markets to serve, personnel, R&D, and corporate image. For example, IBM might decide to serve business and home users with its personal computers, and McDonald's might decide to enhance its corporate image as the preeminent family restaurant chain.

Marketing objectives follow from the corporate strategy. Firms usually state their marketing objectives in terms of expectations for market share, sales, or profits over a period of time. Finally, the firm develops marketing strategies to specify how it will achieve its marketing objectives. In this chapter and the next we focus on the key factors that influence firms in formulating these marketing strategies.

Wind and Robertson (1983) have developed a useful framework for structuring the marketing elements that firms consider in developing their strategies (Exhibit 5.1). The framework has three main sections:

Section I: A traditional assessment of market opportunities and business strengths:
  a. An analysis of opportunities and threats in the market and environment
  b. An analysis of business strengths and weaknesses

Section II: The marketing strategy core:
  c. Segmentation and positioning analysis (identifying market segments and the benefits they seek)
  d. Opportunity analysis (linking the benefits the segments seek with business strengths and weaknesses)
  e. Synergy analysis (the positive and negative synergies in advertising, distribution, manufacturing, etc., among products, segments, and marketing-mix components)

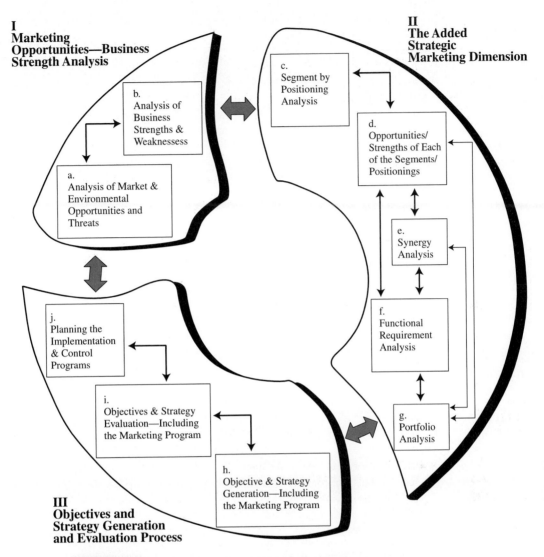

EXHIBIT 5.1
A marketing-oriented approach to strategy formulation and evaluation. *Source*: Wind and Robertson 1983, p. 16.

    f. Functional requirement analysis (specification of what products, services, and support each segment requires and the company's ability to satisfy those requirements)

    g. Portfolio analysis, the analytical core of the process (an integrated view of the strategic process, both for existing and new business)

Section III: The objective and strategy generation and evaluation process:

    h. Generation of objectives and strategies

    i. Evaluation of objectives and strategies

    j. Implementation, monitoring, and control of the program

Limitation of Typical Marketing Strategy (Wind & Robertson 1983)	The Marketing Engineering Solution
1. Improper analytic focus	Market definition and understanding of market structure
2. Functional isolation	Integration, especially models of cost dynamics (scale and experience effects)
3. Ignoring synergy	Marketing-mix/product-line methods
4. Short-run analysis	Dynamic models, especially product life-cycle analysis models
5. Ignoring competition	Competitive-analysis models
6. Ignoring interactions	Proper market-definition models
7. Lack of an integrated view	Integrated models including shared-experience models such as PIMS, product-portfolio models and normative resource-allocation models

EXHIBIT 5.2
Seven limitations of typical marketing strategy and the type of market strategy models that can be used to address these limitations.

Wind and Robertson claim that this framework helps firms to overcome seven important limitations of marketing analysis (Exhibit 5.2); the analytic model-based approaches can be used to address those limitations.

Improper analytic focus: In Chapter 3 we argue that customer needs and values, rather than the physical characteristics of products, define a market. We can use the methods for defining a market described in Chapter 3 in any program to develop a marketing strategy. The size, growth, and development of the market are necessary inputs in developing a strategic process. In addition we must understand key forecasting issues.

Functional isolation: Analyzing functional requirements is integral to the process of formulating and evaluating a strategy (Exhibit 5.1). Marketing strategy is intimately linked to research and development activities, financial issues, logistics, and manufacturing. In this chapter we will address one aspect of the integration of functions with respect to cost dynamics; in Chapter 7 we describe new product development methods, and in Chapter 9 we deal with several related logistical challenges such as location analysis.

Ignoring synergy: In Chapter 2 we sketched out how response models could accommodate the effect of multiple marketing-mix elements.

Short run analysis: Most short-run analyses ignore dynamic effects. We will focus on market dynamics at several points in the book, particularly with the ADBUDG model (Chapter 8) and the Bass diffusion model (Chapter 7); in this chapter we explore the factors that underlie the product life cycle.

Ignoring competition: In today's saturated markets, many companies gain sales only at the expense of others; hence a focus on competition is central to the development of sound marketing strategy. In Chapters 2, 6, and 10 we describe models that incorporate the effect of competition.

Ignoring interactions: A major weakness of many market strategy studies is their lack of attention to interactions between products and across market segments. In Chapter 3 we discuss how to define markets properly, which can lessen this problem: In well-defined markets competition occurs within market boundaries but there is little competition across the defined boundaries.

Lack of an integrated view: The models we describe in Chapter 6 incorporate an integrated view of strategic marketing. In particular, shared experience models such as PIMS and product portfolio models such as GE/McKinsey accommodate an integrated view of strategic decisions.

The marketing strategy component of Exhibit 5.1 has as part of its foundation the size and growth of the market or markets that the firm is or plans to operate in. We discuss the critical issue of analyzing market demand and trends next.

MARKET DEMAND AND TREND ANALYSIS*

Defining a market is critical to developing any market-based model. Marketing strategy, with its focus on the long term, depends on defining the market and the market's evolution and dynamics. In this section we deal with assessing market demand and analyzing trends for products that have had some sales history or market experience; we deal with demand estimation for new products in Chapter 7.

In developing market forecasts one needs to carefully define the level of the market under study. We distinguish five levels here (although coarser or finer grain classifications are possible) and illustrate them using Budweiser beer as an example:

The *potential market* is the set of all customers who show interest in a product or service; survey methods can be used to determine its size.

The *available market* is the set of all customers who have not only interest but sufficient income and access to the product or service. We can determine the available market by linking the potential market to demographic and distribution data.

The *qualified available market* is the set of customers who pass the availability screen and who are qualified to buy. For example, for beer the qualified market might be that part of the available market that is over 21 years old, that is, legal drinkers.

The *served or target market* is the part of the qualified market that the company decides to pursue. Budweiser may decide that (for analysis purposes) the southeast and midwest regions constitute its target market.

The *penetrated market* is the set of all customers who have already bought the product or service. For the beer example the penetrated market is all buyers of all brands of beer in the served markets.

Predicting the course of a company's or an industry's market sales is essential if a company is to plan and control its business operations. As markets fluctuate and become more unstable, it becomes an increasingly critical task for marketing management. Without some form of sales projection, firms would have no reasonable starting point for making strategic marketing decisions.

---

*This section draws on a note by Venkatesh Shanker.

Vital as they are, forecasts are estimates at best. Some firms do better jobs than others, but no one has come up with a perfect method; many companies are beginning to rely on several independent forecasting methods (Exhibit 5.3), hoping to converge on a reliable approach.

Prominent forecasting techniques include judgmental methods, market and survey analyses, time-series analyses, and causal analyses (Exhibit 5.3).

Judgmental methods

There are three main judgmental methods of forecasting the market—through salesforce-composite estimates, using a jury of executive opinion, and Delphi and related methods:

Salesforce-composite estimates: Many company managers turn to members of the salesforce for help when assembling clues about future sales. However, few use their estimates without some adjustments. In the first place, sales representatives are biased observers. They may be characteristically pessimistic (if their quotas are related to their forecasts) or optimistic (if they want to expand their set of accounts), or they may go from one extreme to the other because of a recent sales setback or success (recency bias).

If these biasing tendencies can be countered, sales representatives often have more knowledge of or better insight into developing trends than any other single group. They are often especially knowledgeable when the product is fairly technical and subject to a changing technology. And when they participate in the forecasting process, the sales representatives may have greater confidence in the derived sales quotas, and this confidence may increase their incentive to achieve those quotas.

Jury of executive opinion: A common judgmental approach is to combine the views of key stakeholders in hopes of gaining a sounder forecast than might be made by a single estimator. Those stakeholders may be company executives but may also include dealers, distributors, suppliers, marketing consultants, and professional associations.

The main problems with using juries of executives are (1) a tendency to give too much weight to their opinions, (2) the need to infringe on executives' time, and (3) deciding how to weight the individual forecasts to get a consensus (Chase Econometrics, Data Resources, and Wharton Econometrics are secondary sources that provide expert opinion data). Armstrong (1985) provides some useful guidelines on how to solve these problems.

Delphi and related methods: In gathering informed opinion, a number of companies are relying on the Delphi method for forecasting, especially for medium- or long-term forecasting. Developed by the RAND corporation in the 1950s, the Delphi method has three key features: (1) anonymous response, in which the study director uses formal methods to obtain anonymous opinions and assessments; (2) interaction and controlled feedback, in which the director organizes interaction through a multiround process with controlled feedback between rounds; and (3) statistical group response, where group opinion is the aggregate of

Judgmental	Market and Survey Analysis	Time Series	Causal Analyses
Salesforce composite	Buyer intentions	Naive methods	Regression analysis
Jury of executive opinion	Product tests	Moving averages	Econometric models
		Exponential smoothing	Input-output analysis
Delphi methods		Box-Jenkins method	MARMA
		Decompositional methods	Neural networks

EXHIBIT 5.3
A classification of market forecasting approaches.

individual opinions in the final round. These features mitigate the effects of dominant individuals, irrelevant comments, and group pressure toward conformity.

Several experiments have shown that the Delphi method does indeed perform rather well (Jolson and Rossow 1971, and Martino 1983). Larréché and Montgomery (1977) use the Delphi method to determine the likelihood that marketing managers will use a number of well-known marketing models. Delphi methods are becoming more popular with the development of "groupware" products like Lotus Notes that can facilitate the process. RAND originally developed the Delphi method to forecast which cities Russia would attack in a nuclear war—a situation in which there was no objective basis for forecasting.

EXAMPLE

The University of Michigan's Office for the Study of Automotive Transportation conducted a Delphi study with 300 auto industry executives to forecast the sales of electric vehicles 10 years into the future. The surprising result: The consensus favors hybrid (electric-combustion engines), and if the estimates are realized we should see roughly 150,000 hybrid-drive vehicles on the road in 2003 (Thomas and Keebler 1994).

Market and product analysis

Buying intentions: Marketing forecasting is the art and science of anticipating what buyers are likely to do under a given set of conditions. This definition immediately suggests that a most useful source of information would be the buyers themselves. Ideally the firm draws up a probability sample of potential buyers and asks each buyer how much of a product he or she will buy in a given future time period under stated conditions. It also asks buyers to state what proportion of their total projected purchases they will buy from a particular firm or at least what factors would influence their choice of supplier. With this information the firm seems to have an ideal basis for forecasting its sales.

Unfortunately this method has a number of limitations in practice, the most important of which are (1) the relationship between stated intentions and actual behavior and (2) potential nonresponse bias. (The second problem is particularly critical in industrial markets composed of few buyers.) The value of this method then depends on the extent to which the buyers have clearly formulated intentions and then carry them out. (Haley and Case (1979) and Morrison (1979) discuss stated intentions versus actual behavior.)

Secondary source surveys about buyer intentions are available for both consumer and industrial products. Two indices provide data related to consumer durable purchases and contain information about consumers' present and anticipated future financial positions and their expectations about the economy: the "Consumer sentiment measure" from the Survey Research Center at the University of Michigan and the "Consumer confidence measure" from Sindlinger and Company. For industrial products the best known surveys are published by the U.S. Department of Commerce, the Opinion Research Corporation, and McGraw Hill. Most of their estimates have been within 10 percent of the actual outcomes.

Market tests: The usefulness of opinions, whether those of buyers, sales representatives, or other experts, depends on their cost, availability, and reliability. When buyers typically do not plan their purchases carefully or are very erratic in carrying out their intentions or when experts are not very good guessers, firms need a more direct market test of likely behavior. Unlike forecasts based on buying intentions, which rely on what *people say*, forecasts based on market tests rely on what *people do*. A direct market test is especially desirable for forecasting the sales of a new product or the likely sales of an established product in a new distribution channel or a new territory. When a firm wants a short-run forecast of likely buyer response, a small-scale market test is usually a good solution. (We describe this approach in more detail in Chapter 7.)

Time-series methods

As an alternative (or complement) to surveys, opinion studies, and market tests, many firms prepare forecasts based on statistical analysis of past data (past data arranged in temporal order are referred to as a *time series*). The logic of this approach is that past data incorporate enduring causal relationships that will carry forward into the future and that can be uncovered through quantitative analysis. Thus the forecasting task becomes, in essence, a careful study of the past plus an assumption that the same relationships will hold in the future.

There are a number of time-series analysis and forecasting methods, differing mainly in the way past observations are related to the forecast values.

Naive methods: The simplest time-series forecasting procedure is to use the most recently observed value as a forecast: a naive forecast is equivalent to giving a weight of one to the most recent observation and zero to all other observations. Other naive methods may modify this procedure by adjusting for seasonal fluctuations. These methods are used mainly as a basis for comparing alternative forecasting approaches.

Slightly more sophisticated methods include the following:

- Freehand projection, which is a visual exploration of a plot of time-series observations. This method has the advantage of delivering a forecast quickly and cheaply, and it is easy to understand. However, it is of low accuracy, especially for nonlinear series, and two people may make very different projections.
- Semiaverage projection, in which the analyst divides a time series in half, calculates averages for each half, and draws a line connecting the average points, which the analyst projects to produce a forecast. This method has the same advantages and disadvantages as freehand projection.

Smoothing techniques: The notion underlying smoothing methods is that there is some pattern in the values of the variables to be forecast, which is represented in past observations, along with random fluctuations or noise. Using smoothing methods the analyst tries to distinguish the underlying pattern from the random fluctuations by eliminating the latter.

One way to lessen the impact of randomness in individual short-range forecasts is to average several of the past values. The *moving-average* approach is one of the simplest procedures for doing so. It weights the past N observations with the value $1/N$, where N is specified by the analyst and remains constant. The larger N is, the greater will be the smoothing effect on the forecast. If a year's worth of monthly data were available, the moving-average method would forecast the next period as 1/12 of the total for the past year. When new data become available, they are used, with the newest observation replacing the oldest. In this sense the average is moving. Typically the method of moving averages is used for forecasting only one period in advance. It does not adapt easily to pattern changes in the data.

Formally, for simple moving averages let

S_t = forecast at time t,

X_t = actual value at time t, and

N = number of values included in average.

Then forecasting with moving averages can be represented as

$$S_{t+1} = \frac{1}{N} \sum_{i=t-N+1}^{t} X_i = \frac{X_t - X_{t-N}}{N} + S_t. \tag{5.1}$$

This equation makes it clear that the new forecast S_{t+1} is a function of the preceding moving-average forecast S_t. Furthermore, if X_t corresponds to a change (e.g., step change) in the basic pattern of variable X, it is difficult for the method to account for that change. Note also that the larger N is, the smaller $(X_t - X_{t-N})/N$ will be and the greater the smoothing effect will be.

Advantages of this technique are that a forecast can be produced in little time, at low cost, and with little technical knowledge. Low accuracy and an arbitrary choice of the number of observations in calculating forecasts are among its disadvantages. Furthermore, simple moving averages are not very effective in the presence of complex data patterns, such as trend, seasonal, and cyclical patterns.

Using another procedure, the *double moving average*, one starts by computing a set of single moving averages and then computes another moving average based on the values of the first.

With a trend, a single or double moving average lags the actual series. Also, the double moving average is always below the simple moving average. Thus it is possible to forecast by taking the difference between the single moving average and the double moving average and adding it back to the single moving average. This forecasting technique is called the *double moving averages with trend adjustments*.

The *exponential-smoothing* approach is very similar to the moving-average method, differing in that the weights given to past observations are not constant—they decline exponentially so that more recent observations get more weight than earlier values. Choice of the smoothing factor is left to the analyst. Most often the analyst selects a value experimentally from a set of two or three different trial values. As with moving-average methods, exponential smoothing has limitations when basic changes are expected in the data pattern. These methods cover a variety of procedures, some of which make adjustments for trends and for seasonality. In essence most adjust the data in some way before applying an exponential-smoothing procedure.

With the foregoing notation, the procedure can be represented by

$$S_{t+1} = \alpha X_t + (1 - \alpha)S_t, \tag{5.2}$$

where $0 \leq \alpha \leq 1$ is selected empirically by the analyst. A high value of α gives past forecasts and past data (included in S_t) little weight, whereas a low value of α weights the most recent period very lightly compared with all other past observations.

The method of *double exponential smoothing* is analogous to that of double moving averages, and easily adapts to changes in patterns, such as step changes.

Smoothing methods are based on the idea that a forecast can be made by using a weighted sum of past observations. In the case of simple moving averages, the individual weights are $1/N$. For exponential smoothing the analyst has to postulate the declining weighting factor. *Adaptive filtering* is another approach for determining the most appropriate set of weights. It is based on an iterative process that determines weights that minimize forecasting error.

Specifically, all the methods outlined so far are based on the idea that a forecast can be made as a weighted sum of past observations:

$$S_{t+1} = \sum_{i=t-N+1}^{t} W_i X_i, \tag{5.3}$$

where

S_{t+1} = forecast for period $t + 1$;

W_i = weight assigned to observation i;

X_i = observed value at i, as before; and

N = number of observations used in computing S_{t+1} (and so the number of weights required).

Adaptive filtering attempts to determine a best set of weights. The usual criterion is that the weights should minimize the average mean-squared forecasting error.

The *Box-Jenkins (ARMA)* method is a philosophy for approaching forecasting problems. It is the most general of the short-term forecasting techniques and one of the most powerful available today. Using it an analyst can develop an adequate model for almost any pattern of data. However, it is so complex that its users must have a certain amount of expertise.

Box and Jenkins propose three general classes of models for describing any type of stationary process (processes that remain in equilibrium about a constant mean level): (1) autoregressive (AR), (2) moving average (MA), and (3) mixed autoregressive and moving average (ARMA).

If a series is increasing or decreasing with time, we can remove this (trend) by taking differences,

$$\Delta Y_t = Y_t - Y_{t-1}, \tag{5.4}$$

and then developing an ARMA model for ΔY_t. The original series Y_t can be recovered by successively adding in the ΔY_t, starting at Y_0. If the trend is nonlinear, several successive differences (d) may be required to produce a stationary ARMA series. (Recall that if you differentiate $Y = X^2$ twice—d^2Y/dX^2—you get a constant, 2. The differencing operation here is analogous and produces the same result.) Again, the original series can be recovered by summing d times. Such a series is called an integrated ARMA series, denoted as ARIMA (p, d, q), where p is the order (number of periods used) of the AR part, q is the order of the MA part, and d is the level of difference used to produce stationarity. Multivariate extensions of the ARMA models, known as multivariate ARMA, or MARMA, have been developed. They combine powerful time-series forecasting techniques with explanatory variables and causal models (Hanssens, Parsons, and Schultz 1990). Applying the ARMA and MARMA methods requires more technical expertise and experience than many of the other methods we describe.

EXAMPLE

Exhibit 5.4 shows how some of these forecasting methods perform on data drawn from the National Bureau of Economic Research. Using the mean-absolute-percent error (MAPE) as the measure of forecasting ability, Box-Jenkins does best in this case. However, the naive method is the third best out of the six methods, suggesting that more sophisticated methods do not always perform better than simple ones. (Note that moving average and exponential smoothing methods are available through Excel's "analysis tools" add-in.)

Year	Q1*	Q2	Q3	Q4
1969	11,445	11,573	11,516	11,990
1970	11,704	11,050	11,069	10,705
1971	10,729	10,931	11,832	12,172
1972	12,472	12,840	12,865	13,491
1973	14,324	14,684	14,689	15,473
1974	16,483	16,634	17,245	17,177
1975	16,230	16,562	17,614	18,318
1976	19,148	19,730	19,184	19,424
1977	20,774	21,184	21,052	22,121

* Q1 = quarter 1, and so on.

(a)

1978	(1) Actual	(2) Naive	(3) Averaged on Four Previous Quarters, Moving Average	(4) Moving Average with Trend Adjustment
Q1	22,433	22,121	21,283	22,666
Q2	23,792	22,433	21,698	23,219
Q3	23,980	23,792	22,350	23,772
Q4	25,840	23,980	23,082	24,325
MAPE*	3.78	3.78	7.85	2.53

Exponential Smoothing

1978	(5) $\rho = 0.90$	(6) $\rho = 0.50$	(7) Optimal Box-Jenkins
Q1	22,014	21,397	23,168
Q2	22,391	21,915	23,509
Q3	23,652	22,853	24,133
Q4	23,947	23,416	25,141
MAPE*	4.10	6.65	1.95

*MAPE = mean-absolute-percent error $= \frac{1}{n} \Sigma$ (|actual − forecast| / actual) x 100.

(b)

EXHIBIT 5.4
A comparison of the forecasting accuracy of six forecasting methods; (a) gives actual data for fabricated metal products while (b), columns (2) through (7), gives the forecasting accuracy of six methods. *Source*: National Bureau of Economic Research Series MDCSMS.

Decompositional methods: The forecasting methods described thus far are based on the idea that we can distinguish an underlying pattern in a data series from noise by smoothing (averaging) past values. The smoothing eliminates noise so that we can project the pattern into the future and use it as a forecast. These methods make no attempt to identify individual components of the basic underlying pattern. However, in many cases we can break the pattern down (decompose it) into subpatterns that identify each component of the series separately. With such a breakdown we can frequently improve accuracy in forecasting and better understand the series.

Decompositional methods assume that all series are made up of patterns plus error. The objective is to decompose the pattern of the series into trend, cycle, and seasonality:

$$X_t = f(I_t, T_t, C_t, E_t),\tag{5.5}$$

where

X_t = time series at time t;

I_t = seasonal component (or index) at t;

T_t = trend component at t;

C_t = cyclical component at t; and

E_t = error or random component at t.

The exact functional form of Eq. (5.5) depends on the decompositional method used. The most common form is a multiplicative model:

$$X_t = I_t \times T_t \times C_t \times E_t.\tag{5.6}$$

An additive form is used often, as well.

Although there are a number of decompositional methods, they all seem to follow the same basic process:

1. For the series X_t compute a moving average of length N, where N is the length of the seasonality (e.g., $N = 12$ with monthly data). This averaging will eliminate seasonality by averaging seasonally high periods with seasonally low periods; and because random errors have no systematic pattern, it reduces randomness as well.
2. Separate the outcome of the N-period moving average from the original data period to obtain trend and cyclicality. If the model is multiplicative, you do this by dividing the original series by the smoothed series, leaving seasonality and error:

$$\frac{X_1}{T_t + C_t} (= \text{moving average}) = I_t \times E_t.\tag{5.7}$$

3. Isolate the seasonal factors by averaging them for each data point in a season over the complete length of the series.
4. Specify the appropriate form of the trend (linear, quadratic, exponential) and calculate its value at each period T_t. You can do this by using regression analysis or moving averages with trend adjustments.
5. Use the results to separate out the cycle from the trend + cycle (i.e., the moving average).
6. When you have separated the seasonality, trend, and cyclicality from the original data series, you can identify the remaining randomness, E_t.

Decompositional methods are widely used and have been developed empirically and tested on thousands of series. Although they do not have a sound statistical base, the methods are intuitive and geared to the practitioner and, therefore, the opposite of such procedures as the Box-Jenkins approach, which is derived from theory. Decompositional methods appear to be most appropriate for short- or medium-term forecasting and are mainly suited to macroeconomic series.

Causal methods

The models we have described assume that little is known about the underlying cause of demand and that the future will be pretty much like the past. For these reasons, these time-series methods are most useful for short- or medium-term extrapolations (usually less than a year in the future).

An alternative approach, especially useful when market conditions are not inherently stable, is to express demand as a function of a certain number of factors that determine its outcome. Such forecasts are not necessarily time dependent, which makes them useful for longer-term predictions. In addition, developing an explanatory or causal model facilitates a better understanding of the situation.

Regression and econometric models typically specify the structure of the relationship between demand and its underlying causes.

EXAMPLE

In industrial markets firms often want to relate product-demand needs to published data for those Standard Industrial Classification (SIC) codes they think have high potential. In these analyses they often use the number of employees as the most readily available surrogate for customer size.

The Machinco Company makes high-technology components and currently has 17 customers. Exhibit 5.5 shows the number of employees for each customer and the volume of purchases from Machinco.

Customer Number	No. of Employees	Sales in $1000s*
1	110	9.8
2	141	21.2
3	204	14.7
4	377	22.8
5	395	48.1
6	502	42.3
7	612	27.8
8	618	40.7
9	707	59.8
10	721	44.5
11	736	77.1
12	856	59.2
13	902	52.3
14	926	77.1
15	1045	74.6
16	1105	81.8
17	1250	69.7

Total = 823.0

*Regression of sales versus employees gives
sales = $8.52 + 0.61 \times$ no. of employees, $R^2 = 0.77$.

EXHIBIT 5.5
Data on Machinco's customers, their number of employees and current sale level, providing input for a regression model of demand. *Source*: Lilien and Kotler 1983, p. 342.

If we use number of employees as a rough predictor of sales potential, we might relate sales to the number of employees via a linear equation:

$$\text{Sales} = a_0 + a_1(\text{number of employees}). \tag{5.8}$$

Through linear regression, we find that $a_0 = 8.52$ and $a_1 = 0.061$. The U.S. Census of Manufacturers reports that the organizations that are prospective customers for Machinco's product have a total of 126,000 employees. With this information and Eq. (5.8), we find

$$\text{(Potential) sales} = 8.52 + (0.061 \times 126,000) = 7695. \tag{5.9}$$

This value is nearly 10 times the current sales of Machinco (823), which indicates that Machinco could greatly expand its sales to other prospects.

Suppose that the company has two prospects. Company A has 1600 employees, and B has 500 employees. A good guess for the sales potential for company A is $8.52 + (0.061 \times 1600)$, or 106 units. Similarly we get 39 units as the potential for company B. (A regression tool is one of Excel's "analysis tool" add-ins.)

Input-output analysis, more widely used in the 1960s and 1970s than today, views the economy as an interrelated system. The input-output principle is the conservation of mass. Everything that is produced has to go somewhere, and when demand for finished products increases, this derives demand for other intermediate (industrial) products.

In a complex and diversified economy, direct consumer sales frequently represent only a portion of the output of a given industry. The rest of its output consists of intermediate products used by its purchasers as input into other production processes. Final demand is that part of the output of an industry that is not sold to another industry but rather is sold to domestic consumers or the government, is exported, or is put into inventory. The sum of final demand in a national input-output table is the gross national product.

Thus we can develop a series of accounting equations:

$$\text{Output of any industry} = \text{Sales to intermediate users} + \text{Final demand}. \tag{5.10}$$

EXAMPLE

A system of equations like (5.10), one for each industry, is called a transactions matrix. To explain it, we will use an example of a simple economy with three sectors: agriculture, manufacture, and consumers (Exhibit 5.6).

		Outputs		
	— Processing Sector —		Final Demand	
Inputs	**Agriculture**	**Manufacture**	**(Consumers)**	**Output Total**
Agriculture	50	40	110	200 stacks of flour
Manufacture	28	12	60	100 bars of soap
Consumers	160	360	80	600 hours

EXHIBIT 5.6
Example of transactions matrix for input-output analysis.

The agricultural sector produces 200 sacks of flour, the manufacturing sector produces 100 bars of soap, and consumers provide 600 hours of labor. Exhibit 5.6 shows the intersectoral flows. For example, agriculture turned out 200 sacks of flour but used up 50 in the process and sent 40 to the soap manufacturers; the consumers got the rest. Manufacturing sent 28 bars of soap to agriculture, used 12 itself, and sent the remaining 60 bars to consumers.

Each column represents the input structure of the sector. To produce 200 sacks of flour, the farmers needed to consume 50 sacks, to use 28 bars of soap, and to absorb 160 hours of labor. Manufacturing needed 40 sacks of flour, 12 bars of its own soap, and 360 hours of labor to produce 100 bars of soap. And consumers spent the incomes that they received for supplying 600 hours of labor on 110 sacks of flour, 60 bars of soap, and 80 hours of direct services of labor.

To be useful, an input-output table must have many more entries. In practice the intersectoral flows are generally represented in a common unit (dollars) for convenience.

If we now take the output of sector i as absorbed by sector j per unit of total output, we get the input coefficient of a product of sector i into sector j. Mathematically we get

$$a_{ij} = \frac{x_{ij}}{X_j},$$ (5.11)

where

a_{ij} = input coefficient from industry i to industry j;

x_{ij} = sales of industry i to industry j; and

X_j = total sales of industry j.

A complete set of input coefficients for all sectors of a given economy—arranged in the same way as the transactions matrix—is the structural matrix of an economy. Exhibit 5.7 shows the structural matrix of our three-sector economy with a sack of flour = $2, a bar of soap = $5, and an hour of labor = $1.

To interpret this table, we note that an input coefficient measures the input required from one industry to produce $1 of output in another industry. For example, for every dollar of output in manufacturing, we need $.16 from agriculture, $.12 from manufacturing itself, and $.72 from consumers (labor).

From	To		
	Agriculture	**Manufacture**	**Consumers**
Agriculture	0.25	0.16	0.37
Manufacture	0.35	0.12	0.50
Consumers	0.40	0.72	0.13
	1.00	1.00	1.00

EXHIBIT 5.7
Structural matrix for input-output analysis, showing the proportion of each input needed for a unit of output.

Practically, input-output forecasts provide estimates of industrial growth, of the markets that account for that growth, and of the inputs the industry will require to achieve that growth. However, many firms are not in a single industry, and they must adapt the input-output analysis. One way to do this is to insert the product of an organization as a row in the available tables. Then the company can estimate sales to the various sectors specified in the input-output study and can calculate how much each industry requires from it per dollar of output. It adjusts the row coefficients suitably. The firm can enter itself as a column, and the new structure can be used to produce a forecast for an individual company or a product. Alternatively the firm can expand the input-output matrix by making a detailed analysis of its target markets, inserting them as sectors in the economy. This may require customized data collection.

Artificial neural networks: In many situations in marketing, a manager might say, "I can tell you what factors I take into account in forecasting sales, but I can't tell you exactly what the relationship is." Artificial neural networks allow users to develop and use models in such situations.

An artificial neural network is a special kind of model that relates inputs (e.g., advertising) to outputs (e.g., sales) and (arguably) emulates the organization of the human brain. The network consists of an interlinked set of simple processing nodes (neurons), which represent complex relationships among inputs and outputs. The basic ideas behind neural networks come from researchers who are trying to understand how the brain processes information and to develop computer representations of those processing mechanisms.

A commonly used artificial neural network is a multilayered *feedforward* network, as shown in Exhibit 5.8. This network has *three layers*, each layer consisting of a set of neurons. Analysts feed data into the nodes in the input layer, which then process the data and transmit their outputs to each node in the intermediate layer(s), which do further processing before transmitting the transformed data as outputs in the output layer. The output of a neural net is the combined pattern of signals that come from the output nodes. This network is called *feedforward* because the data move along in only one direction, from the input layer to the output layer.

Each node (also called neuron, processing element, or perceptron) in the hidden intermediate layer of the network performs a simple computational task: it combines all the input signals x_i that it receives into a single signal value Z as follows:

$$Z = \sum_i w_i x_i, \qquad (5.12)$$

where

w_i = weight associated with the link between a node and its ith input source,

$(-\infty \leq w_i \leq \infty)$; and

x_i = the data value (signal) the node receives from its ith source.

Each node also transforms Z into an output signal (Y) that can take any real value $(-\infty \leq Y \leq \infty)$ given real-valued inputs. However, we can use one of several "activation functions" to restrict the range of values output by a node. For example, if we define a threshold value of T for the node, then Y can be transformed into a binary digit (0 or 1) as follows:

$Y = 1$ if $Z \geq T$,

    $= 0$ otherwise. $\qquad (5.13)$

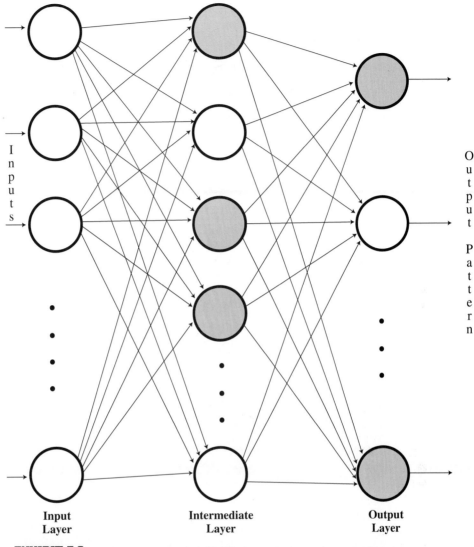

EXHIBIT 5.8
A three-layered feedforward network. The information coming into the input layer is transformed into an internal representation by nodes in the intermediate layer and is then transformed into an output pattern by the nodes in the output layer.

Nodes that generate a binary output are called hard limiters. Other transformations of Z are also frequently used in neural networks. A common form is the sigmoidal activation function that transforms Y to fall in the range $0 \leq Y \leq 1$:

$$Y = f(Z - T) = \frac{1}{1 + e^{-(Z-T)}}, \tag{5.14}$$

Hard limiter nodes where the value of Z is higher than the threshold (i.e., $Z > T$) are said to be "active" and have a value equal to 1 (shown shaded in Exhibit 5.8). Corresponding to each pattern of input, the final output of the network is an associated pattern of activation of the output nodes, some active, some not. Thus the neural net transforms an input pattern

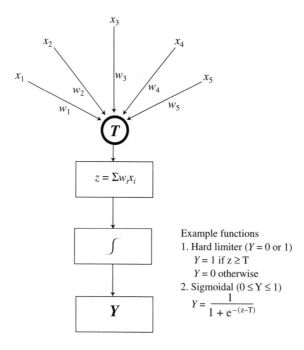

$$z = \Sigma w_i x_i$$

Example functions
1. Hard limiter ($Y = 0$ or 1)
   $Y = 1$ if $z \geq T$
   $Y = 0$ otherwise
2. Sigmoidal ($0 \leq Y \leq 1$)
   $$Y = \frac{1}{1 + e^{-(z-T)}}$$

T = Threshold associated with node
$w_1, w_2, ...$ = Network weights associated with incoming signals
$x_1, x_2, ...$ = Input signal values
Y = Output signal from node

EXHIBIT 5.9
Nodes in the intermediate and output layers of a neural network use processing mechanisms like those shown here to transform inputs into outputs.

to an associated output pattern. The computations performed by a node are shown in Exhibit 5.9.

To ensure that a neural net associates the correct outputs with a specific set of inputs, you must "train" the net to strengthen signals (i.e., adjust weights w_i and thresholds T) that most efficiently lead to the correct output, and to weaken incorrect or inefficient signals. Starting with a set of random weights, a computer representation of the network updates the weights and sometimes the thresholds by minimizing an error measure computed from feedback (usually given by the model developer) regarding the correctness of the output in sample cases; thus the network "learns" to associate the correct outputs with specified sets of inputs. The network then retains this learning and uses it when processing new inputs—that is, when it is used for forecasting. One common method for updating weights is called "back propagation," in which error at the output layer is sequentially propogated backward across the network as errors attributable to individual neurons in the intermediate layers.

Theoretically one can design a multilayered feedforward network with a sigmoidal activation function (given in Eq. (5.14)) to represent any functional relationship at any desired accuracy, if the network contains enough intermediate neurons between the input and output layers. This does not mean, however, that you can train any neural network to correctly represent a sampled relationship. There is no known method for determining just the right number of nodes and levels to represent an unknown response function most appropriately.

Compared with multiple linear regression for representing the relationship between inputs and outputs, neural networks offer two advantages:

1. The user need not specify the structure of the model beforehand. Multilayered networks of the form we have described are general nonlinear estimators that accommodate many kinds of complex nonlinear relationships between inputs and outputs.
2. Neural networks yield more robust fitting and predictions than multiple linear regression when data is incomplete or missing. Because neural networks use redundant connections, they are less sensitive than regression to such data problems.

Neural nets have disadvantages as well: even a trained neural net is a black box, and it is difficult to interpret the weights on the network. However, if the primary objective of using the network is to forecast, rather than to provide detailed explanations for a forecast, a neural net may be useful. Neural net forecasting performance depends on several factors including the number of layers in the network, the strength of the learning parameter (slow versus fast learning), and whether the model is overfitted (i.e., whether the model incorporates too many chance variations). Overfitting is similar to the problem of having too many explanatory variables in a regression analysis—you can fit the model perfectly to your data, but the model may be poor at predicting. In the software accompanying the book, part of the data is used for training the neural net, and the rest of the data is used for predictive validation to minimize the chances of overfitting.

Neural nets are so new in the marketing area that no one has developed definitive guidelines on their use, but the method has reported successes as the following example suggests.

EXAMPLE

First Commerce Corporation, a leading asset banking company, uses a neural network to determine which customers from its database to target for its direct marketing campaigns based on the past behavior of these customers. The company claims that the neural network has helped it increase the response to its direct marketing programs by a factor of four to eight depending on the market segment. The bank conducted an experiment comparing the neural network model with its traditional profiling method (i.e., models that identify customers with desirable profiles). The bank sent out 25,000 letters to customers whose names it had identified as targets using the neural network. These letters did not include prior credit approval. The bank also sent out 100,000 letters to customers whose names were selected in the traditional way and included prior credit approval. The result: while the larger mailing generated 50 more auto loans than the smaller mailing, the smaller mailing generated 100 more loans of all types.

In a comprehensive study comparing neural networks to traditional time-series analysis using more than 1000 data sets, Hill, O'Connor, and Remus (1996) report that neural networks outperform all other methods tested in terms of average forecast accuracy and variance of the forecast errors. They attribute this superior performance to the ability of neural networks to better handle "discontinuities" in most data.

What method to choose?

The man with many clocks never knows the correct time; so it is with forecasting methods. We have described a range of methods. You may ask which one is best. Armstrong (1985) gives some rough guidelines (Exhibit 5.10).

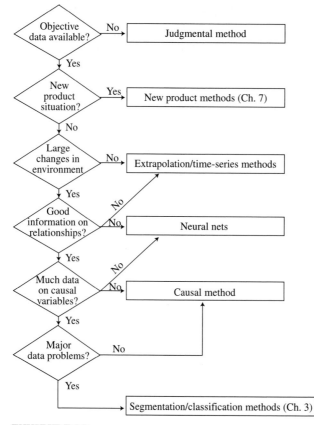

EXHIBIT 5.10
Suggested decision rules for choosing the appropriate forecasting method. Adapted from Armstrong 1985.

- If no objective data are available or possible, you should use judgmental methods.
- If the product is a new product, you should use one of the methods described in Chapter 7.
- If the environment has not changed, you should use extrapolation or time-series methods.
- If you have no good data on relationships, you should use time-series methods or neural nets.
- If you have a lot of data on causal variables, you should use causal methods (or perhaps neural nets).
- If you have all the foregoing data, but have major problems with the data regarding subsegment differences in relationships, you should use cross-classification and segmentation methods, like those we developed in Chapter 3. (For a good review of available forecasting software, see Yurkiewicz (1996).)

None of the methods we described in this chapter is appropriate for new products. Here is why: First, by definition new products have little sales history, and therefore you cannot use most procedures based on time series. In addition, the structure of new product sales tends to be much less stable than that for existing products. An important objective is to predict the terminal share of a product or the product's performance after its sales have settled down.

The information at the marketer's disposal varies by product class and may include diary-panel data, pre-test market evaluations, usage rates, relative penetrations, first purchase and repeat rates, and so on. Methods for forecasting new product sales are varied and are based on different behavioral assumptions and different data sources; we explore them in Chapter 7.

THE PRODUCT LIFE CYCLE

An important concept underlying most dynamic business-planning models is the product life cycle. Because a product's sales position and profitability can be expected to change over time, the firm needs to revise its product's strategy periodically. Using the concept of the life cycle, the firm tries to recognize distinct phases in the sales history of the product and its market and to develop strategies appropriate to those stages.

The life-cycle concept comes from many sources. Biological life forms are born, grow, mature, and die. Many human enterprises (like the Roman Empire) have a birth, a heyday, and a decline or death. The length of the product life cycle varies from product to product; it is long for such commodity items as salt, peanut butter, and wine, and short for more differentiated products such as California wine coolers and Darth Vader Halloween masks. Several factors affect the length and form of the product life cycle, including changing needs and wants, changes in technology that lead to close substitutes, and how quickly a new product is adopted in a market.

The importance of the life-cycle concept is not that all products have such a product life cycle, or even that a life cycle has specific, distinct stages. Rather, by using the life cycle firms can anticipate how sales might evolve for a product, and they can develop strategies to influence those sales. For example, in the introductory stage the firm should devote considerable resources toward advertising to increase customer awareness of the new product, and in the mature stage the firm should devote resources to differentiating and positioning its offering with respect to those of competitors.

In most discussions of the product life cycle (PLC), people portray the sales history of a typical product as following an S-shaped sales curve (Exhibit 5.11). This curve is typically divided into four stages known as introduction, growth, maturity, and decline. *Introduction*

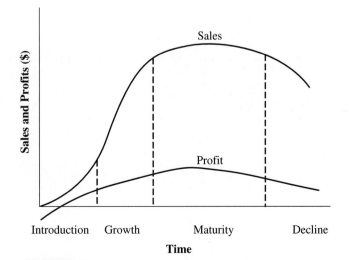

EXHIBIT 5.11
Typical stages in the sales and profit cycles, showing that profit typically lags the growth of sales.

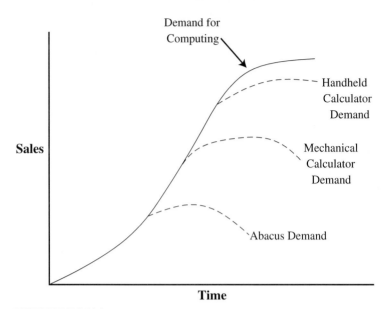

EXHIBIT 5.12(a)
The demand for computing is satisfied over time by different technologies that substitute for one another.

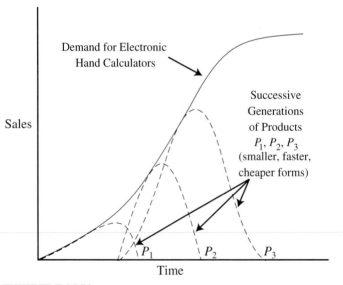

EXHIBIT 5.12(b)
The demand for a product class is driven by the replacement of one generation (product form) by another.

is a period of slow growth as the product is introduced in the market. The profit curve in Exhibit 5.11 shows profits as low or negative in this stage because of the heavy expenses of product introduction. *Growth* is a period of rapid market acceptance and substantial profit improvement. *Maturity* is a period of slowing sales growth, because the product has been accepted by most of its potential buyers. Profits peak in this period and start to decline because of increased marketing outlays needed to sustain the product's position against com-

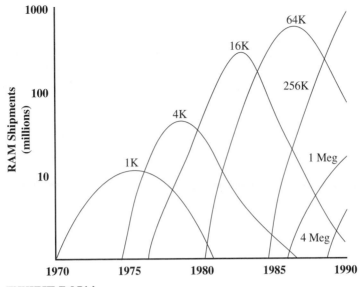

EXHIBIT 5.12(c)
Technological life cycles for random access memories, showing greater peaks and shorter cycle time (a pattern that has continued in the market). *Source*: Urban and Star 1991, p. 96.

petition. Finally, *decline* is the period when sales show a strong downward drift and profits erode toward zero.

We can understand this phenomenon as follows. Assume that a human need or want (e.g., calculating power) exists and that a product (e.g., a calculator) satisfies that need. Exhibit 5.12(a) shows how different technologies can successively substitute for one another (leading to a sequence of technology cycles within an overall demand cycle). Exhibit 5.12(b) breaks things down further, showing how successive product forms can replace one another within the context of a single technology cycle. Exhibit 5.12(c) illustrates the effect with actual data from random access memory chips.

The empirical evidence of the existence and applicability of the product life-cycle concept is uneven. In a literature review, Rink and Swan (1979) identified 12 types of product life-cycle patterns. For example, Cox (1967) studied the life cycles of 754 ethical drug products and found that the most typical form was a cycle-recycle pattern (Exhibit 5.13). He explains that the second hump in sales is caused by a promotional push during the decline phase. In another study, Buzzell (1966) reported a scalloped life-cycle pattern (Exhibit 5.13), representing a succession of life cycles based on the discovery of new product characteristics, new uses, or new markets. Exhibit 5.14 shows the cycle-recycle pattern for the Boeing 727 and 747, where redesigns provided several sparks of rejuvenation to the product.

Harrell and Taylor (1981) and Thorelli and Burnett (1981) found that growth rates are only one aspect of the product life cycle; such elements as market innovation, market concentration, competitive structure, economic cycles, supply constraints, and replacement sales affect the structure of the life cycle as well.

In fact research results are further confounded by differences in the level of product aggregation and by difficulties with the definition of a new product. Typically there are three possible levels of aggregation: product class (cigarettes), product form (plain filter

Cycle-Recycle Pattern

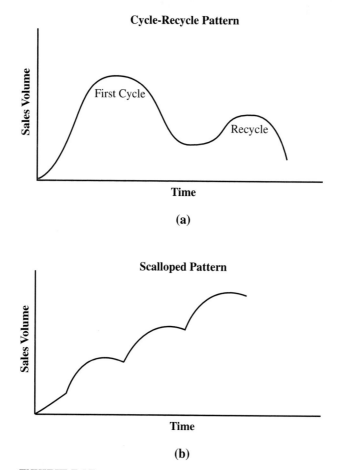

(a)

Scalloped Pattern

(b)

EXHIBIT 5.13
Two anomalous life-cycle patterns, both featuring forms of rejuvenation after a slowdown or decline in growth.

cigarettes), and brand (Philip Morris, regular or nonfilter). The PLC concept is applied differently in these three cases. Product classes have the longest life histories, longer than particular product forms, and certainly longer than most brands. The sales of many product classes can be expected to continue in the mature stage for an indefinite duration because they are highly related to population (cars, perfume, refrigerators, and steel). Product forms tend to exhibit the standard PLC histories more faithfully. Product forms, such as the dial telephone and cream deodorants, seem to pass through a regular history of introduction, rapid growth, maturity, and decline. On the other hand, a brand's sales history can be erratic because changing competitive strategies and tactics can produce substantial ups and downs in sales and market shares, even to the extent of causing a mature brand to suddenly exhibit another period of rapid growth. Two problems life-cycle researchers tackle frequently are the forecasts of stage transitions and phase duration. Lambkin and Day (1989) explicitly develop such a model to describe and explain the product life cycle.

Although some success has been claimed for these methods, they typically rely on data from one phase to forecast the timing and length of the next stage. Accurate long-range forecasting is quite difficult, and therefore little is known about the length and sequence of life-cycle phases (Day 1981). The problems of forecasting phase change and phase length are made more difficult by the widely held belief that life cycles are becoming shorter.

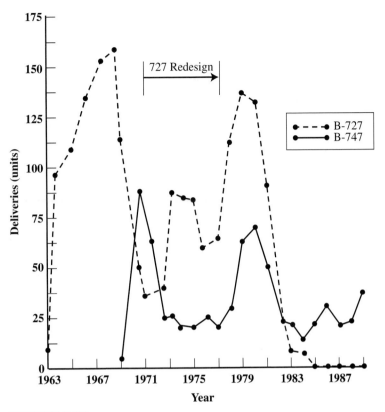

EXHIBIT 5.14
The life cycle of the Boeing 727 and 747, showing the 727's rejuvenation after a redesign in 1971, and a similar pattern for the 747. *Source*: Boeing Commercial Airplane Group 1988, p. 7.

What are we to make of this? A realistic view is that life-cycle analysis is only one important element in the overall analysis of marketing opportunities. The life cycle acts as a classification device and suggests conditions under which market growth, for example, may occur. During market growth competitors are better able to enter the market, and new opportunities for product offerings are available in selected market segments. Price and advertising elasticities change over the product life cycle as well, so while there continues to be much discussion concerning definition and measurement, the product life cycle is clearly critical in determining appropriate marketing strategies (Thietart and Vivas 1984). In Chapter 7 we describe several useful tools for developing life-cycle planning models, especially in the introduction and growth stages of the product life cycle.

COST DYNAMICS: SCALE AND EXPERIENCE EFFECTS

Another phenomenon affecting marketing strategy is cost dynamics. One of the most widely discussed findings of the profit impact of marketing strategy (PIMS) program (Chapter 6) is that market share is a primary determinant of business profitability: the PIMS results show that on average a difference of market share between competitors of 10 percent translates into a 5 percent difference in pretax return on investment. One reason for this increase in profitability is that firms with larger market shares have lower costs, partly because of *economies of scale*—very large plants cost less per unit of production to build and run—and partly because of the *experience effect*—the cost of many products declines 10 to 30 percent in real terms each time the company's experience in producing and selling them doubles.

Although researchers have long observed that manufacturing costs seem to fall with cumulative experience and not just with product scale, only recently have they studied this phenomenon carefully and quantified it (Yelle 1979). Initially people believed that only the labor portion of manufacturing costs decreased with cumulative production. The commander of the Wright-Patterson Air Force Base noted in the 1920s that the number of hours required to assemble a plane decreased as the total number of aircraft increased. The relationship between cumulative production and labor costs became known as the *learning curve*.

In the 1960s evidence began mounting that the phenomenon was broader. The Boston Consulting Group (1970), in particular, showed that each time the cumulative volume of production of a product doubled, total value-added costs—sales, administration, and so on—fell by a constant percentage. This relationship between total costs and cumulative production became known as the *experience curve*.

The simplest form of the learning or experience curve is the log-linear model:

$$C_q = C_n \left(\frac{q}{n} \right)^{-b},$$

(5.15)

where

q = cumulative production to date;

n = cumulative production at a particular, earlier time;

C_n = cost of nth unit (in constant dollars);

C_q = cost of qth unit (in constant dollars); and

b = learning constant.

In practice, experience curves are characterized by their *learning rate*. Suppose that each time experience doubles, cost per unit drops to 80 percent of the original level. Then the 80 percent is known as the learning rate. The learning rate is related to the *learning constant* as follows:

$$r = 2^{-b} \times 100,$$

(5.16)

or

$$b = \frac{\ln 100 - \ln r}{\ln 2}$$

(5.17)

where

r = learning rate (percentage); and

b = learning constant.

Exhibit 5.15 shows how costs fall with experience for various learning rates and levels of experience.

Alberts (1989) contends that most cost declines are caused partly by innovations and partly by economies of scale. Innovation-based causes of cost reductions include

1. Operator innovations—in which workers figure out how to procure, manufacture, and distribute goods more efficiently with current technology

Ratio of Old Experience (n) to New Experience (q)	Learning Rate (r)					
	70%	75%	80%	85%	90%	95%
1.1	5	4	3	2	1	1
1.25	11	9	7	5	4	2
1.5	19	15	12	9	6	3
1.75	25	21	16	12	8	4
2.0	30	25	20	15	10	5
2.5	38	32	26	19	13	7
3.0	43	37	30	23	15	8
4.0	51	44	36	28	19	10
6.0	60	52	44	34	24	12
8.0	66	58	49	39	27	14
16.0	76	68	59	48	34	19

EXHIBIT 5.15
The amount of cost reduction with different levels of learning and production experience.
Source: Abell and Hammond 1979, p. 109.

2. Management innovations—in which supervisors and managers figure out how to improve operations with existing technologies
3. Process innovations—in which new technologies for procurement, assembly order processing, and distribution lead to increased efficiency

Scale-based causes of cost reductions include

1. Reduction of excess capacity—which reduces the ratio of fixed costs per unit of production
2. Scale-dependent substitutions—in which larger assembly, procurement, and distribution systems are more cost-effective per unit
3. Increased procurement power—in which increases in procurement volume lead to better deals and lower unit prices

Exhibit 5.16 outlines Alberts's (1989) view of the experience "hypothesis," although he contends that neither repetition nor growth "cause" process innovations—rather they arise through R&D investments that may or may not be linked to volume or experience. According to Alberts, experience by itself does not cause cost declines; rather it provides the opportunity for such declines. Many of the effects of experience (work specialization, for example) may become possible because the size of the operation increases, and therefore they are part of a scale effect. In fact, growth in experience usually occurs at the same time the size of an operation grows, although firms can use scale effects to bypass experience (as the Japanese did in the steel industry). And it is clear that process innovations will not just happen—they come from an R&D program targeted at such cost reductions.

While the experience concept is rather simple, its application in a model requires ingenuity. It is important to (1) adjust prices for inflation; (2) plot cost versus experience (not time); (3) consider cost components separately, because each may have different learning rates; (4) correct for *shared experience*, where two or more products share a common resource or activity; (5) adjust for different experience rates between competitors (firm A, a late entry, may benefit from B's experience, may be able to exploit shared experience that B cannot, may have a different proportion of value added than B, etc.); (6) begin at the right starting point choosing n and C_n in Eq. (5.15); (7) measure costs properly over a reasonably long time frame; (8) properly define the unit of analysis (a firm may have a large share of a small market yet have less experience than a competitor with a small share in a much

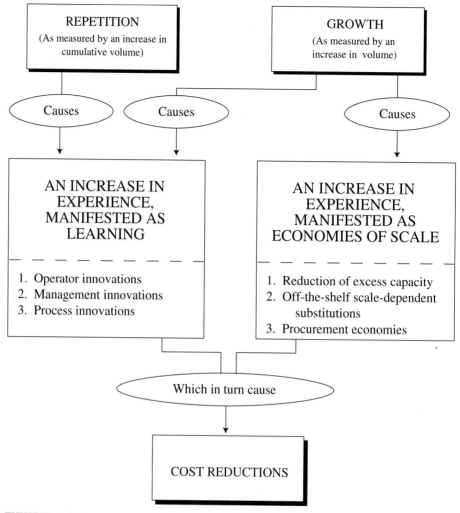

EXHIBIT 5.16
The classical view of production cost reductions: they arise from both learning and scale economics. *Source:* Alberts 1989, p. 40.

larger market!); and (9) treat process innovation effects as separately budgeted effects. These and other practical considerations in developing and using the experience curve are discussed by Abell and Hammond (1979), The Boston Consulting Group (1970), Hax and Majluf (1982), Day (1986), Day and Montgomery (1983), and Alberts (1989).

The experience-curve concept is of strategic importance in business planning for many industries. In stable industries, where profit margins remain at a constant percentage of cost, the experience curve allows for long-range projections of cost, price, and profit.

Many situations are similar to the one illustrated in Exhibit 5.17. In phase A costs exceed prices, as is often the case in a *start-up* situation. In phase B the market leader maintains a *price umbrella* over higher-cost producers entering the market, trading future market share for current profit. In phase C, the *shake-out period*, one producer begins lowering prices at a faster rate than costs are declining, perhaps because of overcapacity. In phase D *stability* occurs when profit margins return to normal levels, paralleling industry costs again. This illustration suggests the importance (and the risks) associated with a market-dominance

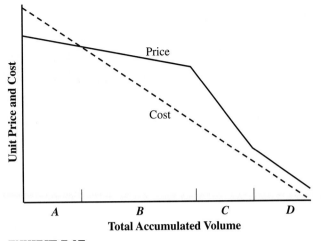

EXHIBIT 5.17
A typical price-cost relationship with costs going down faster than price during phases A, B, and C before settling down to commodity phase D. *Source:* The Boston Consulting Group, Inc. 1970, p. 21.

strategy. While being the market leader and operating at a low-cost position are desirable, a firm can precipitate a shake-out period (phase C) in a market by aggressively pursuing market share.

In Chapter 10 we discuss using the experience curve to develop an optimal *monopoly-pricing* strategy, using software called learning curve pricing. Making informed strategic decisions in response to experience-curve cost declines requires information about market growth, competitive costs, and likely competitive reaction. When you can carefully model and forecast experience-curve cost declines, you can use them in business planning.

SUMMARY

In this chapter we introduced the notion of marketing strategy as an umbrella concept within which firms must make marketing decisions. We stressed the interconnectedness of all these decisions, particularly functional interactions, synergies between marketing-mix elements, and functional interactions.

To devise a marketing strategy, we must define a market appropriately and assess and forecast the demand for that market. We outlined the most common and emerging methods of forecasting sales for established products.

The structure and dynamics of markets have led marketers to develop two other key planning concepts: the product life cycle and cost dynamics. The product life cycle makes using traditional time-series and econometric forecasting methods difficult. And the dynamics of product costs—the experience-curve effect—affects market strategy and planning.

We will apply these concepts and tools in the forthcoming chapters, particularly in Chapter 6.

Models for Strategic Marketing Decision Making

In Chapter 5 we described several building blocks for marketing strategy. In this chapter we discuss some important marketing-strategy problem areas in which the marketing engineering approach has been effective:

- Market entry and exit decisions—how to time market entry and exit and the issues associated with market pioneering and order of entry
- Shared experience models—how we can learn from the experiences of successful firms
- Product portfolio models—how to manage products and businesses as an integrated group
- Models of competition—how the nature of the market and competitive response influences marketing strategy

Decisions in these areas all depend on the key strategic-marketing decision: what is the best way to allocate the firm's marketing resources in the long term? Deciding when to enter or exit a market is a question of timing: when is the best time to invest (or divest)? Shared experience models can help us learn from the investment experience of successful organizations to benchmark and improve our own marketing investment strategy. Product portfolio models help us to establish internal consistency in our investments: when marketing investment alternatives compete for scarce resources, how should we prioritize and allocate those resources? Finally, models of competition help us analyze the likely reaction of competitors to our investment decisions and how we should address those reactions.

MARKET ENTRY AND EXIT DECISIONS

A critical issue in formulating a dynamic market strategy is timing market entry in light of market-pioneering or first-mover advantages. Lieberman and Montgomery (1980) suggest that first-mover advantages arise from three sources:

1. Technological leadership that comes from being further down the learning curve than competitors (experience-curve effect) or from success in R&D or patents.

2. Preemption of scarce assets such as limited raw materials, channels of distribution, shelf space, and scarce, specially skilled employees.
3. Switching costs and buyer risk aversion, which influence buyers to avoid switching from their current product; late entrants must invest more (provide lower prices or more value) to overcome the costs and risks buyers incur in switching.

Robinson and Fornell (1985) use the PIMS database to show that pioneers on average had higher market shares than early followers. The early followers in turn had higher market shares than late followers. Their explanation of these effects is that early entry affects four factors: product quality, breadth of product line, product price, and product cost. Urban et al. (1986), in a study of 129 consumer packaged goods, also found that entry order had a significant effect on market share, as did Parry and Bass (1990), who found differences based on industry type and end-user purchase amount.

Kalyanaram, Robinson, and Urban (1995) summarize their findings about entry timing in three generalizations:

Generalization 1: For mature consumer and industrial goods, there is a negative relationship between the order of market entry and market share.

Generalization 2: For consumer packaged goods, the entrant's forecasted market share divided by the first entrant's market share roughly equals one divided by the square root of the order of market entry.

Generalization 3: In mature consumer and industrial goods markets, early entrant market share advantages slowly decline over time.

These generalizations and others (Lilien and Yoon 1990) provide important information about the likely outcomes of market entry decisions. In addition to timing, the firm should consider the likely consumer reaction to the product, the likely competitive response, market evolution, and the like.

EXAMPLE

Yoon and Lilien (1985) studied the success rate of a sample of 112 new industrial products as measured by the market share of those products after one year (Exhibit 6.1). They classified the products as

Original new products (ORNPs), technological breakthroughs, often relying on technologies never before used in the industry (also called new product lines and new-to-the-world products)

Reformulated new products (RFNPs), extensions or modifications of existing products, which usually reduce costs or enlarge the range of possible uses (also called cost reductions, improvements, and additions)

The success of these new products is related to the firm's delay in launching the product after it is technically ready. For ORNPs they found that first-year market share increases with delay up to a certain point and decreases thereafter. For RFNPs they found that first-year market share steadily decreases with delay. This contrast between product types may reflect the level of market development; the market is ready for RFNPs: the longer an incremental innovation takes to get to market, the greater its risk of failure due to changing market conditions, competitive response, or further technological advances.

First Year Market Share Versus Entry Delay Time

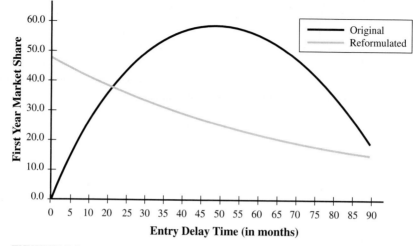

EXHIBIT 6.1

New product success for a sample of industrial products, showing that market share at the end of the first year is highest when reformulated new products are introduced immediately, whereas for original new products a delay helps. *Source*: Yoon and Lilien 1985, p. 142.

EXAMPLE

In a study sponsored by the U.S. Department of Energy (DOE), Kalish and Lilien (1986) looked at market-entry timing for a demonstration program for the residential use of photovoltaics (solar batteries). DOE was considering funding a proposal from a developer in the southwestern United States to incorporate photo-voltaics in a 100-home development. At the time of the proposal (1980) photo-voltaic products were not technically ready, and the results of a survey and expert judgments suggested that a demonstration program at that time (when the risk of failure or even fire damage to a home's roof was not insubstantial) could have a negative impact on the rate of penetration into the marketplace. Kalish and Lilien developed a market penetration model (a modification of the Bass diffusion model we describe in Chapter 7) to look at the likely rate of diffusion of the product into the market.

Their formal analysis showed that given DOE's objective of maximizing market penetration after 10 years, it was better for DOE to delay the demonstration program for 5 years (and get the bugs out of the technology) than to demonstrate the current state of the technology. In addition, by delaying the DOE would save money. Partly on the basis of this analysis, the DOE did not fund the residential demonstration program.

The empirical generalizations and the examples above demonstrate that the timing of market entry should depend on the nature of the product (new versus reformulated), of the market (industrial versus consumer; mature versus immature), and of competition (number in market before you—entry order). Premature market entry can be a mistake that is as costly as excess delay.

How can we address the timing of market entry? We describe a set of methods that rely on new product diffusion theory in the next chapter. Here we describe decision analysis or decision-tree analysis, which can also be used to address these issues.

The reactions of the market, consumers, and competitors to the entry of a new product are uncertain, and marketing managers deal with uncertainty in several ways. Some do worst-case analyses and go ahead with product launches only if the launch is still projected to pay off with poorer market response and higher costs than projected. Others run a series of spreadsheet scenarios, looking at a number of possible futures, and choose among them.

The increasing availability of various kinds of decision support software makes these kinds of decisions easier to quantify. One of the methods that is most appropriate for handling decisions under uncertainty is decision analysis. Decision analysis is appropriate for solving problems with the following characteristics:

Decision Analysis

- A choice or sequence of choices must be made among various courses of action.
- The choice or sequence of choices will ultimately lead to some consequence; but the decision maker cannot be sure in advance what the consequence will be, because it depends not only on his or her decisions but also on an unpredictable event or sequence of events.

The choice of action should depend on the likelihood that the decision maker's action will have various possible consequences, as well as the desirability of the various consequences.

The decision-analysis approach usually includes four steps:

1. *Structuring the problem*: To structure the problem one must define general objectives, specify measures of effectiveness, identify restrictions on actions, and characterize the problem chronologically. One should also identify alternative courses of action.
2. *Assigning probabilities to possible consequences*: One needs to assess the possibilities of various consequences occurring, depending on managerial actions. This assessment can be purely subjective or can include analysis of past system behavior.
3. *Assigning payoffs to consequences*: The decision maker must explicitly include his or her preferences for possible outcomes. (These preferences, or payoffs, relate to the objectives and goals we outlined in Chapter 2.)
4. *Analyzing the problem*: To analyze the problem we use a method called averaging out and folding back, which we illustrate with the following example.

EXAMPLE

This example is based on Keeney (undated notes). The QRS Company must decide whether or not to introduce a new product now. If it chooses to introduce the product, sales will either be high or low. For simplicity we assume that the firm's objective is to maximize expected profits. The firm is considering a market survey to collect information on expected sales. The market research firm contacted will report one of three results: great, good, or poor, where great means that high sales are likely. Marketing management feels that if the firm introduces the product now, its probability of high sales is 0.4. The company has had past experience with this market research firm and knows that 60 percent of high-sales products in the past had great survey results, 30 percent had good survey results, and 10 percent had poor survey results. Similarly, 10 percent of its low-sales products had great survey results, 30 percent had good survey results, and 60 percent had poor survey results. If sales are high, the firm expects net profits (excluding the cost of the survey) to be $100,000; if sales are low, it expects a net loss of $50,000 (excluding survey costs).

This problem can be structured as a decision tree (Exhibit 6.2). The chronology of events begins on the left and flows to the right. The first thing that happens is that marketing management must decide whether or not to run a market survey. If it does run a survey, it then learns the results and decides whether or not to introduce the product. Finally, it learns sales results.

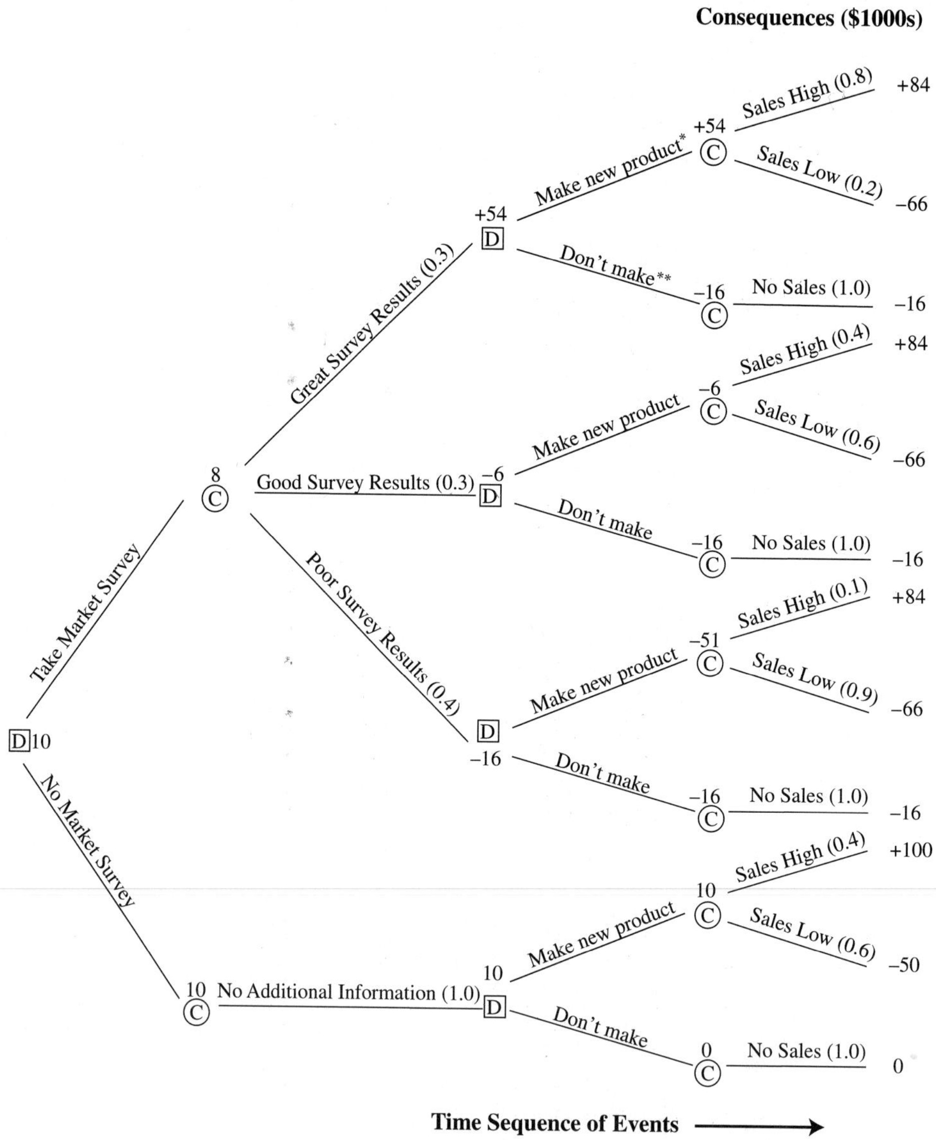

Consequences ($1000s)

Time Sequence of Events ⟶

* Read as: Introduce new product now.
** Don't introduce new product now; delay introduction or "kill" the project.

EXHIBIT 6.2
Structure of decision tree for QRS Company, where the nodes marked D are decision nodes and those marked C are chance nodes.

A decision tree has two types of nodes: decision nodes (marked D), meaning management has control over the course of action; and chance nodes (marked C), where the decision maker has no control.

At the end of each path of the decision tree, the consequences of the several courses of action are indicated. For instance, if the firm runs a market survey, that survey reports great results, the firm manufactures the product, and sales are high, the result is a net gain of $84,000: $100,000 less the $16,000 survey cost. All consequences are measured against the do-nothing strategy of no survey, no manufacturing, and no sales.

Beside those segments of the tree beginning at chance nodes are the conditional probabilities (the numbers in parentheses) that the event associated with that segment occurs, given that everything else up to that point in the tree *does* occur. Thus, for instance, the probability that the survey is *great*, given that the firm runs the survey, is 0.3, or 30 percent. The conditional probability that sales are high, given that survey results are great and the firm decides to manufacture, is 0.8, or 80 percent.

To summarize the given information, the firm knows from past experience that

$$
\begin{aligned}
p(\text{great survey} \mid \text{high sales}) &= 0.6, \\
p(\text{good survey} \mid \text{high sales}) &= 0.3, \\
p(\text{poor survey} \mid \text{high sales}) &= 0.1, \\
p(\text{great survey} \mid \text{low sales}) &= 0.1, \\
p(\text{good survey} \mid \text{low sales}) &= 0.3, \\
p(\text{poor survey} \mid \text{low sales}) &= 0.6, \\
p(\text{high sales}) &= 0.4, \\
p(\text{low sales}) &= 0.6.
\end{aligned}
\tag{6.1}
$$

To get the probability that the survey would be great, we use the theorem of total probabilities:

$$
\begin{aligned}
p(\text{great survey}) &= p(\text{great survey} \mid \text{high sales})p(\text{high sales}) \\
&\quad + p(\text{great survey} \mid \text{low sales})p(\text{low sales}) \\
&= 0.6 \times 0.4 + 0.1 \times 0.6 = 0.3.
\end{aligned}
\tag{6.2}
$$

Similarly

$$
\begin{aligned}
p(\text{good survey}) &= 0.3, \\
p(\text{poor survey}) &= 0.4.
\end{aligned}
$$

To get $p(\text{high sales} \mid \text{great survey})$, we use Bayes's theorem:

$$
\begin{aligned}
p(\text{high sales} \mid \text{great survey}) &= \frac{p(\text{great survey} \mid \text{high sales})p(\text{high sales})}{p(\text{great survey})} \\
&= \frac{0.6 \times 0.4}{0.3} = 0.8.
\end{aligned}
\tag{6.3}
$$

Similarly we get

$$
\begin{aligned}
p(\text{high sales} \mid \text{good survey}) &= 0.4, \\
p(\text{high sales} \mid \text{poor survey}) &= 0.1,
\end{aligned}
$$

p(low sales | great survey) = 0.2,

p(low sales | good survey) = 0.6,

p(low sales | poor survey) = 0.9.

We can now use these probabilities to average out and fold back. The numbers beside each node represent the expected profit associated with being at that node. If we conduct a market survey, have great results, and introduce the product now, then there is an 80 percent chance of high sales, implying a net profit of $84,000, and a 20 percent chance of low sales, with a net loss of $66,000. Thus the expected profit (averaging out) of being at that chance node is

$$(0.8)(\$84,000) - (0.2)(\$66,000) = \$54,000. \qquad (6.4)$$

At the node immediately below, if we have the same great results on the survey and then choose not to manufacture, we will lose $16,000.

Now backing up (folding back) to the decision node before these chance nodes, the firm can either introduce the product with expected profit of $54,000 or not introduce the product now with an expected loss of $16,000. The best choice is to make the product; therefore the expected profit of that decision node is $54,000. In addition, if we fold back to the start, we find the best choice is not to do the survey.

Decision analysis is a powerful tool that can help managers to structure decisions of this type and others. The tree can easily be expanded to include market entry timing. For example, suppose an alternative decision at each "introduce" decision node is to delay one quarter. Suppose management judges that a competitor can enter the market with probability = 0.20 (i.e., a 20 percent chance of not being the pioneer, with an associated lower reward, even for a successful product). But if that delay allows the firm to develop a better quality product (product quality improvement over time as happened with photovoltaics in our example and with other truly new products), the likelihood of high sales may increase. Decision trees provide a convenient framework within which managers can make such judgments and trade-offs explicit and quantified, and currently available software makes constructing such decision trees simple. Through cut-and-paste operations, users can easily duplicate such trees (introduce now, wait one period, wait two periods, etc.) and obtain other important diagnostics: "What probability of success—after a good market survey, for example—would make us just indifferent between introducing and not introducing the product?" "What would the consequences be of an increase or decrease of 10 percent in the return from this project." These diagnostics also give the user two other pieces of useful information: the expected value of sample information and the expected value of perfect information.

The expected value of sample information is the most the firm should pay for a survey. What price on the survey would make the decision maker just indifferent between running the survey and doing no marketing research?

EXAMPLE

From our analysis we learned that the survey information the firm could obtain was not worth $16,000. Just how much is it worth? If we label the survey cost as S and average out and fold back, we find that the value of being at the first chance node is $24,000 minus S. If S is $14,000, the firm is indifferent between making a survey and not making it, since the decision "no market survey" is worth an expected $10,000. This amount is the maximum one should pay for the survey.

The expected value of perfect information is the most the firm should pay for a "perfect" survey—one that told it reliably if the product were going to succeed or fail.

EXAMPLE

The expected value of perfect information is important, because no survey can give us perfect information and thus the value of perfect information is the most one should ever pay for sample information.

By "perfect information" we mean a forecast such that

$$p(\text{high forecast} \mid \text{high sales}) = 1,$$
$$p(\text{low forecast} \mid \text{low sales}) = 1, \qquad\qquad (6.5)$$

and other outcomes have probability zero of occurring.

If sales are forecast as high, the best strategy is to introduce the product. This forecast will occur with probability 0.4:

$$p(\text{high forecast}) = p(\text{high sales}) = 0.4. \qquad\qquad (6.6)$$

The net profit of this consequence is $100,000 minus R, where R is the cost of the perfect information. Similarly the probability of the forecast being low is 0.6, and in that case the best strategy is not to make the product. This strategy has a net profit associated with it of minus R.

Therefore the expected profit with perfect information is

$$(0.4)(\$100,000 - R) + (0.6)(-R) = \$40,000 - R. \qquad\qquad (6.7)$$

When $R = \$30,000$ the marketing manager should be indifferent between obtaining the perfect information and not doing a market survey. Both strategies would have an expected net profit of $10,000. Thus the expected value of perfect information is $30,000.

Thus decision analysis not only helps resolve decisions under uncertainty, it helps determine how much it is worth to collect information that reduces that uncertainty. In our experience (Brown, Lilien, and Ulvila 1993) it often takes a surprisingly small reduction in market uncertainty to justify fairly substantial market research expenditures, and decision analysis is quite useful for that justification task.

In the preceding discussion we assume that such information can affect management decisions. If management is already committed to a new-product-entry decision, say, then the best one can do using decision analysis is to provide the (expected) opportunity cost of the inappropriate decision. While we think that the wider availability of marketing engineering tools will help systematize such decisions, so far they have not.

EXAMPLE

(From Ulvila and Brown 1982, pp. 134–135.) How will Honeywell's defense division grow? In late 1979 the manager of planning for the defense systems division of Honeywell, Inc., faced the task of planning the division's growth over the next 10 years. A major part of the work involved finding how to stay within the R&D budget and yet pursue new product opportunities to increase the division's sales and profits.

After he screened the new product opportunities according to their fit with the rest of the division, the manager needed forecasts of the products' sales, profits, and investment requirements. The products' successful development, the strength of competition, and their eventual market success were all uncertain. In addition the chances for success of some of the products were interrelated, and several products offered the chance of significant collateral business.

The approach the analysts took was to build a composite forecast for the division by combining decision-tree analyses of individual products. During the project Honeywell's planners worked closely with decision-analysis consultants and, by the time they finished, acquired the skills needed to carry out the analyses in-house. This type of analysis is now a regular part of Honeywell's project evaluation, planning, and forecasting activity.

The analysts developed a model for each product. The analysis team worked closely with each project manager and his or her staff to build the decision tree, assess probabilities and values, and discuss results and sensitivities.

The two analyses differed significantly, however, in a number of ways. First, the results of Honeywell's analysis were to be used for forecasting as well as for decision making. This use meant that the analysts would need to model additional factors and would have to make the form the outputs took suitable for forecasting.

Second, because the success of some products was related to the success of others, the analysts had to include in the analysis such factors as common investments, collateral business opportunities, and marketing interactions.

Third, Honeywell's problem presented no clear single criterion according to which management could make a decision. Honeywell considered several financial criteria such as internal rate of return, net present value, and yearly streams of profits, investments, and return on investment.

Honeywell developed a forecast based on decision-tree analyses of three main products and two collateral business opportunities. The analysts first developed decision trees for each product to determine the distributions of sales in the event that a market sufficient to support full production either did or did not emerge. Then they developed a second level of analysis to model the key interdependencies among the products; specifically, the probability of any particular product being in full production depended on which other products were also in full production.

That forecast showed that low sales were expected from the products for the first seven years. After that sales for the next six years were expected to be about $75 million per year. That amount was not certain, however. The forecast, for instance, showed a 24 percent chance of sales being below $25 million in 1989.

The supporting decision-tree analyses were useful for explaining the shape of each year's forecast. For example, because of uncertainty about which products would have sufficient markets to support full production by 1988, the forecast for sales were "lumpy." The reasons for these uncertainties are detailed in the decision-tree analyses.

This analysis helped Honeywell to assess the chances that these products would meet sales goals, the uncertainties in the assessment, and the reasons for the uncertainties. By detailing the chain of events that would produce different levels of sales, it also identified points of leverage—places where Honeywell could take action to change probabilities and improve sales.

The analysts also used the decision trees to forecast yearly profits, fund flows, assets, research and development investments, and the related financial quantities of net present value, internal rate of return, and annual return on investment. Their forecasts indicated that these products could be expected to exceed requirements on all factors and that, unless Honeywell was very risk averse, they were attractive.

Honeywell's managers compared forecasts to decide which product opportunities to pursue. These comparisons provided an additional screen since some products were clearly worse than others on *all* factors. But because the analysis did not show the relative importance of each factor—some products were projected to perform better on certain factors (for example, internal rate of return and net present value) and other products were projected to perform better on other factors (for example, return on investment)—an unambiguous ordering of the products was impossible. Honeywell's managers might have had such an ordering if their analysts had used techniques like multiattribute utility methods or the Analytic Hierarchy Process (described later in this chapter).

Urban and Hauser (1993) provide other examples of the use of decision analysis for planning new products, and Raiffa (1968) provides a good basic treatment of decision-analysis concepts. Decision analysis can also be used to assess the responses of the market and competition to other strategic and tactical moves. If the firm is considering a price increase, it can use decision analysis to structure the likely competitive and market response, assigning values to various scenarios and the likelihood of those scenarios so that the firm can choose the best course of action. The Treeage software (included with this book) gives you an opportunity to experiment with and explore this methodology. It allows you to focus on representing and formulating the problem, and it handles all the associated computations automatically.

SHARED EXPERIENCE MODELS: THE PIMS APPROACH

People use a wide variety of other tools in practice to support market-strategy decisions; these approaches can be roughly classified as follows:

1. Shared-experience models (the PIMS approach)
2. Product portfolio models
   a. Standardized
   b. Customized
   c. Financial
3. Normative-resource-allocation models

All of these approaches explicitly or implicitly incorporate life-cycle analysis, experience-curve effects, market definition effects, and market structure effects. We describe shared experience models and product portfolio models in this chapter; see Wind and Lilien (1993) for a discussion of the normative-resource-allocation models.

The PIMS (profit impact of marketing strategy) project began in 1960 at General Electric as an intrafirm analysis of the relative profitability of its businesses. It is based on the notion that the pooled experiences of diverse successful and unsuccessful businesses will provide useful insights and guidance about the determinants of business profitability. By the term *business*, we mean a strategic business unit, which is an operating unit selling a distinct set of products to an identifiable group of customers in competition with a well-defined set of competitors. By the mid-1980s the PIMS database of about 100 data items per business included about 3000 businesses from about 450 participating firms.

Perhaps the most publicized use of the PIMS data is the PAR regression model, which relates return on investment (ROI = pretax income/investment averaged over four years of data) to a set of independent variables (Buzzell and Gale 1987). Exhibit 6.3 presents the results of that analysis for the entire PIMS database. The most widely cited results of the PIMS studies are those relating to market selection and strategic characteristics associated with profitability (Exhibit 6.4).

Firms participating in the PIMS program receive PAR reports for their business, which compare its actual return on investment and return on sales (ROI and ROS) with the ROI and

Profit Influences	Impact on	
	ROI	ROS
Real market growth rate	0.18	0.04
Rate of price inflation	0.22	0.08
Purchase concentration	0.02**	
Unionization, %	-0.07	
Low purchase amount and		
Low importance of purchase***	6.06	1.63
High importance of purchase	5.42	2.10
High purchase amount and		
Low importance of purchase	-6.96	-2.58
High importance of purchase	-3.84	-1.11**
Exports minus imports, %	0.06**	0.05
Customized products	-2.44	-1.77
Market share	0.34	0.14
Relative quality	0.11	0.05
New products, %	-0.12	-0.05
Marketing, % of sales	-0.52	-0.32
R&D, % of sales	-0.36	-0.22
Inventory, % of sales	0.49	-2.09
Fixed capital intensity	-0.55	-2.10
Plant newness	0.07	0.05
Capacity utilization, %	0.31	0.10
Employee productivity	0.13	0.06
Vertical integration	0.26	0.18
First in first out inventory valuation	1.30*	0.62

R^2	.39	.31
F	58.3	45.1
Number of cases	2,314	2,314

Note: All coefficients, except those starred, are significant ($p < .01$). ROI = Return on investment
   * Significance level between .01 and .05.   ROS = Return on sales
  ** Significance level between .05 and .10.
 *** Products for which the typical purchase amount is low and the importance of the purchase to customers is also low.

EXHIBIT 6.3
Multiple-regression equation for return on investment (ROI) and return on sales (ROS) for the entire PIMS database. *Source:* Buzzell and Gale 1987, p. 274.

Some market characteristics associated with high profitability
- A growing market
- Early life cycle
- High inflation
- Few suppliers
- Small purchase levels
- Low unionization
- High exports/low imports

Some strategic factors associated with high profitability
- High market share
- Low relative costs
- High perceived quality
- Low capital intensity
- Intermediate level of vertical integration

EXHIBIT 6.4
Some general PIMS principles relating market selection and strategic planning to profitability. *Source*: Buzzell and Gale 1987, p. 274.

ROS (ROS = pretax income/sales averaged over four years of data) that PIMS predicts for that business (based on its market and strategic characteristics). This type of analysis, showing the deviation of the actual ROI from the PAR ROI, yields insights into how well and why the business has met its strategic potential. Another useful output from PIMS is the Limited Information Report (LIM), containing the results of an abbreviated version of the PAR ROI model. The Limited Information Model contains only 18 variables, which can be assessed using a subset of the total data required for PIMS (Exhibit 6.5).

EXAMPLE

(Drawn from Sudharshan 1995.) The Central Air Conditioner Division of Scott-Air Corp. invested $85 million to increase its capacity to produce 1 1/2- to 10-ton air conditioners. With this new capacity its break-even sales volume was $56 million, higher than the previous year's record volume of $52 million. More important, corporate management demanded at least a 22 percent return on capital. The division manager used the PIMS LIM report to guide his strategy to accomplish this objective.

	This Business (%)	Losers (%)	Winners (%)
Actual ROI	18.0	5.9	26.2
Cash flow/investment	−3.0	−1.3	4.7
Total R&D/sales	6.2	4.8	2.8
Total marketing/sales	1.2	9.1	11.4
Relative % new products	0.0	3.7	−2.6
Fixed-capital intensity	44.0	57.0	33.1

EXHIBIT 6.5
The PIMS Limited Information Report compares the focal business to winners and losers in the same market. The Limited Information Model requires only a subset of the data that the full PIMS model requires. *Source*: Cole and Swire 1980.

CAC management used the LIM report to examine the impact of increasing sales to $100 million per year; however, when considering the whole market that volume amounted to only about an 8.3 percent market share, a share too low to be consistent with the high ROI target. That low market share was consistent with poor market position, poor distribution, and low capacity utilization, leading to the low ROI figures.

On the basis of that analysis the CAC managers decided to focus on narrow market segments: modernization and replacement. If Scott could achieve its $100 million sales target in these narrower market segments (where it had both product and strategic strengths), its projected segment market share (28 percent rather than 8.3 percent) would be consistent with a PIMS ROI of more than the 22 percent target. The LIM report in this case helped the managers to identify a strategy in which the firm's goals would at least be consistent with the performance of the businesses in the PIMS database.

This brief example illustrates the benefits and some of the risks associated with using a model like PIMS for benchmarking. On the one hand, firms can use PIMS as a diagnostic device to indicate what range of outcomes (for ROI and related performance measures) are consistent with a business's market position and strategy. On the other hand, a firm is on a weak foundation if it uses the model for making specific strategy recommendations like "by defining our market more narrowly, we will increase our market share and hence our ROI." (For a direct challenge to this type of focus on market share, see Anterasian, Grahame, and Money (1996).) Because PIMS has been the most widely publicized and widely supported source of cross-sectional information about business strategy, the results emerging from the program have undergone considerable scrutiny both by academics (who question the way the data have been collected and the structure of the models) and by practitioners (who challenge the relevance of both the specific recommendations and the data—most of which were collected more than a decade ago—to current business problems). Our view is that PIMS is simply a good method of benchmarking. It provides reference points and allows managers to ask questions about business performance and the relevance of specific business strategies, but thePIMS results should not be used normatively to recommend policies by themselves. (The portfolio analysis exercise helps you to explore the PIMS models in detail.) Another good method of benchmarking is the use of the ADVISOR model (Chapter 8).

PRODUCT PORTFOLIO MODELS

Wind (1981) classifies the many product portfolio models as standardized models, customized models, and financial models.

All standardized product portfolio models assume that the value of market position or market share depends on the structure of competition and the stage of the product life cycle. Thus in one way or another competitive strength and rate of market growth play prominent roles in all such models.

The Boston Consulting Group (BCG) approach

The earliest and most widely cited standardized approach is the growth/share matrix developed by the Boston Consulting Group (BCG). In this approach the company classifies all of its strategic business units (SBUs) in the business portfolio matrix (also called the growth/share matrix), shown in Exhibit 6.6. There are several things to notice:

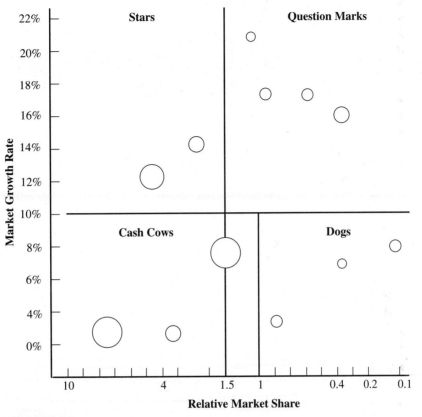

EXHIBIT 6.6
The BCG business portfolio matrix. *Source*: Lilien, Kotler, and Moorthy 1992, p. 554.

■ The vertical axis, the market growth rate, shows the annualized rate at which the various markets in which each business unit is located are growing. Market growth is arbitrarily divided into high and low growth by a 10 percent growth line.

■ The horizontal axis, relative market share, shows the market share for each SBU relative to the share of the industry's largest competitor. Thus a relative market share of 0.4 means that the company's SBU stands at 40 percent of the leader's share, and a relative market share of 2.0 means that the company's SBU is the leader and has twice the share of the next-strongest company in the market. Relative market share conveys more information about competitive standing than absolute market share; an absolute market share of 15 percent may or may not mean market leadership until we know the leader's share. The more SBUs with a relative market share greater than 1.5 that a company has, the more markets it leads. The relative market share is drawn on a logarithmic scale.

■ The circles depict the growth/share standings of the company's various SBUs. The areas of the circles are proportional to the SBUs' dollar sales.

■ Each quadrant represents a distinct type of cash flow situation, leading to the following classification of SBUs:

1. *Stars* are high-growth, high-share SBUs. They often use cash because they need cash to finance their rapid growth. Eventually their growth will slow down, and they will turn into cash cows and become major cash generators supporting other SBUs.

2. *Cash cows* are low-growth, high-share SBUs. They throw off a lot of cash that the company uses to meet its bills and to support other SBUs that are cash using.

3. *Question marks* (also called problem children or wildcats) are low-share SBUs in high-growth markets. They need a lot of cash to maintain and increase their shares. Managers must think hard about whether to spend more to build these question marks into leaders; if they do not, they will have to phase the question marks down or out.

4. *Dogs* (also called cash traps) are low-growth, low-share SBUs. They may generate enough cash to maintain themselves, but they do not promise to be large sources of cash.

- The higher an SBU's market share, the higher its cash generating ability, because higher market shares are accompanied by higher levels of profitability. On the other hand, the higher the market growth rate, the higher are the SBU's requirements for cash to help it to grow and maintain its share.

- The distribution of the SBUs in the four quadrants of the business portfolio matrix suggests the company's current state of health and desirable future strategic directions. The company in Exhibit 6.6 is fortunate in having some large cash cows to finance its question marks, stars, and dogs.

- As time passes SBUs will change their positions in the business portfolio matrix. Many SBUs start out as question marks, move into the star category if they succeed, later become cash cows as market growth falls, and finally turn into dogs toward the end of their life cycles.

- Management's job is to project a future matrix showing where each SBU is likely to be, assuming no change in its strategy. By comparing the current and future matrices, management can identify the major strategic issues facing the firm. Its task in strategic planning is then to determine what role it should assign to each SBU in the interest of allocating resources efficiently. Managers usually evaluate four basic strategies:

1. Build or improve market position and forgo short-term earnings to achieve this goal.
2. Hold or preserve the current market position.
3. Harvest or get a short-term increase in cash flow regardless of the long-term effect.
4. Divest, sell, or liquidate the business because the firm can use its resources better elsewhere.

The main concept behind the BCG approach is that of cash balance—that the long-run health of the corporation depends on some products generating cash (and profits) and others using that cash to grow. Unless a company has an unusually favorable cash flow, it cannot afford to sponsor too many products with large cash appetites. On the other hand, if resources are spread too thin, the company may end up with a number of marginal businesses and reduced capacity to finance promising future opportunities.

The GE/McKinsey approach

While easy to understand, the BCG approach has been criticized by some as too inflexible and simplistic to be universally applicable. Indeed the growth/share dimensions of the BCG approach can be viewed as elements (or as a special case) of the multifactor portfolio matrix pioneered by General Electric (GE): the *GE/McKinsey multifactor matrix*. In the GE/McKinsey approach businesses are displayed against two composite dimensions: *industry attractiveness* and the company's *business strength*. These dimensions in turn are composed of a series of weighted factors that make up the composite dimension. Both the factor weights and the factors themselves may vary from one application to another. For example, industry attractiveness includes measures of market size, growth rate, competitive intensity, and the like, while business strength includes such measures as market share, share growth, and product quality.

Management gives each business a rating for each factor and gives each factor a weight. These factor ratings are multiplied by the weights and summed to arrive at a position in the strength/attractiveness matrix.

The matrix has nine cells. The three cells in the upper right are those in which the company has a strong position and should be considered for investment and growth. The three cells along the diagonal are of intermediate overall attractiveness, and the company should consider a policy selectively enhancing businesses in those cells to generate earnings. Finally, the cells in the lower left corner are low in overall attractiveness, and the company should consider harvesting and divesting businesses in those cells.

EXAMPLE

(From Sudharshan 1995.) Ford Motor Company's tractor division uses the GE/McKinsey approach to evaluate a portfolio of country markets (Exhibit 6.7). In this application, they defined business attractiveness for tractors in a country as follows:

Business attractiveness = Market size

$+ 2 \times$ Market growth

$+ 0.5 \times$ Price control/Regulation rating

$+ 0.25 \times$ Ratification requirements

$+ 0.25 \times$ Local content and compensatory report requirements

$+ 0.35 \times$ Inflation

$+ 0.35 \times$ Trade Balance

$+ 0.30 \times$ Political factors.

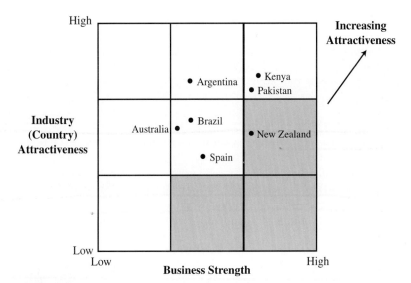

EXHIBIT 6.7
Portion of GE/McKinsey matrix for Ford's tractors' multinational portfolio. *Source*: Sudharshan 1995, p. 258.

Note that the factors Ford uses to address business attractiveness are quite specific to a portfolio-of-countries problem; for other applications, even for tractors, the factors might be quite different.

While more complete than the BCG approach, the GE approach shares the benefits and problems associated with all standardized portfolio approaches. Its benefit is that it is easy to implement, communicate, and understand. Its limitation is that it attempts to boil down business strategy to the interplay of a small number of somewhat arbitrary dimensions that may ignore important specific aspects of the business planning environment.

In contrast to the standardized portfolio approaches, customized approaches do not pre-specify dimensions or objectives. (The GE portfolio planning software allows you to build a customized matrix and the portfolio analysis exercise allows you to apply this tool to a product portfolio problem.)

The product-performance matrix approach (Wind and Claycamp 1976) allows managers to select dimensions. In an application at a major industrial firm, management selected four dimensions: industry sales, product sales, market share, and profitability. In allocating resources this approach follows the BCG method, but it is based on projected sales response to alternative marketing strategies.

Financial models

The analogy between the business portfolio problem and the stock portfolio problem has prompted the adaptation of financial portfolio models to this problem area. Financial portfolio analysis deals with investments in holdings of securities generally traded through financial markets. The objective is typically to create an efficient portfolio—one that maximizes return on investment for a given level of risk or that minimizes risk for a specified level of return. To apply this approach to business portfolios, managers must be able to assess the expected rate of return, the variance of that return, and the correlation between returns for any pair of businesses.

The approach is theoretically appealing. In practice, however, it has proved difficult to obtain reliable estimates of the key data inputs needed and it has seen limited application. Anderson (1979, 1981) and Cardozo and Wind (1980) discuss its applications further.

Analytic Hierarchy Process

The Analytic Hierarchy Process (AHP) is another approach for assessing and allocating resources in a portfolio. AHP is particularly useful when a firm can bring a logical structure to a problem but has great difficulty making quantitative assessments of the economic consequences of alternatives, a frequent problem in strategic-marketing decisions.

The AHP is an interactive structured process that brings together the key decision makers who represent diverse functions and experiences. As a group they integrate "objective" market data with subjective management judgment. The process is based on three steps:

1. Structuring the problem as a hierarchy of levels (Exhibit 6.8). In constructing the hierarchy the decision makers generate creative options and identify the criteria for their evaluation.

Overall Goal
1.00

| Level 1 | Compatibility (.108) | Market Opportunity (.446) | Inventory & Cost (.065) | Competitive Advantage (.262) | Risk (.119) |

Level 2   Consistency (.047)   Growth (.183)   Fixed Costs (.022)   Differentiation (.209)   Technical (.060)
          Support (.062)   Geographic   Marketing (.024)
                               Concentration (.041) Variable Costs Current Position Distribution
                               Volume (.041)   (.035)   (.052)   (.024)
                               $$$Level (.116)   Substitution   Conjuncture
                                                     Costs (.007)   (.012)

Level 3   Support
(example) Creation (.047)
          Expansion
          (.027)
          Milking (.015)

Criterion	Definition
$$$ LEVEL	Expected price acceptance level
COMPETITIVE ADVANTAGE	Competitive advantage with respect to proposed solution
COMPATIBILITY	Compatibility of solution with overall group strategy
CONJUNCTURE	Sensitivity to conjuncture
CONSISTENCY	Apparent consistency with overall objectives
CURRENT POSITION	Current position on the relevant market
DIFFERENTIATION	Differentiation toward competition
DISTRIBUTION	Risk of physical distribution failure
FIXED COSTS	Fixed costs of solution (mid entry)
GEO CONCENTRATION	Geographic dilution of the relevant market
GROWTH	Growth of relevant segment
INVESTMENTS & COSTS	Investments and costs required by solution
MARKETING	Commercial risk of failure
MARKET OPPORTUNITIES	Market opportunities of solution
RISK	Uncertainty raised to solution
SUBSTITUTION COSTS	Costs of substitution (disengagement)
SUPPORT	Likeliness of affiliated support
TECHNICAL	Technical risk of failure
VARIABLE COSTS	Variable costs of solution (margin)
VOLUME	Volume of the relevant market

EXHIBIT 6.8
This decision hierarchy for the Ciba-Geigy example has two levels of criterion importance (levels 1 and 2) and their evaluation of one node for the three alternatives (level 3).

2. Evaluating the elements at each level along each of the criteria at the next higher level of the hierarchy. The decision makers use a nine-point scale to make the evaluation and base it on a series of paired comparisons.
3. Weighting the option. The model uses a weighting algorithm to determine the importance of their options in relation to multiple criteria or objectives. The algorithm is based on the idea that pairwise comparisons recover the relative weights (importance) of items or objects at any level of a hierarchy.

Given, for example, n objects, $A_1, \ldots, A_n$ and an unknown vector of corresponding weights $w = (w_1, \ldots, w_n)$, we can then form a matrix of pairwise comparisons of weights:

$$A_1 \cdots A_n$$

$$A = \begin{array}{c} A_1 \\ \vdots \\ A_n \end{array} \begin{bmatrix} \dfrac{w_1}{w_1} & \cdots & \dfrac{w_1}{w_n} \\ \vdots & \ddots & \vdots \\ \dfrac{w_n}{w_1} & \cdots & \dfrac{w_n}{w_n} \end{bmatrix}. \tag{6.8}$$

We can recover the scale of weights, $w_1, \ldots, w_n$ through some simple matrix calculations such that the computed weights recover the respondents' pairwise judgments as closely as possible. (The procedure also synthesizes the weights at each level of the hierarchy to obtain overall priorities for each decision alternative.) Unlike the product portfolio model where the user directly provides the weights assigned to the criteria, the AHP model infers these weights based on a set of simple pairwise judgments.

This process produces explicit guidelines for selecting a strategy based on the decision makers' prioritization of the strategic options. The resulting strategy can be made to satisfy the corporate mission and a set of multiple objectives under alternative environmental scenarios and time horizons.

Secondary output from the AHP includes explicit weights for the objectives or criteria used for evaluating the options. The AHP provides a consistency index for a set of pairwise judgments (a good guide to the quality of those judgments) and also provides a simple way to conduct sensitivity analysis on the results. Through its computer software (Expert Choice, included with this book) the process also helps identify areas requiring the collection of additional information—those relationships on which people cannot reach consensus and for which the results can vary significantly depending on which of the conflicting views is accepted.

EXAMPLE

Ciba-Geigy, one of the top 10 pharmaceutical groups in the world, needs to determine a long-term international strategy for its dermatological unit. The dermatological unit is a part of Ciba-Geigy's Other Therapeutic Areas (OTA) Division, and it is a relatively small but profitable business. The promotional efforts for dermatological products have been irregular; the world market share has dropped correspondingly. Nevertheless, a new segment of this market is developing. The corporation can count on significant competitive advantages for a market entry because of its research and development efforts in the field. Management identified three possible strategies for the dermatological unit:

1. Milking the existing business based on its topical cortisone (TC) products and a product to be launched in the near future. It would abandon or license products in development. This option uses the minimal R&D efforts and marketing expenses necessary to maintain a presence in the marketplace.

2. Expand the existing business. It would launch TC products in development to improve performance in this segment. R&D and marketing efforts would be set accordingly.

3. Expand the existing business and create a new segment. Develop and launch nonsteroidal topical products, greatly increasing R&D and marketing expenses.

The strategy guidance committee is in charge of evaluating the strategic consistency of product groups' actions in terms of market opportunities and resource allocations. Its objective is to ensure maximization of results based on compatibility with overall strategy and objectives, organizational constraints and political aspects of the decision, market opportunities, investment and costs, competitive advantages, and risk. The committee used the AHP model to assess the alternatives identified for the dermatological unit with respect to the foregoing objectives.

The committee constructed a three-level hierarchy to help it determine the appropriate strategy to follow. Exhibit 6.8 gives two levels of criteria; for example, one criterion (level 1) is compatibility and consists of two criteria at a secondary level: consistency and support. Exhibit 6.9 shows the output of the analysis: for these input values, the third option (to expand and create a new segment) is best along all criteria except the level of risk.

The analytic procedure and the associated software facilitate structuring strategic decision problems like these and enable simple sensitivity analyses.

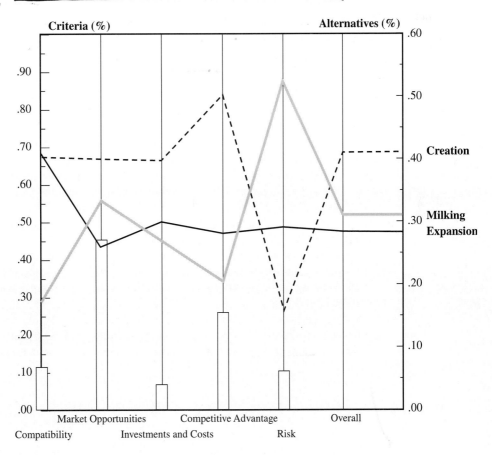

EXHIBIT 6.9
For the Ciba-Geigy example, the "creation" alternative performs well on all criteria except the level of risk.

AHP has broad applicability for marketing strategy. Saaty and Vargas (1994) report its use in pricing new products, developing corporate strategy, determining the market attractiveness of developing countries, and other applications.

COMPETITION

Substitutes exist for most products, and it is naive to assume that a firm can investigate marketing strategy without regard to competition. Dolan (1981) presents an overview of approaches to competition from microeconomics and marketing, as well as empirical evidence about types of competition from various industry studies.

In the cases of monopoly and perfect competition, microeconomic theory provides unambiguous results for optimal marketing-mix decisions. But for oligopoly the problem of specifying competitors' behavior makes it difficult to determine what the optimal marketing mix should be. The models of oligopoly provide no single solution or strategy for a firm to follow (Singer 1968).

Considering the entire sequence of moves and countermoves by competitors is hopelessly complex. Instead, Baumol (1972) proposes one of two approaches: (1) ignore the interdependence between competitors or (2) assume each competitor is a rational economic agent and then determine a likely set of actions that will allow it to maximize its expected utility.

These two approaches relate to work on *reaction functions*, first proposed by Cournot in the nineteenth century, and to *game-theory* models. The classical reaction-function hypothesis is that each seller assumes the output (action) of rival firms to be fixed and then sets a price to maximize profits. This approach leads to unrealistic results that are apparently nonoptimal (Mansfield 1979; Scherer 1980), although Green and Krieger (1991) claim this approach closely approximates actual market behavior.

Dolan (1981) points out that many people in marketing think that game-theory models would solve many competitive issues if only some critical mathematical hurdles could be overcome. This is unlikely to be the case: game theory has "insuperable problems as a prescriptive theory of rational decisions in conflict situations [and] the prescriptive aspect of game theory ought to be written off" (Rapoport 1966, pp. 202–203). A main problem is that game-theoretic results depend critically on assumptions about the objectives, on the level of information, and on the analytical capabilities of *all* competitors, factors the decision-making firm is unlikely to know. However, the models are quite important for gaining insight into market structure and operation (Lilien, Kotler, and Moorthy 1992, especially Chapters 4–6). (For some assessments of the uses and limitations of game theory, see Aumann (1987) and Rubinstein (1991).)

Another approach to understanding competition comes from the area of industrial organizations, which explores the nature of the structural variables that influence competitive behavior. Porter (1980) attributes the type and intensity of competition to eight major factors:

1. Number and size distribution of competitors
2. Industry growth rate
3. Cost structure and storage costs
4. Extent of product differentiation
5. Divisibility of capacity additions
6. Diversity of competitors
7. Importance of the market to firms
8. Heights of exit barriers

Dolan (1981) has examined a number of industry studies to determine the extent to which these structural variables determined the mode of competition. He summarizes his results in four lessons:

1. High fixed costs promote competitive responses to share gain attempts.
2. Low storage costs reduce competitive reactions.
3. Growing primary demand reduces competitive reactions.
4. Large firms avoid price competition.

He suggests that structural dimensions of the market affect the likelihood of market response and the form of that response, but these are broad guidelines at best.

An econometric approach to modeling competition uses *reaction matrices*. We illustrate a reaction matrix with an example. Two competitors in the market compete on price (P) and advertising (A). Exhibit 6.10 shows their reaction matrix. Under the assumption that these elasticities are constant and stable over time and that a multiplicative function is a reasonable representation of the structure of interaction, the η's (elasticities) in Exhibit 6.10(a) can be estimated via the equations

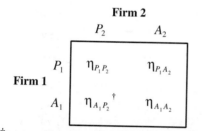

†$\eta_{A_1 P_2}$ = percentage change in A_1 with a 1% change in P_2.

EXHIBIT 6.10(a)
Reaction matrix: two firms, two marketing variables.

	Firm 2	
	Price	Advertising (Lagged)
Firm 1 Price	0.664† (0.030)	1.898† (0.825)
Firm 1 Advertising	0.008 (0.005)	0.273† (0.123)

† Significant at the 0.05 level.

EXHIBIT 6.10(b)
Partial reaction-function example showing that firms not only react in kind (price decline following price decline, for example) but firm 2 increases advertising when firm 1 lowers price. *Source*: Lambin, Naert, and Bultez 1975, p. 119.

$$\log P_1(t) = a_1 + b_1 \log P_2(t) + b_2 \log A_2(t), \tag{6.9a}$$

$$\log A_1(t) = a_2 + b_3 \log P_2(t) + b_4 \log A_2(t); \tag{6.9b}$$

then b_1 is an estimate of η_{P1P2}, b_2 is an estimate of η_{P1A2}, and so on. A portion of the reaction matrix for the application reported in Lambin, Naert, and Bultez (1975) is reproduced in Exhibit 6.10(b). All the diagonal elements are significantly different from zero, signifying that firm 2 reacts directly to any change in the marketing mix of firm 1 (it changes price in response to a price change, for example). In addition, the lagged advertising-price elasticity is also significant, showing that indirect responses are important as well. This example shows that reaction behavior is complex, involving multiple responses and potential lags in time; therefore tracking direct responses could lead to mistaken inferences.

Bensoussan, Bultez, and Naert (1978) have used this approach to optimize marketing-mix decisions in a competitive environment. Lambin (1976) and Hanssens, Parsons, and Schultz (1990) report additional applications of the approach for assessing competitive behavior. Hanssens (1980) extends the basic model to explicitly represent multiple competitors and to develop interrelationships among the marketing elements within a particular firm, and Carpenter and colleagues (1988) show how to address markets where competitive effects are differentially and asymmetrically distributed among competitors.

One of the main insights and contributions of this approach is the measurement of what drives the sales that result from a firm's action in a competitive market. A firm can gain sales in a market by increasing its market share or by maintaining its share while the market grows. The market can grow as a direct result of what the firm does (increasing its advertising) or as an indirect result as competitors respond to the firm's actions: competitors respond to the firm's advertising program by increasing their advertising as well, leading to an indirect effect, an increase in total market sales. Formally this approach decomposes sales elasticity as follows:

$$\text{Sales elasticity} = \text{Share effect} + \text{Size effect}; \tag{6.10}$$

$$\text{Share effect} = \text{Direct effect} + \text{Competitive-response effect}; \tag{6.11}$$

$$\text{Size effect} = \text{Direct effect} + \text{Competitive-response effect}. \tag{6.12}$$

This decomposition permits a more careful assessment of the firm's marketing-mix options as well as their direct and indirect effects. The Acme liquid cleanser exercise with the competitive advertising software illustrates some of the complexities of studying competitive response.

Sudharshan (1995) brings an interesting perspective to the analysis of competition by looking at four domains that have studied competition extensively: industrial organization economics (IO), sports games, military operations, and evolutionary ecology. Each domain can be characterized by the key elements in the way it handles competition, and the types of competitive strategy guidelines or insights one can glean from studying the area.

Exhibit 6.11 summarizes Sudharshan's evaluation of these approaches. For example, industrial organizational economics recognizes strategic groups and mobility barriers as key to the critical asymmetries among competing firms and identifies three ways firms can isolate themselves from competition: they can differentiate their product offerings, they can lower their costs, or they can collude. Industrial organization economics focuses largely on the mechanisms a firm can use to isolate itself from competition.

The sports game approach focuses on the relationship between prior planning and execution, on the role of time (single play, game, season), and multiple routes to success.

Strategy	Key Elements	Generic Strategies	Key Limitations
Organizational economics	Competition versus collusion Isolating mechanisms	Cost competition Product differentiation Strategic group competition (inter- versus intra-group)	Interaction between cost and quality Nature of "mixed" strategies Stability of groups
Sports games	Planning and coordination Importance of time Impact of rule change	Offensive Defensive Imitative Innovative	Territorial logic of the game Fixed rules Degree of control
Military	The role of signaling Direction vs. surprise Multiple time periods	Direct confrontation Flanking Guerrilla Avoidance	Focus on conflict Importance of terrain Focus on external factors and logistics
Evolutionary ecology	Scope of competition Forms of organization Interaction between firms and their markets	Generalist Specialist Niche	Nature of competition Level and unit of analysis Every species has a "niche"

EXHIBIT 6.11
An overview of competitive strategy analogies and their potential application to marketing-strategy problems. *Source*: Sudharshan 1995, p. 55.

In addition rules are most codified in sports (second most in the industrial organization perspective and the least in the other two paradigms), making changes in rules critical in the selection and modification of competitive strategies.

As we stressed in Chapter 1, the marketing engineering approach to solving marketing decision problems provides structure and insight as well as direct policy recommendations. Perhaps this value is best illustrated in the domain of analyzing competitive market strategies, where an understanding of analogous situations provides insight, but where it is risky to apply that insight directly to a marketing problem. These analogies expand our thinking and the set of theories and tools that we can combine and apply in developing competitive marketing strategy.

SUMMARY

In making marketing-strategy decisions we must allocate marketing resources over time. A key strategic decision is to time market entry and exit. We have identified some key determinants of success in that decision and a method (decision analysis) that can prove handy. Deciding when to enter the market and analyzing a firm's portfolio of products and markets are central to allocating strategic-marketing resources. Such tools as shared experience models, product portfolio models, and the Analytic Hierarchy Process can be very helpful to those who must structure and facilitate these resource-allocation decisions.

To determine marketing strategy one must consider the competition. Our competitive-analysis toolkit is primitive, but it is far from empty. We can combine sound competitive intelligence with such approaches as market simulations, reaction-matrix analysis, and the study of analogs to better understand the benefits and consequences of our strategic allocation decisions.

**Part III:
Developing
Marketing
Programs**

CHAPTER **7**

New Product Decisions

In this chapter we

■ Provide a conceptual framework to highlight the major decisions in developing a new product

■ Describe conjoint analysis, a method useful for making product design decisions and for evaluating new product opportunities

■ Describe methods for forecasting the sales of a new product both before and shortly after it is introduced into the market

INTRODUCTION

A product is anything that can be offered in the market for attention, acquisition, use, or consumption that might satisfy a want or a need. Most of the products we think of are *physical products*. But products also include *services*, such as concerts, overnight package delivery, management consulting, vacation tours, on-line services such as CompuServe and America Online, and MBA programs. Even such entities as the American Red Cross can be viewed as products in the sense that a transaction with the Red Cross makes us feel positive toward it and about ourselves.

Marketing managers view products at three levels:

Core product: The core product is the most fundamental aspect of a product: the need or want that the customer satisfies by buying the product. As Ted Levitt (1960) noted, a customer buys a three-inch hole, not a 3-inch drill-bit, or as Charles Revson of Revlon put it: "In the factory, we make cosmetics; in the store, we sell hope."

Tangible product: Marketing managers must transform the core product into a tangible product, consisting of features, styling, quality level, brand name, and packaging. They make the core product into something that customers can buy. A vacation package by Club Med helps transform customers' desires for adventure, excitement, finding a mate, or getting away from it all into a tangible product that they can conveniently purchase. A Visa credit card transforms customers' desire for secure, convenient, and quick access to credit into a tangible product.

Augmented product: The augmented product includes enhancements to the tangible product in the form of additional services and features to make the product competitively attractive, such as toll-free customer information, installation guides, delivery, warranty, and after-sale services.

The product is the most important element of the marketing mix. To develop and manage successful products managers must make key decisions during the new product development process and in managing the portfolio of existing products. Here we focus primarily on new product development (NPD), which consists of several stages (Exhibit 7.1) (Urban and Hauser 1993).

In the first stage, *opportunity identification*, people generate ideas and articulate the market opportunities associated with the ideas. For example, R. J. Reynolds Tobacco Company came up with the idea of the "smokeless cigarette" to address the opportunity represented by increasing social objections to smoking. Gillette came up with the idea of a spring-mounted

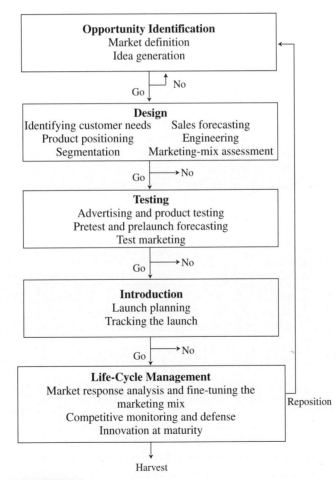

EXHIBIT 7.1
An outline showing the various stages and decisions of the new product development (NPD) process. Adapted from Urban and Hauser 1993, p. 38.

razor that would provide a closer and smoother shave than any other razor available in the market. If the firm decides that the new idea is attractive, it proceeds to the next stage.

In the *design* stage, the firm transforms the idea into a physical or psychological entity by giving it form, features, and meaning. For example, the smokeless cigarette was designed to heat the tobacco instead of burning it, thus reducing the "environmental" tobacco smoke in the air by 65 to 99 percent as compared with a regular cigarette. Other features included a sleek package with thin golden diagonal lines on a white background to convey the image of a "cleaner cigarette" and the brand name "Premier" to indicate a superior product.

During the design stage managers also seek a better understanding of the market segments for the product, explore alternative ways to position the product in those segments (Chapter 3), work with engineers in making cost-benefit trade-offs for various product features, develop and evaluate product prototypes, develop initial marketing plans, and generate sales forecasts for selected product designs.

In the *testing* stage, managers assess whether the product will gain market acceptance when it is introduced and whether the product will meet the firm's goals for profit and market share under a proposed marketing plan. Testing also offers diagnostic information about what changes to the product or marketing program will improve its chances of success. If the various tests (e.g., taste tests, advertising copy tests, and simulated shopping tests) indicate success, the firm introduces the product.

In the case of Premier cigarettes, test market results indicated that consumers did not value "social benefits" highly enough to overcome its perceived poor taste (it leaves a charcoal-like aftertaste) and to a lesser extent its higher price and its "strangeness" (each package contained special instructions on how to light the cigarette). Most test stores reported high trial but low repeat-purchase rates. Not surprisingly, R. J. Reynolds did not introduce Premier nationally.

Introducing the product into the market calls for decisions on such issues as coordination of production and marketing plans, fine-tuning product design for manufacturability, and managing the distribution pipeline. It also calls for continuous monitoring of market performance to refine the introduction strategy (e.g., price and advertising copy).

If the firm successfully introduces the new product, it puts in place a *life-cycle management* process to maintain the growth and profitability of the product. Successful products invite competition, and the firm thus needs defensive strategies. Successful products also draw organizational resources away from other products. The firm must use portfolio management strategies across the entire product line to ensure both short-term and long-term profitability of its entire portfolio of products (Chapter 6).

At each of the five stages the firm makes a go or no go decision to move to the next stage (Exhibit 7.1). The foregoing process represents an ideal, and individual firms customize the process depending on the requirements of a specific product and the capabilities of the firm. In some cases a firm may skip a stage (e.g., testing) or iterate several times between stages before moving forward.

The costs and risks associated with new products are high. Most new products fail to achieve the objectives managers set for them, and they are withdrawn from the market. Urban and Hauser (1993, p. 61) estimate that the average costs (in 1987 dollars) were $700,000 for opportunity identification, $4.1 million for design, $2.6 million for testing, and $5.9 million for introduction. (The projects they analyzed included 60 percent industrial, 20 percent consumer durables, and 20 percent consumer nondurables.) In other categories short product cycles (e.g., a few weeks for new movies, a few months for new notebook computers) require that managers get the product right the first time rather than refining it after introduction.

Several research studies indicate that using a disciplined approach to developing new products improves the likelihood of success. For example, Hise et al. (1989) report that firms that use the full range of up-front activities associated with the stages shown in Exhibit

7.1 have a 73 percent success rate as compared with a 29 percent success rate for firms that use only a few of the up-front activities.

NEW PRODUCT DECISION MODELS

The NPD process is coming under close scrutiny as companies operating in today's competitive markets scramble to develop new products that simultaneously accomplish several objectives. New products today should be competitive in global markets, offer good value to customers, be environment-friendly, enhance the strategic position of the company, and enter the market at the right time. To meet these challenging objectives companies are embracing new concepts and techniques to support changes in their NPD processes. These new approaches include such *techniques* as quality function deployment and stage-gate reviews, such *measures* as cycle time, and such *organizational mechanisms* as cross-functional teams (see, for example, Griffin 1993; Zangwill 1993). An accompanying trend has been the growth of computer models to facilitate decision making at every stage of the NPD process (Rangaswamy and Lilien 1997). We mention some of these models in the next section. In the remaining sections of this chapter we describe in detail selected models for which we provide software implementations with this book.

Models for identifying opportunities

Generating ideas: Creativity in NPD requires both divergent thinking (lateral thinking) and convergent thinking. Using such divergent thinking techniques as free association and the synectics process, people can generate a large number of ideas. They can then use convergent thinking to sort through those ideas and decide which are the most promising. Several commercial software packages are available to support the creative process, based on the premise that interaction between people and software enhances creativity.

Mindlink is a software package that implements the well-known synectics process, which combines structured problem solving with techniques for stimulating creative thinking. The user starts by stating a problem (e.g., increase battery life of notebook computers). The program encourages divergent thinking by using "wish triggers" (I wish computers could store energy the way cacti store water) and "idea triggers" (ways to realize the wishes—e.g., a battery mechanism dispersed throughout the body of the notebook computer). The software also uses a mechanism called "option triggers" to help users to evaluate ideas and to select those that are likely to be most effective in resolving the problem.

Other software for generating ideas include IdeaFisher and Inspiration. IdeaFisher encourages divergent thinking for making nonobvious connections through free associations. The software combines two databases: one with 65,000 words and phrases linked by an extensive set of cross-references, and the other with a bank of about 700 questions (e.g., how would a child solve this problem?) organized in categories. When the user enters a word or phrase, the software retrieves associated words and phrases. For example, the term *new product* would retrieve such associated terms as *marketing, imagination,* and *research experiments,* and each of these in turn triggers other connections (e.g., imaginary people and places). This process may be continued iteratively.

The Inspiration software program offers a visual environment to facilitate the creative process. Starting from a core concept, the user "spans outward" to develop links to other concepts related to the core concept using such visual aids as charts, maps, symbols, and outlines. For example, starting with the core idea of developing a notebook computer with a 10-hour battery life, the user can link this visually (with arrows) to other activities such as "check patent office for battery technology," "contact R&D in sister company," and "initiate feasibility study within the company." Each of these actions can then be visually linked to other concepts. Concepts put on a computer screen may be easily rearranged during the process.

Software packages for idea generation typically provide only minimal support for evaluating those ideas. Other decision models are available for evaluating ideas in terms of their potential value to the company and their likelihood of success if introduced.

Evaluating ideas: The Analytical Hierarchy Process (described in Chapter 6) is useful for prioritizing several new product projects based on user-provided criteria and subcriteria. The manager first establishes a hierarchical structure of criteria and subcriteria on which to evaluate the new product. Next the manager provides pairwise evaluations of the alternatives at each level on the hierarchy. The software synthesizes these evaluations across the entire hierarchy to come up with numerical scores that indicate the overall relative attractiveness of the new product ideas. AHP is particularly useful for conducting visual sensitivity analyses to explore how changes in the importance of a criterion alter the relative attractiveness of each alternative. Exhibit 7.2 shows a hierarchical model for evaluating new pharmaceutical products.

The *NewProd* model helps a firm to evaluate a new product idea in terms of the associated business risks and rewards and to determine the organizational resources needed to improve the product's chances of success. NewProd incorporates a model based on the research of Cooper (1986, 1992), who analyzed the determinants of new product success in 195 projects using 80 independent variables. The database has been updated and enlarged since the

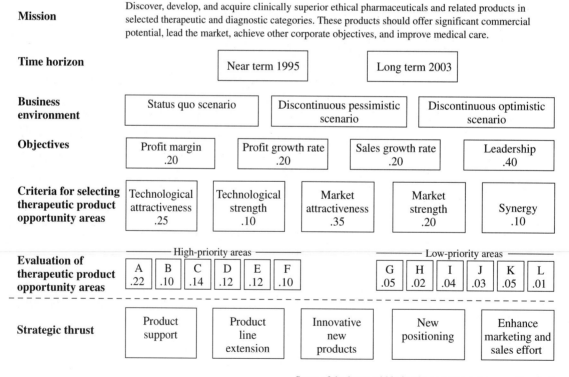

Some of the items within levels, and all numbers are disguised.
Source: Jerry Wind, The Wharton School

EXHIBIT 7.2
An example showing how a pharmaceutical firm used the Analytic Hierarchy Process (AHP) to assign numerical priorities to 12 different product opportunity areas (A through L).

original study, and the current model is based on 30 of the 80 variables (reduced to nine orthogonal factors) that were most instrumental in explaining the products' degrees of success.

Firms use NewProd under the guidance of a trained facilitator. Project members independently provide data on the 30 variables identified in Cooper's research and then meet to discuss differences in their inputs, repeating the process until there is general agreement about the inputs. The NewProd program compares this input profile of the new product (summarized on nine factors) with its internal database of factor scores to determine the percentile position of the new product as compared with the factor scores of products in the database. This evaluation may be customized by industry (e.g., consumer packaged goods, business markets, or electronics and communications). Several reports help the project members to determine whether the new product score on each factor is consistent with that of a successful or unsuccessful product and indicate what they should do to improve the new product's chances of success. Firms can also use this software to evaluate a number of products at different stages of development, thereby evaluating a new product in the context of the entire portfolio of new products under development. In many ways NewProd operates like PIMS, ADVISOR, and other shared experience models (Chapters 6 and 8).

Models for product design

Many products and services can be viewed as bundles of product attributes—that is, products can be represented as combinations of levels of product attributes. For example, a Toyota Camry car could be described as SIZE = midsize, TYPE = sedan, MPG = 30 in city, ENGINE = V-6 fuel-injection, OPTIONS = sunroof, and so forth. In purchasing products customers make trade-offs between the various attributes, for example, between a sunroof and a V-6 engine. Conjoint analysis is a formal technique for examining these trade-offs to determine an effective combination of attribute levels that will perform well in the marketplace. In particular, conjoint analysis is useful for deciding what attributes should be designed into a new product to maximize its expected performance in a market already containing competitors and for determining which market segment(s) will find a particular product configuration most appealing. In short, conjoint analysis is a formal method by which a firm can have its customers design the products that would appeal most to them. We describe conjoint analysis in detail in the next main section.

A different approach to designing new products to meet customers' needs is the BUNDOPT model (Green and Kim 1991). The BUNDOPT model is particularly useful for deciding what combination of features to offer in a new product. For example, in designing a car the firm could incorporate a number of optional features such as cruise control, a roof rack, a hood air deflector, or a trailer hitch. The possible options could number 25 or more, but most customers would probably not be willing to pay for more than 5 or 10 of these. However, each customer may want different features. The manufacturer must decide which features to offer to ensure that the car will appeal to the maximum number of customers. The BUNDOPT model uses data obtained from potential customers to address this problem. It can also be used to identify which segments prefer a particular set of features, and the desirability of a particular combination of features to a target segment.

Models for new product forecasting and testing

In Chapter 5 we described several forecasting methods. Most of them require historical data. However, managers must forecast sales and success of new products before they generate any historical data. Good forecasts help firms to minimize the risk of failing in the market and maximize their use of opportunities associated with the product. For example, better forecasts might have minimized the losses on such products as Ford's Edsel, Apple's Newton Personal Digital Assistant (PDA), and General Motors' Wankel engine. Improved forecasts would also have enhanced the profits earned by such products as Mazda's Miata and Mattel's Cabbage Patch dolls, both of which were in short supply.

We can categorize new product forecasting situations based on whether the success of the product depends more on customers' first purchase (i.e., adoption) of the new product or on customers' repeat-purchase behavior. Forecasting first purchase is important for "discontinuous" innovations that *may* require customers to change their current behavior. For example, a customer who is thinking of replacing a Rolodex with an electronic personal information manager (PIM) such as a Filoflex may be reluctant to type information on a keypad instead of writing by hand. Likewise, someone adopting a microwave oven has to learn new ways to cook. These two products were made possible by enabling new technologies (inexpensive integrated chips for the PIM, and controlled microwave generation in a compact unit in the case of microwave ovens), but this need not always be the case (e.g., Chrysler used existing technologies to develop a new category of automobiles, the minivan). However, some innovations based on new technologies do not require customers to change their purchase or use behavior significantly (e.g., DirecTV satellite-based transmission of digital TV signals). Firms in business-to-business markets also need to forecast new product sales, for example, when they introduce new types of manufacturing equipment.

Forecasting repeat-purchase behavior is important for products that are purchased frequently (e.g., packaged goods such as detergents, or industrial supplies). Here the customer may already have a base of experience with which to evaluate the new product. Firms often test their new products in real or simulated markets to develop sales forecasts for them.

Most forecasting is conditional upon a specific marketing plan. Good forecasting models provide diagnostic information on how best to improve the proposed marketing plans, if necessary, by helping the firm identify those controllable variables (e.g., price, product positioning, or advertising) that are most important in driving the sales of the new product.

In the last two main sections of this chapter we describe the Bass model for forecasting first purchase and the ASSESSOR model for forecasting repeat purchase. These are well-established models for forecasting the sales of new products.

CONJOINT ANALYSIS FOR PRODUCT DESIGN

Introduction

It is helpful to view many products and services as bundles of product attributes. For example, a pizza is a composite of several attributes such as type of crust and topping, and the amount of cheese. An attribute can have many options or levels (e.g., the topping can consist of pepperoni, veggie, or plain cheese). A bundle is a specific product composed of one option (or level) of each attribute selected for analysis.

Conjoint analysis uses data on customers' overall preferences for a selected number of product bundles and decomposes these overall preferences into utility values (part-worths) that the customer attaches to each level of each attribute. The set of decomposed utility values is referred to as the *part-worth function*.

In the data collection stage of conjoint analysis, the firm obtains data on respondents' preferences for a carefully selected set of product bundles. The selected bundles typically do not include those that dominate other bundles on all attributes of interest. The respondents rate or rank order the bundles to indicate their degree of preference for each bundle. In this evaluation process respondents are forced to make trade-off judgments between attributes because one product bundle may have the preferred levels of an attribute (e.g., pepperoni topping) while containing less preferred levels of other attributes (e.g., higher price). The preference data enable the firm to obtain part-worth functions, which can then be used to estimate respondent preference for any product (i.e., any combination of attribute levels) *including those not directly evaluated by the respondents*. As a result managers can efficiently determine the value to respondents of many more product design options than the respondents could evaluate directly. The use of numeric part-worth functions also allows managers to develop quantitative forecasts for the sales or market shares of alternative product concepts under consideration, and to price out noneconomic attributes (e.g., delivery in three weeks versus four weeks is worth $X to the respondents).

EXAMPLE

Designing a pizza: To illustrate the basic concepts of conjoint analysis, let us see how it can be used by a packaged foods firm to design a new frozen pizza. We start by assuming that pizza can be described by combinations of attributes—type of crust, type of toppings, amount and type of cheese, price, and other attributes. Suppose that the firm is considering three types of crusts (thin, thick, and pan), four types of toppings (veggie, pepperoni, sausage, and pineapple), three types of cheese (mozzarella, Romano, and mixed cheese), quantity of cheese at three levels (two, four, or six ounces), and priced at one of three levels ($7.99, $8.99, and $9.99). The pizzas are identical in all other respects, such as size, type of tomato sauce, and brand name. Even with this limited set of options there are 324 ($3 \times 4 \times 3 \times 3 \times 3$) different types of pizzas that the company can make by varying the crust, topping, type and amount of cheese, and price. Which of these will be among the most preferred by customers in a target segment?

In the typical conjoint study marketing researchers would present potential customers in selected target segment(s) with several carefully chosen pizza alternatives. The pizzas can be described in words, shown in pictures, or better still (in this case), actually provided in samples to be taste tested. Here the respondents would evaluate as few as 16 selected pizzas out of the 324 possibilities. Because only 16 ($= 3 + 4 + 3 + 3 + 3$) discrete levels of the attributes are under study, fewer than 16 parameters need to be estimated by the model. Thus it is technically possible to estimate the part-worth that a respondent associates with each attribute level by having that respondent evaluate as few as 16 product bundles. With the information the firm obtains from this respondent's evaluation of the small number of alternatives, it can still assess how this customer will evaluate any of the 324 pizza combinations. This is possible because the basic outputs of conjoint analysis are (1) the (imputed) relative importance that each respondent attaches to each pizza *attribute* (e.g., type of topping is three times as important as amount of cheese), and (2) each respondent's part-worth for each *level of each attribute* (e.g., on a scale of 0 to 30, a customer values veggie topping at 10 points and pepperoni topping at 30 points). Exhibit 7.3 illustrates how one adds up these part-worths to compute any respondent's (or customer segment's) valuation of any possible pizza.

From the part-worths for the respondent shown in Exhibit 7.3, we can compose the ideal pizza (the pizza with the highest preference) for this respondent: a thick crust pizza with pepperoni topping, 6 oz of mozzarella, priced at $7.99, giving a utility score of 100. This respondent's lowest rated pizza would be a pan pizza with pineapple topping, 2 oz of Romano cheese, priced at $9.99, giving a

Crust (15 points)	Amount of cheese (10 points)
Pan (0)	2 oz (0)
Thin (10)	4 oz (8)
Thick (15)	6 oz (10)

Topping (30 points)	Price (35 points)
Pineapple (0)	$9.99 (0)
Veggie (10)	$8.99 (20)
Sausage (25)	$7.99 (35)
Pepperoni (30)	

Types of cheese (10 points)
Romano (0)
Mixed cheese (3)
Mozzarella (10)

Ratings of three alternative pizzas for this customer based on the part-worth function

Aloha Special	Meat-Lover's Treat	Veggie Delite
Pan (0)	Thick (15)	Thin (10)
Pineapple (0)	Pepperoni (30)	Veggie (10)
Mozzarella (10)	Mixed cheese (3)	Romano (0)
4 oz (8)	6 oz (10)	2 oz (0)
$8.99 (20)	$9.99 (0)	$7.99 (35)
Utility = 38	Utility = 58	Utility = 55

Among these three pizzas, this customer most prefers the Meat-Lover's Treat.

EXHIBIT 7.3
An example of conjoint analysis showing one customer's part-worth function for frozen pizza. The numbers in parentheses are the part-worths. For this customer the topping attribute is worth 30 points (on a scale of 0 to 100), and the crust attribute is worth half as much at 15 points. Within the topping attribute, going from a pineapple topping to a veggie topping is worth 10 points and going from veggie to sausage is worth an incremental 15 points.

utility score of 0. The other 322 possible pizzas will have scores between 0 and 100. For example, the Aloha Special has a score of 38, the Veggie Delite has a score of 55, and the Meat-Lover's Treat has a score of 58. Note also that this respondent prefers pepperoni (30) to veggie (10) by 20 points (30 − 10); this respondent also prefers paying $8.99 to paying $9.99 by the same 20-point difference, implying that pepperoni topping is worth an incremental $1 to this respondent ($9.99 − $8.99) as compared with a veggie topping.

Although the firm could produce a pizza that will have a utility score of 100 for this customer, it is far from clear that doing so would be profitable. First, all the pizzas do not cost the same to produce, which means that the firm must balance customer preferences for attributes, including price, with costs to determine which pizza would generate the most profit. Second, all customers do not have preferences identical to those of the respondent shown in Exhibit 7.3. Within a target segment, customers will vary in their preferences. Although most customers in the target segment may prefer to pay the lowest price and prefer pepperoni topping, they may differ in their preferences for the type and amount of cheese and the type of crust. Thus no single pizza would be the best for everyone in the target segment. Therefore the firm might seek to develop several pizzas that are among the more preferred options for a large number of customers in a segment, a more complicated problem than simply putting together a pizza with the highest average utility score for the target segment.

As suggested by the preceding example, conjoint analysis is particularly useful for designing products that maximize measured utilities for customers in a target segment. Using the resulting information the firm can modify existing products and services and develop new products that appeal maximally to customers. Early applications of conjoint analysis were of this type. However, increasingly firms are using conjoint analysis for making strategy decisions, such as selecting market segments for which a given product delivers high utility, for planning competitive strategy, and for analyzing pricing policies (Wittink and Cattin 1989).

Conjoint analysis procedure

Conjoint analysis studies typically comprise three stages. In the first stage we design the study. In the second stage we obtain data from a sample of respondents from the target segment. In the third stage we use the data to set up simulations to explore the impact of alternative decision options (Exhibit 7.4).

Stage 1: Designing the conjoint study

Step 1.1: Select attributes relevant to the product or service category. One way to identify these attributes is by conducting a focus group study of target customers (e.g., design engineers in an industrial marketing context). Another possibility is to ask the new product development team what features and benefits it is considering. Yet another approach is to use secondary data, such as *Consumer Reports*, to identify an appropriate set of attributes. Studies that cover more than six attributes may become unwieldy, although studies have been conducted with a large number of attributes. Wind et al. (1989) describe the design of the Courtyard by Marriott hotel using a conjoint study with 50 attributes.

Step 1.2: Select the levels of each attribute to be used in the study. We can start by asking the new product development team what specific design options it is considering.

Stage 1—Designing the conjoint study:
      Step 1.1: Select attributes relevant to the product or service category.
      Step 1.2: Select levels for each attribute.
      Step 1.3: Develop the product bundles to be evaluated.
Stage 2—Obtaining data from a sample of respondents:
      Step 2.1 Design a data-collection procedure.
      Step 2.2 Select a computation method for obtaining part-worth functions.
Stage 3 —Evaluating product design options:
      Step 3.1 Segment customers based on their part-worth functions.
      Step 3.2 Design market simulations.
      Step 3.3 Select choice rule.

EXHIBIT 7.4
Steps in designing and executing a conjoint study.

In selecting the levels of attributes, we must keep in mind several conflicting considerations:

- To improve the realism of the conjoint study, we should choose attribute levels that cover a range similar to that actually observed in existing products. We should include both the highest prevalent attribute level (e.g., highest mpg among the competing cars) and the lowest prevalent level (e.g., lowest tensile strength).
- We should include as few attributes and attribute levels as possible to simplify the respondents' evaluation task. Typically studies use between two and five levels for each attribute.
- To avoid biasing the estimated importance of any attribute, we should include roughly the same number of levels for each attribute. Otherwise, as shown by Wittink, Krishnamurthi, and Nutter (1982), some attributes may turn out to be more important simply because respondents have more levels (options) to evaluate for those attributes. We can equalize the number of levels in attributes by redefining attributes, combining two or more attributes, or breaking up an attribute into two or more attributes.

To summarize, we should use a range of attribute levels that are consistent with those observed in the marketplace and we should try to have roughly the same number of levels for each attribute, both to simplify the evaluation task for the respondents and to avoid misleading results on the importance of attributes.

Step 1.3: Develop the product bundles to be evaluated. Here we define a product as a combination of attribute levels. As in the frozen pizza example, it is unreasonable to expect a respondent to evaluate every possible combination. We must choose the product bundles (also called profiles) presented to the respondents carefully. Instead of full-factorial designs (i.e., including all possible combinations of attribute levels), we use fractional-factorial designs to reduce the number of products we ask respondents to evaluate. A common approach is to select orthogonal combinations of attribute levels to reduce the number of product bundles respondents must evaluate and, at the same time, to permit one to measure the independent contribution of each attribute to the utility function. Exhibit 7.5 presents a set of products conforming to an orthogonal design for the pizza example. We could also use nonorthogonal (or more saturated) designs to incorporate interactions between attributes. For example, if we believe that customer utility for price of a pizza depends on the type of topping, we should consider more complex designs. Green (1974) describes several such designs.

In some circumstances orthogonal designs can result in unrealistic products, such as when respondents perceive some of the attributes used in the study to be correlated—automobile horsepower (hp) and gas mileage (mpg) typically have a high negative correlation, but orthogonal designs could result in hypothetical products that combine high hp with unrealistically high levels of mpg. If a product is unrealistic in an orthogonal combination, there are several possible remedies: (1) We can combine the attributes and develop a new set of levels for the combined attribute. (For example, hp and mpg might be combined into a "performance" attribute with high performance associated with high hp and low mpg, and low performance associated with low hp and high mpg.) (2) We can replace unrealistic products by substituting other combinations (perhaps generated randomly, but not duplicating the retained combinations). While this approach compromises orthogonality, it will rarely affect the estimated utility functions significantly if we replace only a few bundles (say, less than 5 percent). (3) We can select other orthogonal combinations (although this remedy requires special expertise).

To minimize respondent fatigue we recommend a maximum of 25 product bundles (preferably 16 or fewer) for evaluation. When using traditional assessment procedures

Product bundle #	Crust	Topping	Type of cheese	Amount of cheese	Price	Example preference score
1	Pan	Pineapple	Romano	2 oz.	$9.99	0
2	Thin	Pineapple	Mixed	6 oz.	$8.99	43
3	Thick	Pineapple	Mozzarella	4 oz.	$8.99	53
4	Thin	Pineapple	Mixed	4 oz.	$7.99	56
5	Pan	Veggie	Mixed	4 oz.	$8.99	41
6	Thin	Veggie	Romano	4 oz.	$7.99	63
7	Thick	Veggie	Mixed	6 oz.	$9.99	38
8	Thin	Veggie	Mozzarella	2 oz.	$8.99	53
9	Thick	Pepperoni	Mozzarella	6 oz.	$7.99	68
10	Thin	Pepperoni	Mixed	2 oz.	$8.99	46
11	Pan	Pepperoni	Romano	4 oz.	$8.99	80
12	Thin	Pepperoni	Mixed	4 oz.	$9.99	58
13	Pan	Sausage	Mixed	4 oz.	$8.99	61
14	Thin	Sausage	Mozzarella	4 oz.	$9.99	57
15	Thick	Sausage	Mixed	2 oz.	$7.99	83
16	Thin	Sausage	Romano	6 oz.	$8.99	70

Notes:
Preference scores could be rank orders (1 to 16), relative preference ratings (on a scale of 1 to 100), or allocation of a constant sum (e.g., 100 points) across the 16 bundles.

We can compute the relative utility of an attribute level by averaging the preference scores for the bundles in which that level occurs. For example, to compute the preference score for pan crust, compute the average of the scores of bundles 1, 5, 11, and 13, which gives a value of 45.5. Likewise, the average preference score for thick crust is 60.5, and for thin crust is 55.5. Thus, the customer gets an incremental utility of 15 points from having thick crust instead of pan crust and 5 incremental utility points from thick crust instead of thin crust. (For purposes of illustration, we made these relative utilities the same as those shown in Exhibit 7.3. As an exercise, compute the relative utilities for the other attribute levels.)

EXHIBIT 7.5
An example showing 16 product bundles that form an orthogonal design for the frozen pizza study.

we should try to have about twice the number of products for evaluation as there are parameters to be estimated by the model.

The software accompanying this book uses a more flexible interactive utility assessment procedure than traditional methods, so that the number of products evaluated can be about 25 to 50 percent more than the number of parameters to be estimated. The number of independent parameters to be estimated is equal to

$$\left\{ \sum_{i=1}^{N} (n_i - 1) \right\} - 1,$$

where N is the number of attributes and n_i is the number of levels of attribute i. For each product attribute we can arbitrarily set the lowest utility value (say, equal to 0). We can also arbitrarily set the maximum total utility from any product (say, equal to 100). For the frozen pizza example the number of parameters estimated is equal to 10.

Stage 2: Obtaining data from a sample of respondents

Step 2.1: Design a data-collection procedure. Once we design the study, the next stage is to obtain evaluations of the selected product bundles from a representative sample of respondents in the target segment(s). We can present the products verbally, pictorially, or physically (using prototypes). Pictures have some advantages. They make the task more interesting and they are superior to verbal descriptions for some products (e.g., a picture of a vacation property is better than a description). Physical prototypes, while desirable, are expensive, and they are not often used in conjoint studies. Once we decide on the presentation mode, there are a number of ways to obtain data from customers:

- *Pairwise evaluations of product bundles*: One way to obtain respondent evaluations of products is to present the products two at a time and ask the respondent to allocate 100 points between the two. This task is simple, but the respondent may have to make many pairwise comparisons. For example, if there are 16 product bundles, the respondent has to evaluate 120 pairs ($(16 \times 15)/2$), a tedious and burdensome task. (Hauser and Shugan (1980) provide further details of this approach.) Exhibit 7.6 shows a pairwise comparison for two of the alternatives from Exhibit 7.5.
- *Rank ordering product bundles*: In this method the respondent ranks (or sorts) the products presented, with the most preferred having rank 1 and the least preferred having a rank equal to the number of products presented. If necessary, the respondent can first sort the products into piles of similarly valued products, then sort within each pile, and then finally sort the entire set. We can then use special-purpose programs such as MONANOVA (monotonic analysis of variance) or LINMAP to transform the ordinal rank order data into a part-worth function that recovers the rank orders as closely as possible. (Ordinary regression analysis often gives satisfactory results even with rank-ordered data.)
- *Evaluating products on a rating scale*: In this method the respondent evaluates each product on a rating scale (e.g., on a scale of 0 to 100), with larger numbers indicating greater preference. Alternatively and more difficult, the respondents can allocate a constant sum (say 100 points) across the products presented to them. The assumption is that respondents are able to indicate how much more they prefer one product bundle to others. The advantage of this type of measurement is that we can use ordinary least squares (OLS) regression analysis with dummy variables to compute part-worth functions. Given the widespread availability of regression analysis packages, this approach is the most convenient for managers, and it is the approach used in the software accompanying this book. The last column of Exhibit 7.5 lists sample ratings for a customer in the frozen pizza study.

Step 2.2: Select a computation method for obtaining part-worth functions. Regardless of which of the foregoing methods we choose, respondents may find the evaluation

Product 1		Product 10
Pan pizza		Thin crust
Pineapple	**OR**	Pepperoni
Romano		Mixed cheese
2 oz. cheese		2 oz. cheese
$9.99		$8.99

Strongly
Prefer   1—2—3—4—5—6—7—8—9
Product 1

Strongly
Prefer
Product 10

EXHIBIT 7.6
Example of pairwise comparison for products 1 and 10 from Exhibit 7.5.

task difficult if they have to evaluate many product bundles. Several approaches are available to simplify the task:

- *The hybrid conjoint model*: Here we first obtain "self-explicated" preferences, and then we combine them with a reduced set of data obtained by the traditional methods. As the name suggests the hybrid model combines two methods. In the self-explication phase (Green and Srinivasan 1990) the customer first evaluates the levels of each attribute separately on a desirability scale (say 0 to 10, with the least desirable level having a value of 0 and the most desirable 10). The respondent is then asked to allocate points (say 100) across the attributes to reflect the relative importance of each attribute. We then obtain the initial part-worths for the attribute levels by multiplying the importance weights and the respective attribute-level desirability scores. We augment the self-explicated data with data obtained from each respondent on a smaller set of complete product bundles. Finally we compute the adjusted part-worth functions for each respondent. See Green (1984) for further details.

- *Adaptive conjoint analysis*: Another way to reduce respondent burden is adaptive conjoint analysis, which uses a computer program to obtain data from respondents interactively. The respondent first puts the attributes in rough order of importance (a simpler version of self-explication) and then refines the trade-offs between the more important attributes using pairwise comparisons. The program selects the pairs of product bundles to maximize the information content of the responses, given the respondent's previous responses. See Johnson (1987) for further details.

- *Bridging designs*: Yet another way to handle a large number of attributes is to use sophisticated designs, asking respondents to evaluate the product bundles only on a subset of attributes and on "bridging" attributes that are common across several respondents. This distributes the burden of evaluating a complete set of product bundles across several respondents. (For a discussion of these approaches, see Green and Srinivasan (1978, 1990).)

The software accompanying this book draws on ideas used in hybrid conjoint and adaptive conjoint analysis to simplify the evaluation task. The respondent first provides self-explicated preferences. The program then orders the orthogonal set of product bundles according to decreasing preference as determined from the self-explicated ratings. (The study designer can also develop customized nonorthogonal designs externally and import them into the software.) Next the customer rates each product on a scale of 0 to 100. An attractive feature of this software is that it allows respondents to view a graph of their part-worth function and fine-tune the function directly to more closely reflect their preferences. This is an interactive and iterative process, combining self-explication, ratings, and part-worth refinements.

Our software uses dummy variable regression to compute the part-worth function separately for each respondent, from the ratings the respondents provided:

$$R_{ij} = \sum_{k=1}^{K} \sum_{m=1}^{M_k} a_{ikm} x_{jkm} + \varepsilon_{ij}, \tag{7.1}$$

where

j = a particular product or concept included in the study design;

R_{ij} = the ratings provided by respondent i for product j;

a_{ikm} = part-worth associated with the mth level ($m = 1, 2, 3, \ldots, M_k$) of the kth attribute;

M_k =   number of levels of attribute k;

K =   number of attributes;

x_{jkm} =   dummy variables that take on the value 1 if the mth level of the kth attribute is present in product j and the value 0 otherwise; and

ε_{ij} =   error terms, assumed to be normal distribution with zero mean and variance equal to σ^2 for all i and j.

The a_{ikm}'s obtained from regression are rescaled so that the least preferred level of each attribute is set to 0 and the maximum preferred product combination is set to 100, producing results that are more easily interpreted. Letting $\tilde{a}_{ikm}$'s denote the estimated (rescaled) part-worths, the utility u_{ij} of a product j to customer i is equal to

$$u_{ij} = \sum_{k=1}^{K} \sum_{m=1}^{M_k} \tilde{a}_{ikm} x_{jkm}. \tag{7.2}$$

Note that product j can be any product that can be designed using the attributes and levels in the study, including those that were not included in the estimation of the part-worths in Eq. (7.1).

Stage 3: Evaluating product design options

Step 3.1: Segment customers based on their part-worth functions. At this stage we can segment the market by grouping customers who have similar part-worth functions. In the frozen pizza example we might find a segment of customers who prefer thin crust pizza and another segment of customers who prefer pan pizza, with preferences on the other attributes being roughly similar for the two segments. Furthermore, we may find that these two segments differ systematically in terms of their demographic characteristics (e.g., age) and media habits (e.g., watching MTV). A simple way to identify such segments is through traditional cluster analysis (Chapter 3). There are also more sophisticated models, such as clusterwise regression, that can simultaneously segment customers and estimate a common utility function for each segment.

Step 3.2: Design market simulations. A major reason for the wide use of conjoint analysis is that once part-worths ($\tilde{a}_{ikm}$'s) are estimated from a representative sample of respondents, it is easy to assess the likely success of a new product concept under various simulated market conditions. We might ask: What market share would a proposed new product be expected to achieve in a market with several specific existing competitors? To answer this question we first specify all existing products as combinations of levels of the set of attributes under study. If more than one competing product has identical attribute levels, we need to include only one representative in the simulation.

Step 3.3: Select choice rule. To complete the simulation design we must specify a choice rule to transform part-worths into the product choices that customers are most likely to make. The three most common choice rules are maximum utility, share of utility, and logit, all of which are options in the software:

- *Maximum utility rule*: Under this rule we assume that each customer chooses from the available alternatives the product that provides the highest utility value, including a new product concept under consideration. This choice rule is most appropriate for high-involvement purchases such as cars, videorecorders, equipment, and other durables that customers purchase infrequently.

We can compute the market share for a product by counting the number of customers for whom that product offers the highest utility and dividing this figure by the number of customers in the study. In computing overall market shares it may sometimes be necessary to weight each customer's probability of purchasing each alternative by the relative volume of purchases that the customer makes in the product category:

$$m_j = \frac{\sum_{i=1}^{I} w_i p_{ij}}{\sum_{j=1}^{J} \sum_{i=1}^{I} w_i p_{ij}}, \tag{7.3}$$

where

I = number of customers participating in the study;

J = the number of product alternatives available for the customer to choose from, including the new product concept;

m_j = market share of product j;

w_i = the relative volume of purchases made by customer i, with the average volume across all customers indexed to the value 1; and

p_{ij} = proportion of purchases that customer i makes of product j (or equivalently, the probability that customer i will choose product j on a single purchase occasion).

■ *Share of utility*: This rule is based on the notion that the higher the utility of a product to a customer, the greater the probability that he or she will choose that product. Thus each product gets a share of a customer's purchases in proportion to its share of the customer's preferences:

$$p_{ij} = \frac{u_{ij}}{\sum_j u_{ij}} \quad \text{for } j \text{ in the set of products } J, \tag{7.4}$$

where u_{ij} is the estimated utility of product j to customer i.

We then obtain the market share for product i by averaging p_{ij} across customers (weighting as in Eq. (7.3) if necessary). This choice rule is particularly relevant for low-involvement, frequently purchased products, such as consumer packaged goods.

This choice rule is widely applied in conjoint studies and often provides good estimates of market shares. However, as Luce (1959) notes, this rule requires that utilities be expressed as ratio-scaled numbers, such as those obtained from constant-sum scales where the customer allocates a fixed number of points (say 100) among alternatives. Unfortunately, data from most conjoint studies do not satisfy this requirement.

■ *Logit choice rule*: This rule is similar to the share-of-utility rule, except that the underlying theoretical rationale is different. To apply the share-of-utility model we assume that the utility functions are basically accurate—but an element of randomness occurs in translating utilities into choice. In applying the logit choice rule we assume that the computed utility values are mean realizations of a random process, so that the brand with the maximum utility varies randomly, say from one purchase situation to the next. The choice rule then gives the proportion of times that product j will have the maximum utility:

$$p_{ij} = \frac{e^{u_{ij}}}{\sum_j e^{u_{ij}}} \quad \text{for } j \text{ in the set of products } J. \tag{7.5}$$

Both the share-of-utility and the traditional logit rules share a questionable property known as IIA (independence from irrelevant alternatives). The choice probabilities from any subset of alternatives depend only on the alternatives included in the set and are independent of any alternatives not included. This property implies that if, for example, you prefer light beers to regular beers, then adding a new regular beer (an irrelevant alternative) to your choice set would nevertheless lower your probability of choosing a light beer, a counterintuitive result.

One way to choose among these three rules is this: First compute the predicted market shares of just the existing products with each rule. Then use the choice rule that produces market shares that are closest (in the sense of least squares) to the actual market shares of these products (this assumes that we are using a representative sample of customers for the study).

Contexts best suited for conjoint analysis

Conjoint analysis is one of the most widely used modeling techniques in marketing, with over 25 years of usage. Based on a survey, Wittink and Cattin (1989) determined that it is most commonly used for new product identification, competitive analysis, pricing, market segmentation, and product positioning. In a survey of industrial firms Anderson, Jain, and Chintagunta (1993) report that conjoint analysis is used for demand forecasting and determining price, product positioning, and new investment decisions. They also report that 85 percent of the firms classified their use of conjoint analysis as being successful for assessing how customers value products.

Conjoint analysis is a sophisticated method that has to be applied with care. The following checklist will help one to decide whether conjoint analysis is suitable in a decision context:

1. In designing the product, we must make trade-offs between various attributes and benefits offered to customers.
2. We can decompose the product or service category into basic attributes that managers can act on and that are meaningful to customers.
3. The existing products are well described as combinations of attribute levels, and new product alternatives can be synthesized from those basic attribute levels.
4. It is possible to describe the product bundles realistically, either verbally or pictorially. (Otherwise, we should consider using actual product formulations for evaluations.)

There are several limitations of the method. As indicated by Eq. (7.2), a customer's overall utility for a product is equal to the sum of the utilities of the component parts. A highly valued option on one attribute can compensate for an unattractive option on another attribute. Thus a low price can compensate for the fact that a pizza does not have pepperoni topping (Exhibit 7.3). However, in many situations customer choices are noncompensatory—

for example, no matter how good a car is on other attributes, you may not want one with a stick-shift transmission. To the extent that a problem context includes noncompensatory processes, conjoint analysis can give misleading conclusions.

The validity of the study also depends on the completeness of the set of attributes. However, including too many attributes increases respondent fatigue, leading to inaccurate responses. A typical commercial application uses about 16 product bundles, which allows for about five attributes with three or four levels each.

Finally, the market-share simulation assumes that customers consider all available alternatives when choosing among them. Again, customers may idiosyncratically eliminate some alternatives from consideration (e.g., ignore all cars with stick-shift transmissions). Some conjoint analysis techniques allow for this possibility (e.g., Jedidi, Kohli, and DeSarbo 1996).

FORECASTING THE SALES OF NEW PRODUCTS

Overview of the Bass model

The Bass model for forecasting first purchase has had a long history in marketing. It is most appropriate for forecasting sales of an innovation (more generally, a new product) for which no closely competing alternatives exist in the marketplace. Managers need such forecasts for new technologies or major product innovations before investing significant resources in them.

The Bass model offers a good starting point for forecasting the long-term sales pattern of new technologies and new durable products under two types of conditions: (1) the firm has recently introduced the product or technology and has observed its sales for a few time periods; or (2) the firm has not yet introduced the product or technology, but it is similar in some way to existing products or technologies whose sales history is known. The model attempts to predict how many customers will eventually adopt the new product and when they will adopt. The question of *when* is important, because answers to this question guide the firm in its deployment of resources in marketing the innovation.

EXAMPLE

While the Windows 95 operating system, or its successors, will eventually replace earlier Windows versions in home-based PCs, the timing of that replacement or substitution is critical to Microsoft and other stakeholders in the PC industry. Microsoft is also developing an industrial strength version of its operating system called Windows NT; the speed with which customers adopt NT and their expectations about its development will also influence how rapidly Windows 95 sells and how many units it will eventually sell. Microsoft needs this information to plan its production and distribution logistics, to make financial forecasts, and to inform their channel members and computer hardware and software developers (Intel, Gateway, Lotus, etc.) whose decisions and operations depend on forecasts of the timing and penetration of Windows 95.

Exhibit 7.7 shows the "sales" trajectories for a number of innovations, including several innovative scientific articles. Some start with explosive growth, but sales fall off almost from the start. Others exhibit a "sleeper" pattern (S-shaped) where sales start out slow, then pick up momentum, and eventually decline. Surprisingly, a simple and elegant model (Bass 1969) with just three easily interpretable parameters can represent all these patterns quite well.

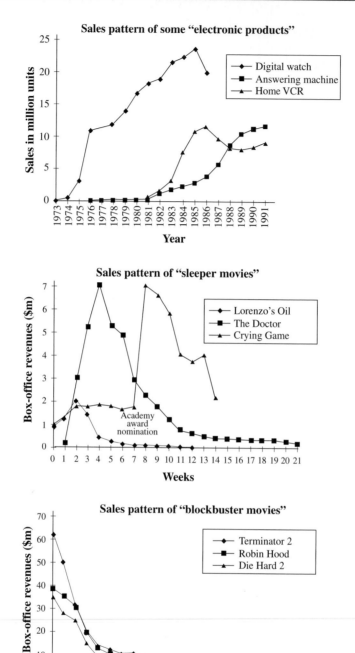

EXHIBIT 7.7
These graphs show the pattern of total sales (cumulative sales) for several products in different product categories.

Technical description of the Bass model

Suppose that the (cumulative) probability that someone in the target segment will adopt the innovation by time t is given by a nondecreasing continuous function $F(t)$, where $F(t)$

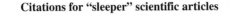

Citations for "sleeper" scientific articles

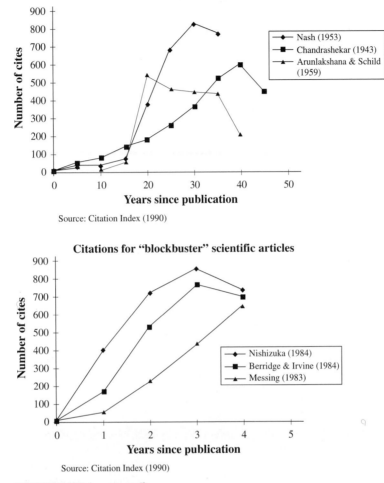

Source: Citation Index (1990)

Citations for "blockbuster" scientific articles

Source: Citation Index (1990)

EXHIBIT 7.7 (continued)

approaches 1 (certain adoption) as t gets large. Such a function is depicted in Exhibit 7.8(a), and it suggests that an individual in the target segment will eventually adopt the innovation. The derivative of $F(t)$ is the probability density function, $f(t)$ (Exhibit 7.8b), which indicates the rate at which the probability of adoption is changing at time t. To estimate the unknown function $F(t)$ we specify the conditional likelihood $L(t)$ that a customer will adopt the innovation at exactly time t since introduction, given that the customer has not adopted before that time. Using the foregoing definition of $F(t)$ and $f(t)$, we can write $L(t)$ as (via Bayes's rule)

$$L(t) = \frac{f(t)}{1 - F(t)} \tag{7.6}$$

Bass (1969) proposed that $L(t)$ be defined to be equal to

$$L(t) = p + \frac{q}{N} N(t), \tag{7.7}$$

where

$N(t)$ = the number of customers who have already adopted the innovation by time t;

$\overline{N}$ = a parameter representing the total number of customers in the adopting target segment, all of whom will eventually adopt the product;

p = coefficient of innovation (or coefficient of external influence); and

q = coefficient of imitation (or coefficient of internal influence).

Equation (7.7) suggests that the *likelihood* that a customer in the target segment will adopt at exactly time t is the sum of two components. The first component (p) refers to a constant propensity to adopt that is independent of how many other customers have adopted the innovation before time t. The second component in Eq. (7.7) $[(q/\overline{N})N(t)]$ is proportional to the number of customers who have already adopted the innovation by time t and represents the extent of favorable interactions between the innovators and the other adopters of the product (imitators).

Equating Eqs. (7.6) and (7.7), we get

$$f(t) = \left[p + \frac{q}{\overline{N}} N(t) \right] [1 - F(t)]. \tag{7.8}$$

Noting that $N(t) = \overline{N}F(t)$ and defining the number of customers adopting at exactly time t as $n(t) (= \overline{N}f(t))$, we get (after some algebraic manipulations) the following basic equation for predicting the sales of the product at time t:

$$n(t) = p\overline{N} + (q - p)N(t) - \frac{q}{\overline{N}} [N(t)]^2. \tag{7.9}$$

If $q > p$, then imitation effects dominate the innovation effects and the plot of $n(t)$ against time (t) will have an inverted U shape. This is likely to be the case for new movies, new records, or such new technologies as cellular radios. On the other hand, if $q < p$, then innovation effects will dominate and the highest sales will occur at introduction and sales will decline in every period after that (e.g., blockbuster movies). Furthermore, the lower the value of p, the longer it takes to realize sales growth for the innovation. When both p and q are large, product sales take off rapidly and fall off quickly after reaching a maximum. By varying p and q, we can capture all the patterns shown in Exhibit 7.7 reasonably well.

Generalized Bass model: Bass, Krishnan, and Jain (1994) propose a general form of Eq. (7.8) that incorporates the effects of marketing-mix variables on the likelihood of adoption:

$$f(t) = \left[p + \frac{q}{\overline{N}} N(t) \right] [1 - F(t)] x(t), \tag{7.10}$$

where $x(t)$ is a function of marketing-mix variables in time period t (e.g., advertising and price).

Equation (7.10) implies that by increasing marketing effort, a firm can increase the likelihood of adoption of the innovation—that is, marketing effort speeds up the rate of

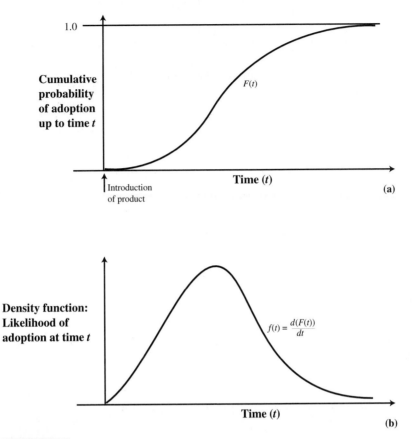

EXHIBIT 7.8
Graphical representation of the probability of a customer's adoption of a new product over time; (a) shows the probability that a customer in the target segment will adopt the product before time *t*, and (b) shows the instantaneous likelihood that a customer will adopt the product at exactly time *t*.

diffusion of the innovation in the population. In the software accompanying the book, marketing effort is measured relative to a base level indexed to 1.0. Thus if advertising at time t is double the base level, $x(t)$ will be equal 2.0.

Estimating the Bass model parameters: There are several methods to estimate the parameters of the Bass model. These methods can be classified based on whether they rely on historical sales data or judgment for calibrating the model. Linear and nonlinear regression can be used if we have historical sales data for the new product for a few periods (years). Judgmental methods include using analogies or conducting surveys.

Linear regression: Discretize the model in Eq. (7.9) by replacing continuous time t by discrete time periods, where t is the current period, $t + 1$ is the next period, and so on. We can then estimate the parameters of the following linear function (a, b, and c) using ordinary least squares regression:

$$n(t) = a + bN(t - 1) + cN^2(t - 1), \tag{7.11}$$

where

$n(t)$ = Sales in period t and $N(t)$ = cumulative sales to period t.

We can then calculate the Bass model parameters:

$$\bar{N} = \frac{-b - \sqrt{b^2 - 4ac}}{2c} \ ;$$

$$p = \frac{a}{\bar{N}} \ ; \text{ and}$$

$$q = p + b.$$

We need sales data for at least three periods to estimate the model. To be consistent with the model, $\bar{N} > 0$, $b \geq 0$, and $c < 0$.

Nonlinear regression: By discretizing the model in equation (7.8) and multiplying both sides by $\bar{N}$ we get:

$$n(t) = \left[p + \frac{q}{\bar{N}} N(t-1) \right] \left[\bar{N} - N(t-1) \right]. \tag{7.12}$$

Given at least four observations of $N(t)$ we can use nonlinear regression to select parameter values $(\bar{N}, p, q)$ to minimize the sum of squared errors. This is the approach used in the Bass model software implemented in this book, and for obtaining the parameter estimates summarized in Exhibit 7.9. An important advantage of this specification is that users need not know *when* the product was introduced into the market. They only need to know the cumulative sales of the product for estimation periods.

Using analogous products: This approach has proved very useful in practice. First identify previous innovations that are analogous to the current product. We can then determine p and q from the sales trajectories of these previous innovations. By combining this with $\bar{N}$ estimated for the current innovation (or obtained using managerial judgment) we can forecast the sales pattern for the new product. The advantage of this approach is that instead of directly guessing the sales of a new product, managers guess the inputs to a well-established model, and the model provides a structure for incorporating these inputs in generating forecasts.

We must be careful in how we choose analogous products. Analogies based on similarities in expected market behavior work better than analogies based on product similarities. For example, in forecasting the sales path of digital cameras, it may be better to use CD-ROM drive as an analog rather than 35mm SLR camera. Thomas (1985) recommends that in selecting analogs we consider similarities along five bases: environmental context (e.g., socioeconomic and regulatory environment), market structure (e.g., barriers to entry, number and type of competitors), buyer behavior (buying situation, choice attributes), marketing-mix strategies of the firm, and characteristics of the innovation (e.g., relative advantage over existing products and product complexity). If necessary, we can consider multiple analogs and take the (weighted) average of their p and q values.

It took 27 years to sell 1 million telephones, 11 years for that many TV sets, 6 years for as many VCRs, 5 years for CDs, and 2 years for Hewlett Packard's OfficeJet all-in-one printer-fax-copier-scanner. Exhibit 7.9 provides a summary of parameter estimates that have been reported for various innovations (we have included these estimates within the software to help in selecting analogs).

Product/Technology	Period of Analysis	p	q	$\bar{N}$
Agricultural				
Tractors (units)	1920–1964	.000	.142	5,144.0
Hybrid corn	1926–1941	.000	.797	100.0
Artificial insemination	1942–1959	.028	.307	73.2
Bale hay	1942–1959	.013	.455	92.2
Medical equipment				
Ultrasound imaging	1964–1978	.000	.534	85.8
Mammography	1964–1978	.000	.729	57.1
CT scanners (50–99 beds)	1979–1993	.036	.375	57.5
CT scanners (>100 beds)	1973–1993	.028	.292	94.5
Production technology				
Oxygen steel furnace (USA)	1954–1980	.000	.503	62.9
Oxygen steel furnace (France)	1960–1980	.013	.374	85.2
Oxygen steel furnace (Japan)	1958–1975	.044	.325	85.3
Steam (vs. sail) merchant ships (UK)	1810–1965	.006	.259	86.7
Plastic milk containers (1 gallon)	1963–1987	.021	.245	101.5
Plastic milk containers (half gallon)	1963–1987	.000	.280	25.5
Stores with retail scanners (FRG, units)	1980–1993	.001	.605	16,702.0
Stores with retail scanners (Denmark, units)	1980–1993	.076	.540	2,061.0
Electrical appliances				
Room air conditioning	1949–1979	.006	.185	60.5
Bed cover	1948–1979	.008	.130	72.2
Blender	1948–1979	.000	.260	54.5
Can opener	1960–1979	.050	.126	68.0
Electric coffee maker	1954–1979	.056	.000	127.6
Clothes dryer	1948–1979	.009	.143	70.1
Clothes washer	1922–1979	.000	.111	96.4
Coffee maker ADC	1973–1979	.077	1.106	32.2
Curling iron	1973–1979	.101	.762	29.9
Dishwasher	1948–1979	.000	.213	47.7
Disposer	1948–1979	.000	.179	50.4
Fondue	1971–1979	.166	.440	4.6
Freezer	1948–1979	.013	.000	129.7
Frypan	1956–1979	.142	.000	65.6
Hair dryer	1971–1979	.055	.399	51.6
Hot plates	1931–1979	.056	.000	26.3
Microwave oven	1971–1990	.002	.357	91.6
Mixer	1948–1979	.000	.134	97.7
Range	1924–1979	.004	.065	63.6
Range, built-in	1956–1979	.038	.014	32.6
Refrigerator	1925–1979	.017	.188	101.1
Slow cooker	1973–1979	.000	1.152	34.4
Steam iron	1949–1979	.033	.116	102.1
Toaster	1922–1979	.030	.000	123.8
Vacuum cleaner	1922–1979	.000	.066	120.3
Consumer electronics				
Cable television	1980–1994	.100	.060	68.0
Calculators	1972–1979	.145	.495	101.1
CD player	1987–1992	.157	.000	68.8
Home PC (units)	1981–1988	.121	.281	25.8
Telephone answering device	1987–1992	.259	.041	53.6
Television, black and white	1948–1979	.106	.235	98.1
Television, color	1964–1979	.059	.130	103.1
VCR	1980–1994	.025	.603	76.3
Average across studies, including many not listed here (Sultan et al. 1990)		0.03	0.38	

Compiled by Christophe Van den Bulte
Unless indicated, the model was estimated on penetration data collected in the USA.

EXHIBIT 7.9
Parameters of the Bass model in several product categories.

Estimating the parameters of the generalized Bass model: Bass, Krishnan, and Jain (1994) use a modified version of nonlinear regression (described above) for estimating the parameters of the generalized Bass model.

The software accompanying this book incorporates only the effects of advertising and pricing in the generalized Bass model. We can still use any of the foregoing methods for estimating p and q of the traditional Bass model. In addition the software asks managers to provide their best guesses for the advertising and pricing coefficients.

Once we determine the parameter values by estimating or by using analogs, we can put these values into a spreadsheet to develop forecasts (Exhibit 7.10). The software has built-in options for sales forecasting using estimates either from the nonlinear least squares method (if there are sufficient market data for estimation) or by directly selecting p and q from analogous products.

Extensions of the basic Bass model

The Bass model makes several key assumptions. We can relax many of these assumptions by using more sophisticated models as summarized by Mahajan, Muller, and Bass (1993). However, the basic model has been widely applied. The key assumptions and possible extensions of the Bass model follow:

- *The market potential ($\bar{N}$) remains constant*: This assumption is relaxed in models in which $\bar{N}$ is a function of price declines, uncertainty about technology performance,

Sales in each period (reported every quarter)

Quarter	Sales	Cumulative sales
0	0	0
1	160	160
4	425	1,118
8	1,234	4,678
12	1,646	11,166
16	555	15,106
20	78	15,890
24	9	15,987

Example computations (from Equation 7.9)

Sales in Quarter 1 =

$$0.01 * 16{,}000 + (0.41 - 0.01) * 0 - (0.41 / 16{,}000) * (0)^2 = 160$$

Sales in Quarter 2 =

$$0.01 * 16{,}000 + (0.41 - 0.01) * 160 - (0.41 / 16{,}000) * (160)^2 = 223.35$$

Sales in Quarter 4 =

$$0.01 * 16{,}000 + (0.41 - 0.01) * 692.9 - (0.41 / 16{,}000) * (692.9)^2 = 424.8$$

EXHIBIT 7.10
Example computations showing how to use the Bass model to forecast the sales of an innovation (here, room temperature control unit). The computations are based on the estimated values of $p = 0.1$ and $q = 0.41$, and market potential ($\bar{N}$) = 16,000 units (in thousands).

and growth of the target segment. The software includes an option to specify the growth rate of the target segment.

- *The marketing strategies supporting the innovation do not influence the adoption process*: Considerable research has been devoted to incorporating the impact of marketing variables, particularly price, advertising, and selling effort. We described the generalized Bass model, which represents one way to relax this assumption.

- *The customer decision process is binary (adopt or not adopt)*: This assumption is relaxed in several models that incorporate multistage decision processes in which the customer goes from one phase to another over time: awareness → interest → adoption → word of mouth.

- *The value of q is fixed throughout the life cycle of the innovation*: One would, however, expect interaction effects (e.g., word of mouth) to depend on adoption time, being relatively strong during the early and late stages of a product's life cycle. This assumption is relaxed in models that incorporate a time-varying imitation parameter.

- *Imitation always has a positive impact (i.e., the model allows only for interactions between innovators and noninnovators that favor the innovation)*: Several models are available that allow for both positive and negative word of mouth. When word-of-mouth effects are likely to be positive (e.g., "sleeper" movies such as *Ghost*), it may be wise to gradually ramp-up marketing expenditures, whereas when word-of-mouth effects are likely to be negative (e.g., the "mega-bomb" movie *Waterworld*), it may be better to advertise heavily initially to generate quick trials before the negative word of mouth significantly dampens sales.

- *Sales of the innovation are considered to be independent of the adoption or non-adoption of other innovations*: Many innovations depend on the adoption of related products to succeed. For example, the adoption of multimedia software depends on the adoption of more powerful PCs. Likewise such innovations as wide area networks and electronic commerce complement each other and have to be considered jointly to predict their sales. Several models are available for generating forecasts for products that are contingent on the adoption of other products.

- *There is no repeat or replacement purchase of the innovation*: There are several models that extend the Bass model to forecast purchases by both first-time buyers and by repeat buyers.

Although the basic Bass model and its enhancements have wide applicability, these models share several limitations, perhaps the most important of which being that they have been predominantly used for describing how successful innovations have diffused through the marketplace rather than for forecasting. As a result, if we consider only those innovations that have succeeded as analogs, the model would predict strong market forecasts for any new product! This type of result adds to the bias that is already present because new product managers usually make optimistic forecasts for their innovations. To overcome this bias one must evaluate the probability of the product failing. Unfortunately, we have very little information available about the sales patterns of innovations that failed.

A second limitation is that we can estimate the Bass model well from data only after making several observations of actual sales. However, by this time the firm has already made critical investment decisions. While the use of analogs can help firms make forecasts before introducing the innovation into the market, choosing a suitable analog is critical and requires careful judgment. There is clearly a need for ways to calibrate the diffusion model before product launch, perhaps using laboratory measurement methods.

In the next section we describe a very successful method for forecasting the sales of new products that is used in the packaged goods industry. It relies on laboratory measurements.

PRETEST MARKET FORECASTING

According to a Food Institute Report more than 22,000 new products were introduced in 1995 into U.S. supermarkets in the food and beverage categories alone. Over 90 percent of these were line extensions and minor modifications of existing products. Most of these products will not achieve the objectives set for them and will be withdrawn within two years of introduction. Most of the costs incurred for these new products occur after they are introduced into the market. To minimize these costs we need methods that will better forecast the sales of a new product before it is introduced into the market. We also need methods that will give firms diagnostic information so that they can identify potential problems with the product and improve its chances of success before introducing it.

Several successful pretest forecasting models have been developed and widely used in the last 20 years, primarily in the packaged goods industry. Models such as NEWS, TRACKER, SPRINTER, BASES, ASSESSOR, and LTM are available commercially. Shocker and Hall (1986) provide an overview of several of these models and summarize the similarities and differences among them. Here we describe of the ASSESSOR model, which is similar to the other models in its underlying concepts and features, and the details of this model are available publicly. The following description of the model is based on Silk and Urban (1978) and Urban (1993).

Pretest market forecasting and analysis occur after the product and packaging are available (at least in trial quantities), advertising copy is ready, and the firm has formulated a preliminary plan for the marketing-mix elements such as the price, channels of distribution, and the marketing budget. Given these inputs ASSESSOR is intended to

1. Predict the new product's long-term market share and sales volume over time
2. Estimate the sources of the new product's share—that is, whether it draws its market share from competitors' brands or from other products of the same firm ("cannibalization")
3. Generate diagnostic information to improve the product, the advertising copy, and other launch materials
4. Permit rough evaluation of alternative marketing plans, including different prices, package designs, and the like

Overview of the ASSESSOR model

Exhibits 7.11 and 7.12 summarize the overall structure of the model and the measurement approach for calibrating the model. ASSESSOR consists of two models: a preference model and a trial-repeat model. If these two models provide similar forecasts, it strengthens our confidence in the forecasts. If they provide very different forecasts, an analysis of the sources of discrepancies should provide us with useful diagnostic information.

The laboratory phase of the study is conducted in a testing facility (e.g., a room in a mall or a specially equipped trailer) located in the immediate vicinity of a shopping center. The participants are about 300 individuals who have been screened to be relevant for the study and to be representative of the target segment. The respondents are given about $10 each for participating.

Upon arriving at the testing facility the participants fill in a self-administered questionnaire regarding their "consideration set" (i.e., those brands that they are aware of and would consider buying in the category), the brands that they have purchased in the category in the immediate past, and their preferences for the major products (competing brands) within the consideration set. The participants then watch five or six commercials, one for each product including the new product. To avoid systematic position effects the researchers rotate the order in which the participants see the commercials.

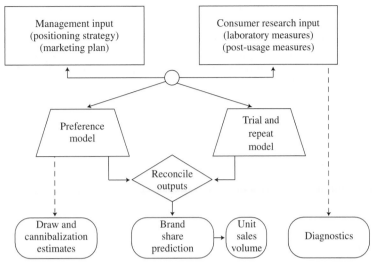

EXHIBIT 7.11
Overview of ASSESSOR modeling sequence. The model uses managerial judgment and consumer research data to make sales forecasts (brand share and sales volume) and offer diagnostics (e.g., draw and cannibalization estimates and reasons for purchase of new product). *Source*: Silk and Urban 1978, and Urban and Katz 1983.

Design	Procedure	Measurement
O_1	Respondent screening and recruitment (personal interview)	Criteria for target-group identification (e.g., product-class usage)
O_2	Premeasurement for established brands (self-administered questionnaire)	Composition of "relevant set" of established brands, attribute weights and ratings, and preferences
X_1	Exposure to advertising for established brands and new brand	
$[O_3]$	Measurement of reactions to the advertising materials (self-administered questionnaire)	Optional, e.g., likability and believability ratings of advertising materials
X_2	Simulated shopping trip and exposure to display of new and established brands	
O_4	Purchase opportunity (choice recorded research personnel)	Brand(s) purchased
X_3	Home use, or consumption of new brand	
O_5	Post-usage measurement (telephone interview)	New-brand usage rate, satisfaction ratings, and repeat-purchase propensity; attribute ratings and preferences for "relevant set" of established brands plus the new brand

EXHIBIT 7.12
Overview of ASSESSOR data-collection procedure. *Source*: Silk and Urban 1978, p. 174, Table 1.

The participants are then sent to a simulated store, which consists of a shelf display of products in the test category along with the representative prices for all the products. They can use their $10 to purchase any product or combination of products in the category. (Participants may choose not to buy anything and keep their $10.) Those who do not purchase the new product receive a quantity of it free after all buying transactions are completed.

This procedure parallels market behavior where some participants will try a new product on their own after seeing an ad, and others will try it if they get free samples. After allowing respondents time to use the new product at their homes, the researchers contact them by telephone for a post-usage survey. They offer participants an opportunity to repurchase the new product (to be delivered by mail) and ask them to respond to the same questions (perception and preference measurements) that they were asked in the laboratory (testing facility). The laboratory measurements provide the inputs for calibrating both the preference model and the trial-repeat model.

The preference model

The preference model transforms the measured preferences of the participants (from observations O_2 in Exhibit 7.12) into choice probabilities indicating the probability that the participants will purchase each of the products in their consideration set:

$$L_{ij} = \frac{V_{ij}^b}{\sum_{k \in C_i} V_{ik}^b}, \tag{7.13}$$

where

V_{ij} = participant i's stated preference for product j measured on a suitable scale;

L_{ij} = an estimate of the probability that participant i will purchase product j;

C_i = the consideration set of customer i; and

b = a parameter that is estimated from the data.

$L_{ij} = 0$ for those products j that are not in the consideration set of participant i. The sum in the denominator is over all the products in participant i's consideration set. If participants differ significantly in product usage rates, L_{ij} can be weighted by usage index w_i to convert probability of purchase into market shares of the products, in a fashion similar to Eq. (7.3).

The parameter b in Eq. (7.13) is an index that indicates the rate at which preferences for products will convert to purchase probabilities for the products. If $b > 1$, then high-preference brands will have disproportionately high probabilities of purchase as compared with low-preference brands. In typical applications b will be between 1.5 and 3.0. The maximum likelihood estimation procedure offers a way to estimate a value for b that maximizes the likelihood of recovering the actual product choices the participants made at *their most immediate previous purchase occasion* (as measured at O_2 in Exhibit 7.12).

To forecast the purchase probability of the new product, we measure preferences for both the new product and the existing products after the participant has used the new product for a trial period. Because the participants are aware of the new product and have had the opportunity to try it, we can assume that the new product will be in the consideration set of all the participants. We can use an equation similar to (7.13) to estimate the probability of purchase for all products, including the new product, after the participants have had an opportunity to use the new product:

$$L'_{ij} = \frac{V'^b_{ij}}{V'^b_{in} + \sum_{k \in C_i} V'^b_{ik}}, \tag{7.14}$$

where

V'_{ij} = post-use preference rating by the ith consumer for the jth product;

n = an index to denote the new product; and

L'_{in} = the probability that consumer i will choose the new product, after having used it.

In Eq. (7.14) we assume that in the laboratory setting all participants will include the new product in their consideration sets. In Eq. (7.14) b is the estimate we obtain from Eq. (7.13).

The market share obtained from (7.14) for the new product will be an optimistic forecast because not everyone in the marketplace will include the new product in their consideration sets. One way to adjust for this is to obtain estimates of the percentage of those in the target segment who will include the new product in their consideration sets and then adjust L'_{in} as follows:

$$M'_n = E_n \sum_i \frac{L'_{in}}{N}, \qquad (7.15)$$

where

E_n = proportion of participants who include the new product in their consideration set;

M'_n = the projected market share for the new product; and

N = the number of participants in the study.

To assess *draw* and *cannibalization* from other products, we first partition the participants into two hypothetical groups: those who would include the new product in the consideration set (equal to the proportion E_n) and those who would not include the new product in the consideration set (proportion equal to $1 - E_n$). (One estimate of E_n is the proportion of customers in the target segment who would eventually try the new product—a number that is estimated as part of the trial-repeat model described in the next section.) Then NE_n participants would include the new product in the consideration set, and $N(1 - E_n)$ would not. For those who do not include the new product in the consideration set, the best estimates of their choice probabilities are those provided by Eq. (7.13), which reflect product choices before trying the new product. Likewise, for those who include the new product in their consideration set, the best estimates of their choice probabilities are those provided by Eq. (7.14). Thus we obtain the best estimate of the sources of market share for the new product as follows. First we compute the market shares of the existing products j before and after the new product is introduced:

$$M_j = \sum_i \frac{L_{ij}}{N}, \qquad (7.16)$$

$$M'_j = E_n \sum_i \frac{L'_{ij}}{N} + \left(1 - E_n\right) \sum_i \frac{L_{ij}}{N}, \qquad (7.17)$$

where

M_j = the market share for product j before the new product is introduced, and $j = 1, 2, \ldots, J$, where J is the number of existing products in the competitive set (i.e., products that belong in the consideration set of at least one customer); and

M'_j = the market share for product j after the new product is introduced.

In this model M'_j will be equal to at most M_j for all existing products. Given these estimates the extent to which the new product draws from product j is given by

$$D_j = M_j - M'_j \qquad (7.18)$$

Note that the sum of the draws across the existing products (i.e., $\sum_{j \in j} D_j$) is equal to the market share for the new product (M'_n). The proportion of the new product's sales that is drawn from other products sold by the firm is considered to be cannibalized; the remaining part drawn from competitors' brands is called incremental sales. A new product whose sales are primarily due to cannibalization has to be further evaluated carefully for its financial contribution to the firm, even though the ASSESSOR model may forecast that it will have high market share.

In Exhibit 7.13 we provide a numerical illustration of the computations given in Eqs. (7.13) to (7.18).

Trial-repeat model

ASSESSOR uses a standard formula to generate the long-run market share of the new product using the new product trial and repeat measures obtained from the laboratory experiment:

$$M_n = trw, \qquad (7.19)$$

where

t = the cumulative proportion of the target segment that will eventually try the new product;

r = the proportion of those trying the new product who will become long-run repeat purchasers of the new product; and

w = relative usage rate, with $w = 1$ being the average usage rate in the market.

ASSESSOR estimates the trial rate (t) as follows:

$$t = \underbrace{FKD}_{\substack{\text{those} \\ \text{who try}}} + \underbrace{CU}_{\substack{\text{those} \\ \text{given} \\ \text{samples}}} - \underbrace{(FKD)(CU)}_{\substack{\text{adjustment for} \\ \text{double counting}}}, \qquad (7.20)$$

where

F = the long-run probability of trial given unlimited distribution and total awareness of the new product in the target segment, the proportion of the participants who purchase the product in the simulated store (O_4 in Exhibit 7.12);

K = the long-run probability of awareness, estimated based on management judgment and the projected advertising plan;

Customer	Preference ratings								
	V_{ij} (Pre-use)				V'_{ij} (Post-use)				
	B1	**B2**	**B3**	**B4**	**B1**	**B2**	**B3**	**B4**	**New product**
1	0.1	0.0	4.9	3.7	0.1	0.0	2.6	1.7	0.2
2	1.5	0.7	3.0	0.0	1.6	0.6	0.6	0.0	3.1
3	2.5	2.9	0.0	0.0	2.3	1.4	0.0	0.0	2.3
4	3.1	3.4	0.0	0.0	3.3	3.4	0.0	0.0	0.7
5	0.0	1.3	0.0	0.0	0.0	1.2	0.0	0.0	0.0
6	4.1	0.0	0.0	0.0	4.3	0.0	0.0	0.0	2.1
7	0.4	2.1	0.0	2.9	0.4	2.1	0.0	1.6	0.1
8	0.6	0.2	0.0	0.0	0.6	0.2	0.0	0.0	5.0
9	4.8	2.4	0.0	0.0	5.0	2.2	0.0	0.0	0.3
10	0.7	0.0	4.9	0.0	0.7	0.0	3.4	0.0	0.9

Customer	Choice probabilities								
	L_{ij} (Pre-use)				L'_{ij} (Post-use)				
	B1	**B2**	**B3**	**B4**	**B1**	**B2**	**B3**	**B4**	**New product**
1	0.00	0.00	0.63	0.37	0.00	0.00	0.69	0.31	0.00
2	0.20	0.05	0.75	0.00	0.21	0.03	0.03	0.00	0.73
3	0.43	0.57	0.00	0.00	0.42	0.16	0.00	0.00	0.42
4	0.46	0.54	0.00	0.00	0.47	0.50	0.00	0.00	0.03
5	0.00	1.00	0.00	0.00	0.00	1.00	0.00	0.00	0.00
6	1.00	0.00	0.00	0.00	0.80	0.00	0.00	0.00	0.20
7	0.01	0.35	0.00	0.64	0.03	0.61	0.00	0.36	0.00
8	0.89	0.11	0.00	0.00	0.02	0.00	0.00	0.00	0.98
9	0.79	0.21	0.00	0.00	0.82	0.18	0.00	0.00	0.00
10	0.02	0.00	0.98	0.00	0.04	0.00	0.89	0.00	0.07
Unweighted market share (%)	38.0	28.3	23.6	10.1	28.1	24.8	16.1	6.7	24.3
New product's draw from each brand (unweighted %)					9.9	3.5	7.5	3.4	
New product's draw from each brand (weighted by E_n in %)					2.0	0.7	1.5	0.7	

EXHIBIT 7.13

Example computations associated with the ASSESSOR model. There are 10 customers and four brands (B1 to B4). To convert preference ratings to choice probabilities, we used a value of 1.9 for the parameter b (Eq. 7.13). To obtain the new product's weighted draw from other brands we set E_n, the proportion of customers including the new product in their consideration set, to 0.2.

D =   the long-run probability that the product will be available where the target customers shop, based on managerial judgment and expectations regarding the proportion of outlets that will eventually carry the product;

C =   the probability that a customer in the target segment will receive a sample of the new product, estimated based on the introduction plan for the new product; and

U = the probability that a customer who receives a sample will use it, estimated based on past experience and managerial judgment.

The first term in Eq. (7.20), FKD, represents the proportion of customers who will be aware of the new product, have it available where they shop, and will then try it. The second term, CU, represents the proportion of customers who will obtain a trial sample. The third term, $(FKD)(CU)$, adjusts for double counting those who both purchase the new product and receive a sample. Unlike the preference model, the trial-repeat model does not provide estimates of draw and cannibalization, which are important to a firm in developing its marketing plan for the new product.

We estimate the repeat rate (r in Eq. (7.19)) from the information in the post-usage telephone survey (O_5 in Exhibit 7.12). We first formulate a brand switching matrix that shows the proportion of customers who switch into and out of the new product at each time period:

$$ t \begin{array}{c} t+1 \\ \begin{bmatrix} p_{nn} & p_{no} \\ p_{on} & p_{oo} \end{bmatrix} \end{array}, \tag{7.21} $$

where

p_{nn} = the probability that a customer who purchases the new product at time period t will also purchase it at time period $t+1$, estimated as the proportion of customers who purchased the new product in the test facility and say in the post-usage survey that they will buy the new product at the next purchase occasion;

p_{no} = $1 - p_{nn}$;

p_{on} = the probability that a customer who purchases another product at time t will purchase the new product at time $t+1$, estimated as the proportion who did not purchase the new product in the test facility but say in the post-usage survey that they will buy the new product at the next purchase occasion; and

p_{oo} = $1 - p_{on}$.

Given the switching matrix, we are interested in determining what proportion of the customers who bought the new product at some period t would buy the new product in the next period ($t+1$) if the pattern embedded in the matrix is repeated period after period indefinitely—that is, what would be the equilibrium repeat rate? The answer turns out to be given by a simple formula:

$$ r = \frac{p_{on}}{1 - p_{nn} + p_{on}}. \tag{7.22} $$

The trial-repeat model summarized in Eqs. (7.19) to (7.22) provides an independent estimate of the market share for the new product, which one can compare with the estimate obtained from the preference model. When these two estimates are close, they increase managers' confidence in the forecasted market share of the new product.

The validity and value of the ASSESSOR model

Those marketing commercially available pretest market models all claim good success rates. However, ASSESSOR is one of the few models whose validation studies have been reported in academic journals (Urban and Katz 1983). The success rate of new products that go through an ASSESSOR evaluation is 66 percent, compared with a success rate of 35 percent for products that do not undergo a formal pretest model analysis. At the same time, only 3.8 percent of products that failed in ASSESSOR and were then introduced in the market succeeded. In a study of 44 new products that had undergone analysis with ASSESSOR, the average forecasted market share was 7.77 while the actual achieved market share averaged 7.16 with a standard deviation of 1.99. The correlation between the forecast and the actual market share was 0.95.

Urban and Katz (1983) also compare the average monetary gains for firms using the ASSESSOR model and for those using no market-based testing to decide whether to introduce a new product. The average incremental gain associated with the use of ASSESSOR is $11.7 million, a substantial return compared with the investment of $50,000 for the ASSESSOR model. Firms that use both ASSESSOR and a regular test market still make an incremental gain of over $300,000 by using ASSESSOR.

In summary, pretest market models have been one of the most successful areas of application of marketing engineering. These models are particularly useful for forecasting and evaluating a new product entering a well-defined category. The preference model in ASSESSOR provides diagnostic information that is useful to a firm in designing the marketing plan for introducing the new product. The preference model is likely to be accurate only in well-defined product categories where (1) customers learn about new products rapidly enough that preferences stabilize quickly and (2) the customers' usage rate for the product category would not change as a result of the new product.

We have provided a software implementation of ASSESSOR that includes both the trial-repeat and preference models, along with data for the Johnson Wax case.

SUMMARY

Firms recognize that a neverending quest for new products is a strategic necessity to thrive. In this chapter we outlined the major stages of new product development (NPD) and the many decision models that firms can use to improve their decisions. We highlighted three models: conjoint analysis, the Bass model, and the ASSESSOR pretest market forecasting model. Firms can use these models in the early stages of developing a new product to help them make effective decisions about how much to invest in the product.

CHAPTER **8**

Advertising and Communications Decisions

In this chapter we will discuss the marketing engineering approach to advertising and some other communications-mix decisions. The communications mix that marketers can use includes

Advertising: Any paid form of nonpersonal presentation and promotion of ideas, goods, or services by an identified sponsor

Direct marketing: The use of mail, telephone, and other nonpersonal contact tools to communicate with or solicit a response from specific customers and prospects

Sales promotion: Short-term incentives to encourage people to try or purchase a product or service

Public relations and publicity: Various programs designed to promote or protect a company's image or its individual products

Personal selling: Face-to-face interaction with one or more prospective purchasers for the purpose of making sales

We focus on advertising in this chapter, and we discuss the major elements of the rest of the communications mix in the next two chapters.

In this chapter, then, we deal with the following topics:

- The bewildering nature of advertising
- Advertising effects: response, media, and copy
- Advertising budgeting decisions
- Media decisions
- Advertising copy development and decisions

Software packages that are relevant for this chapter are the ADBUDG spreadsheet, developed to accompany the Blue Mountain Coffee case; ADVISOR, designed to accompany the Convection Company case; and ADCAD, a knowledge-based system for designing advertisements.

THE BEWILDERING NATURE OF ADVERTISING

One of the most important and bewildering promotional tools of modern marketing management is advertising. No one doubts that it can be effective in presenting information to, or persuading, potential buyers. Everyone agrees that it can influence customers' preferences for a product, enhance a company's image, and affect customers' purchasing behavior. Even when advertising does not directly influence sales, it may affect image and preference, which influence sales. In fact, small changes in people's preference for a product can have lasting impact, resulting in increased sales over time.

Advertising is bewildering because, among other reasons, its effects typically play out over time, may be nonlinear, and can interact with other elements in the marketing mix in creating sales. Currently no one knows what advertising really does in the marketplace. However, what advertising is supposed to do is fairly clear: Advertising is supposed to increase company sales and profits. However, it rarely can create sales by itself. Whether the customer buys also depends on the product, price, packaging, personal selling, services, financing, and other aspects of the marketing process.

Even more than for other elements for the marketing mix, advertising decisions and their effectiveness are influenced by their interaction with marketing objectives, with product characteristics, and with other elements of the marketing mix. Here are some examples:

Personal selling: When personal selling is an important element in the marketing mix (in industrial markets, for example), the role of advertising is diminished. Personal selling is a far more effective (although more expensive) communication method than advertising. But because of its extra expense, it can be used most effectively when the expected level of sales to a single prospect is large (generally, sales to industrial customers, wholesalers, and retailers).

Branding: If a company produces several variations of its product under a family or company name (Kellogg's cereal, Campbell soup), it can advertise the entire line, giving attention to a special brand from time to time. When a firm carries different brand names (Procter and Gamble's Tide, Bold, and Cheer detergents, for example), the company can advertise each brand independently and make separate advertising budget, copy, and media decisions.

Pricing: The copy or message and media placement of the advertising must reinforce and be consistent with the brand's price position. A premium-priced brand should emphasize differentiating qualities, whereas a low-priced brand should stress its low price.

Distribution: The length of the distribution channel and the overall marketing strategy dictate different targets for advertising messages. To influence wholesalers or retailers a firm can use two different strategies: push versus pull. In a push strategy the firm directs its marketing efforts at salespeople or the trade, with the objective of pushing the product through the distribution channel; in a pull strategy the firm aims its marketing strategy at the ultimate consumer, with the objective of stimulating consumer demand to pull the merchandise through the distribution channels.

Aaker and Myers (1987) define three major decisions for advertising: (1) setting objectives and budgeting (how much to spend), (2) developing copy (what message), and (3) choosing media (what media to use). Although we address these three points separately here, they are closely interrelated: advertising objectives drive copy decisions, and copy effects, which vary by response group, and affect media decisions. In addition, time is an issue for all three decision areas. For budgeting, dollars must be spent over time, and firms must evaluate pulsing versus more continuous spending policies. Furthermore, advertising copy varies in its effectiveness over time, eventually wearing out, and firms must create new copy and phase it in. Finally, firms must decide what media to use in conjunction with timing and scheduling their messages.

ADVERTISING EFFECTS: RESPONSE, MEDIA, AND COPY

Advertising response phenomena

Little (1979) identifies three areas of controversy associated with advertising sales response models:

> *Shape* refers to the long-term level of sales expected at each level of advertising. Is the relationship linear? S-shaped? What are sales when advertising is zero? Is there a supersaturation point, where large amounts of advertising actually depress sales?

> *Dynamics* refers to the speed of the sales increase when advertising is increased and the rate of decay when advertising is decreased. One question is whether hysteresis exists—that is, whether advertising can move sales to a new level at which it will stay without further advertising input. Although carryover effects have been found in many empirical studies, there is little agreement about how long they last (Clarke 1976).

> *Interaction* refers to the interplay and synergy (positive and negative) between advertising and other elements in the marketing mix, such as sales promotion, personal selling, and price.

Little (1979) also reviews many empirical examples in an attempt to identify important advertising response phenomena. Exhibit 8.1 shows that advertising increases the sales rate of a packaged good: After heavy advertising, sales increased substantially. The sales rate increased within a month or so, substantially faster than many managers believe is the case.

The exhibit also shows sales leveling off during the period of heavy advertising: apparently it achieved its total effect before spending returned to its usual level.

Finally, the exhibit shows the beginning of a decay in sales following the decrease in advertising. Furthermore, sales seem to decline more slowly than they grow. Two separate phenomena are involved: the rise is related to advertising, while the decline is related to product experience, a different phenomenon, and we should expect a different rate.

Exhibit 8.2 shows sales for a line of products that have never been advertised. Supermarkets and department stores are full of house brands, price brands, and other products that have quite healthy sales even though they are not advertised. Therefore an advertising response model should admit the possibility of sales with zero advertising.

Perhaps the most interesting aspects of response to advertising are nonlinearities in the response curve. Logic suggests that a linear response curve is unreasonable: optimal advertising for a product with a linear response would be either zero or infinity, and one could increase its sales by continued increases in advertising spending. On the other hand, nonlinearity covers many alternatives, most importantly diminishing returns and an S shape. Exhibit 8.3 shows the sales of two products that display concavity, or diminishing returns to advertising spending.

Finally, Little (1979) summarizes his observations with a list of five phenomena that a good advertising response model should admit:

1. Sales move dynamically upward in response to increases in advertising and downward in response to decreases of advertising and frequently do so at different rates.
2. Response to advertising can be concave or S-shaped, and sales will often be positive at zero advertising.

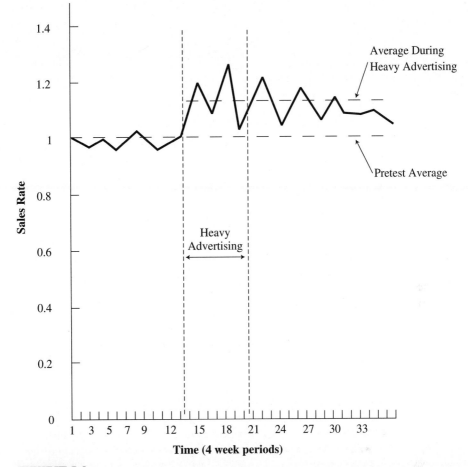

EXHIBIT 8.1
The sales rate of a packaged good rose quickly under increased advertising but declined slowly after it was removed. The vertical axis shows the ratio of sales in test areas to sales in control areas that did not receive the heavy advertising. *Source*: Little 1979, p. 637.

3. Competitive advertising affects sales, usually negatively.
4. The dollar effectiveness of advertising can change over time because of changes in media, copy, and other factors.
5. Sales of products sometimes respond to increased advertising with an increase that falls off even as advertising is held constant.

An advertising response model: Vidale and Wolfe (1957) developed a classical advertising response model to explain the rate of change of sales when advertising had both immediate and lagged effects:

$$\frac{\Delta Q}{\Delta t} = \frac{rX(V - Q)}{V} - \alpha Q, \tag{8.1}$$

where

Q = sales volume;

$\Delta Q/\Delta t$ = change in sales at time t;

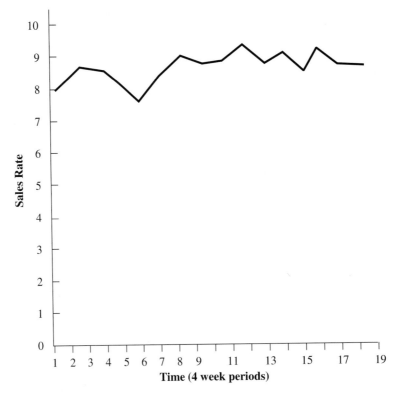

EXHIBIT 8.2

The healthy sales of a line of unadvertised food products show that advertising is not always required to sell something. *Source:* Little 1979.

X = advertising spending rate;

V = market volume;

r = sales-response constant (sales generated per dollar of advertising, X, when sales, $Q = 0$); and

α = sales-decay constant (proportion of sales lost per unit of time when advertising, $X = 0$).

The right-hand side of Eq. (8.1) means that the change in the rate of sales, $\Delta Q/\Delta t$, depends on several factors: it will be greater for higher levels of r, X, and $(V - Q)/V$ (untapped potential), and it will be lower for higher values of α and Q. Thus $\Delta Q/\Delta t$ is equal to the response rate, r, per dollar of spending times the number, X, of marketing dollars spent reduced by the percentage of unsaturated sales, $(V - Q)/V$, less sales lost through decay, αQ. The implications of this model for an advertising program of a given level of intensity that is stopped are shown in Exhibit 8.4.

Lodish et al. (1995a) provide some interesting results on how advertising works, based on split-cable TV ads. They find that in general increasing advertising does not increase sales. They also find that advertising is most likely to increase sales when it is accompanied by changes in the product (e.g., a new product), in the advertising copy, or in the

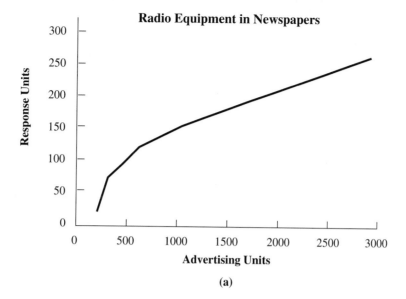

(a)

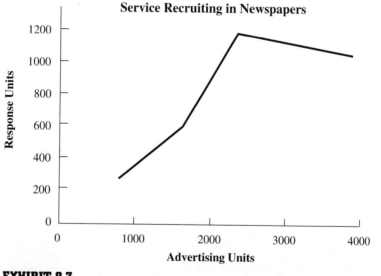

EXHIBIT 8.3
In these two examples of nonlinear response, returns diminish as advertising increases.
Source: Little 1979.

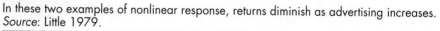

media strategy and when the ads are used for product categories for which in-store merchandising effort is low. In particular 67 percent of the tests showed no increase in sales
with increased advertising for established products, and 61 percent of the tests that used
existing advertising copy showed no increase in sales with increased advertising. For established products advertising elasticity averaged 0.05; that is, a 100 percent increase in advertising would lead to a 5 percent increase in sales. Marketing researchers need to do
more work of this type to determine when and how sales respond to advertising in their own
product categories.

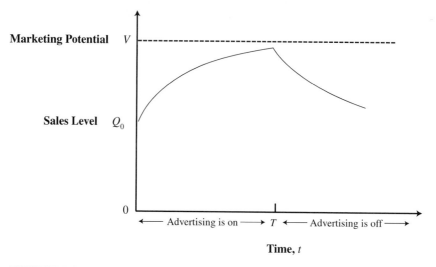

EXHIBIT 8.4
According to the Vidale-Wolfe model, during an advertising campaign of duration T during which spending is constant, sales increase, showing a concave response. When advertising ceases sales decline gradually, at a different rate than they increased.

Frequency phenomena

In planning and scheduling media for advertising it is critical to understand the effect of advertising exposure over time.

The theory concerning the effects of advertisement frequency is based on laboratory research in psychology and can be traced to the work of Ebbinghaus in the late 1800s in which he showed that the forgetting rate is slowed by repeated learning of the same lessons. Zielski (1959) later applied Ebbinghaus's findings to ads for grocery products.

Appel (1971) and Grass (1968) show that response to a simple stimulus first increases, then passes through a maximum, and finally declines (Exhibit 8.5). From studies for a number of DuPont products, Grass concludes that attention increases and maximizes at two exposures, while the amount of learned information increases and maximizes at two or three exposures. Krugman (1972), based on his studies of brain waves and eye movements, advocates the idea that the third and subsequent exposures reinforce the effects of the second exposure.

McDonald (1971) reports on the effects of frequency, based on records 255 homemakers kept on their exposure to newspapers, magazines, and radio and TV ads for 50 product fields over a 13-week period. He found that over 9 product fields, homemakers were on average 5 percent more likely to switch to a particular brand if, between two purchases of that commodity, they saw two or more ads for that brand than if they saw zero or one ad. McDonald also found that the effect was stronger for advertising seen within four days before the second purchase.

In a study conducted for four advertisers, Ogilvy and Mather (1965) asked respondents to keep television viewing diaries; they tracked their brand preferences and related them to their number of exposures. Their study showed (1) no more than minimal effects for one exposure in an eight-week period, (2) major differences by time of day, and (3) major differences by brand. Naples (1979) reports another study within a split-cable television market in which respondents kept diaries recording their purchasing. The results indicated that at least two exposures were needed for maximum effectiveness. He also found that the brands that showed the greatest response were those with the highest share of advertising in their

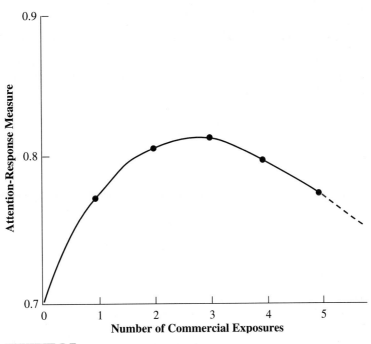

EXHIBIT 8.5
As the exposure to a TV commercial increases, people pay less attention to it. *Source*: Grass 1968.

categories. On the basis of these studies and a review of others, Naples (1979, pp. 63–81) offers the following conclusions:

1. Optimal frequency appears to be three or more exposures within a purchase cycle.
2. Beyond three ad exposures, effectiveness continues to increase but at a decreasing rate.
3. Advertising frequency by itself does not cause wear-out, although it can speed the decline of an effective campaign.
4. Response to advertising appears smaller for the brands with the highest market share.

Cannon (1987) lists 27 propositions (e.g., "Proposition 25: Vivid images will require low frequency since they provide unique and memorable experiences," p. 41) that summarize his feeling that frequency is an individual-, copy-, and situation-specific phenomenon and that a media schedule can at best segment the market appropriately and select media vehicles and a schedule that works best for each of those segments. (See also Cannon and Goldring (1986), and Wenzel and Speetzen (1987), and for industrial ads, Cort, Lambert, and Garret (1982).)

Copy effects

People interested in copy or message effectiveness are most concerned with the sales effect of copy relative to media spending (advertising intensity). For example, Aaker and Carman (1982) reviewed 48 AdTel advertising experiments and reported that 30 percent showed significant results on advertising intensity while 47 percent involving ad copy showed significant results. Similarly, Fulgoni (1987) reported on more than 400 BehaviorScan tests, with from 40 to 55 percent showing response to intensity (depending on the year) while 75 percent showed a significant response to copy. Carroll et al. (1985) reported no effect of intensity in an experiment concerning an enlistment program for the Navy but did report statistically significant results for copy tailored to the local area. Eastlack and Rao (1989), reviewing 19 advertising experiments at Campbell soup, concur, reporting that "good copy in the right media will produce sales increases without increases in budget" (p. 70). Using data on 92 British TV advertising tests, Stewart (1990) reported 48 percent of the tests showed a significant increase in sales in response to new copy and 31 percent of the tests showed a significant sales increase for an advertising intensity test for established brands.

Given that advertising copy is so important, people have good reason to want to know what makes a good ad. Those in copy research investigate myriad phenomena from how the physical and mechanical aspects of ads relate to recognition, recall, and other measures (Hendon 1973) to the humor and seriousness of TV commercials (Wells, Leavitt, and McConnell 1971). In his review of a large number of copy-testing studies Ramond (1976) provides the following principles:

- The bigger the print ad, the more people will recognize it later (Starch 1966; Trodahl and Jones 1965; Twedt 1952; Yamanaka 1962), possibly as a function of the square root of the size increase.
- More people recognize color ads than black-and-white ads (Gardner and Cohen 1966; Twedt 1952).
- The shorter its headline, the greater the recognition of an ad (unpublished Leo Burnett bulletin).
- People recall shorter TV commercials as well as longer ones, and product class has a significant effect on recognition and recall of both TV and print ads.
- People's awareness and attitudes change with changes in the execution of TV commercials, and these changes can predict changes in brand choice (Assael and Day 1968; Axelrod 1968).
- People do not need to believe ads to remember them (Leavitt 1962; Maloney 1963).

These observations, while simplistic, have lead to some contingency theories of copy and message effects—that is, what messages to use in what circumstances (Rossiter and Percy 1987). Other research in this area is promising as well. For example, Hanssens and Weitz (1980) reported that recall and readership scores for industrial ads were strongly related to such characteristics as size and position in magazines. Sewall and Sarel (1986) performed a similar analysis for radio commercials, and Goodwin and Etgar (1980) report relationships between communication effects and the type of advertising appeals. For a good treatment of what seems to drive effective TV ads, see Stewart and Furse's (1986) study of 1000 commercials.

ADVERTISING BUDGET DECISIONS

Firms must often decide how much to spend on advertising. We will describe four of the more common methods for making this decision. Patti and Blasko (1981) and Blasko and Patti (1984) give some statistics about the use of these methods by industrial marketers (*I*) and consumer marketers (*C*) respectively. We put the percentages of each type of firm that reports using each method in parentheses following the method.

Affordable method (I = 20%, C = 33%): Many executives set the advertising budget based on what they think the company can afford. As one advertising executive explained:

Why it's simple. First, I go upstairs to the controller and ask how much they can afford to give us this year. He says a million and a half. Later, the boss comes to me and asks how much we should spend, and I say, "Oh, about a million and a half." Then we have an advertising appropriation. (Seligman 1956, p. 123)

Setting budgets in this manner is tantamount to saying that the relationship between advertising expenditure and sales results is at best tenuous: the company should spend whatever funds it has available on advertising as a form of insurance. The basic weakness of this approach is that it leads to a fluctuating advertising budget that makes it difficult to plan for long-range market development.

Percentage-of-sales method (Anticipated: I = 16%, C = 53%; Past year's: I = 23%, C = 20%): Many companies set their advertising expenditures at a specified percentage of sales (either current or anticipated) or of the sales price. For example, a railroad company executive once said:

We set our appropriation for each year on December 1 of the preceding year. On that date we add our passenger revenue for the next month, and then take two percent of the total for our advertising appropriation for the new year. (Frey 1955, p. 65)

Furthermore, automobile companies typically budget a fixed percentage for advertising based on the planned price of each car, and oil companies tend to set the appropriation as some fraction of a cent for each gallon of gasoline sold under their own label.

People claim a number of advantages for this method. First, advertising expenditures are likely to vary with what the company can afford. Second, it encourages managers to think in terms of the relationship between advertising cost, selling price, and profit per unit. Third, to the extent that competing firms spend approximately the same percentage of their sales on advertising, it encourages competitive stability.

In spite of these advantages the percentage-of-sales method has little to justify it. It uses circular reasoning in making sales the determinant of advertising rather than its result. And it leads executives to set the appropriation for advertising according to the availability of funds rather than according to the available opportunities. Furthermore, the method provides no logical basis for choosing a specific percentage, except what has been done in the past, what competitors are doing, or what the costs will be. Finally, it does not encourage firms to appropriate funds for advertising constructively on a product-by-product and territory-by-territory basis but instead suggests that all allocations be made at the same percentage of sales.

Competitive-parity method (I = 21%, C = 24%): Some companies set their advertising budgets specifically to match competitors' outlays—that is, to maintain competitive parity.

Two arguments are advanced for this method. One is that competitors' expenditures represent the collective wisdom of the industry. The other is that maintaining a competitive parity helps to prevent advertising wars. But neither of these arguments is valid. There are no a priori grounds for believing that the competition is using logical methods for determining outlays. Advertising reputations, resources, opportunities, and objectives are likely to differ so much among companies that their budgets are hardly guides for other firms. Furthermore, there is no evidence that appropriations based on the pursuit of competitive parity do in fact stabilize industry advertising expenditures.

Knowing what the competition is spending on advertising is undoubtedly useful information. But it is one thing to have this information and another to copy it blindly.

Objective-and-task method (I = 74%, C = 63%): In using the objective-and-task method advertisers develop their budgets by (1) defining their advertising objectives as specifically as possible, (2) determining the tasks that must be performed to achieve these objectives, and (3) estimating the costs of performing these tasks. The sum of these costs is the proposed advertising budget (Colley 1961; Wolfe, Brown, and Thompson 1962).

Firms should develop their advertising goals as specifically as possible to guide them in developing copy, in selecting media, and in measuring results. The stated goal "to create brand preference" is much weaker than "to establish 30 percent preference for brand X among Y million women in the 18 to 34 age category by next year." Colley listed 52 specific communication goals, including the following:

- Announce a special reason for buying now (price premium, etc.).
- Build familiarity and easy recognition of the package or trademark.
- Place the advertiser in a position to select preferred distributors and dealers.
- Persuade the prospect to visit a showroom and ask for a demonstration.
- Build the morale of the company's salesforce.
- Correct false impressions, misinformation, and other obstacles to sales.

This method has strong appeal and popularity among advertisers. Its major limitation is that it does not indicate how to choose the objectives and how to evaluate them and decide whether they are worth the cost of attaining them. Indeed Patti and Blasko (1981) report that 51 percent of major consumer advertisers use quantitative methods to set their budgets, although the figure for industrial advertisers is a disappointing 3 percent (Blasko and Patti 1984).

Model-based approaches: Many researchers have worked to develop decision models for setting advertising budgets. In their articles they focus on the size and allocation of the advertising budget. While the research efforts differ widely in their purpose and methodology, most are closely related to the following general approach:

Find $A_i(t)$ to

$$\max Z = \underbrace{\sum_i \sum_j \sum_t S_i\left(t \mid \{A_i(t)\}, \{C_{ij}(t)\}\right) \times m_i}_{\text{Gross Profit}} - \underbrace{\sum_i \sum_t A_i(t)}_{\text{Advertising spending}}, \qquad (8.2)$$

subject to

$$\sum_i \sum_t A_i(t) \le B \text{ (budget constraint)},$$

$$L_i \le \sum A_i(t) \le U_i \text{ (regional constraints)},$$

where

$S_i(t \mid \{A_i(t)\}, \{C_{ij}(t)\})$ = sales in area i at time t as a function of current and historical brand and competitive advertising;

$C_{ij}(t)$ = competitive advertising for competitor j in area i at time t;

$A_i(t)$ = advertising level in area i at time t;

m_i = margin per unit sales in area i;

$\{A_i(t)\}$ = entire advertising program over the planning horizon;

U_i, L_i = upper, lower regional constraints; and

B = budget constraint.

The quantitative models we discuss differ most importantly in their specifications of the form of $S_i(t)$.

As we discussed in the last section, a response model should include certain advertising phenomena. But models vary in form and incorporate these phenomena to different extents. We describe two of the simplest decision models below and a third approach (ADVISOR) based on the formal development of budgeting norms.

EXAMPLE

Rao and Miller's (1975) approach: Rao and Miller's model combines data from multiple markets over time. Their basic idea is that many national advertising campaigns provide a set of quasi-experimental conditions because exposure rates and other characteristics vary from market to market. The idea is to derive an advertising-response coefficient from each of a number of sales districts and then to combine those coefficients in a way that produces a general sales-response function.

Rao and Miller assume that advertising has an immediate effect and a lagged effect and that the lagged effect decays exponentially. Although they show how to handle price offers and other trade promotions, we concentrate here only on the aspects of the model that relate to advertising. Their individual-market model is

$$S_t = c_0 + c_1 A_t + c_1 \lambda A_{t-1} + c_1 \lambda^2 A_{t-2} + \ldots + \mu_t, \tag{8.3}$$

where

S_t = market share at t;

A_t = advertising spending at t;

c_0, c_1, λ = constants ($0 < \lambda < 1$); and

μ_t = random disturbance.

This equation means that an incremental expenditure of one unit of advertising in a given period will yield c_1 share points in that period, $c_1 \lambda$ in the following period, $c_1 \lambda^2$ in the period after that, and so on.

The distributed lag form in Eq. (8.3) can be simplified by multiplying both sides by λ,

$$\lambda S_{t-1} = \lambda c_0 + \lambda c_1 A_{t-1} + \lambda^2 c_1 A_{t-2} + \ldots + \lambda \mu_{t-1}, \tag{8.4}$$

and subtracting Eq. (8.4) from Eq. (8.3):

$$S_t = c_0(1 - \lambda) + \lambda S_{t-1} + c_1 A_t + \mu_t - \lambda \mu_{t-1}. \tag{8.5}$$

Note that the short-run effect of advertising here is

$$\frac{dS_t}{dA_t} = c_1 \ \text{(short-run effect)}, \tag{8.6}$$

while the long-run effect is c_1 in the first period, then $\lambda c_1 + \lambda^2 c_1 + \ldots$ in subsequent periods, or

$$c_1 + \lambda c_1 + \lambda^2 c_1 + \cdots = \frac{c_1}{(1 - \lambda)} \ \text{(long-run effect)}. \tag{8.7}$$

Now if

I =   industry sales per year in the district;

P =   the district population; and

AV =   the average rate of advertising during the period,

then with k periods per year, by Eq. (8.6) a $1000 increase in advertising produces a share increase of $c_1/(1 - \lambda)$. Thus the sales increase of an additional $1000 in advertising is

$$y_i = \Delta sales_i = \frac{c_1}{(1 - \lambda)} \frac{I}{K} \quad \text{(in market } i\text{)} \tag{8.8}$$

at a per capita advertising rate of $AV_i/P = x_i$. In other words, Eq. (8.8) can be interpreted as the derivative of a general market-share response curve at the per capita spending rate AV/P.

This procedure gives a set of values (y_i, x_i) for each market i, where the $\{y_i\}$ are the derivatives of a more general response function $g(x)$, so that $y = dg/dx$. Assuming that $g(x)$ is S-shaped, Rao and Miller propose using a polynomial in x to approximate it; specifically they assume that $g(x)$ can be modeled as a cubic function in x, while $y(x)$ is a quadratic function in x:

$$y = k_1 + k_2 x - k_3 x^2 + k_4 z, \tag{8.9}$$

where

z =   percent share of premium brands (an empirical adjustment factor that accounts for variability in marginal response); and

$k_1, \ldots, k_4$ =   parameters to be estimated.

Given a set of $\{y_i\}$ and $\{x_i\}$ (as well as $\{z_i\}$) we can estimate the coefficients in Eq. (8.9) using standard econometric methods. We can obtain the total advertising-response function simply by integrating Eq. (8.9). After integration they obtain

$$g(x) = k_0 + k_1 x + \frac{k_2}{2} x^2 - \frac{k_3}{3} x^3 + k_4 z, \tag{8.10}$$

with k_0 unspecified. The authors assume $k_0 = 0$ (zero advertising equals zero sales), but this model can clearly accommodate a nonzero sales level at zero advertising, in line with Little's second phenomenon. Then Eq. (8.10) can be used in Eq. (8.1) to allocate an advertising budget over districts and over time.

The basic procedure is illustrated with applications to five brands. The average value of the coefficients of determination (R^2) for the within-market models, Eq. (8.5), was 0.89; and the average R^2 for the response curves, Eq. (8.9), was 0.60. Thus the fits appear adequate. Exhibit 8.6(a) graphs the relationship between marginal sales due to advertising and average expenditure levels for one of the five brands (brand B), while Exhibit 8.6(b) shows the associated advertising-response function. The authors show how this model can be used to evaluate alternative advertising policies, and they make a case for pulsing (sporadic high levels of advertising followed by lower levels) when the response is S-shaped.

Companies have applied this method widely, expanding the model to incorporate dealing and price effects as well (Rao 1978; Eastlack and Rao 1986, 1989).

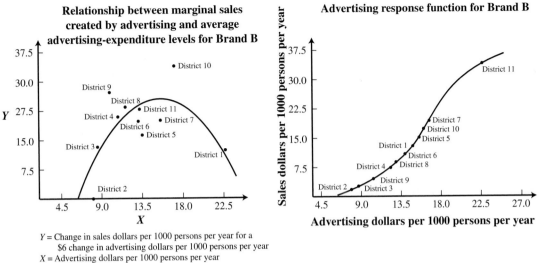

Relationship between marginal sales created by advertising and average advertising-expenditure levels for Brand B

Advertising response function for Brand B

Y = Change in sales dollars per 1000 persons per year for a
     $6 change in advertising dollars per 1000 persons per year
X = Advertising dollars per 1000 persons per year

(a)   (b)

EXHIBIT 8.6

Rao and Miller's econometric model for advertising decisions. Graph (a) shows the inverted U-shaped relationship between advertising and the per capita change in sales, and graph (b) shows the response function that results from integrating curve (a). *Source*: Rao and Miller 1975, p. 13.

Some products show S-shaped responses, whereas others show concave responses. Like most other econometric models this modeling approach has a variety of weaknesses. Of Little's desirable phenomena it includes only the second, a possible S-shaped response. However, the model could be extended to include competitive effects (phenomenon 3), and copy and media effectiveness could be included as an effectiveness factor in the x's. Equation (8.4) does not readily admit differing rise and decay times. And with all econometric-based models, the data quality and its variability determine the acceptability of the model fit. In addition, while the authors report an S-shaped response, Hanssens, Parsons, and Schultz (1990) criticize their statistical methodology.

In conclusion this approach, while it has some flaws, is both simple and useful. It uses econometric methods to estimate the local conditions of a (postulated) global response curve. Furthermore, it blends well with the type of data typically collected for frequently purchased packaged goods.

The ADBUDG model: Little (1970) introduced the judgmental, decision calculus approach with his ADBUDG model. Like Rao and Miller, Little focuses on market-share response to advertising spending without explicitly considering competitive effects. Little bases the ADBUDG model on the following assumptions (Exhibit 8.7):

1. If advertising is cut to zero, brand share will decrease; but there is a floor, or minimum, to which the share will fall from its initial value by the end of one time period.
2. If advertising is increased a great deal, say, to something that could be called saturation, brand share will increase; but there is a ceiling, or maximum, on how much can be achieved by the end of one time period.

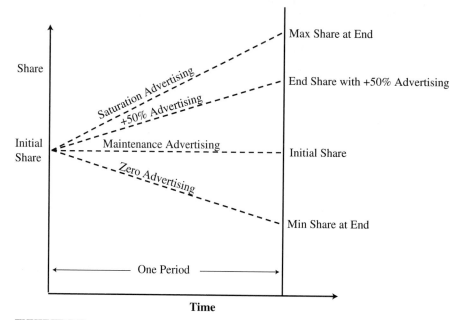

EXHIBIT 8.7
Assumptions about the one-period response for Little's ADBUDG model that can be used to develop a response function.

3. There is some advertising rate that will maintain initial share.
4. An estimate can be made based on data analysis or managerial judgment of the effect on share by the end of one period of a 50 percent increase in advertising over the maintenance rate.

These assumptions are represented as four points on a share-response-to-advertising curve in Exhibit 8.8. This is the ADBUDG function from Chapter 2:

$$\text{share} = b + (a - b)\frac{\text{adv}^c}{d + \text{adv}^c} . \tag{8.11}$$

The constants a, b, c, and d are implicitly determined by the input data. Equation (8.11) represents a versatile but nevertheless restricted set of response relations.

The value specified for the increase in market share with a 50 percent increase in advertising is an important determinant of the advertising rate, while the values of a (maximum) and b (minimum) restrict changes to a meaningful range.

Although Exhibit 8.8 shows an S-shaped curve, Eq. (8.11) need not provide such a shape. If $c > 1$, the curve will be S-shaped; for $0 < c < 1$, it will be a concave function. The particular c will depend on the input data.

The description so far has omitted consideration of time delays. To take these into account, the model assumes

1. In the absence of advertising, share would eventually decay to some long-run minimum value (possibly zero).
2. The decay in one time period will be a constant fraction of the gap between current share and the long-run minimum; that is, decay is exponential.

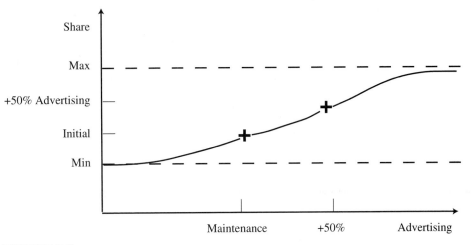

EXHIBIT 8.8
The ADBUDG model uses the data generated from the assumptions in Exhibit 8.7 to develop a smooth advertising-response function.

Let long-run min denote the long-run minimum and persistence denote the fraction of the difference between share and long-run minimum that is retained after a period of decay. Under the foregoing assumptions,

$$\text{persistence} = \frac{\text{min} - \text{long-run min}}{\text{initial share} - \text{long-run min}} \, ;$$

$$\text{share}_t = \text{long-run min} + \text{persistence} \times [\text{share}_{t-1} - \text{long-run min}]$$

$$+ \, (a - b) \, \frac{\text{adv}_t^c}{d + \text{adv}_t^c} \, . \tag{8.12}$$

This is a simple, dynamic model. It is easy to explain, and it behaves reasonably. It could be further generalized by permitting some of the constants to change with time, but that does not seem desirable at the moment.

What exactly do we mean by *advertising*? Dollars? Exposures? A product manager worries about spending rates, media, and copy. Let us construct two time-varying indices: (1) a media efficiency index, and (2) a copy effectiveness index. We will assume both have reference values of 1.0. We then hypothesize that the delivered advertising, that is, the adv_t that goes into the response function in (8.10), is given by wtd adv_t, weighted advertising:

$$\text{wtd adv}_t = \text{media efficiency}_t \times \text{media effectiveness}_t \times \text{adv dollars}_t. \tag{8.13}$$

We can determine the media efficiency and copy effectiveness indices subjectively, but better alternatives exist. Copy testing is helpful, and we can use data on media cost, exposures by market segment, and relative value of market segments to develop a media index. (We can include other effects such as product class sales effects, promotion, competition, and price in this model, but we will not deal with them here.) To summarize the model:

1. Share

$$\begin{aligned}
\text{adjusted share}_t = \ & \text{long-run min} \\
& + \text{persistence} \times [\text{share}_{t-1} - \text{long-run min}] \\
& + (a - b)\ \frac{\text{wtd adv}_t^c}{d + \text{wtd adv}_t^c}.
\end{aligned} \tag{8.14a}$$

2. Brand sales

$$\text{adjusted sales}_t = \text{product class sales index}_t \times \text{adjusted share}_t. \tag{8.14b}$$

3. Profits

$$\begin{aligned}
\text{contribution to profit after adv}_t = \ & \text{contribution per sales unit}_t \\
& \times \text{brand sales}_t \\
& \times \text{adv dollars}_t.
\end{aligned} \tag{8.14c}$$

The spreadsheet that accompanies the Blue Mountain Coffee case provides an implementation of the ADBUDG model that you can easily adapt to other situations.

Several of the problems with the ADBUDG model are that it does not include competition, that the one-period response limits (max and min) are independent of the market share at the beginning of the period, that advertising is independent of other marketing-mix effects, and that in the long run enough advertising can make market share exceed 100 percent. However, the model is simple and easy to understand, and it incorporates both single-period and carryover effects in an intuitively appealing manner.

As Little (1979) noted, models for budgeting advertising are seldom used. We hope that the software in this book will both demonstrate the ease with which ADBUDG can be implemented and also encourage its wider use.

Given that the effects of advertising are little understood and difficult to measure, it is not surprising that firms rely on the guidelines and informal rules of thumb outlined above as well as more formal guidelines like the ADVISOR approach.

The shared experience approach—ADVISOR: The ADVISOR models follow the PIMS, shared experience approach (Chapter 6), but they focus more narrowly on the strategy for setting a budget for marketing industrial products. Begun in 1973 at MIT, the ADVISOR studies were sponsored by more than 80 companies who provided data on more than 300 industrial businesses.

Researchers analyzed the decision processes the sponsoring firms used in budgeting and also reviewed earlier studies. They found that models of marketing-communications spending should incorporate the effect of interaction between product and market characteristics, such as stage in the product life cycle and degree of product complexity, and should allow for a non-linear relationship between the level of spending and those product and market characteristics.

The level of spending on advertising or marketing is dictated primarily by the sales level of the product as measured by last year's sales, and by the number of customers the marketing effort must reach. The firm then modifies that spending level to accommodate such factors as stage in the life cycle of the product, customer concentration, and technical complexity of the product.

A simple model that reflects these concepts is multiplicative:

$$\text{marketing}_t = b_0 \times \text{sales}_{t-1}^{b_1} \times \text{users}_2^{b_2} \times \text{var}_3^{b_3} \times \cdots \times \text{var}_9^{b_9}, \tag{8.15}$$

where

$b_0, \ldots, b_9$ = regression coefficients;

marketing = spending on marketing, in dollars (primarily personal selling, technical service, and marketing-communication expenditures);

sales = sales dollars (lagged one year);

users = number of individuals the marketing program must reach; and

var_i = other variables (stage in life cycle, product plans, etc.).

Exhibit 8.9 gives the main results of the ADVISOR models. Both advertising and marketing are strongly and positively related to sales (column 1). As sales increase, advertising gets less of the marketing dollar, perhaps because the number of trade journals is limited, while no such limit exists on the salesforce (row 2). As the number of users increases, firms spend more money on marketing and on advertising, but there is no obvious effect on the A/M ratio (column 2).

Researchers have developed other models to consider media selection, choice of distribution channels, changes in spending patterns, and use of trade shows (Lilien 1979, 1993). Furthermore, Lilien and Weinstein (1984) have replicated the results of these studies for a sample of 80 products in Europe, with remarkably consistent results. The Convection Company case provides you with a context in which to use the ADVISOR model to evaluate industrial-marketing budgeting decisions.

Thus advertising causes many different responses in the market, many of which have been reported in empirical studies (Leone 1995; Lodish et al. 1995b; Kaul and Wittink 1995). Still we need more knowledge about the dynamics of the effects and their estimation. Advances in measurement through electronic point-of-sale equipment and purchases on the Internet will improve our understanding of advertising phenomena, and this will permit us to further refine advertising models and make better advertising decisions.

MEDIA DECISIONS

Ad agencies specialize in two major decision areas: the creative decision, discussed next, and the media decision. In selecting media the agencies try to find the best way to expose the target audience to a message the desired number of times and to schedule those exposures over the planning period.

We will elaborate on the concept of "desired number of exposures." Presumably the advertiser wants a response to its advertising from the target audience. Assume that the desired response is a certain level of product trial, which depends on, among other things, the level of brand awareness in the audience. Suppose product trial increases at a diminishing rate with the level of audience awareness (Exhibit 8.10a). Then if the advertiser wants to achieve a product trial rate of T^*, it must achieve a brand-awareness rate of A^*, and the task is to find out how many exposures E^* it needs to produce this awareness.

The effect of an advertisement on audience awareness depends on that ad's reach, frequency, and impact:

Reach (R): The number of persons or households exposed to a particular ad at least once during a specified time period. The media model assumes that if someone is exposed to a particular media vehicle carrying an ad, then that person is also "exposed" to the ad.

Dependent Variable	Continuous Variables						Dichotomous Variables			Constant	$\dfrac{R^2}{F}$	$\dfrac{SSE}{N}$
	Sales (LSLS)	Number of Users (LUSERS)	Customer Concentration (LCONC)	Fraction of Sales Made to Order (LSPEC)	Prospect/Customers Product Attitudes Difference (DIFF)	Sales Direct to Users (LDIR-USER)	Stage in Life Cycle (LCYCLE)	Product Plans (PLANS)	Product Complexity (PROD)			
Advertising (LADV)	+0.618 (9.1)	+0.104 (3.6)	-1.881 (3.1)	-1.989 (4.4)	a	a	-0.892 (3.2)	-1.503 (6.0)	a	-0.651	0.59 – 25.0	1.12 – 110
A/M [Logit (A/M)]	-0.232 (4.5)	a	a	a	+0.383 (2.0)	-0.255 (2.1)	a	a	-0.230[b] (1.2)	+0.544	0.24 – 7.5	0.91 – 100
Marketing (LMKTG)	+0.712 (12.6)	+0.082 (3.1)	-1.633 (3.1)	-0.993 (2.8)	-0.305 (1.7)	-0.194[b] (0.6)	-0.424 (2.0)	-0.809 (3.9)	+0.528 (2.5)	+0.185	0.72 – 28.2	0.91 – 110

Note: t statistics in ( ); all equations significant at $\alpha < 0.001$. [a]Variable insignificant and logically irrelevant. [b]Variable retained for logical consistency.

EXHIBIT 8.9

ADVISOR model coefficients for advertising (A), the advertising-to-marketing (M) ratio ([logit(A/M) = log[A/(M − A)]), and marketing. LMKTG means that the equation for advertising (ADV) is linear after taking logs (Eq. 8.15). *Source*: Lilien 1979.

Average frequency (F): The average number of times within the specified time period that a person or household in the target segment is exposed to the message.

Impact (I): The qualitative value of an exposure through a given medium (thus a food ad would have a higher impact in *Good Housekeeping* than it would have in *Popular Mechanics*).

Exhibit 8.10(b) shows the relationship between audience awareness and reach. Audience awareness is greater the higher the exposures' reach, frequency, and impact. Furthermore, there are trade-offs among reach, frequency, and impact. For example, suppose the media planner has an advertising budget of $1 million and the cost per thousand exposures of average quality is $5. Then he can buy 200 million exposures (equal to $1,000,000 × 1000/$5). If he seeks an average exposure frequency of 10, then he can reach 20 million people (equal to 200,000,000/10) with the $1 million budget. But if he wants to use higher-quality media, costing $10 per thousand exposures, he can reach only 10 million people, unless he is willing to decrease the frequency of exposures.

The following concepts capture the relationship among reach, frequency, and impact:

Total number of exposures (E) is the reach times the average frequency, that is, $E = R \times F$. It is also called gross rating points (GRP). If a given media schedule reaches 80 percent of the homes with an average exposure frequency of three, the media schedule is said to have a GRP of 240 (80 × 3). If another media schedule has a GRP of 300, it can be said to have more weight, but we cannot tell from GRP alone how this weight breaks up into reach and frequency.

Weighted number of exposures (WE) is the reach times the average frequency times the average impact, that is,

$$WE = R \times F \times I. \tag{8.16}$$

We can view the problem of planning as follows. With a given budget what is the most cost-effective combination of reach, frequency, and impact to buy?

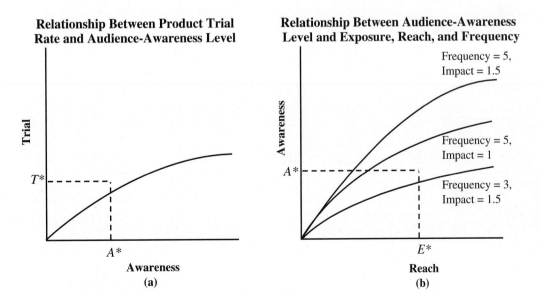

Relationship Between Product Trial Rate and Audience-Awareness Level

Relationship Between Audience-Awareness Level and Exposure, Reach, and Frequency

EXHIBIT 8.10
Relationship among trial, awareness, and the exposure function: Increasing the reach of an ad leads to an increase in the level of awareness (b), which in turn leads to an increase in trial for a new product (a).

In choosing a combination of media types, the media planner considers (1) the media habits of the target audience, (2) the characteristics of the product, (3) the message, and (4) the relative costs. On the basis of media impacts and costs, the planner chooses specific subgroups within each media type (PC magazines, daytime TV, daily newspapers in 20 major markets) that produce the desired response in the most cost-effective way. He or she then makes a final judgment on which specific vehicles will deliver the best combination of reach, frequency, and impact for the money.

Some agencies (and firms) use mathematical models to help them in making media plans. The media-decision problem can be stated as follows:

Given a media budget, an advertising message and copy, a set of media alternatives, and data describing the audiences and the costs of the media alternatives, decide (1) what media alternatives to use, (2) how many insertions in each and their timing, and (3) what type of advertising units (e.g., the size and color for print ads) for each of the media alternatives in such a way that you maximize the effect (measured in some way) of the media budget. The output of the media-decision process is called the media schedule, and it actually depends on your choice of an objective function. The most desirable measure of the effect of different media schedules is their impact on company profits. However, most media models do not presume a knowledge of the current or long-run sales or profit that advertisements placed in different media will generate. Instead they use various communication surrogates to measure the effectiveness of advertising when future sales would be difficult or impossible to measure. In media models the surrogate that is used most often is the number of exposures to members of the target audience—that is, the weighted number of exposures, defined in (8.16). To determine the total weighted-exposure value of a media schedule we must know two things: (1) the net cumulative audience of each media vehicle as a function of the number of exposures and (2) the level of audience duplication across all pairs of vehicles. In the case of two media alternatives we would typically use the following equation for net coverage:

$$R = r_1(X_1) + r_2(X_2) - r_{1,2}(X_{1,2}),\tag{8.17}$$

where

$R =$ reach of media schedule (i.e., total weighted-exposure value with replication and duplication removed);

$r_i(X_i) =$ number of persons in audience of media i; and

$r_{1,2}(X_{1,2}) =$ number of persons in audience of both media vehicles.

With three media alternatives, their reach would be

$$R = r_1(X_1) + r_2(X_2) + r_3(X_3) - r_{1,2}(X_{1,2}) - r_{1,3}(X_{1,3}) - r_{2,3}(X_{2,3}) + r_{1,2,3}(X_{1,2,3}).\tag{8.18}$$

In this case net coverage is found by summing the separate reaches of the three vehicles with the triplicated group and subtracting all the duplicated audiences. This equation can be generalized to the case of n media alternatives.

Obtaining data on the size of audience overlap for different sets of media vehicles requires large and expensive samples. Agostini (1961) has developed a useful estimation formula based on data from a French study of media-audience overlap, showing that total reach for magazine insertions can be estimated by

$$C = \frac{1}{K(D/A) + 1}\,A,\tag{8.19}$$

where

C = total reach;

K = constant, estimated as 1.125;

$$A = \sum_{j=1}^{n} r_j\left(X_j\right)$$

= total number of persons in audiences of media 1, 2, . . ., n; and

$$D = \sum_{j=1}^{n} \sum_{k=j+1}^{n} r_{jk}\left(X_{jk}\right),$$

= total of all pairwise duplicated audiences.

This relationship with parameter $K = 1.125$ has been shown to be a useful approximation for American and Canadian magazines as well (Bower 1963). See Claycamp and McClelland (1968) for an analytical interpretation of the formula. In a review of reach models, Rust (1986) recommends using the Agostini model to estimate the reach of a single vehicle and recommends Hofmans's (1966) model for two or more vehicles. Rust also provides an excellent review of models that have been developed to estimate audience overlap and exposure frequency. For some other methods for estimating both reach and frequency, see Rice (1988) Rust, Zimmer, and Leone (1986), Lancaster and Martin (1988), and Danaher (1989).

Media-scheduling models can work with a sales objective function, an effective-exposure value, or with reach and frequency separately. The most appropriate measures of sales and effective exposure are also the most difficult to use, because they are the most difficult to model and measure.

There are usually three components in models for media decisions: (1) the objective function, which assigns a value (e.g., profit or effective exposures) to an insertion schedule, (2) the solution strategy (e.g., heuristic or optimization), and (3) the constraints (e.g., the budget).

There are generally five principal components of the objective function:

1. The vehicle exposure measure—used to measure the net reach, schedule exposure, or GRPs (gross rating points)
2. The repetition effect—the relative impact of successive exposures on the same person
3. The forgetting effect—the forgetting between exposures and the nature of the decay
4. The media-option source effect—the relative impact of exposures from different sources
5. The segmentation effect—who is exposed and the fraction of the audience that represents target segments

We can classify media models by their solution approaches: optimizing models and nonoptimizing approaches. Optimizing models include several classes of mathematical-programming models, and nonoptimizing approaches include heuristic-programming, stepwise or marginal-analysis procedures, and simulation models.

In the early and mid-1960s researchers working on media models focused on linear-programming approaches. The main constraints they included were the size of the advertising budget, the minimum and maximum uses of specific media vehicles and media categories, and the desirable, minimum exposure rates to different target buyers. Choosing a best plan required them to specify an effectiveness criterion, which for media selection was usually the weighted number of exposures.

These models, and others such as MEDIAC (Little and Lodish 1966), were very sophisticated and required a lot of data, many managerial judgments, and vast computer power to generate schedules. After a decade of trial, advertising agencies developed heuristic procedures embedded in decision support systems that generate very good (if not optimal) schedules in much less time and with much less effort and cost than the more sophisticated methods (Simon and Thiel 1980). In addition, media planners could understand these methods more easily.

The increasing availability of single-source data (combining purchasing patterns and exposures to advertising and other forms of communication) and flexible database-management software makes it likely that new models will be developed (Eskin 1985; Kamin 1988). See Rust (1986) and Leckenby and Ju (1989) for reviews of media models.

ADVERTISING COPY DEVELOPMENT AND DECISIONS

Much of the effect of an advertising exposure depends on the creative quality of the ad itself. But rating the quality of ads is extremely difficult, and much controversy surrounds copy testing. An advertisement may have very good aesthetic properties and win awards, and yet it may not do much for sales (e.g., Nissan's introductory ad for its Infiniti car that did not include a picture of the car). Another advertisement may seem crude and offensive (e.g., the classic Wisk "ring around the collar" ad), and yet it may be a major force behind sales. Such properties in advertisements as humor, believability, informativeness, simplicity, and memorability have not shown consistent relationships with sales generation. In this section we discuss three topics: testing copy and measuring its copy effectiveness, rating the creative quality of ads, and a new approach to designing ads.

Copy effectiveness

Copy strategy is based on advertising objectives. For a new brand, copy is oriented toward building broad awareness and inducing trial, whereas for established brands it focuses on reminding individuals to use the brand, increasing the rate of use, and distinguishing the brand from other brands. Thus in creating an ad, one must find the facts and ideas that match what a brand delivers with the objectives for the copy.

The goal of copy testing is to determine if an ad is likely to work. Two elements are involved in copy testing: measuring the dependent variable (e.g., response) and the setting for the measurement. The possible measures of response include the following:

1. Attention and impression—the ability of the ad to attract attention and be memorable
2. Communication and understanding—the ability of the ad to convey the message clearly and unambiguously to people in the target market
3. Persuasion—the ability of the ad to modify people's attitudes and beliefs about the product on certain key attributes or to change their overall purchase intentions
4. Purchase—the ability of the ad to positively affect purchasing behavior

The latter two measures, while most appropriate, are also the most difficult to measure.

Copy tests can also be classified by whether they use a laboratory setting, a simulated natural environment, or a totally natural environment (i.e., market tests). Laboratory and simulated-natural-environment methods include focus group interviews and a variety of physiological recording devices, including eye cameras (measuring eye movement), polygraphs and related devices (measuring emotional or psychological responses), and pupilometers (measuring pupil dilation, which occurs when people see something interesting).

In simulated natural environments, researchers usually bring subjects to a theater, where they measure their interest, liking, and often likelihood of purchase before and after exposing them to the advertising copy. Some procedures provide on-line measurements during exposure. For example, Schwerin shows ads embedded in TV programs and measures changes in brand liking arising from the ad.

A number of companies provide market tests. Usually they limit their campaigns to a small region and ask respondents (both those exposed to the ad and those not exposed) to answer various measures of recall and preference. Burke's AdTel and IRI's BehaviorScan can use split-cable techniques and personal interviews, along with a mail panel, to measure the effects of ads.

These methods provide some measures that may (or may not) be related to product sales. In an interesting cross-cultural comparison of advertisers' attitudes toward copy testing, Boyd and Ray (1971) found that market testing companies emphasize predictive validity, explanatory power, and reliability and do not use sales as a criterion because of measurement problems.

EXAMPLE

Developing AT&T's cost-of-visit campaign: Kuritsky et al. (1982) developed and tested a new ad copy program for AT&T Long Lines—the *cost-of-visit* campaign. Their research took five years, cost over $1 million, and comprised four "projects": (1) a segmentation study of the residential long-distance market, (2) tracking studies to test customer awareness of interstate phone rates, (3) qualitative research on customer attitudes to develop an ad concept, and (4) a large-scale, split-cable experiment that measured the effect of the advertising program in the marketplace.

In the segmentation study they established that there was a light-user group that looked (demographically) just like the heavy-user group, but it was composed of people who thought phoning was expensive: they had a price barrier. The second phase showed that most people overestimated the cost of long-distance phoning by over 50 percent. The third phase established the *cost-of-visit* theme, which included four elements:

1. *Surprise* that the cost is so low

2. *Appropriateness* of a 20-minute "visit" on the phone

3. *Maximum cost* ($3.33 or less)

4. *Taxes included* (no hidden costs)

The fourth phase of the study was the AdTel, split-cable experiment. In the AdTel system two cables distribute TV programming to households. AdTel divides a geographic area into small cells of 40 to 50 subscribers in a checkerboard pattern, each of which receives either signal A or signal B. (On a checkerboard, the red squares would get program A, the black squares program B.)

AdTel tested the cost-of-visit campaign against AT&T's very successful reach-out campaign using a panel of 16,000 households. Because there is no (necessary) delay between the time an ad is shown and when someone can make a call, and because AT&T automatically records data on calls, one can read the response to advertising in this setting much more clearly than in other field environments.

The experiment lasted for over two years and had three phases: (a) pre-assessment (5 months), (b) treatment period (15 months), and (c) post-assessment (6 months).

During the pre-assessment phase AT&T tracked the records of all households to establish a norm for their calling behavior. In addition the company sent all respondents a questionnaire to determine whether their attitudes were the same as those in an earlier study and whether the test and control groups were demographically balanced (they were).

During the treatment period AT&T aired the two ad campaigns at a rate that gave each household about three exposures per week. The objective of the *cost-of visit* campaign was to encourage all user groups, but particularly the light-user group, to call during the 60-percent-off, deep-discount period (nights and weekends). The results of the study showed that, overall, an average household made an additional one-half long distance call during the deep-discount period while the targeted light-user group made about an additional one and a half calls. (These results were significant at the 0.01 level.) In addition there was an overall increase in revenue of about 1 percent overall, and the targeted light-user group yielded a 15 percent increase in revenue.

To make these assessments and to project them to the rational level, AT&T used the following model:

USDF $\;=\;$ usage difference between the test group (cost-of-visit) and the control group (reach-out)

$\;=\;$ (Average usage during treatment for the test $-$ average usage during pre-assessment for the test group) $-$

(Average usage during treatment for the control group $-$ average usage during pre-assessment for control group)

UNOFF $\;=\;$ dummy variable

$$= \begin{cases} 0 \text{ for pretest weeks,} \\ 1 \text{ for test weeks,} \end{cases}$$

$\varepsilon \;=\;$ disturbance.

The regression model:

$$\text{USDF} = \alpha + \beta \times \text{UNOFF} + \varepsilon \tag{8.20}$$

models the difference in usage/household/week as a preperiod constant (a) and a treatment constant ($a + b$). So the statistical significance of b for any segment (light users in a deep-discount period, for example) can be read from standard confidence limits resulting from linear regression analysis.

To project the results to the national level, AT&T used the following model:

$$y = \sum_{i=1}^{I} \left(n_i \sum_{j=1}^{J} z_{ij} p_{ij} \right), \tag{8.21}$$

where

y = projected usage in a given area, assuming a given level of advertising exposure;

i = index of usage segment (light, regular, etc.), $i = 1, \ldots, I$;

j = index of calling category (rate period), $j = 1, \ldots, J$;

z_{ij} = usage measure per household in cell i for calling category j;

n_i = number of households of segment type i in the area; and

p_{ij} = fraction increase or decrease in cell i, category j with "cost-of-visit" versus "reach-out."

The national or any regional projection can be made by summing over the appropriate areas.

The results of the analysis showed that AT&T was projected to earn more than $100 million more from the light-user segment without any increase in capital expenditures by introducing this new ad copy.

This study is one of the few that has demonstrated a significant impact on purchase and usage behavior based on a variation in ad copy strategy. It demonstrates the effectiveness of a systematic approach for testing ad copy. We expect that as electronic commerce and direct marketing become more prevalent, we will see more experiments of this type.

Estimating the creative quality of ads

Several researchers have tried to relate desirable characteristics of ads to quantifiable mechanical and message elements. Most have focused on readership or recall scores for print ads, the easiest types of ads and response variables to measure. In an interesting early study of this type, Twedt (1952) regressed readership scores of 151 advertisements in *The American Builder* against a large number of variables and found that the parameters of size of the advertisement, size of illustration, and number of colors account for over 50 percent of the variance in advertising readership. Interestingly, these mechanical variables explained advertising-readership variation better than many of the content variables that Twedt also tried out in the regression.

Diamond (1968) performed a well-known regression study of the effect of advertising-format variables on readership scores. His data were 1070 advertisements that appeared in *Life* between February 7 and July 31, 1964. For each advertisement he had six different (Starch) readership scores: "noted," "seen-associated," and "read most" for both men and women readers. In addition to these six readership scores, he measured 12 variables related to each ad: product class, past advertising expenditure, number of ads in the issue, size, number of colors, bleed/no bleed, left or right page, position in the magazine, layout, number of words, brand prominence, and headline prominence.

Diamond fitted several regression models and used the coefficients to draw conclusions about the effects of different variables on readership score. He found that the readership score was higher the larger the advertisement, the greater the number of colors, and the fewer the number of advertisements in the issue; he found that right-hand-page advertisements gained more attention than left-hand-page advertisements; and that advertisements with photographs did better than advertisements with illustrations, and both did better than nonpictorial advertisements.

In a study of the effectiveness of industrial print ads, Hanssens and Weitz (1980) related 24 ad characteristics to recall, readership, and inquiry generation for 1160 industrial ads in *Electronic Design*. They used a model of the form

$$y_i = e^a \prod_{j=1}^{p_t} x_{ij}^{b_j} \prod_{j=p_t+1}^{p} \left(1 + x'_{ij}\right)^{b_j} e^{\mu_i}, \qquad (8.22)$$

where

y_i = effectiveness measure for ith ad;

x_{ij} = value of jth nonbinary characteristic of the ith ad (page number, ad size), $j = 1, \ldots, p_t$;

x'_{ij} = value (0 or 1) of jth binary characteristic of ith ad (bleed, color, etc.);

e^a = scale factor; and

μ_i = error term

($\prod$ means product or "times" ($\times$)).

They segmented 15 product groups into three categories—routine purchase items, unique purchase items, and important purchase items—by factor analysis of purchasing-process similarity ratings obtained from readers of the magazine. Their results are similar to those of Twedt (1952) and Diamond (1968): they found that advertising characteristics account for more than 45 percent of the variance in the "seen" effectiveness measure, more than 30 percent of the "read-most" effectiveness measure, and between 19 and 36 percent of the variance in inquiry generation. Thus the variance explained by the "seen" measure is significantly greater than that explained by the "read-most" measure, which in turn is greater than that explained by the inquiry measure. These results are consistent across the three product categories. They are also in line with a hierarchy-of-effects model, which postulates that communication variables typically have a greater effect on lower-order responses (awareness) than on higher-order responses (behavior).

Hanssens and Weitz also found that both recall and readership were strongly related to format and layout variables (ad size, colors, bleed, use of photographs/illustrations, etc.), while the effects were weaker for inquiry generation. The effects of some factors, such as ad size, were consistently related across product groups and effectiveness measures, while others, such as the use of attention-getting methods (woman in ad, size of headline, etc.), were specific to the product category and the effectiveness measure.

As noted earlier, the only reported similar study for broadcast ads was that of Sewall and Sarel (1986). Much of the research cited here and in the previous section uses some recall measure(s) as dependent variable(s) (rather than an action measure) and neglects the effect of timing of exposures, measures of advertising believability, validity and reliability assessment, and the like. (See Rossiter and Percy (1987) for a good discussion of the practical issues involved in ad testing.)

Advertising design

Can we, in some sense, reverse the foregoing process: that is, use information about what copy platforms work best to develop a complete advertising design? A system called ADCAD is designed to aid advertisers of consumer products in developing advertising objectives and copy strategy and in selecting communication approaches. An implementation of ADCAD is included with this book.

ADCAD is a rule-based expert system that allows managers to translate their qualitative perception of marketplace behavior into a basis for deciding on advertising design. Exhibit 8.11 shows an overview of the stages of the advertising-design process and the operation of the ADCAD system. The ADCAD system assumes that before purchasing a brand a consumer must (1) have a need that can be satisfied by purchasing this brand, (2) be aware that the brand can satisfy this need, (3) recognize the brand and distinguish it from its close substitutes, and (4) have no other behavioral or attitudinal obstacles to purchasing the brand. Advertising can address one or more of these issues: it can stimulate demand for the product category, create brand awareness, facilitate brand recognition, and modify beliefs about the brand that might be barriers to purchase.

ADCAD starts by asking for background information about the product, the nature of competition, the characteristics of the target audience(s), and so on, and it then develops a communication strategy for each target audience. Exhibit 8.12 lists a sample of rules for setting objectives for a specific application.

ADCAD then selects communications approaches to achieve the advertising and marketing objectives based on the characteristics of the consumers, the product, and the environment. It makes recommendations concerning the position of the ad, the characteristics of the message, the characteristics of the presenter, and the emotional tone of the ad. Exhibit 8.13 lists a sample of rules that ADCAD uses in considering each of these issues.

Where do these rules (the *knowledge base*) come from? The rules and judgments come from three sources: published theoretical results, published empirical studies, and ad agency experience. To go from these rules, or the knowledge base, to concrete recommendations the program uses what is called an inference engine, which logically processes the rules and facts in a way that solves the problem the user poses. Specifically, ADCAD requests information on the name and product class of the brand to be advertised and the name of the target segment. It then uses the rules in a goal-driven procedure (called backward chaining) to search for alternative communication approaches and copy strategies that best meet the conditions specified by the user. ADCAD asks the user for the minimal information it needs to evaluate the current set of alternatives that it cannot infer from the user's past responses. When it seeks only a single answer or conclusion about a variable (e.g., the life-cycle stage of the product), ADCAD stops seeking further answers to that variable as soon as it gets one answer. When it could expect multiple responses regarding a variable (e.g., benefits sought), ADCAD seeks multiple answers (or recommendations).

Exhibits 8.14 and 8.15 show the inference process for a consultation on the Suave Shampoo case (Albion 1984a,b). Exhibit 8.14 shows sample input and output (ADCAD's recommendations). Exhibit 8.15 shows how the system links user inputs with rules in the knowledge base to reach conclusions.

The Suave case describes the shampoo market as mature, competitive, and highly fragmented. Eighteen- to thirty-four-year-old women are traditionally the heaviest users of shampoo. Suave management segments this market into three groups: loyal Suave users (22 percent), consumers who have tried Suave but now use other brands (28 percent), and consumers who have never tried Suave (50 percent). The firm is targeting the third group, and the user enters this information.

ADCAD first asks the user questions to identify the firm's marketing objectives. When requesting information, the system provides a "What" facility in which the user can find detailed definitions regarding the terminology the system uses in questions and a "Why" facility in which the user can learn why it is using a certain piece of information in the particular decision. In the Suave example ADCAD infers that, because shampoo is a mature

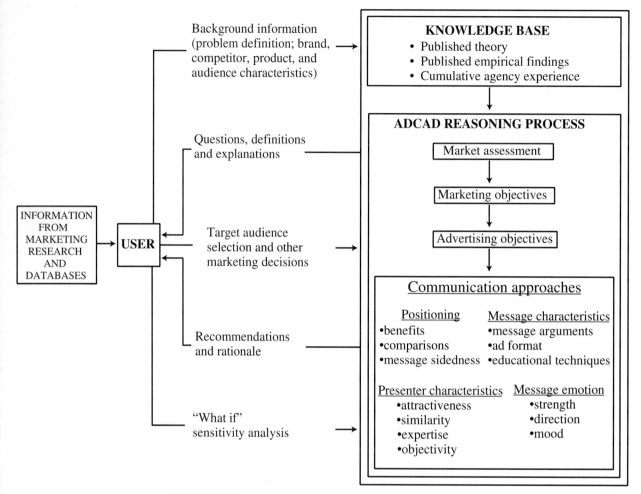

EXHIBIT 8.11
Overview of the major steps in advertising design and user interaction with ADCAD, showing the interaction of the user with the environment and the role of ADCAD's knowledge base and reasoning process in generating recommendations.

product and most consumers use it often, it is not necessary to increase primary demand. The target audience has not used Suave, and so ADCAD suggests stimulating brand trial.

Next ADCAD tries to determine appropriate advertising objectives. The user states that the motivation of the audience in purchasing a brand of shampoo is not to clean hair, but to enhance self-esteem and achieve social approval, and so ADCAD proposes that advertising should communicate a brand image, mood, or lifestyle (Rossiter and Percy 1987; Wells 1981). The case includes the information that buyers make brand decisions at the point of purchase, and so the system recommends that advertising should enhance brand recognition (Bettman 1979).

ADCAD then tries to choose a benefit to be featured in the advertisement and to determine effective communication approaches. Suave sells at a much lower price than its competitors but offers similar product features. The price attribute is important to the target audience, and so ADCAD recommends positioning on value. However, the user anticipates the introduction of low-priced competing shampoos, and he or she overrides this suggestion and chooses instead to enhance the quality image of Suave. The image-oriented creative strategy dictates a one-sided message.

Marketing Objectives (11 rules)
- IF product life cycle stage = introduction AND innovation type = discontinuous THEN marketing objective = stimulate primary demand
- IF brand usage = none THEN marketing objective = stimulate brand trial
- IF current brand usage = some AND (brand switching = high OR product usage rate = fixed) THEN marketing objective = stimulate repeat purchase/loyalty
- IF current brand usage = some AND brand switching = low AND product usage rate = variable THEN marketing objective = increase rate of brand usage

Advertising Objectives (18 rules)
- IF marketing objective = stimulate primary demand AND product purchase motivation direction = negative THEN ad objective = convey product category information
- IF marketing objective = stimulate brand trail AND brand purchase motivation direction = positive THEN ad objective = convey brand image
- IF time of brand decision = at point of purchase AND package visibility = high AND package recognition = low THEN ad objective = increase brand recognition
- IF marketing objective = increase rate of brand usage AND new brand uses = yes THEN ad objective = convey new brand uses

EXHIBIT 8.12
Examples of the rules ADCAD employs in selecting marketing and advertising objectives, set up in the format of rule-based models.

At the end of the consultation ADCAD presents its conclusions. Because shampoos are inexpensive, perceived brand differences are small, and health risks are minimal, ADCAD infers that the purchase decision is low involvement. ADCAD suggests that the firm use an endorsement by an attractive, recognizable, female celebrity to attract the audience's attention and communicate the quality image (Petty, Cacioppo, and Schumann 1983; Young and Rubicam 1988). The ad should be appealing, capture what the consumer feels, and use visual stimuli, imagery, and music to enhance the emotional response (Mehrabian 1982; Rossiter 1982; Young and Rubicam 1988). To make salient the audience's motivations in purchasing a brand, ADCAD proposes an emotional tone of apprehension followed by flattery (Rossiter and Percy 1987). Since the audience's evaluation of brand performance is subjective (visible benefit in use is low) and its motivation to process a message is likely to be low, ADCAD recommends making extreme claims for brand performance (Maloney 1962) and showing surrogate indicators of performance (e.g., thick suds, rich colors) (Runyon 1984). To increase brand recognition ADCAD suggests using large color photographs or extended close-ups of the brand's package (Diamond 1968; Holbrook and Lehmann 1980; Starch 1966). The user can explore how ADCAD reached a conclusion, and the system will report the underlying rationale for the recommendation.

The user can review and revise the input information and examine the impact of the revised information on the recommendations. In the Suave example the user considers an alternative scenario in which consumers perceive significant differences between brands. Because they are motivated by social approval and self-esteem, ADCAD infers that the psychosocial risk and involvement for the shampoo decision are now high, and it revises a number of its recommendations. The audience may be somewhat more critical of message claims, and so ADCAD suggests using strong claims with supporting information (Petty, Cacioppo, and Schumann 1983). The audience is more likely to be interested in the brand message, and so ADCAD proposes using the testimonial of an attractive presenter with whom the audience can identify (Brock 1965; Young and Rubicam 1988). ADCAD no longer recommends instilling apprehension in the ad because it assumes that the purchase motivation already exists (Rossiter and Percy 1987).

Positioning (24 rules)
- IF objective = convey brand image or reinforce brand image AND brand purchase motivation = social approval AND brand usage visibility = high THEN possible benefit = "status" (cf. Holbrook and Lehmann 1980)
- IF an objective = convey brand information or change brand beliefs AND perceived differences between brands = small or medium AND perceived relative performance = inferior or parity AND relative performance = superior AND current brand loyalty = competitor loyal THEN message comparison = direct comparison against competition (Gorn and Weinberg 1983)
- IF ad objective = convey brand information or reinforce brand beliefs AND conflicting information = likely AND education = college or graduate AND product knowledge = high AND involvement = high THEN message sidedness = two-sided (McGuire and Papageorgis 1961)

Message Characteristics (80 rules)
- IF ad objective = increase top-of-mind awareness THEN technique = jingle, rhyme, or slogan (MacLachlan 1984)
- IF ad objective = convey brand information or reinforce brand beliefs AND market share > 18.5 AND brand switching = high AND product type = existing THEN technique = sign off (Stewart and Furse 1986)
- IF ad objective = convey brand information or change brand beliefs AND message processing motivation = low AND message processing ability = low THEN ad format = problem solution (Schwerin and Newell 1981)

Presenter Characteristics (20 rules)
- IF ad objective = convey brand information or change brand beliefs AND message processing ability = low THEN presenter expertise = high (Rhine and Severance 1970)
- IF presenter expertise = high THEN time of identification in message = early (Sternthal, Dholakia, and Leavitt 1978)
- IF ad objective = convey brand information or change brand beliefs AND involvement = high THEN presenter objectivity = high (Choo 1964)

Message Emotion (35 rules)
- IF ad objective = convey brand image or reinforce brand image or change brand image THEN emotional direction = positive (Young and Rubicam)
- IF ad objective = convey brand image or reinforce brand image AND brand purchase motivation = sensory stimulation AND message processing motivation = high THEN emotional tone = elation (Rossiter and Percy 1987)
- IF ad objective = change brand beliefs AND message processing motivation = low AND purchase anxiety = low AND brand use avoids fearful consequences = yes THEN emotional tone = high fear (Ray and Wilkie 1970)

EXHIBIT 8.13
Example rules for selecting advertising communication approaches for ADCAD.

ADCAD is a marketing expert system that can help an individual who has little marketing expertise; it incorporates some of the existing knowledge in a package that is readily available and inexpensive. Its major value is its ability to consistently apply research findings and insights to decisions. ADCAD is far from a perfect system: it reasons sequentially, in a buildup procedure rather than holistically; it is not programmed to generate new, creative responses; it is not currently linked to outside databases, and its knowledge base is neither complete nor dynamic—it can become outdated.

On the plus side ADCAD is an emerging, marketing engineering approach to developing advertising copy, and it or its successors may provide great value in developing better ad copy.

A final decision regarding advertising copy is how many ads to create. ADCAD generally suggests a single ad platform, but most ad agencies do not (and should not) stop once they have created a single ad. The first creative idea may be the best, but typically it is not. Often clients want the agency to create and test a few alternative ideas before making a selection. The more advertising campaign themes the agency creates and pretests, the higher is the probability that it will find a really first-rate one. But the more time it spends trying to create alternative themes and advertisements, the higher its costs are. Therefore there must be some optimal number of alternative advertising themes that an agency should try to create and test for the client.

INPUT: Market Assessment

Audience Characteristics:

Sex = female	Past brand usage = none
Product category usage = frequent	Product purchase interval = short
Perceived brand differences = small	Benefit "value" important = yes
Current loyalty = unfavorable brand switcher	Time of brand decision = at point of purchase
Brand purchase motivation = self-esteem, social approval	Package recognition = low

Product-Class Characteristics:

Life-cycle stage = maturity	Complexity = low
Possible to demo. "quality" = yes	Competition = heavy

Brand/Competitor Characteristics:

Brand market share = 2.0	Relative performance = parity
Brand price = $1.40	Competitor price = $3.60
Package visibility at purchase = high	Brand usage visible = low
"Quality" visibility in ad = high	"Quality" visibility in use = low
Benefit "value" unique = yes	Benefit "value" deliverable = yes
Physical/health risks = low	

OUTPUT: Marketing and Advertising Objectives

Marketing objective = stimulate brand trial	Advertising objectives = create/increase brand recognition, communicate brand image/mood/lifestyle

OUTPUT: Communication Approaches

Positioning:

Featured benefit = quality (user replaced recommend benefit = "value")	Message comparison = none
Benefit claim = extremely positive	Message sidedness = one-sided
	Number of benefits = few

Message Characteristics:

Format = demonstration of product in use, endorsement by celebrity, vignette	Technique = closeup, color illustration, long package display, music, visual stimuli/imagery, surrogate indicators of performance, capture consumer emotions

Presenter/Principal Character:

Identity = celebrity	Sex = female
Likability = high	Attraction = high
Identification in message = early	Recognizability = high

Message Emotion:

Strength = high	Direction = positive
Tone = apprehension/flattery	Authenticity of portrayal = high

EXHIBIT 8.14

ADCAD input and output values for a sample consultation on the Suave Shampoo case.

If the client reimbursed the agency for the costs of creating and pretesting advertisements, then the agency might create the optimal number of advertisements for pretesting. Under the normal compensation system, however, the agency's main income is a 15 percent commission on media billings. The agency has no incentive to go through the expense of creating and pretesting many alternative advertisements. Gross (1972) studied this question in an ingenious way and concluded that agencies generally create too few advertisements for pretesting. This result means that the advertiser does not typically get the best possible ad for its money but only the best (one hopes) of the few that the agency created.

To illustrate this point Gross used some "conservative" figures for the variables in his analysis to show that the optimal expenditure for developing and testing copy should be about 15 percent of the advertising budget, more than five times the "typical" value.

Although these types of results have been challenged earlier (see Longman (1968), for example), Gross's basic result has important implications for pretesting procedures. He found that the value of pretesting depended more on the validity of the pretest (how the ad related to sale effectiveness) than on its reliability (how well the measurement is repeated

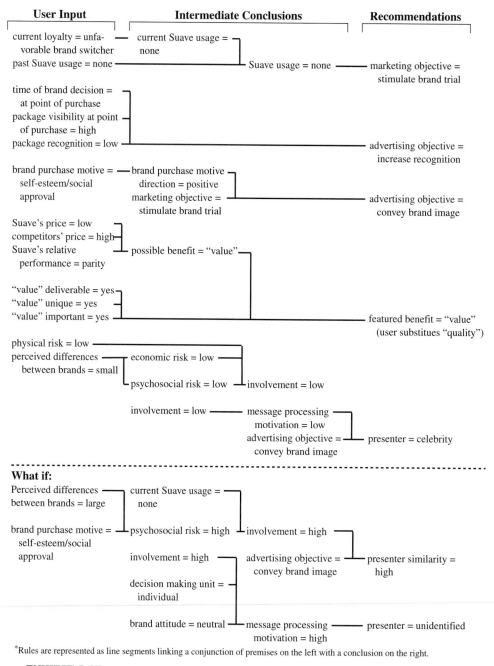

User Input	Intermediate Conclusions	Recommendations

current loyalty = unfavorable brand switcher
past Suave usage = none
— current Suave usage = none
— Suave usage = none —— marketing objective = stimulate brand trial

time of brand decision = at point of purchase
package visibility at point of purchase = high
package recognition = low
—— advertising objective = increase recognition

brand purchase motive = self-esteem/social approval
— brand purchase motive direction = positive
marketing objective = stimulate brand trial
—— advertising objective = convey brand image

Suave's price = low
competitors' price = high
Suave's relative performance = parity
— possible benefit = "value"

"value" deliverable = yes
"value" unique = yes
"value" important = yes
—— featured benefit = "value" (user substitues "quality")

physical risk = low
perceived differences between brands = small
— economic risk = low
— psychosocial risk = low —— involvement = low

involvement = low —— message processing motivation = low
advertising objective = convey brand image —— presenter = celebrity

- -

What if:
Perceived differences between brands = large
brand purchase motive = self-esteem/social approval
— current Suave usage = none
— psychosocial risk = high —— involvement = high

involvement = high — advertising objective = convey brand image —— presenter similarity = high

decision making unit = individual

brand attitude = neutral —— message processing motivation = high —— presenter = unidentified

*Rules are represented as line segments linking a conjunction of premises on the left with a conclusion on the right.

EXHIBIT 8.15
Illustration of the ADCAD reasoning process for the Suave Shampoo case.

in consecutive evaluations). Furthermore, he found that the higher the validity of the pretest, the greater was the justification for a large sample size to increase reliability.

Although advertisers and agencies pay lip service to Gross's idea of creating more alternatives, Jones (1986, p. 268) comments that "the system is not really concerned with generating a wide range of creative alternatives. It is really concerned with finding one alternative; the elimination of the others becomes a tool for selling this selected one."

SUMMARY

Advertising is at once one of the most potent and problematic elements of the marketing mix. Its effects are often hard to establish outside of an experimental situation. Nonetheless, managers need whatever decision support they can obtain to make informed advertising decisions.

We focused on three advertising decisions in this chapter. In budgeting advertising the notion of the advertising-response function is central, and we explored three approaches: using judgmental information (ADBUDG and the Blue Mountain Coffee case), using historical cross-sectional and time-series data to assess likely market response (the Rao and Miller approach), and using historical norms (ADVISOR and the Convection Company case). While we have a lot to learn, these approaches make the sizing and budget allocation process more systematic.

Media-scheduling models mostly involve heuristic models (although several decades ago, optimization models were popular). The availability of expert systems and single-source data promises to revitalize interest in formal models.

Developing and deciding on advertising copy has traditionally been left to the "creative types." An expert system—ADCAD—can provide firms with decision support for making decisions about copy development.

CHAPTER **9**

Salesforce and Channel Decisions

In this chapter we

- Highlight those salesforce decision problems that are most amenable to analytical modeling
- Describe the Syntex model for determining the size of the salesforce and allocating sales effort among products and markets
- Summarize the main elements of models for designing sales territories and compensation plans for the salesforce
- Describe the CALLPLAN model that helps salespeople to improve their call productivity
- List important channel decisions and describe the gravity model for selecting retail sites.

INTRODUCTION TO SALESFORCE MODELS

Sales-response models for representing the effects of sales activities

In scope and cost, selling is the most important element in the marketing mix. About 10 percent of the workforce is engaged in sales and related occupations. In addition, many company employees and other individuals perform sales functions even though their job titles do not indicate it. For example, company presidents, partners in accounting firms, management consultants, college military recruiters, and TV evangelists perform several selling functions. Many firms rely largely on the salesforce to implement their marketing strategy.

Personal selling has the following characteristics:

1. It enables the firm to target its marketing effort selectively: to high-value prospects and accounts, for example.
2. Because of the interactive nature of selling, salespeople can customize their messages: for example, they can identify and resolve specific customer problems, use visual aids or working models to demonstrate products, address specific objections, and get

feedback and information from customers that the firm can use to improve its products and customer service.

3. It involves people—recruiting, training, motivating, rewarding, and retaining employees—which makes it more complex than the other elements in the marketing mix. In particular, firms cannot change their investments in human beings as easily as they can their investments in advertising or promotions.

4. Compared with advertising, the costs per sales contact are high. *Forbes* magazine (August 28, 1995) estimates that the average cost of a single sales call was $500 in 1995, up from $71 in 1975. In contrast, a $500,000 ad insertion that reaches 20 million viewers costs just a few cents per contact.

As with other marketing investments, it is important for the firm to understand the relationship between selling effort and sales. The nature and structure of this relationship is especially difficult to determine because of the numerous functions salespeople perform:

Prospecting: Finding and cultivating new customers

Communicating: Providing information about the company's products and services to existing and potential customers

Selling: Making presentations, answering objections, closing the sale, and the like

Problem solving: Understanding customers' problems (both actual and potential) and figuring out how to solve them using the firm's products and services

Servicing: Rendering technical assistance, arranging financing, expediting delivery, and organizing after-sale service

Building relationships: Establishing long-term partnerships with customers by developing goals for the relationship, understanding customers' needs and decision-making processes, and developing shared objectives with the customer

Information gathering: Gathering information about customers and competitors (market intelligence) and recording selling activities

Analyzing and allocating: Assessing sales potential and allocating effort accordingly

Traditionally salespeople have been used primarily to generate "targeted sales volume" while marketing and company management focused on profits. However, as firms become market-driven they require their salespeople to pursue multiple objectives. In addition to tracking sales to measure their salespeople's performance, firms now use such performance measures as customer satisfaction, account relations, profit contribution, share of customers (share of product-category sales), and customer retention.

Salespeople perform a number of activities besides just selling, and their effectiveness can be measured in several ways, as just mentioned. Quantifying the link between a salesperson's input (what a salesperson does) and the outputs (what the firm observes) in the form of sales-response functions is the basis for some of the most effective implementations of salesforce modeling. These response functions may be specified at the level of the individual salesperson or at the level of the salesforce.

Our main objective in this chapter is to describe several models that can help firms improve the productivity of their field salesforce and their marketing channels. Although the salesforce models can be adapted by firms that use telemarketing or rely on external reps, we do not explore those issues specifically here. We focus on models for which we have software implementations, namely the Syntex and CALLPLAN models for allocating sales effort and the gravity model for locating retail stores. We also describe models for designing sales territories and compensating the salesforce and indicate what commercial software packages are available to address these problems.

Salesforce management decisions

Exhibit 9.1 highlights the three major categories of decisions (organization, allocation, and control) for which salesforce managers are responsible (Vandenbosch and Weinberg 1993). The four boxes and the connecting arrows offer a simple way to conceptualize decisions regarding salesforce management. The goals and objectives provide the link between the overall strategic plan for the firm and the three salesforce decision areas. The bidirectional nature of this link indicates that goals and objectives determine and are determined by each decision. Furthermore, each decision area influences and is influenced by the other decision areas. Decisions concerning the organization of the salesforce determine the internal (firm-based) context and structure for deploying the sales effort. The allocation decisions partition the total sales effort among revenue-generating entities (e.g., market segments), and control decisions are intended to motivate salespeople to adopt the firm's objectives as their own.

Salesforce organization: In organizing a salesforce the firm must decide whether to have its own direct salesforce, employ outside sales representatives, or rely on a mixture of the two. If it hires and trains its own salespeople, the firm will have greater control over which products and market segments they emphasize; outside reps, who typically handle the products of many firms, may not fully internalize the selling priorities of the firm. On the other hand, "owning" the salesforce also increases the firm's current and future fixed costs

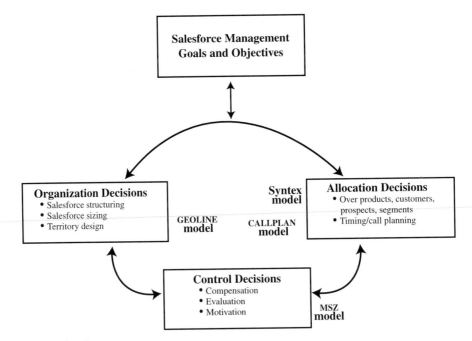

EXHIBIT 9.1
A conceptual outline of salesforce management decisions, showing the overall relationships between salesforce goals and objectives and the three major decision areas: organization, allocation, and control. In this chapter we describe the GEOLINE model for territory design, the Syntex and CALLPLAN models for allocation, and the Mantrala, Sinha, and Zoltners (MSZ) model for controlling effort deployment through compensation design.

(salary, benefits, and overhead), while commission-based reps give the firm more flexibility by making all costs variable.

Maintaining its own direct salesforce is likely to be a better choice for a firm when

1. Its salespeople have product-specific or firm-specific know-how that is not readily available in the marketplace.
2. Evaluating sales reps' performance is difficult because the firm cannot relate selling effort to sales with certainty (e.g., are the sales due to the superb selling skills of the salesperson or to a favorable market environment?).
3. The firm sells a product line so complex that salespeople must develop detailed knowledge of those products.
4. In conjunction with (1), the firm operates in a changing and competitive environment.
5. Effective sales performance requires skills other than selling (e.g., servicing) (Anderson 1985).

EXAMPLE

Quaker Oats used outside reps to sell its frozen food products (Aunt Jemima frozen waffles and Celeste pizza) and its own salesforce to sell its grocery items (e.g., Instant Quaker Oatmeal and Gatorade), even though both call on supermarkets. This strategy makes sense because the two require different call frequencies. The frozen food business is very competitive and the reps can get into the stores each week to maintain shelf space, whereas the firm uses periodic promotions for its grocery products, which are most effectively introduced by company-employed sales representatives. (Quaker Oats sold off its frozen foods business in 1996.)

Although research provides some guidance, which of these options the firm chooses depends on the context. The AHP model (Chapter 6), constructed using the factors mentioned above, offers one way to resolve this issue.

If the firm employs its own salespeople, how should it structure the salesforce: on a geographic, product, market, or functional basis? The answer depends partly on the overall strategy the firm pursues. Exhibit 9.2 lists some factors to consider in structuring the salesforce.

SALESFORCE SIZING AND ALLOCATION

Salesforce sizing (how many salespeople?) and allocation (how should total sales effort be allocated to different products, markets, and sales functions?) are fundamental management issues for all salesforces. Fortunately a number of well-tested models are available to support decision making in this area. However, many firms continue to employ intuitive methods even though these models have proved very effective (e.g., Lodish et al. 1988; Rangaswamy, Sinha, and Zoltners 1990).

Intuitive methods

Firms often determine the size of their salesforce by deciding "what we can afford." Typically they determine how much they can spend on the salesforce by taking a percentage of the forecasted sales for the company; they may base the actual percentage they use on historical

Approach	Influential factors
1. Geographic	Travel expenditures are high Products are mature Administrative support for sales force is low (sales force consists of "lone wolf" salespersons)
2. Customer	Customer needs or behaviors are homogeneous There are a large number of customers The firm as a whole has a market-focused organization
3. Product	Products are complex (e.g., technical content) Firm has a divisional structure organized around products The firm offers a number of products Duplication of calls (multiple salespeople calling on the same customer) is minimal
4. Functional	The buying process is complex (number of people involved, length of buying process, etc.) Effective selling requires a changing mix of skills (e.g., management consulting companies)

EXHIBIT 9.2
Factors to consider when structuring the salesforce.

norms from within the company or on the selling expense ratios for competitors. They divide the average cost of a salesperson into this figure to get the size of the salesforce:

$$\text{Number of salespeople} = \frac{\text{Selling expenses as \% of sales}}{\text{Average cost of a salesperson}}. \tag{9.1}$$

In a study of 41 packaged-goods salesforces DeVincentis and Kotcher (1995) found that the average expense for a salesforce was 3.71 percent of sales, with smaller firms (sales of less than $500 million per annum) spending between 5 and 8 percent and larger firms, about half of that.

Another approach firms use to determine the size of the salesforce is the "breakdown method": the firm divides the sales forecast for the planning horizon by the average revenues generated by a single salesperson in that length of time:

$$\text{Number of salespeople} = \frac{\text{Forecasted sales}}{\text{Average revenues generated by a salesperson}}. \tag{9.2}$$

Once the firm has determined the total number of salespeople, it then allocates the total effort (e.g., total number of calls (visits) available) to accounts and prospects based on their actual or forecasted sales. For example, salespeople may visit accounts with high levels of sales every month and those with low levels of sales once in six months.

Intuitive methods of sizing and allocating salesforce effort are unsatisfactory for two reasons:

1. They do not account for the possibility that some accounts or prospects may respond differently from the "average" account.
2. They do not take into account that a firm cannot determine the best size for the salesforce (i.e., the total sales effort) without knowing how to allocate the total sales effort most effectively (Exhibit 9.3).

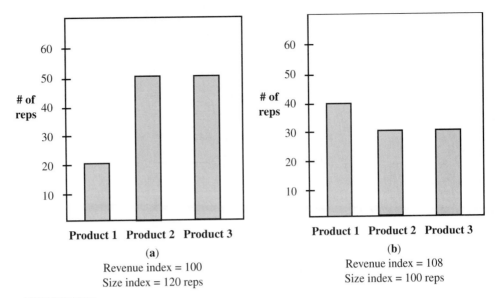

(a)
Revenue index = 100
Size index = 120 reps

(b)
Revenue index = 108
Size index = 100 reps

EXHIBIT 9.3
This exhibit illustrates the salesforce sizing dilemma—how large should the salesforce be? In case (a) (the current situation) the firm has a salesforce of 120. However, more effort is allocated to the (less responsive) products 2 and 3 at the expense of product 1. An analysis reveals that reallocation of effort toward product 1 yields anticipated sales that are higher with fewer sales representatives (case (b)). In this example the firm can realize an 8 percent increase in revenue with a 17 percent decrease in salesforce size by allocating more effort to the more responsive product (1).

Missing from Exhibit 9.3 are the "sales-response functions" that enable managers to quantify what would happen by redeploying sales effort in different ways. We address this issue next.

Market-response methods (the Syntex model)

Market-response methods require firms to estimate response functions, which show the relationship between sales effort and sales in each *sales entity* of interest. A sales entity is anything with which we can associate potential sales for the firm—customer, prospect, market segment, geographic area, product sold by the firm, and so forth. If the firm estimates sales-response functions for each such sales entity, it can use these functions to calculate the levels of effort to allocate to each entity to maximize profits or to achieve other objectives. The sum of the sales effort across a set of nonoverlapping entities is the total sales effort the firm needs. The firm can then divide this total by the average effort of a salesperson (e.g., 750 calls per year) to estimate the number of salespeople it needs.

The Syntex model provides a general approach to the problem of sizing and allocating the salesforce effort. Lodish et al. (1988) developed the model for Syntex Laboratories, and it can be adapted for use by other multiproduct, multisegment firms that employ a field salesforce. When Lodish et al. developed the model in 1982, Syntex was selling seven prescription drugs (e.g., Naprosyn and Anaprox) that it promoted to nine physician specialties (e.g., general practice and dermatology). Syntex was considering increasing its salesforce size substantially with the expectation that this would increase the sales of its portfolio of products in the nine physician segments. Exhibit 9.4 outlines the process used

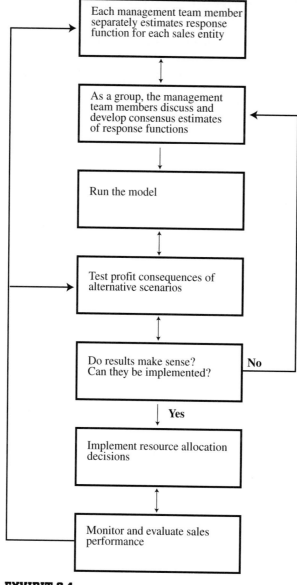

EXHIBIT 9.4

The sequence of steps for developing and implementing the Syntex salesforce resource-allocation model.

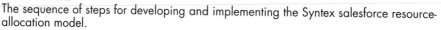

in implementing the Syntex model. We describe the process next; although we formulate the model specifically for Syntex, it is easily generalized to other firms facing similar problems.

Specification and calibration of response models: Syntex used an ADBUDG response function (Chapter 2) to model sales response for each sales entity (product or market segment). To calibrate the model senior managers from the sales, marketing, and research departments, who together had several decades of experience in selling pharmaceutical products, estimated the response functions. These managers separately answered several questions with respect to how sales of each product would respond to sales effort and how each physician segment would respond to varying levels of sales effort. The following question illustrates the type of questions they answered:

> According to Syntex's strategic plan, if salesforce effort is maintained at the current level (indexed to 1) from 1982 to 1985, sales of product A would be the planned level (indexed to 1). What would happen to product A's year 1985 sales (compared with a base of 1 for the present levels) if during the same time period it received

1. No sales effort? $\underline{\quad X_0 \quad}$

2. One-half the current effort? $\underline{\quad X_{0.5} \quad}$

3. 50 percent greater effort? $\underline{\quad X_{1.5} \quad}$

4. A saturation level of sales effort? $\underline{\quad X_\infty \quad}$

After a half-day training session, each manager privately answered the questions. The four answers provided by a manager are denoted X_0, $X_{0.5}$, $X_{1.5}$, and X_∞ respectively. The answers were then summarized by a computer and the summary results provided to each manager participant.

After studying this summary the managers discussed the initial results, contemplated the differences between their own responses and the group mean, and then completed the same questionnaire again. In the Syntex study the second round led to consensus estimates for the questions. (In other situations it may take as many as three or four rounds to obtain consensus estimates; see Rangaswamy, Sinha, and Zoltners (1990).)

These consensus estimates provide inputs to calibrate the ADBUDG function. That is, the parameters a_i, b_i, c_i, and d_i in the following equation are fitted using the estimates of $r_i(X_i)$ provided by the managers at the four levels of X_i given above; the base estimate of $r_i(X_i) = 1$ when $X_i = 1$ provides another data point for the calibration:

$$r_i(X_i) = b_i + \left(a_i - b_i\right)\frac{X_i^{c_i}}{d_i + X_i^{c_i}}, \tag{9.3}$$

where

i = a sales entity, $i = 1, 2, 3, \ldots, I$ (# of sales entities);

X_i = total effort devoted to sales entity i during a planning period measured in number of calls, indexed so that current effort = 1 (for simplicity we treat this as a continuously varying quantity rather than as an integer);

$r_i(X_i)$ = indexed level of sales at entity i if the salesforce devotes X_i amount of effort to that entity;

b_i = minimum sales that can be expected with no sales effort allocated to sales entity i;

a_i = maximum sales that can be expected with an unlimited amount of sales effort allocated to sales entity i;

c_i = parameter that determines the shape of $r_i(X_i)$—whether it is concave or S-shaped; and

d_i = an index of competitive effort levels directed toward sales entity i (the larger this value, the smaller the impact of the firm's own sales effort on sales).

Syntex model description: The Syntex model allocates effort to sales entities to maximize firm profits over a planning horizon, subject to several constraints. Each run of the model requires a constraint specifying a proposed salesforce size. This constraint ensures that the model allocates effort in the best way possible for a given salesforce size. The base model follows:

Find the set of X_i's to

$$\text{maximize } Z = \sum_{i=1}^{I} r_i(X_i)S_i a_i - CF \text{ (profits)}, \tag{9.4}$$

subject to

$$\sum_{i=1}^{I} X_i e_i = F \text{ (salesforce size constraint)}, \tag{9.5}$$

where

S_i = forecasted sales for entity i according to the strategic plan;

a_i = contribution margin per incremental dollar of sales for sales entity i;

C = full costs (salary, benefits, etc.) of a single salesperson;

F = planned salesforce size (number of salespeople); and

e_i = planned deployment of sales effort to entity i according to the strategic plan.

The base model gives the optimal allocation of effort for any given salesforce size F. This model is then solved repeatedly for various levels of F, and the firm should keep adding salespersons as long as the incremental profit associated with each person is positive. At the optimal level of salesforce size, the marginal profit of an additional salesperson is 0 (Exhibit 9.5).

Constraint (9.5) can include more entity-level constraints. For example, the constraints might include minimum and maximum levels of effort allocated to any particular entity. The modified constraint set can be specified as follows:

$$\sum_{i=1}^{I} X_i e_i \leq F; \tag{9.6}$$

$$\text{LB}_i \leq X_i \leq \text{UB}_i. \tag{9.7}$$

LB_i and UB_i are the lower and upper bounds on effort devoted to any particular sales entity. For example, the firm might specify that total effort devoted to Naprosyn should not exceed the equivalent of 100 salespersons (UB) and be at least 50 (LB).

Model usage: Syntex calibrated the model twice: first to allocate sales effort to products, and then to allocate effort to physician specialties. The company used these results to plan for changes in the size of the salesforce. See Syntex Laboratories (A) case (HBS case #584033) for a fuller discussion of how the company used this model. (Note that other models are available for allocating effort simultaneously to both market segments and products, such as those described by Rangaswamy, Sinha, and Zoltners (1990).)

The model can also be used to assess the overall value of the salesforce. In today's competitive environment, firms must justify every investment in terms of its opportunity

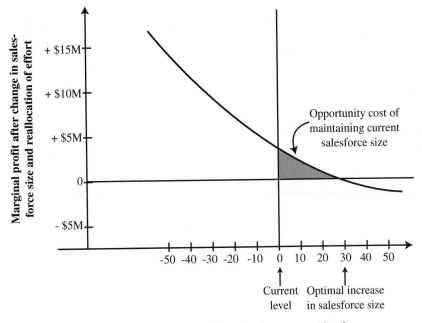

Change in salesforce size from current level

EXHIBIT 9.5
This graph shows how the results from the Syntex model can be organized to indicate
(1) the opportunity cost (the shaded area) of maintaining the salesforce at the current level
and (2) the required change to the current salesforce size to maximize profits.

costs. One way to meaningfully estimate opportunity cost in the context of salesforce investment is by computing the difference between profits calculated for effort levels corresponding to the selected salesforce size and the profits the firm would earn by expending zero sales effort on all sales entities (all upper bounds set to 0).

The Syntex model is available in the software called Sales Resource Allocation model, which can also be adapted to allocate other types of resources. However, the model has several limitations. It is best suited for repetitive buying situations where the number of calls made to accounts is an important determinant of sales. In repetitive buying situations the purchase cycle is short, customers buy from an assortment of products, and the salesperson provides a much more sophisticated version of reminder advertising that one gets from other such media as TV. Here the regular contacts with customers help cement relationships and allow the salesperson to recognize potential problems in advance and deal with them. Some common examples of sales calls in repetitive buying situations are pharmaceutical reps calling on physicians, packaged goods salespeople calling on grocery stores, agricultural product reps calling on stores and farmers, and industrial parts reps calling on distributors.

SALES TERRITORY DESIGN

Firms usually structure large field salesforces geographically at some level within the organization. They assign salespeople exclusive territories in which they are responsible for sales of specified products. An important management question is how should these territories be carved out from the total market area that the firm serves.

A fundamental criterion in designing sales territories is the notion of "balance," that is, ensuring that *opportunities* or *workload* are equal across sales territories. Assigning a salesperson to a territory (a group of accounts) with low market potential, heavy competition, or too many small accounts reduces that salesperson's opportunity to perform well. Territories that do not fully utilize the time available to a salesperson or territories that demand too much work from the salesperson are suboptimal. In the former case the territory imposes a performance hurdle that is outside the control of the salesperson. This could lead to frequent turnover in personnel. In the latter case the firm suffers an opportunity loss when the salesperson does not have the time to call on profitable accounts. According to Andris Zoltners, a leading consultant, "eighty percent of the companies in the United States have imbalanced alignments. They have too many salespeople in one territory and too few in another. This is costing companies two to seven percent in sales losses every year" (quoted by Camparelli 1994).

Balancing territories for potential is particularly important if the "commission" component of the salesperson's compensation package is large. On the other hand, balancing territories by workload is appropriate when salespeople are on straight salary and are not compared on the basis of the sales volume they achieve. In the latter case firms can design territories so that they require about the same number of calls per year.

Sales territories tend to become unbalanced over time because of uneven changes among geographical areas, the differential growth of the firm across sales territories, or personnel changes in salesforce, resulting in misaligned territories with highly uneven sales potential or workload. For example, Cravens (1995) describes a Fortune 500 services company that had a poorly aligned salesforce—the annual sales for 24 salespeople ranged from less than $300,000 to over $60 million! Firms should also evaluate their existing territory alignments when they reorganize or when they merge with other firms.

In addition to balance, firms use several other criteria in designing sales territories:

1. The territories should be easy to administer (e.g., conform to such geographic configurations as counties or zip codes).
2. Sales potential should be easy to estimate (e.g., if average physician prescription levels for each product are available only at the zip code level, then the standard unit of geography should be a zip code).
3. Travel time should be minimized by taking into account topography, natural geographic barriers, and the location of the territory center (home base of the salesperson).

The GEOLINE model for territory design

The GEOLINE model was developed by Hess and Samuels (1971). It is an optimization model that simultaneously tries to accomplish three objectives: (1) to equalize workload or potential (more generally, to equalize along any activity measure of interest to salesforce management), (2) to create territories that are physically contiguous, that is, they consist of adjacent geographical units, and (3) to ensure compactness, that is, the shape of the territory minimizes travel time. The model takes the total geographic area of interest (e.g., entire United States, region, or state) and breaks it down into standard geographic units (SGUs) such as zip codes or counties. The model assigns each SGU to one or more territories (Exhibit 9.6).

Given the number of territories (I) and a starting location for the territory centers, the model assigns each SGU to a territory to minimize an objective function called the "moment of inertia." At the start each SGU is assigned to the nearest territory center. This will ensure contiguity. The objective function is the weighted sum of squared distances from a proposed territory center to all SGUs located in that territory, where the weights are determined from

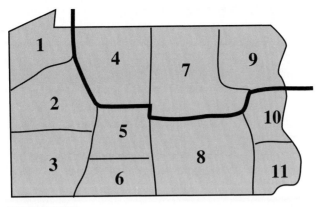

EXHIBIT 9.6
In this example, 11 SGUs have been allocated to two territories: 4, 7, and 9 to territory 1, and 1, 2, 3, 5, 6, 8, 10, and 11 to territory 2.

a measure of the magnitude of the activity for that SGU. Defining an appropriate measure is essential. An activity measure can be a general index of potential (e.g., purchasing power of consumers in an SGU) or workload (e.g., number of sales calls per year). Alternatively, an activity measure can be a specific index of potential (e.g., number of dermatologists or number of Chinese restaurants) or workload (e.g., number of sales calls to dermatologists). The number of territories can be set equal to the number of salespersons, so that each salesperson has a territory. The model also imposes two constraints: an equal activity constraint and a constraint to ensure that every SGU is assigned to at least one territory.

The model is
find $\{X_{ij}\}$ to

$$\text{minimize} \sum_j \sum_i c_{ij} X_{ij} a_j \text{ (moment of inertia)}, \tag{9.8}$$

subject to

$$\sum_j X_{ij} a_j = \frac{1}{I} \sum_j a_j \text{ for } i = 1, 2, 3, \ldots, I \text{ (equal activity constraint)}, \tag{9.9}$$

$$\sum_i X_{ij} = 1 \qquad \text{for } j = 1, 2, 3, \ldots, J \text{ (complete assignment of SGUs)}, \tag{9.10}$$

$$X_{ij} \geq 0 \qquad \text{for } i = 1, 2, 3, \ldots, I \text{ and } j = 1, 2, 3, \ldots, J \text{ (nonnegativity)}, \tag{9.11}$$

where

X_{ij} = proportion of SGU j assigned to territory i ($i = 1, 2, 3, \ldots, I$ and $j = 1, 2, 3, \ldots, J$);

a_j = activity measure associated with SGU j; and

c_{ij} = the contribution to the moment of inertia when SGU j is assigned to territory i, calculated as the square of the distance from a proposed territory center to the location of the center of SGU j.

After the first run the model assigns territories to minimize the moment of inertia relative to the starting territory centers. However, there may be two problems with the initial solution: (1) some SGUs may be split between two or more territories, and (2) the initial territory centers may not be central to the SGUs assigned to each territory. The split-SGU problem can be addressed by reassigning split SGUs wholly to just one territory. Managers can do this judgmentally by adjusting territory centers in light of the SGUs assigned to the territories, or the model can assign each SGU automatically to the territory for which its share of activity is the largest. The model can also be programmed to automatically locate the centers at the weighted center of the territory's activity measure. These changes will disrupt the optimality of the solution, and so we must rerun the model with the new territory centers. This process must be repeated until the model output converges to a reasonably stable set of SGU assignments and territory centers.

Since Hess and Samuels (1971) developed the GEOLINE model, researchers have made several modeling enhancements in both data and computer technologies (Zoltners and Sinha 1983). A number of databases are now available from commercial sources that incorporate various geographically referenced activity measures. For example, SCAN/US sells a geo-demographic database that has built-in activity measures such as buying potential and the income, age, and gender composition of each SGU. SGUs can now be defined at the level of nine-digit zip codes or even at the level of a city block. Furthermore, the database and related software packages incorporate such features as accessibility of SGUs (proximity to major highways) and nontraversibility (e.g., unbridged waterways or mountains). These data are important because GEOLINE places more weight on achieving territory compactness than on territory contiguity; that is, the moment-of-inertia criterion tends to place territory centers near the "center of gravity" of the activity measures rather than at the most accessible location.

New developments also permit managers to employ user-friendly PC software to make judgmental adjustments to results obtained from formal models such as GEOLINE. One such program is MAPS (Manpower Assignment Planning System), available from ZS Associates and widely used in the pharmaceutical and medical equipment industries. In addition to considering physical limitations (e.g., nontraversibility), it permits managers to make judgmental adjustments to the "optimal" territory alignment to account for personnel considerations, such as when a new salesperson replaces another. It is also likely that by balancing territories the firm will not necessarily be maximizing profits. This may require further judgmental adjustments to improve firm profits by relaxing the balance criterion.

EXAMPLE

(Adapted from Camparelli 1994.) In early 1993 Jerry Acuff, vice president and general manager of Hoescht Roussel, the pharmaceutical arm of Hoescht Celanese, realized that to stay competitive he had to take a closer look at who his customers were, where they were, and whether his 640-member salesforce was aligned properly. Market conditions were changing rapidly in the pharmaceutical industry. Traditionally salespeople sold primarily to private care physicians. However, managed care HMOs were beginning to change physicians' roles in prescribing drugs. In their new roles physicians are members of a team that may include HMO administrators, who recommend bulk purchases of certain standard drugs. Could he realign his salesforce to take advantage of the changing marketplace?

Before he plunged into realignment, Acuff surveyed his customers to find out what they wanted. He conducted a five-month-long research project to gather information from customers and from cross-functional teams comprising individuals from all levels within Hoescht Roussel. According to Acuff, before the research project, "our sales force went out there with the general assumption that 65 percent of the physicians write 94 percent of the prescriptions. But when we learned that data was available that would let us know which of these 65 percent we should be focusing on and which ones we shouldn't, we decided to take action."

In reorganizing the salesforce the firm used a sales-territory-alignment model to plan the realignment around the redefined customer groups: primary care physicians' offices, managed care companies, and hospitals. Before the end of 1993 Hoescht Roussel had completed its research and modeling efforts. The model results suggested the following realignment: reduce the number of regions from nine to six and eliminate 125 sales reps. Many of these reps sold directly to physicians. In implementing these decisions the company created the position of regional operations manager. These managers would be responsible for training and deploying salespeople at the regional level (a function the home office had handled previously). Prior to the realignment, says Acuff, "the whole sales force was deployed based on where physicians and hospitals were located. The new organization takes into account the impact of managed care." Also, within each region the company had identified high-volume and low-volume customers (the activity measure in this modeling effort was physician prescription volume). The salesforce focused on high-volume customers, and the firm devised a plan to reach lower-volume customers with direct mail and telemarketing. According to Acuff this realignment was expected to reduce sales costs by about 14 to 15 percent, saving more than $10 million.

SALESFORCE COMPENSATION

The compensation plan for salespeople serves several objectives: (1) *compensation*, to reward individuals for their effort or performance, (2) *motivation*, to encourage salespeople to work harder and accomplish more, and (3) *direction*, to channel sales effort toward activities that are in the firm's best interests (e.g., to establish long-term relationships with customers or to emphasize new products).

Companies compensate their salespeople in a number of ways for their efforts and for their sales performance. Compensation plans may include both monetary and nonmonetary components. The monetary components can include *salary*, money in return for time worked; *commission*, money for sales revenues generated; and *bonus*, money for attaining a goal or quota. Among the possible nonmonetary components are *recognition programs* (e.g., salesperson of the month, preferred parking spots, Millionaire club), *contests* (e.g., salesperson with highest sales revenues for a month), and *noncash awards* (e.g., all-expense-paid trips, personal use of business car).

According to surveys of salesforce compensation by the Dartnell group, the most popular monetary compensation scheme is a combination plan that has a base salary component and an incentive component (commission or bonus). Even firms in the securities industry, which have traditionally relied on 100 percent commission plans, are moving toward combination plans. Approximately 70 percent of all U.S. companies use a combination plan, about 20 percent use only a straight-salary plan, and the remaining companies use all-commission plans. Smaller firms are more likely to use a commission-only plan than larger firms. Most popular is a combination of salary and bonus.

In designing a compensation plan, managers should keep several issues in mind. In most cases they are not able to fully observe the selling efforts of their field salespeople. Thus the firm often cannot determine how much of a salesperson's results should be attributed to effort and how much to happenstance. Furthermore, sales are affected by many factors other than selling effort, such as the quality of the product, the reputation of the firm, and its advertising program. Therefore salespeople are uncertain about the sales consequences of their efforts. Also differences between salespeople, including differences in abilities, preferences for leisure versus work, and territory potential, can account for differential results. Finally, a good compensation plan should be perceived to be equitable (i.e., perceived to offer roughly equivalent earning opportunities among the salespeople), be easy to understand, and be simple to implement. Mantrala, Sinha, and Zoltners (1994) have developed and implemented a model to design bonus plans that takes into account the foregoing issues. This model, the MSZ model, is useful for designing a bonus plan for selling in a repetitive buying environment.

Using conjoint analysis to design a bonus plan (the MSZ model)

The MSZ compensation model helps management to (1) set individual sales quotas that take into account differences in territory potentials and (2) design a common bonus plan that awards all salespeople the same amount of money for the same achieved percentages of their quotas. Thus, for example, all salespeople who exceed their quotas by 20 percent receive identical bonus amounts, regardless of the actual levels of the quotas assigned to the different salespeople. To design such a bonus plan, the firm first needs two types of information:

> *Measure(s) of sales potential in each territory*: In such industries as pharmaceuticals, where MSZ implemented this model, data on territory potential are available from syndicated data sources. In some other industries geodemographic databases (described in the last main section of this chapter) can be used.

> *Salespeople's assessments of how sales of various products are likely to respond to their individual efforts (i.e., their individual sales-response functions) and their preferences for income versus leisure*: The firm can obtain this information from the salespeople by using a specially designed conjoint analysis procedure, described below. (In Chapter 7 we describe the basics of conjoint analysis.)

With this information a firm can predict how salespeople are likely to behave under various bonus plans, and it can design a good bonus plan.

The core of the MSZ model are sales-response functions, which are specified as the modified exponential described in Chapter 2:

$$r_{ij}(X_{ij}) = b_{ij} + \left(a_{ij} - b_{ij}\right)\left(1 - e^{-c_{ij}X_{ij}}\right) \tag{9.12}$$

where

X_{ij} = effort per period on product i by salesperson j; $i = 1, 2, 3, \ldots, I$ (# of products) and $j = 1, 2, 3, \ldots, J$ (# of salespeople);

$r_{ij}(X_{ij})$ = expected sales of product i per period attributable to salesperson j;

a_{ij} = maximum sales of product i that can be expected with a saturation (infinite) level of effort by salesperson j;

b_{ij} = minimum sales of product i if there is no selling effort in the territory handled by salesperson j; and

c_{ij} = parameter that determines the rate at which sales ($r_{ij}(X_{ij})$) approach the maximum (a_{ij}) with increasing effort (X_{ij}).

In the MSZ model a_{ij} and b_{ij} are determined from external data sources, while c_{ij} is inferred from the responses that salespeople provide to the conjoint analysis task. We briefly describe the conjoint analysis task and the optimization model the firm uses to determine a good bonus plan. (For technical details of the model, see Mantrala, Sinha, and Zoltners (1994).)

Equation (9.12) can be "inverted" to determine the effort required for any desired level of sales (quota), by solving for X_{ij} as a function of sales $r_{ij}(X_{ij})$. These effort levels are then summed to determine the total effort across the products a salesperson sells, which is a function of all the c_{ij}'s associated with the products the salesperson sells. The salesperson derives "utility" from the bonus compensation, but a "disutility" from the total effort needed to get the bonus. (The larger the bonus, the higher the utility; the higher the total effort devoted to selling, the higher the disutility.) The actual trade-off between the utility value of the bonus and the disutility of work is idiosyncratic to each individual salesperson. To determine both the utility and the disutility functions and the response function coefficients (c_{ij}), the firm gives the salespeople a "conjoint ranking task," an example of which is shown in Exhibit 9.7.

We can use an ordinal regression procedure and the rank orders the salespeople provide in the conjoint task to estimate the "utility function" for each salesperson. The estimated utility function depends on the bonus amount, the territory potential, and the responsiveness parameters c_{ij} estimated from the responses to the conjoint-ranking task.

The firm then incorporates the utility functions of all the salespeople into an optimization model that selects a *common* bonus plan (i.e., the amounts it would pay for achieving sales levels corresponding to various percentages of the quota) for all salespersons. The optimization model maximizes total firm profits generated by the entire salesforce, assuming that each salesperson will act to maximize his or her own utility and subject to an additional restriction that any new bonus plan should at least maintain the past satisfaction (utility) levels of the salespeople.

Below are nine different bonus plans for products A and B. Also listed are possible sales objectives (quotas) for the next six-month period and the bonus that will be awarded if you achieve 100% of the sales objectives. Please rank these nine plans from "1" to "9" in terms of your preference, with "1" indicating your most preferred plan and "9" your least preferred plan.

Bonus plan	Product A sales objective	Product B sales objective	Bonus (for achieving 100% of **total** sales objectives)	Rank
1	$316,000	$45,000	$2,100	_____
2	316,000	75,000	3,200	_____
3	316,000	105,000	4,900	_____
4	526,000	45,000	4,000	_____
5	526,000	75,000	4,250	_____
6	526,000	105,000	5,100	_____
7	737,000	45,000	4,700	_____
8	737,000	75,000	5,300	_____
9	737,000	105,000	6,400	_____

EXHIBIT 9.7
An example questionnaire for the MSZ model for estimating utility function of a salesperson (adapted from Figure A1 of Mantrala, Sinha, and Zoltners 1994). The table should be customized for each salesperson so that product sales objectives are set to lie between the minimum sales for the salesperson's territory (b_{ij}) and the maximum sales for the territory (a_{ij}).

One may question whether salespeople would misrepresent their preferences in responding to the questionnaire if they know that their responses are being used to design the bonus plan. The authors, however, report that this is rarely a problem for at least four reasons: (1) the salespeople have incomplete information about the model and therefore are unable to systematically misrepresent preferences; (2) the salespeople know that the objective of management is to set a common bonus plan rather than an individual-specific bonus plan; (3) the salespeople would find it difficult to collude to share the bonus payments; and (4) management has the ability to detect and penalize gaming behavior over time.

The MSZ model and its variants have been implemented in a number of pharmaceutical and medical products firms. In describing an early application of this model, the authors show that a new quota-bonus plan could potentially increase firm profits by 10 percent for a 12-person salesforce in an eight-month period.

We need to further develop and deploy operational models for sales compensation. In particular, existing models are weak in evaluating combination plans (salary + incentive compensation), in considering cross-product costs and sales interdependencies, and for developing compensation plans in team-selling situations.

IMPROVING THE EFFICIENCY AND EFFECTIVENESS OF SALES CALLS

In most markets customers and prospects are not all equally responsive to the efforts of the salesperson. Some customers have been buying from the firm for years and need no reselling, while some prospects need a lot of selling effort before they buy from the firm. Some customers buy large quantities of the product with each order, while others buy small quantities. Most salespeople intuitively recognize these differences. However, without formal methods they may not fully capitalize on these differences by spending more effort where likely response is high and less effort where likely response is low.

A single sales call can cost $500. According to a survey by the Dartnell Corp. (*American Salesman*, August 1995), sales professionals make an average of 3.4 calls per day, or about 750 calls per year. In salesforces that sell packaged goods to supermarkets, salespeople ("account managers") are each responsible for two to four accounts, consisting of 40 to 120 stores, and they handle 2 to 18 products (100 to 5000 stock keeping units (SKUs)). The average duration of a call is 60 to 90 minutes, of which the average time spent selling is 11 to 15 minutes (DeVincentis and Kotcher 1995). In industrial salesforces the percentage of time that salespeople spend in actual face-to-face selling has been around 35 percent for years (Hise and Reid 1994). Given these statistics it is not surprising that by improving the efficiency and effectiveness with which they manage sales calls, firms with large salesforces can increase their profits.

The CALLPLAN model

CALLPLAN (Lodish 1971, 1974) is an interactive call-planning system that helps salespeople to determine how many calls to make to each client and prospect (equivalently, to each category of clients and prospects) in a given time period to maximize the returns from their calls. The system determines call frequencies with respect to an *effort* period, which is the planning period used by the salesperson (e.g., one quarter). The model is based on the assumption that the expected sales to each client and prospect over a *response* period, which is the planning period of the firm (e.g., a year), is a function of the average number of calls per effort period during that response period. The response period selected should be long enough to accommodate potential carryover effects from each effort period.

Specifying response functions: We will use a simple version of CALLPLAN to illustrate the central issues. Like the Syntex model, CALLPLAN depends on the specification of response functions. Again we use an ADBUDG response function (Chapter 2):

$$r_i(X_i) = b_i + (a_i - b_i) \frac{X_i^{c_i}}{d_i + X_i^{c_i}}, \qquad (9.13)$$

where

i = 1, 2, 3, . . ., I (# of accounts or prospects);

X_i = average level of effort, measured in number of calls, expended on account i during an effort period. X_i formalizes informal statements that salespeople make of the form "I will call on this customer twice a month";

$r_i(X_i)$ = indexed level of sales at account i if the salesperson devotes X_i amount of effort at that account;

b_i = minimum sales that can be expected with no sales effort at account i;

a_i = maximum sales that can be expected with an unlimited amount of sales effort to account i;

c_i = parameter that determines the shape of $r_i(X_i)$, whether it is concave or S-shaped; and

d_i = an index of competitive effort levels directed toward account i (the larger this value, the smaller the impact of the salesperson's effort).

The response model can be calibrated using managerial judgment as described in Chapter 2. The salesperson estimates a separate response function for each account. The salesperson can adjust the response functions based on account-specific profit-margin factors f_i if different accounts offer different levels of profitability.

Model specification: Once the response functions are specified, CALLPLAN tries to develop an effective way for the salesperson to allocate effort across the different accounts. The model assumes that the salespeople seek to maximize contribution (profits) from their selling efforts; however, they have limited time and therefore they wish to use this resource as effectively as possible. A sales territory is assumed to be divided into mutually exclusive geographic areas (e.g., zip codes). The salesperson makes trips to some or all areas in the territory in each effort period. In each trip to an area the salesperson incurs variable costs for expense items such as travel and lodging. In a trip to an area the salesperson calls on any given account at most once.

Before we describe the formal model, we define its parameters:

n_j = number of trips per effort period to area j, where j = 1, 2, 3, . . ., J. Because the salesperson calls on an account at most once during a trip, n_j is also equal to the maximum number of calls made to any account in territory j;

c_j = variable costs incurred when making a trip to area j;

t_i = time that the salesperson spends with the customer when making a call to account i (t_i may be set to be the same for all customers);

U_j = time it takes to get to area j;

e = number of effort periods in a response period (if the effort period is a month and the response period is a year, then $e = 12$);

T = total work time available to a salesperson in an effort period, which includes both selling and nonselling times;

a_i = a customer-specific profit-adjustment factor that reflects the profit contribution of sales to that customer.

The optimization model maximizes profits (Z) for a single sales territory taking into account both the costs of visiting the accounts and the expected contribution from all the accounts and prospects:

Find the set of X_i to

$$\text{maximize profits } Z = \sum_i a_i r_i(X_i) - e \sum_j n_j C_j,$$

subject to

$$\sum_i X_i t_i + \sum_j n_j U_j \le T, \tag{9.14}$$

$$n_j = \max_i \left(X_i \text{ in geographic area } j\right), \tag{9.15}$$

$$\text{LB}_i \le X_i \le \text{UB}_i. \tag{9.16}$$

Constraint (9.14) ensures that the total time (visit time plus travel time) used in an effort period does not exceed the time available to the salesperson; constraint (9.15) equates the number of trips to territory j to the maximum number of calls made to any specific account in that territory, thus ensuring that in any trip to territory j the salesperson does not call on any account more than once; constraint (9.16) allows the salesperson to incorporate judgment-based lower and upper bounds on the number of calls made to any account i in an effort period.

Model usage: We recommend that the model be run first with no upper bounds in constraint (9.16) and with a lower bound of 0 for all i. Then the model is likely to suggest that the salesperson never call on some accounts and call on some accounts too often. The salesperson may feel that such an allocation is not reasonable and can then specify minimum and maximum constraints for each account to modify these results. These judgments account for the effects of factors not explicitly included in the model. (For example, some accounts may be beta-test sites that help with testing a new product before release. However, sales effort on those accounts may not necessarily lead to increased sales.)

A salesperson should include both accounts and prospects in a calling portfolio. However, prospects typically respond weakly to sales efforts as compared with existing accounts; therefore the model will tend to exclude them from the calling plans it develops. One way to give adequate treatment to both is to run the model separately for accounts and for prospects: Run the analysis for prospects by setting aside time equal to $T_P < T$ in constraint (9.14) to be allocated to prospects. Do the same for accounts by setting aside time equal to T_A for existing accounts such that $T_A + T_P = T$, the total time available to the salesperson. A comparison of the results with and without time set aside for prospects shows how much of the current profit the salesperson is willing to forgo to cultivate long-term prospects.

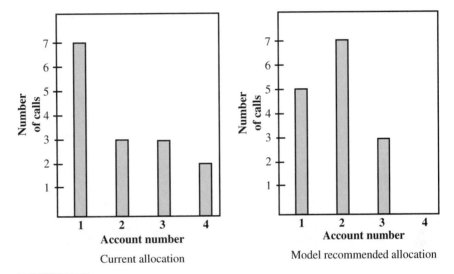

		Number of calls									
		1	2	3	4	5	6	7	8	9	10
	1	100	300	600	400	300	225	160	110	70	50
Account	2	1400	1100	850	650	490	360	250	165	85	15
number	3	3600	1800	800	200	100	75	50	40	30	25
	4	180	170	160	150	140	135	130	125	120	115

The numbers in each row of the matrix correspond to the response function for that account, showing incremental contribution per call at that call level.

☐ Indicates marginal contributions at current level of deployment

⬭ Indicates marginal contributions at the optimal level of deployment

Current allocation

Model recommended allocation

EXHIBIT 9.8
Example of optimization procedure in CALLPLAN. The table at the top is a numerical representation of sales-response functions in four accounts. The bar charts at the bottom show the current and model-recommended allocation of effort to the four accounts when the salesperson makes a total of 15 calls.

EXAMPLE

To understand the "incremental analysis" the CALLPLAN model uses to determine the optimal allocation of effort, consider a simple example with four accounts, summarized in Exhibit 9.8. Suppose that the salesperson is currently devoting 15 calls to these accounts as shown, bringing in total sales of $11,985. If the cost of a single sales call is $200, the net contribution is then $8985.

An optimization procedure would allocate the first call to account 3, which has the highest marginal contribution ($3600). It will allocate the second call also to this account, which has the next highest marginal contribution ($1800). The third to the fifth calls will be allocated to account 2 with a total contribution of $3350, the sixth call to account 3, the seventh and eighth calls to account 2 with a total contribution of $1140, the ninth to twelfth calls to account 1 with a total contribution of $1400, the thirteenth to account 2, the fourteenth to account 1, and the fifteenth call to account 2. This allocation procedure results in total contributions of $13,000 with a net contribution (after paying for the sales calls) of $10,000, which represents a 11.3 percent improvement over the current net contribution of these 15 calls.

Note that the model recommends making no calls on account 4. The firm should use less costly methods such as telemarketing to contact such accounts. Note also that it would not pay to make any call whose marginal contribution would be less than $200, the cost of a call. Let us explore what would happen if the salesperson is able to make more than 15 calls. Then the eighteenth call will be to account 4, with a marginal contribution of $180. Thus the maximum number of calls the salesperson makes to this set of accounts should be 17. (If the salesperson makes only 15 calls to these accounts, the opportunity loss of not making the sixteenth and seventeenth calls is equal to $25, the net contribution of making the two additional calls. The sixteenth call would be to account 1, and the seventeenth to account 3.)

Exhibit 9.9 summarizes the output from an actual application of CALLPLAN (Lodish 1971). In this example, the salesperson could increase sales by about 20 percent by following model recommendations to shift calls from smaller customers such as Chempro and Polyfin to larger customers such as Chemplst and Ethyln.

Firms increasingly use telemarketing and direct mailing to reach less profitable accounts. For example, W. W. Grainger distributes maintenance, repair, and operating supplies to 1.3 million customers in different market segments such as contractors, service shops, mainte-

	Optimal call in average three-month period	Optimal expected sales in one year	Present policy	Expected sales using present policy
Account				
Balfor	7	75	8	79
Chempro	3	14	6	22
Chemplst	10	195	3	171
Dilctx	5	15	4	8
Emerson	0	0	1	0
Ethlyn	6	64	4	52
F/C	5	37	5	37
M-I	0	0	1	2
Micro	0	0	4	2
Polyfin	1	5	3	8
Slctro	5	36	3	18
Sevema	9	59	6	38
Surf	0	0	3	2
Tri-Pt	5	72	3	36
Brdng	0	0	1	0
Marlow	0	0	1	1
Total	56	572	56	476

EXHIBIT 9.9
Optimal account call policies from an application of CALLPLAN.

nance departments, hotels, and educational facilities. General Motors, its largest customer, accounts for less than 1 percent of its sales. The company has now partitioned its accounts into three groups based on their size and responsiveness. It contacts those that are not profitable enough to justify visits by salespeople through telemarketing and mailings.

A question that often arises is, How do we know these gains from reallocating calls will actually be realized? To answer this question Fudge and Lodish (1977) conducted a study at United Airlines to assess the value of CALLPLAN. One group of salespersons used CALLPLAN to develop call frequencies for their accounts, whereas the control group used manual techniques to plan their call frequencies. However, both groups filled out the questionnaires for CALLPLAN response-function inputs. Fudge and Lodish assigned 10 pairs of "matched" salespersons randomly to each group (10 salespersons in each group) to participate in this study. At the end of the six-month study the CALLPLAN group had an 11.9 percent increase in sales from the previous year, while the control group had only a 3.8 percent increase. As a result the CALLPLAN group had an incremental sales of nearly $1 million over the control group. This difference between these groups was statistically significant at the 0.025 level.

Individual users should assess the value of the model in a similar fashion. A simple way to do this is to run a before-and-after study: track sales performance for six months prior to using the model and compare that with sales performance during six months when using the model. While this approach could lead to misleading results, especially if there are seasonality effects and market changes during the evaluation, it can still provide a useful assessment of the model.

Advantages and limitations of CALLPLAN: Although many salespeople believe that they should focus on high-potential prospects, they often fall back to the routine comfort of calling on friendly established accounts. The CALLPLAN model can help them realize the consequences of such an approach on the bottom line and their commissions and nudge them to try alternative allocation strategies. Lodish (1974) notes:

> A typical first reaction from some sales managers about the procedure is "garbage in, garbage out." They are uncomfortable putting in subjective estimates of sales or odds of conversion at different call levels for each account. However, if maximizing sales or profits is the objective of the sales operation, these estimates are necessary to evaluate the profitability of utilizing the limited manpower resources. . . . After they have utilized the procedure, most managers realize this and become enthusiastic supporters of this concept. (p. 124)

In recent years several account-management software packages have become available commercially. These packages keep track of customer phone numbers and addresses, customer history, correspondence, and the like, and they also contain calendars to schedule appointments. The more sophisticated packages can link to central databases to upload and download information (e.g., sales presentations or price lists). CALLPLAN complements these software packages with analytical support that helps salespeople use account information effectively.

The limitations noted under the Syntex model also apply to the CALLPLAN model. It is best suited for repetitive buying situations. In addition, in its current form the model is likely to be more useful for the "lone wolf" salesperson, but it can be adapted for team-based salesforce applications.

MARKETING CHANNEL DECISIONS

Marketing channels may be "viewed as sets of interdependent organizations involved in the process of making a product or service available for consumption or use" (Stern, El-Ansary, and Coughlan 1996). Decisions about marketing channels influence the effectiveness and the efficiency with which a firm reaches its markets. In addition, because channels require long-term commitment of corporate resources, channel decisions also affect the competitive positioning of the firm. Typically channel decisions encompass three areas:

1. *Strategy*: The firm determines the method for selling products to target markets and the types of contractual mechanisms to employ. The firm can sell directly to customers (e.g., by direct mail or the Internet) or use a variety of intermediaries (e.g., manufacturer's agents, brokers, rack jobbers, drop shippers, wholesalers, and retailers). Possible contractual mechanisms range from complete ownership of the entire marketing channel to relying only on brokers who operate entirely on commissions.

2. *Location*: The firm determines the number and locations of outlets through which it will sell its products and services. In some cases the location decision implies direct investments by the firm (e.g., Wal-Mart). In other cases, although intermediaries made the investments (e.g., McDonald's franchisees), the firm greatly influences location decisions in order to maintain system-wide control over locations.

3. *Logistics*: The firm plans and manages such activities as physical distribution and inventory to maximize the efficiency of channel operations. It tries to provide high service to customers with low transit and inventory costs.

In this section we focus on models for facilitating location decisions. In recent years firms have increasingly used such decision models because relatively inexpensive geodemographic databases have become available. For a discussion of models concerning strategy and logistics, see Lilien, Kotler, and Moorthy (1992).

Location decisions: In selecting a location for an outlet, the firm makes two decisions: it chooses a market area, such as a city, region, or country, in which to establish an outlet, and then it chooses a specific site within that location. The former is referred to as the "macro" decision, while the latter is referred to as the "micro" decision. Many firms choose locations for retail outlets based on information about what real estate is available, deciding if the rent at that location is affordable, and then assessing the neighborhood on such criteria as profit potential and other measures of suitability. They can now use formal models in making both macro and micro location decisions because of the availability of computerized geodemographic databases. These databases overlay demographic and other types of data (e.g., psychographic) on a geocoded database containing the latitude and longitude of most households and firms in the United States. By combining these databases with quantitative computer models, such as the gravity model (Huff 1964), managers can carefully evaluate alternative retail-location options.

The gravity model

Formal models to support location decisions are intended to evaluate the combined effects of such factors as customer profiles, store image, drive times, and the locations of competing retailers on the potential value of a site. The gravity model offers managers a way to assess the impact of these and other factors in a familiar modeling framework—the discrete choice model. In its basic form the gravity model postulates that the probability that a customer or individual i will choose a store j is given by

$$p_{ij} = \frac{V_{ij}}{\sum_{n \in N} V_{in}}, \tag{9.17}$$

where

p_{ij} = probability (proportion of times) individual(s) in geographic zone i will choose the store at the jth location;

V_{ij} = an index to indicate the attractiveness (also called value or utility) of store j to individual(s) in zone i; and

N = the set of stores that will compete with the proposed new store. (In more sophisticated versions of the model, N may be indexed by i to indicate that it may vary from zone to zone.)

Specifically, gravity models propose that value (V_{ij}) depends on several key factors. An important factor will be the size of the store (or shopping center) at location j; the larger the store, the higher the attractiveness. Larger stores typically offer greater variety and better prices. Another important factor is the distance from an individual's home to each of the competing outlets, including a proposed new outlet. The greater this distance, the less attractive a store becomes to individuals in zone i. Finally, the model permits the use of various parameters to modify the relative impact of store size and distance. We describe some examples of such parameters below. Thus shoppers in a geographical area will be "pulled" (whence the term gravity model) toward a store with higher probability if it is located closer to their homes, it is larger, and its retail image is more attractive than that of the existing competitors.

A specific form of V_{ij} in Eq. (9.17) that is used in practice is

$$p_{ij} = \frac{S_j^\alpha / D_{ij}^\beta}{\sum_{n \in N} S_j^\alpha / D_{in}^\beta}, \tag{9.18}$$

where

p_{ij} = probability that individuals in zone i choose store at the jth location;

S_j = size of store at location j (more generally, this can be some index of store image);

D_{ij} = distance of store j from the center of zone i (more generally, this may be viewed as ease of access to the store rather than just distance);

α = a parameter to "tune" the impact of size (or image) on the decision to patronize stores; and

β = a parameter to "tune" the impact of distance (or ease of access) on the decision to patronize stores.

The example in Exhibit 9.10 shows how store choice varies as a result of changes in the parameters α and β. Note the dramatic increase in the probability of choosing store 3 when the distance component becomes more important (from 0.32 when $\alpha = 1$ and $\beta = 1$ to 0.48 when $\alpha = 1$ and $\beta = 2$).

Although gravity models have been around for many years, the recent development of commercial geodemographic databases only now makes it feasible to apply these models broadly. Without these databases it is difficult to specify exact geographic areas for analysis, and it is cumbersome to obtain distance and demographic data for a large number of geographic zones and stores. Recent data and modeling enhancements have also made it easier to use geodemographic databases in making location decisions. Managers no longer have

	Store image (Index averages to 100)	Distance from geographic unit (in miles)	$\dfrac{\text{(Store image)}^{\alpha}}{\text{(Distance)}^{\beta}}$	Choice probability (p_{ij})
$\alpha = 1, \beta = 1$				
Store 1	100	5	20.0	0.17
Store 2	100	3	33.3	0.29
Store 3	75	2	37.5	0.32
Store 4	125	5	25.0	0.22
$\alpha = 1, \beta = 2$				
Store 1	100	5	4.0	0.10
Store 2	100	3	11.1	0.29
Store 3	75	2	18.8	0.48
Store 4	125	5	5.0	0.13
$\alpha = 2, \beta = 1$				
Store 1	100	5	2000.0	0.18
Store 2	100	3	3333.3	0.29
Store 3	75	2	2812.5	0.25
Store 4	125	5	3125.0	0.28

EXHIBIT 9.10

A numerical example illustrating the gravity model. Stores 1, 2, and 3 are existing stores, and store 4 is a proposed new store. The table shows how changes in model parameters influence store choice. The α parameter captures the impact of store image (or size) on customers' probability of selecting each store. As α increases, stores with stronger or weaker images than the average will see greater changes in the probabilities of customers' choosing them (look at changes in choice probabilities for stores 3 and 4). The β parameter captures the impact of distance (or ease of access) of a store from customers' homes on their probability of selecting each store. As β increases, the distance variable becomes more important in influencing customers' store choice (look at changes in choice probabilities for stores 1, 3, and 4).

to evaluate store attractiveness by traditional geographic units such as census tracts or zip codes. Newer databases offer finer detail, such as latitude and longitude corresponding to every geographic entity and microgrids to produce highly accurate boundaries. The user of the software is free to identify an existing or potential market area by combining grids. Also various geographic features such as streets and highways and boundaries of block groups (an area consisting of about 2000 people) are available. In addition, company-specific data (e.g., customer records) can be overlaid on commercial databases using other databases that contain the latitude and longitude of every listed telephone in the United States. These enhancements make it possible for a company such as The Sharper Image to use its customer database of direct mail shoppers to identify potential retail store locations that are geographically close to its existing customer base.

EXAMPLE

(Adapted from Garry 1996.) Supervalue is one of the largest grocery wholesalers in the United States and is also the twelfth largest food retailer. The company serves 4100 food stores and operates nearly 300 retail food stores. Locating its distribution facilities and its food stores in the most appropriate locations is critical to its success. Supervalue was an early adopter of geographic information systems (GIS) and gravity modeling. The company uses GIS to support a number of decisions, such as locating new stores and the mix of products to carry in a given location.

Supervalue uses GIS to evaluate potential new sites from a number of perspectives, including how a site compares with existing store sites, the kind and number of shoppers who live in the trade area, their spending potential, and the market share of competitors. In addition it uses this system to evaluate the suitability of different store formats (e.g., Cub Foods and Shop 'N Save) for a particular market area. It also uses gravity model estimates to evaluate the performance of existing stores. It uses the model to project how much business a particular store should be getting based on the number of customers who reside near the store, their access to competitors, their spending potential, and the road network. It then compares these predictions with actual store sales and associates reasons for underperformance or superior performance with specific factors included in the model.

Steps in implementing gravity models: The software accompanying this book was developed by SCAN/US, a leading provider of geodemographic databases for marketing decision making. Although these databases have many other uses in marketing, we will focus on using them to implement a gravity model. To develop a gravity model you take the following general steps (the software tutorial has more specific instructions for implementing these steps within the SCAN/US software):

Step 1: Define the market area. Identify the geographic area that the proposed outlet is likely to serve and divide that area into its constituent zones. Ideally the zones should be relatively homogeneous in their demographic characteristics and in the availability of competitive stores and movement barriers (e.g., rivers, railway lines, high-crime neighborhoods).

Step 2: Obtain data about existing stores that might compete with the proposed store. In particular get data on the location, size, sales, and other characteristics of each competing store within the market area.

Step 3: Compute distances from each store to each zone. Commercial software packages automatically compute the distances once you specify the zones and locations of stores. (Sometimes the data from steps 2 and 3 alone are enough to indicate the potential value of a location. For example, potentially lucrative locations are likely to exist if these data indicate that sales per square foot in existing stores are much above average or that people have to travel great distances to reach existing stores.)

Step 4: Calibrate the gravity model on the existing competitors in the market area. Specifically, choose a set of parameter values for α and β that fit the existing data well. Good starting values are $\alpha = 1$ and $\beta = 1$, unless you have reason to believe that other values are more likely. For the chosen values of the parameters, compute p_{ij} from Eq. (9.18) using the size and distance information gathered in steps 2 and 3.

a. Next compute market shares for each of the existing competitors by aggregating the p_{ij}'s as follows:

$$m_j = \frac{\sum_{i \in I} P_{ij} T_j}{\sum_{j \in J} \sum_{i \in I} P_{ij} T_j} ; \tag{9.19}$$

T_j is a measure of sales potential in zone j, I is the set of zones in the market area, and J is the number of existing stores in the market area. You can use any suitable index available in the database for measuring potential (T_j) in each zone. The actual index you select depends on the nature of the store and product category. In some cases potential may be a general index such as average annual expenditure per household or total households in a zone. In other cases it may be a product-specific index. Potential can even be indicated by *relative* measures of demographic variables, such as age or income, that are indexed to an average value of 100 (if you use indexed measures, make sure that higher index values indicate higher potential; for example, if lower age indicates higher potential, as it would for the purchase of rock music CDs, then the index should increase with decreasing age). The numerator in Eq. (9.19) is a measure of the sales potential of store j, while the denominator is a measure of the sales potential for all existing stores in the market area.

The demographic information most often included in gravity models concerns such characteristics as income, sex, age, occupation, education, family size, religion, race, and nationality. For a gravity model based on these measures of potential to be useful, these characteristics should be associated with store preferences.

b. Check that the model produces market shares m_j (or sales potential $\sum_{i \in I} P_{ij} T_j$) that are consistent with the actual market shares of sales of the existing competitors. If not, change the values of parameters α and β and repeat step 4 until the procedure settles on a realistic set of values for α and β. (There are statistical methods for choosing α and β. See, for example, Cooper and Nakanishi (1988).)

Step 5: Evaluate the sales potential of a new store at various locations. Introduce a new store k at a proposed location into the model and recompute the p_{ij}'s using the estimated α and β. Compute the sales potential for the new store ($= \sum_{i \in I} P_{ik} T_k$). Repeat this process to consider other locations for the new store.

Step 6: Select the location of the new store. This is where sales potential, $\sum_{i \in I} P_{ik} T_k$, is highest.

For a detailed example of implementing a gravity model in conjunction with geodemographic databases, see Tayman and Pol (1995).

Limitations of the gravity model: Users of the gravity model should carefully scrutinize the assumptions of the model before applying it in a specific decision situation. Customers do not always try to minimize distance traveled nor do they always prefer large stores to small stores. Thus some high-fashion retailers succeed by placing a few small stores in selected locations (e.g., Hermes, the maker of fine silk scarves and ties), while others succeed by locating large stores in selected areas (e.g., Ikea furniture outlets). Despite its limitations the gravity model has turned out to be a remarkably robust method for predicting store choice, at least at the aggregate level.

The gravity model is a special case of the attraction models described in Chapter 2, which are subject to a counterintuitive phenomenon known as "independence from irrelevant alternatives." Suppose that customers are indifferent between shopping in store 1 (S1) and store 2 (S2) as long as these are the only two options, but they prefer to shop in store 3 (S3) four-to-one when offered a choice between S1 and S3, and they would prefer S3 four-to-one over S2 when offered a choice between S2 and S3. In this case, according to the model customers would prefer S3 two-to-one over S1 and S2 when all three stores are available, whereas intuition suggests that S3 should still be preferred four-to-one over S1 and S2. The model forces the ratio of the attractiveness of S3 to S1 (4/1) and S3 to S2 (4/1) to remain the same, regardless of the shopping context. Thus when the customer chooses among all three stores, the probabilities (market shares) are 1/6, 1/6, and 2/3 for S1, S2, and S3 respectively. One way out of this problem is to treat highly similar alternatives as a single choice option. In the foregoing example, you could treat S1 and S2 as just one store-format option for purposes of analysis.

Another limitation of gravity models is that they ignore modes of access to a location. For example, accessibility by bus, by car, or by foot have different implications for distance measures. Where multiple modes of access are common, gravity models will perform poorly. Such situations are more likely outside the United States.

Gravity models are more difficult to interpret than multiple regression models, which are also used for making site-location decisions. The regression approach relates data from a number stores regarding store sales (dependent variable) and various independent variables such as store size, demographic characteristics associated with the store, and characteristics of competitor stores. Regression models can be used to forecast sales in new locations based on the values of the independent variables for these locations. Compared with gravity models, regression models generally do a poor job of accounting for the impact of existing competitors.

The retail world is changing. Current trends include customers making less frequent shopping trips and the growth of megastores, direct marketing, and interactive marketing. These trends are reducing the impact of geographic constraints on shopping behavior. As these trends continue, traditional measures of market potential of a geographic area may prove inappropriate. For example, sales of PCs in N. Sioux City, South Dakota (home to Gateway computers, a leading direct marketer of personal computers), would be a misleading indicator of potential for this geographical unit for the sales of a new computer game through retail outlets.

SUMMARY

In this chapter we highlighted five successful marketing engineering models for managing salesforces and marketing channels: the Syntex model for allocating sales resources, the Hess and Samuels model for aligning sales territories, the MSZ model for designing compensation plans for salespeople, the CALLPLAN model for planning sales calls, and the gravity model for locating new stores. We described how to calibrate each model and provided example applications.

The sales-management models are normative decision models (see Chapter 1) that help managers to choose a course of action from numerous available options, whereas the gravity model is a descriptive/predictive decision model, which helps managers to evaluate a few selected options very carefully. Sales-management models have resulted in incremental profits in the range of 5 to 10 percent over those the firm earned before implementing the model. Although many firms use gravity models, we did not find documented evidence in the public domain showing the incremental benefits associated with such models. However, the repeated use of the model by such companies as Supervalue is an indicator of its positive value in use.

A current trend is for companies to invest in salesforce automation to facilitate the sales process (Young 1995). They are setting up "data warehouse," communications, and supporting services to provide salespeople with current information (e.g., specs for company and competitive products, authorized prices, account history, and order status) and equip salespeople and sales managers with computers so that they can access the data warehouse and upload and download information.

A good salesforce automation system effectively links corporate functions, managers of the field salesforce, and sales reps. The systems enable managers to monitor sales activities readily and focus on mentoring salespeople and developing strategies (not just tactics) to manage each account. The systems can include packaged software for resource allocation, account analysis, time management, and generating proposals and presentations. By linking their corporate databases to geographic information systems, firms can improve their management of channel functions and operations. As the use of information technologies in managing salesforces and marketing channels increases, we expect firms to find further applications for the models (and their variants) that we have described in this chapter.

10

Price and Sales Promotion Decisions

In this chapter we cover

- Pricing decisions—the classical economics approach
- Pricing in practice—orientation to cost, demand, or competition
- Interactive pricing—reference prices and price negotiations
- Price discrimination
- Pricing product lines
- Sales promotional types and effects
- Aggregate models to analyze promotional effects
- Analyzing individuals' responses to promotions

Price is the only marketing variable that directly affects revenue. Indeed if one looks at a profit function as

Profit = (Unit price − Unit cost) × Quantity sold,

one sees that price is involved in all parts of the profit equation. Price affects margin (unit price less unit cost) in two ways: it is the first term (unit price) in the equation by definition, and it has an indirect effect on unit cost, which is often partly determined by the quantity sold. As price affects quantity sold (and hence unit cost indirectly), it is involved in all three components of the foregoing profit equation.

We discuss promotion along with price in this chapter since the most common promotions (deals and coupons) are in fact no more than advertised, temporary price decreases.

PRICING DECISIONS: THE CLASSICAL ECONOMICS APPROACH

From the viewpoint of the classical economist, price is the driving force that allocates goods and services in the marketplace. For the customer it is the cost of a purchase in monetary terms. For the producer or seller it helps determine the level of supply and acts to allocate economic resources on the production side.

A basic relationship in economic theory is known as the Law of Demand, which states that the quantity demanded per period (also known as the time rate of demand) is negatively related to price. This law is based on the postulate of a rational customer who has full knowledge of the available goods and their substitutes, a limited budget, and a singular drive to maximize his or her utility. For a given structure of relative prices, customers will allocate their income over goods (including savings) so as to maximize their utility. If the price relations change, they will normally substitute less expensive goods for more expensive goods; this action will increase their utility.

Central to this model is the concept of price elasticity, defined as the ratio of the percentage change in demand to a percentage change in price:

$$e_{qp} = \frac{\text{Fraction change in demand}}{\text{Fraction change in price}} = \frac{(Q_1 - Q_0)/Q_0}{(P_1 - P_0)/P_0}$$

$$= \frac{\Delta Q/Q}{\Delta P/P} = \frac{\Delta Q}{\Delta P}\frac{P}{Q}, \tag{10.1}$$

where

e_{qp} = elasticity of quantity demanded with respect to change in price;

Q_1 = quantity demanded after price change;

Q_0 = quantity demanded before price change;

P_1 = new price;

P_0 = old price;

$\Delta Q = Q_1 - Q_0$; and

$\Delta P = P_1 - P_0$.

Note that we cannot assess elasticities without specifying a model of how sales (quantity sold) respond to changes in price. In most cases price elasticities are negative. A price elasticity equal to 1.0 means that demand rises (or falls) by the same percentage that price falls (or rises). In such a case total revenue is not affected. A price elasticity greater than one means that demand rises (or falls) by more than the price falls (or rises) in percentage terms, and total revenue rises (or falls). A price elasticity less than one means that demand rises (or falls) by less than the price falls (or rises) in percentage terms, and total revenue falls (or rises).

If we know the price elasticity of demand, we can answer the question of whether the firm's price is too high or too low more precisely. If we want to maximize revenue, the price is too high if the demand elasticity at that price is less than one. Whether this rule holds true for maximizing profit depends on the behavior of costs.

Another measure of the sensitivity of demand to price is the relationship between the price of one good and the quantity demanded of another. This measure is known as the cross-price elasticity of demand, and it is computed for product X as $(\Delta Q_X/\Delta P_Y)(P_Y/Q_X)$, where Y is any other product. If the cross-price elasticity is positive, then products X and Y are substitutes. In this case (for Coke and Pepsi, say), when the price of Coke increases sales of Pepsi will increase, as customers substitute Pepsi for Coke. If the cross-price elasticity is negative, then products X and Y are complements. For example, when the price of computer equipment (hardware) goes down, the demand for related software increases.

Finally, elasticity and marginal revenue are related:

$$\text{Total revenue} = \text{TR} = PQ \text{ (Price} \times \text{Quantity).} \tag{10.2}$$

Therefore

$$\text{Marginal revenue} = \frac{\Delta TR}{\Delta Q} = P + Q\frac{\Delta P}{\Delta Q}$$

$$= P\left(1 + \frac{Q\Delta P}{P\Delta Q}\right) = P\left(1 + \frac{1}{\varepsilon_{qp}}\right). \tag{10.3}$$

This equation shows that marginal revenue varies with both price and the price elasticity of demand.

The Law of Demand does not specify the shape of the price-quantity relationship. In fact the shape varies with the particular product or product class. However, two equation forms are particularly appropriate for representing this relationship: the linear and constant-elasticity forms.

The general linear demand-price equation, where quantity goes down linearly with increases in price, is

$$Q = a - bP, \tag{10.4}$$

where a and b are constants (Exhibit 10.1). This linear relationship need not apply throughout the domain of possible prices but should be approximately true in the neighborhood of the prevailing price.

How can the price elasticity be determined in the neighborhood of a particular price, say P_1, on a linear demand curve? For the linear demand function, $\Delta Q/\Delta P = b$ and

$$\varepsilon_{qp} = \frac{\Delta Q}{\Delta P} \times \frac{P}{Q} = -b \times \frac{P}{a - bP} = -\frac{bP}{a - bP}. \tag{10.5}$$

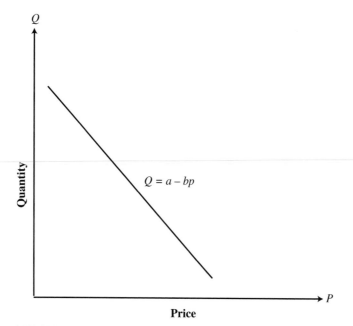

EXHIBIT 10.1
The linear demand-price function, where each $1 decrease in price leads to the same increase (b units) in quantity demanded.

Following from this equation:

1. The price elasticity will be minus one when $P = a/2b$.
2. The price elasticity is high (in absolute terms) at high prices, making it desirable to lower price.
3. The price elasticity is low at low prices, making it desirable to raise the price.

Another popular shape for the demand function is based on the notion of constant elasticity. This function (Exhibit 10.2) is

$$Q = aP^{-b}. \tag{10.6}$$

The exponent b is the price elasticity, which is constant for all prices. This form of demand function has been popular among modelers because it includes an explicit term for elasticity, incorporates nonlinear effects of pricing, and is easy to manipulate mathematically. (The Modeler spreadsheet allows you to investigate these simple price models.)

The classical model is based on several key assumptions that limit its applicability, including the following:

■ The firm's objective in setting a price is to maximize the short-run profits to be realized from a particular product.
■ The only parties to consider in setting the price are the firm's immediate customers.
■ Price setting is independent of the levels set for the other variables in the marketing mix.
■ The demand and cost equations can be estimated with sufficient accuracy.
■ The firm has true control over price—that is, the firm is a price maker not a price taker.
■ Market responses to price changes are well understood.

Each of these limitations leads to modifications of the classical model. To deal with one interesting issue—buyer reactions that vary in response to price changes—classical

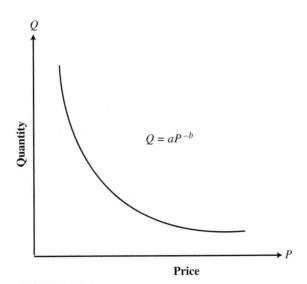

EXHIBIT 10.2
Constant-elasticity price-demand function, where each 1 percent decrease in price leads to a b percent increase in demand.

microeconomic theory usually assumes near-perfect information about market prices and a downward-sloping demand curve. However, all customers will not interpret prices in the same way. A price reduction that would normally attract more customers may not be known to all customers. Furthermore, customers may interpret changes in prices as signifying any of the following:

- The item is about to be superseded by a later model.
- The item has some faults and is not selling well.
- The firm is in financial trouble and may not stay in business to supply future parts.
- The price will come down further and it pays to wait.
- The quality has been reduced.

Conversely a price increase that would normally deter sales may carry a variety of different meanings to potential buyers:

- The item is hot and may soon be unobtainable.
- The item represents an unusually good value.
- The seller is greedy, is charging what the traffic will bear, and may charge more if the potential buyer waits.

Thus demand is affected not only by current price but by the information the price carries and expectations about future prices.

Thus in spite of its conceptual elegance and intuitive appeal, the classical model is not very useful. In practice firms tend to base their pricing decisions on one of three key factors—cost, demand, or competition—and then they rely on models that ignore the other factors.

PRICING IN PRACTICE: ORIENTATION TO COST, DEMAND, OR COMPETITION

Cost-oriented pricing

Many firms set their prices largely or even wholly on the basis of their costs. Typically they count all costs, including an allocation for overhead based on expected operating levels.

The most elementary examples of cost-oriented pricing are markup pricing and cost-plus pricing. They are similar in that price is determined by adding either a fixed amount or a fixed percentage to the unit cost.

Does the use of a rigid, customary markup over cost make logical sense in pricing products? Generally the answer is no. Any procedure that ignores current elasticity of demand in setting prices is not likely to lead, except by chance, to maximum profits, either in the long or in the short run. As demand elasticity changes—as it is likely to seasonally, cyclically, and over the product life cycle—the optimum markup should also change. If markup remains a rigid percentage of cost, then under ordinary conditions it would not lead to maximum profits. However, under special conditions a rigid markup at the right level may lead to optimum profit. These special conditions are (1) that average (unit) costs be fairly constant for different points on the demand curve and (2) that costs be constant over time.

Under these conditions the optimal price is

$$P^* = \left(\frac{\varepsilon}{1 + \varepsilon} \right) \text{MC}, \tag{10.7}$$

where

ε = price elasticity of demand, assumed to be negative; and

MC = marginal cost.

According to this relationship the optimal price (markup over cost) goes down as price elasticity rises (in absolute value). If price = $(1 + \alpha)$MC, then α is the markup. And from Eq. (10.7), if we set $\varepsilon/(1 + \varepsilon) = (1 + \alpha)$, then $\alpha = \varepsilon/(1 + \varepsilon) - 1$. If price elasticity is low, say $(-)2.0$, as it might be in the case of branded frozen pastry, then $\alpha = 1$ and the optimal markup is high (100%). Furthermore, if the price elasticity remains fairly constant over time, then a rigid markup would be consistent with optimal pricing. Both required conditions—constant (marginal) costs and constant elasticity—characterize many retailing situations. This may explain why rigid markups are in widespread use in retailing and why they may be consistent with optimal-pricing requirements. However, for most durable consumer products and for industrial products it is less likely that the two special conditions hold.

In Chapter 5, when considering marketing strategy we described the concept of the experience curve, where costs were shown to fall with cumulative production experience. Indeed empirical studies show that the declines in costs associated with doubling cumulative production generally are in the 5 to 30 percent range (Simon 1989). If such changes in costs can be forecast, then cost-oriented pricing becomes a dynamic phenomenon: that is, the firm can see two effects of lowering price. First, lowering price increases short-term demand. Second, these increases in short-term demand help lower costs (and raise profit margins) through the experience effect. This leads to recommendations contrary to those of the classical model: in the presence of experience-curve cost declines, one generally wants to lower price to accelerate the learning effect and to take advantage of the dynamics of cost reduction. The Price Planning for the ABCOR2000 exercise allows you to explore the impact of the learning curve on pricing decisions.

Demand-oriented pricing

Cost-oriented approaches to pricing center on the costs of producing and distributing the product. Demand-oriented approaches look at the demand for the product at various price levels: they focus on customer value. A central idea behind demand-oriented pricing is to try to charge a higher price when demand is strong and a lower price when demand is weak, even though production costs may remain the same.

Many sophisticated marketers, especially in industrial markets, practice value-based pricing after analyzing the product's value-in-use. The idea behind value-in-use analysis is that the price for a product should be related to the value that product brings to a particular customer. This approach is particularly appropriate for large-volume purchases when the salesperson has discretion in pricing. The idea is for the salesperson to imagine being in the buyer's situation and determine whether it is a good investment for the buyer to adopt the product or to replace the product currently being used with the proposed new product.

The value-in-use of a new product is defined as that price that would make a potential buyer just indifferent between continuing to use the current product and switching to the new product. This calculation is illustrated in the following example.

EXAMPLE

Suppose a chemical plant uses 200 O-rings to seal the valves on pipes that carry corrosive materials. The plant pays $5 for each O-ring and must change them during regular maintenance every two months.

A new product has twice the corrosive resisting power. We can calculate the value-in-use (VIU) of the material:

Solution 1: Annual cost of incumbent product

$$= 200 \text{ (O-rings)} \times 6 \text{ changes per year} \times \$5/\text{O-ring}$$

$$= \$6000$$

$$= 200 \text{ (O-rings)} \times 3 \text{ (changes per year)} \times \text{VIU},$$

or VIU = $10.

Solution 2: The new material allows a longer time between shutdowns—four months vs. two months—and the cost of a shutdown is $5000. Then we get

$$\underbrace{200 \times 6 \times 5}_{\substack{\text{Equipment} \\ \text{Cost}}} + \underbrace{5000 \times 6}_{\substack{\text{Shutdown} \\ \text{Cost}}} = \underbrace{200 \times 3 \times \text{VIU}}_{\substack{\text{Equipment} \\ \text{Cost}}} + \underbrace{5000 \times 3}_{\substack{\text{Shutdown} \\ \text{Cost}}}$$

$$\underbrace{\hspace{4cm}}_{\text{Incumbent}} \qquad \underbrace{\hspace{4cm}}_{\text{New}}$$

or VIU = $35.

When doing value-based pricing it is important to incorporate all costs, both tangible and intangible. Aside from the initial cost and operating costs suggested in the example, you must also consider the buyer's planning horizon, the cost of capital, switching costs (retraining, product reformulation, likely start-up inefficiencies), maintenance cost differences, performance differences, differences in flexibility, and the risk a buyer assumes in adopting a new product.

EXAMPLE

(From Lee 1978.) To calculate the value-in-use of a candidate material, we first calculate the cost of using the incumbent material. We call this its *use cost*. This includes not only the price of that material in cents per pound (or gallon, or square yard, etc.), but also the cost of processing, the cost of any finishing operations, the scrap cost, the inventory charges associated with stocking the material, and any other significant item of cost.

Similarly, the use cost of an incumbent *component part* includes not only its purchase price, but also the costs of assembly, adjustment, and so forth.

Finally, if we are comparing two materials or two components whose useful lives differ, and if the difference is valuable, we should take this into account by calculating use cost per year, or annual use cost. The annual use cost for an incumbent material can be calculated by

$$\text{Annual use cost}_{\text{inc.}} = (QC + C_p + C_f + \cdots)/L, \tag{10.8}$$

where

Q = quantity of incumbent material per unit of finished product;

C = purchase price of incumbent material per unit;

C_p = processing cost per unit of finished product, using the incumbent material;

C_f = finishing cost per unit of finished product, using the incumbent material; and

L = useful life of finished product, using the incumbent material.

We could use a similar equation to express the annual use cost of the candidate material. However, in this equation we insert not the price of the candidate but an unknown, V, which is the value-in-use of the candidate. We then equate the two annual use costs and solve for V.

Let us illustrate: Assume that a firm is producing an industrial fastener out of die-cast alloy, and our candidate material is a sheet metal from which it could fabricate the fastener using a combination punching-forming process. Suppose that the pertinent quantities and costs are those in Exhibit 10.3.

First we calculate the annual use cost of the incumbent material:

$$\text{Annual use cost}_{\text{inc.}} = (QC + C_{\text{fab}} + C_{\text{fin}} + XQC + YQC)/L, \qquad (10.9)$$

where

X = inventory cost, expressed as a decimal fraction; and

Y = scrap cost, expressed as a decimal fraction.

Inserting the numbers from Exhibit 10.3 and solving, we get

$$\text{Annual use cost}_{\text{inc.}} = (QC + 0.05 + 0.02 + 0.05\ QC + 0.1\ QC)/3$$

$$= 0.0281 \text{ (rounded)}.$$

Second we set up a similar equation for the annual use cost of the candidate material and simplify it, as follows:

$$\text{Annual use cost}_{\text{cand.}} = (Q'V + C'_{\text{fab}} + X'Q'V + Y'Q'V)/L'$$

$$= (Q'V + 0.10 + 0.05\ Q'V + 0.2\ Q'V)/7$$

$$= 0.00536\ V + 0.0143. \qquad (10.10)$$

Finally, we equate the two expressions for annual use costs and solve for the value-in-use of the candidate material:

$$0.00536\ V + 0.0143 = 0.0281;$$

$$V = 2.57.$$

Cost element	Die-cast	Sheet metal
Quantity in lbs per finished part	0.05	0.03
Price of material, $/lb	0.25	0.20
Fabricating cost, $/part	0.05	0.10
Finishing cost, $/part	0.02	0
Inventory cost, %**	5	5
Scrap cost, %**	10	20
Useful life of finished parts, years	3	7

** Percentages are based on value of material in finished part.

EXHIBIT 10.3
Industrial fastener cost elements for the sheet metal vs. die-cast alloy value-in-use calculations.

This tells us that if the sheet metal cost is $2.57 per pound, its annual use cost would just match that of the die-cast alloy. In other words, for this application the sheet metal is *worth* $2.57 per pound; that is, its value-in-use is $2.57 per pound. This is so much greater than its assumed price of $0.20 per pound that the fabricator would be wise to adopt the sheet metal and the seller could consider charging considerably more than $0.20 per pound.

To apply value-based pricing on a large scale, the firm normally needs to do in-depth studies at the plants of a sample of key customers to calculate a range of customer values for the product. The firm then has the strategic option of deciding whether to skim the market with the product (setting a high price—say $2.00/lb for sheet metal—and going after that part of the market that sees a high value for its product) or to penetrate the market with a price that makes its product attractive in many uses for many types of customers (charging close to $0.20/lb for sheet metal). Account planning for the ABCOR2000 exercise shows how salespeople can use this concept to customize selling strategies for different accounts.

Competition-oriented pricing

When a company bases its prices chiefly on what its competitors are charging rather than on cost or demand, its pricing policy can be described as competition-oriented. In the most common type of competition-oriented pricing, a firm tries to keep its price at the average level charged by the industry. This is called going-rate or imitative pricing.

Firms use going-rate pricing primarily for homogeneous products like oil, although the market structure itself may vary from pure competition to pure oligopoly. The firm selling a homogeneous product in a purely competitive market actually has no choice in setting its price. In an oligopoly, in which a few large firms dominate, like the plate glass industry, firms also tend to charge the same price as the competition, although for different reasons. Because there are only a few firms, each firm is aware of the others' prices and so are the buyers. The firm with the lowest price is likely to capture the most business, thereby inviting immediate decreases in price from competitors. This situation also discourages single firms from increasing prices.

On the other hand, in markets characterized by product differentiation the individual firm has more latitude in its price decision. Product differences, whether in styling, quality, or functional features, desensitize the buyer to existing price differentials. Firms make their product and marketing programs compatible within each pricing zone, and they respond to their competitors' changes in price to maintain their relative prices.

Competitive bidding is a common form of pricing in markets in which the firm competes with an unknown number of suppliers and has no way to determine their prices. Many manufacturers and service organizations that sell to the Defense Department, municipal governments, original-equipment producers, and so forth must bid against others for the work; the contract usually goes to the lowest bidder. Therefore the seller must carefully think through two issues regarding each bidding opportunity: (1) should the firm bid at all (the decision to bid), and (2) if so, what bid should it make (the bid-size problem)?

If a supplier makes a bid on a particular job, it must search for a price that is above its costs but below (the unknown) competitors' bids. The higher the seller sets its price above its costs, the greater will be the profit if it wins the bid but the smaller will be the probability of getting the contract. The expected profit in a potential bid is the product of the probability of getting the contract and the estimated profit on the contract:

$$E(Z_P) = f(P)(P - C), \tag{10.11}$$

where

$E(Z_P)$ = expected profit with a bid of P;

$f(P)$ = probability of winning contract with a bid of P;

P = bid price; and

C = estimated cost of fulfilling contract.

Each possible price is associated with a certain probability of winning the contract. A company may logically choose the price that it expects to maximize the profits. Exhibit 10.4 shows four alternative bid levels and the associated probabilities and profits for a hypothetical situation. In this example the firm will be tempted to bid $10,000 because its associated expected profit is highest ($216) at this level.

However, the chief problem with this model is guessing the probabilities of winning the contract at various bidding levels. Where price is the buyer's only concern, this probability is the probability of submitting a lower bid than those of all other competitors, and the probability of submitting the lowest bid is the joint probability that the company's bid is lower than each competitor's bid. Assuming that competitors decide their bids independently, the probability of being the lowest bidder is

$$f(P) = f_1(P)f_2(P) \cdots f_j(P) \cdots f_n(P), \tag{10.12}$$

where $f_j(P)$ is the probability that a bid of P is lower than competitor j's bid; that is, the lowest bid has to be lower than that of each of the competitors, leading to a multiplication of probabilities.

Competitors' bids are uncertain but can be based on past bidding behavior, as follows. Assume competitor j has bid on a number of past contracts and that data are available. Then for each bid competitor j's bid is related to your estimate of cost, C:

$$r_j = \frac{P_j}{C},$$

where

r_j = ratio of competitor j's bid to your company's cost;

P_j = past bid by j; and

C = your company's cost at time of bid.

Company's bid	Company's profit	Profitability of getting award with this bid (assumed)	Expected profit
$9,500	$ 100	0.81	$ 81
10,000	600	0.36	216
10,500	1,100	0.09	99
11,000	1,600	0.01	16

EXHIBIT 10.4
Effect of different bids on expected profit, showing that a bid of $10,000 is best.

If for a given contract your cost is C, then we might guess that the probability of competitor j's bid price being greater than ours is $h_j(r_j)$. With k competitors our likelihood of winning is $[h(r)]^k$ if all the competitors are similar, and our expected profit for a bid price of P is

$$E(Z_P) = (P - C)[h(r)]^k. \tag{10.13}$$

In the last step we knew that there would be exactly k bidders. If k is known only probabilistically, then the expected profit is calculated as

$$(P - C)q_0 + (P - C)[h(r)]q_1 + (P - C)[h(r)]^2q_2 + \cdots . + (P - C)[h(r)]^N q_N, \tag{10.14}$$

where N is the maximum number of bidders and q_k is the probability that exactly k competitors submit bids. This equation is the same as (10.13), with each profit level weighted by the probability that 0, 1, 2 . . . up to N competitors actually bid.

The Competitive bidding software and the Paving I-99 exercise allows you to explore these concepts in more detail in a simulated bidding environment.

INTERACTIVE PRICING: REFERENCE PRICES AND PRICE NEGOTIATIONS

We have dealt so far with the concept of price as if it were under the direct control of a decision maker and as if it had little if any direct effect on how customers decide what products are worth. Yet in many real situations these conditions do not hold. For example, when customers cannot directly experience the quality of a product before purchasing it (cosmetics, wines, services), price can serve as an indicator of quality and price discounts may be counterproductive (reducing demand *and* margins!).

A similar and widely discussed phenomenon that undermines many of the recommendations of the classical theory is the concept of reference price; for example, a customer may believe that a four-door sedan should cost no more than $20,000. Roughly speaking, a reference price is a price that customers use to judge the actual price.

The point is that if something like a reference price exists, then the firm must take it into account in making pricing decisions. Consider the following example:

EXAMPLE

Suppose that we use the linear demand-price equation from (10.4):

$$Q = 100 - 2P. \tag{10.15}$$

If marginal production costs are (approximately) constant at $10 per unit, then we can determine profit Z from

$$Z = (P - 10) \times (100 - 2P), \tag{10.16}$$

and the profit-maximizing price P^* is $30.

With a reference price, though, (10.15) might become

$$Q = 100 - 2(P - RP), \tag{10.17}$$

where RP is the reference price. The profit-maximizing price derived from (10.16) and (10.17) is

$$P^* = \frac{120 + 2 \times RP}{4}, \tag{10.18}$$

so that if RP=0, the optimal price from (10.18) is $30 as before; if the reference price is also $30, though, then the optimal price is $45! In general the optimal (profit-maximizing price) will go up as the reference price goes up.

As this example shows, if customers use a reference price in evaluating product offerings, the higher that reference price is, the more the firm can charge for the product and the higher the optimal price will be. Thus in the presence of reference prices it is in the best interest of the seller to consider the reference price in deciding on price and to try to influence the process by which those reference prices are set. For example, the ads for many cars compare that car to a Mercedes, showing how much the consumer can save (for supposedly comparable performance).

A key application of reference-price theory is in developing a price interactively through a bargaining process. To characterize the bargaining process, we often use a concept called *reservation price*, the upper limit on what a customer would be willing to pay for the product or service.

While many consumer markets are driven by posted prices and fixed offerings, in organizational and business markets and in consumer markets where products have high diversity and high utility, such as houses, cars, and boats, prices are generally determined in a bargaining process.

Exhibit 10.5 shows the "zone of agreement"—the zone between the seller's reservation price (or cost) s and the buyer's valuation b. If $s > b$, then there is no zone of agreement. If $s < b$, then the seller and buyer bargain to find a price p such that $s < p < b$. That price, p, then divides the "zone of agreement" $(b - s)$ into two pieces: $b - p$ (called the buyer surplus) and $p - s$ (called the seller surplus or profit).

In a simple one-time bargaining solution, where the buyer and the seller do not consider the elements found in a long-term relationship such as trust, both seek a price p that maximizes their surplus. So how will (or should) they set p?

Nash (1950) proposed an elegant solution to a more general form of this problem, under a set of reasonable assumptions such as *individual rationality* (preferring more to less);

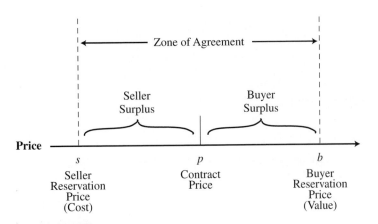

EXHIBIT 10.5
Concepts of a simple distributive bargaining situation where b, the buyer's value, is the most the buyer would pay and s, the seller's cost, is the least a seller would accept. A contract price p splits the agreement zone, providing $b - p$ to the buyer (the buyer surplus) and $p - s$ to the seller (the seller surplus or profit). (Note that if $b < s$, no zone of agreement exists.)

Pareto efficiency (there should be no solution p^* that leaves both parties better off); *symmetry* (or fairness) (the solution on average should leave each party as well off as the other relative to the utility of no agreement). That solution is

$$p \text{ that maximizes } U_s(p - s)U_b(b - p), \tag{10.19}$$

where $U_s(p - s)$ is the utility that the seller, with reservation price s, gets from the price p settled on (and with $U_b(b - p)$ defined similarly).

In several marketing experiments (Neslin and Greenhalgh 1983; Eliashberg et al. 1986) the Nash solution did well at predicting outcomes; however, as Neslin and Greenhalgh (1986) show, many solutions are not Nash-type. If we are to use the Nash solution in real situations, we need other price solutions that include situational contingencies and personal preferences. For example, Roth (1979) relaxes Nash's symmetry assumption to yield the weighted Nash solution

$$p \text{ that maximizes } [U_s(p - s)]^r[U_b(b - p)]^q, \tag{10.20}$$

where the values r and q are the seller's and buyer's bargaining power, respectively. Note the role that the reference price or reservation price plays in the solution. If the buyer can obtain an offer from another supplier of $b^* < b$, then the Nash solution price drops; similarly if the seller can show that circumstances (raw material costs, for example) have forced s upward, the Nash solution price rises.

Most often bargaining on price comes down to discussions about the values of b and s, so that a Nash (or Nash-like) solution will favor the party who makes the most compelling case. Situations in which information is incomplete, where the buyer does not know costs and the seller does not know buyer values, and that explicitly include outside alternatives (see Gupta and Livne 1988, and Gupta 1990, for example) have lead to solutions that differ from those of Nash.

(The Value spreadsheet exercise calculates expected buyer and seller values in a two-issue selling situation and provides a tool that can facilitate such bargaining processes.)

The theoretical and empirical work on interactive price setting shows that each party should use a prenegotiation phase to determine its own reservation values and to estimate the values of the other party. Nash solutions and similar split-the-difference arrangements depend on how both parties view the reference or nonagreement points (the endpoints of the zone of agreement). Most of the negotiation process depends on calculating what those endpoints are, or should be, and then attempting to persuade the other party of one's view on those calculations.

PRICE DISCRIMINATION

Understanding price discrimination

So far we have looked at situations in which the seller seeks the best *single* price that maximizes profits. If customers are homogeneous and the firm can charge only a single price, then that is the best it can do. But if customer valuations differ, then the profit-maximizing firm can increase its profits by charging a variety of prices, that is, by *price discriminating*. We will describe some of the mechanisms for price discrimination and explain how and why they work.

Suppose there are four equal-sized segments of customers in the market for a textbook, each willing to pay a different price for it. Segment A is willing to pay up to $40, segment B up to $30, segment C up to $20, and segment D up to $10. Assume that no customer will buy more than one book and will buy only if his or her *customer surplus* (i.e., reservation price minus the price asked) is nonnegative. Suppose the firm's variable cost per book is $5, there are minimal fixed costs, and the firm wants to determine the best single price to charge. There is no point in charging a price less than $10—everyone is willing to pay at least $10, and so profits increase with a price from $5 to $10. Similarly there is no point in charging a price in between the various reservation prices. So let us begin our analysis with $10. At this price all segments will buy, and so the profits will be $4N(\$10 - 5) = \$20N$, where N is the number of customers in each segment. If the firm charged $20, then it would serve segments A, B, and C and the profits would be $3N(\$20 - 5) = \$45N$; if it charged $30, then it would serve segments A and B and the profits would be $2N(\$30 - 5) = \$50N$; and if it charged $40, then it would serve only segment A and the profits would be $N(\$40 - 5) = \$35N$. So the best single price is $30, yielding $50N$ in profits.

Now suppose that a monopolistic firm can charge four different prices to the four segments. Then it could charge $40 to segment A, $30 to segment B, $20 to segment C, and $10 to segment D. The firm's profits would be

$$N(\$40 - 5) + N(\$30 - 5) + N(\$20 - 5) + N(\$10 - 5) = \$80N.$$

Note the following features of this price-discrimination scheme:

1. The firm extracts every customer's complete surplus. (*Extraction*: "No money is left on the table.")
2. The firm serves every customer who is willing to pay at least as much as the firm's cost (in this case $5: *inclusion*).
3. The firm does not serve any customers whose willingness-to-pay is less than the firm's costs (*exclusion*).
4. Direct price discrimination is *efficient*. That is, no other pricing scheme can be found that will simultaneously improve the welfare of customers and increase the profits of the seller.

A firm trying to implement direct price discrimination in practice faces several difficulties:

1. Identifying customers' reservation prices is difficult. It is unlikely that the observable characteristics of customers will be closely correlated with their reservation prices, and you are unlikely to obtain accurate information by asking them how much they will pay (Morrison 1979).
2. Targeting a particular price to a particular segment is difficult. Most consumer goods, for example, are sold with posted prices and thus are available to everyone equally.
3. It is difficult to prevent *arbitrage*: consumers with low reservation prices may buy up a lot of the product and supply it to high-reservation-price consumers at a price lower than their reservation price.
4. Charging different prices to different segments may be illegal on various grounds, for example, sex and race discrimination, the Robinson-Patman Act governing discrimination among channel intermediaries, and so forth.
5. Customers may view price discrimination as unfair. Customers paying the high price for an item may resent the firm's giving price breaks to others unless it can position that price break positively, perhaps as charity (senior citizen discounts, student discounts). In many situations the seller may "throw in" other items in the package—free service, beneficial financing, free software, and the like—that make the price discrimination less obvious and perhaps more tolerable.

Despite these difficulties direct price discrimination schemes do exist. For example, local telephone companies discriminate between residential and business users in their prices. Senior citizen and student discounts are other forms of price discrimination. And many business products and services, whose terms and conditions of sale are customized, are priced in a discriminatory fashion. Services lend themselves particularly well to direct price discrimination. The seller (e.g., a lawyer) deals with the customer one-on-one and provides services that are difficult to resell. In all these cases the identification, targeting, arbitrage prevention, and legality requirements are satisfied.

Much price discrimination in practice is not as direct as these examples, however. In fact the need for indirectness in the price discrimination scheme is one source of the considerable variety in the pricing schemes we see today. The challenge is to identify correlations between the reservation prices of different segments (Chapter 3) and their preferences for some attributes of the product. If the firm can discover such correlations, then it can tie its different prices to the different levels of the attributes and allow customers to freely choose the level of the attribute they want to buy.

An example of this idea is the airline industry's pricing based on yield management. Airlines offer a variety of fares with various restrictions (and some with no restriction). The higher fares are associated with no advance purchase requirements, no Saturday-stay-at-destination requirement, no cancellation penalties, and so forth. The lower fares, for example, Supersaver fares, have many of these restrictions. The effect is to create a product line differentiated on the "restrictions attribute" with different products in the product portfolio appealing to different segments. The business traveler finds the restrictions costly and opts for the higher unrestricted fares; the vacation traveler, however, finds the lower fares appealing and does not mind the restrictions.

If a market can be segmented by value and those segments can be identified (targeted), then an opportunity for price discrimination exists. The institutional differences of different markets and legal restrictions have led to a number of different methods. *To implement any of these schemes, the seller must analyze customer value carefully (through choice models, conjoint analysis, value-in-use analysis, or one of the other methods we have described), segment the market, and target the various segments (Chapter 3).*

To implement price discrimination, then, the firm must understand how to separate the market segments from one another and how to support the price discrimination program with advertising, distribution, and other marketing instruments. Some of the most common schemes are to rely on geographic and temporal variations in pricing, to use nonlinear pricing (e.g., to base prices on customer characteristics), and to use nonprice marketing instruments.

Geographic price discrimination

In the days of high trade barriers, international borders facilitated price discrimination and made it particularly easy to implement. If the costs of arbitrage exceed the price differential, geographic price discrimination can be effective. The existence of so-called gray markets in many countries suggests that this is not the case. For example:

> Minolta sold cameras to its dealers in Hong Kong for a lower price than in Germany because of lower transportation costs and tariffs. The Hong Kong dealers worked on smaller margins than the German retailers who preferred high markups to high volume. Minolta's Hong Kong wholesalers noticed this price difference and shipped Minolta cameras to German dealers for less than they were paying the German distributor. The German distributor couldn't sell his stock and complained to Minolta. (Kotler 1994, p. 424)

Firms must recognize that improved information combined with lowered trade barriers, lower transportation costs, and lower costs of arbitrage is making geographic price discrimination more difficult to implement. Indeed, the absence of double and triple coupon policies among West Coast U.S. retailers (common on the East Coast) led manufacturers to issue coupons of higher face value in the West than in the East. However, coupon-clipping exchange groups have emerged on the Internet, "marketing" the higher-valued coupons back to the East Coast retail environment.

Temporal price discrimination

The idea behind temporal price discrimination is to introduce a new product at a high price initially, intending to sell it to customers whose reservation price is high, and then lower the price gradually to sell to customers with lower and lower reservation prices. For example, publishers initially introduce books in hardcover at a high price, and after about a year or so they introduce the paperback version at a lower price. One condition necessary for such skimming strategies to work is that the product be a single-purchase item. The other condition is that the customers whose reservation price is high be at least as anxious to consume the product as those whose reservation price is low. For example, the hardcover buyers who have a high reservation price for the book must want to read the book early at least as much as the paperback buyers.

Another place that temporal price discrimination plays an important role is in the service sector, in which demand for services may vary strongly over time. For example, we see

- Time-of-day pricing: peak-load pricing for electricity, discount prices for evening phone charges, afternoon movie rates, early-bird dinner rates, off-peak train fares, and so forth
- Time when purchased: two weeks before flight, day of flight, and the like
- Day of the week pricing: public transportation, museums, theaters, and so forth
- Seasonal pricing: air fares, hotels, vacation packages, fashion goods

In most such cases temporal arbitrage is not feasible because services cannot be stored, making price discrimination very effective.

EXAMPLE

(Smith, Leimkuhler, and Darrow 1992.) American Airlines defines the function of yield management as "selling the right seats to the right customers at the right prices." American Airlines' system is divided into three major functions:

1. Overbooking—intentionally selling more reservations for a flight than there are actual seats to offset the effects of passenger cancellations and no-shows

2. Discount allocation—determining the number of discount fares to offer on a flight, limiting these fares on popular flights to preserve seats for late-booking, high-revenue passengers

3. Traffic management—controlling reservations by passenger origin and destination to provide the mix of markets (multiple-flight connecting markets versus single-flight markets) that maximizes revenue

We will describe how airlines allocate discounts. If the airline were to have only two classes of service, full fare and discount, at any point prior to departure, the system estimates p, the probability of getting a full-fare reservation if a discount fare is rejected. If

$$p \times \$\text{full fare} > \$\text{discount fare},$$

then the discount fare is rejected. In practice the airline updates p many times before the plane departs, depending on the number of remaining available seats, the time until departure, and the distribution of demand. Using a greater number of fare types (full-fare coach, moderate discount, deep discount), American extends this approach in a process called nesting. Let us assume that American has a flight with 100 seats and three classes of service, with 60 seats available for moderate discount and 30 of those 60 for deep discount. The difference in seat availability between the total number of seats and a discount-fare class is the number of seats to protect for all higher-revenue classes. Thus American protects 40 seats exclusively for full fare (100 − 60) and 70 seats (100 − 30) for full fare and moderate discount fares combined. It stops booking full-fare tickets only if the flight reaches its overbooking level.

In the following example there are seven fare classes (which American calls buckets) for a plane, and the company needs an estimate of total demand to do the calculations.

Consider a flight with the passenger and revenue results shown in Exhibit 10.6. If the airline uses no discount controls, it will accept reservations until it reaches the overbooking level. Because leisure customers typically buy the lesser-price reservations far in advance of the flight, this scenario will result in some passengers willing to pay higher prices being displaced by lower-price demand. American estimated the revenue earnings for this case as the least possible revenue that can be obtained by filling the flight to capacity. The revenue the airline would earn for a flight for which it used no discount controls is shown in Exhibit 10.7.

If it used perfect discount controls, American would realize the maximum possible revenue for each flight. In this case it would preserve the number of seats for the higher-price passengers that would exactly match the actual demand. It would turn away only the least-price passengers (and only when it had no more space available). The revenue it would earn for such a flight is shown in Exhibit 10.8.

Total revenue opportunity is defined as the difference between the perfect-controls scenario and the no-controls scenario. This difference is the amount of

Fare class	Passengers			Revenue	
	Boarded	Spilled	Total	Average	Total
Y0	12	0	12	$ 313	$ 3,756
Y1	6	0	6	258	1,548
Y2	10	0	10	224	2,240
Y3	3	0	3	183	549
Y4	30	29	59	164	4,920
Y5	16	5	21	140	2,240
Y6	32	32	64	68	2,176
Total	109	66	175		$17.429

EXHIBIT 10.6

Actual passenger and revenue information for a sample flight. The number of turned away passengers (spilled column) comes from a statistical model. In this example fare classes Y0 through Y3 are filled and no one is turned away. However, 66 passengers are turned away (spilled) and a flight with 138 seats ends up boarding only 109 passengers.

Fare class	Total demand	Passengers boarded	Revenue Average	Total
Y0	12	0	$ 313	$ 0
Y1	6	0	258	0
Y2	10	0	224	0
Y3	3	0	183	0
Y4	59	53	164	8,692
Y5	21	21	140	2,940
Y6	64	64	68	4,352
Total	175	138		$15,984

EXHIBIT 10.7
Passenger and revenue results that would have been achieved with no controls, computed by assuming demand comes from the lowest-valued fare classes first, so that high-revenue demand is turned away. This occurs because lower-fare-using passengers typically book farther in advance than higher-fare-class passengers.

Fare class	Total demand	Passengers boarded	Revenue Average	Total
Y0	12	12	$ 313	$ 3,756
Y1	6	6	258	1,548
Y2	10	10	224	2,240
Y3	3	3	183	549
Y4	59	59	164	9,676
Y5	21	21	140	2,940
Y6	64	27	68	1,836
Total	175	138		$22,545

EXHIBIT 10.8
Passenger and revenue results that would have been achieved with perfect controls, computed by assuming that American knew demand exactly prior to departure, so that they could use ideal discount-allocation controls. Here all the passengers turned away are in fare class Y6.

revenue American could possibly obtain by controlling discount allocations. The airline can measure the amount of revenue it can attribute to controlling discount allocations by calculating the difference between the actual revenue and the no-controls revenue.

Total revenue opportunity through discount controls
= Revenue with perfect-controls − Revenue earned in the no-controls scenario
= $22,545 − $15,984
= $6561 for the example flight.

Revenue earned through discount controls
= Actual revenue − Revenue earned in the no-controls scenario
= $17,429 − $15,984
= $1445 for the example flight.

Thus the percentage of the discount-allocation revenue opportunity the airline earned is 1445 divided by 6561, or 22 percent.

The airline can measure its system-wide performance by calculating the average performance of the individual flights.

According to R. L. Crandall, president and CEO of American Airlines,

[Y]ield management is the single most important technical development in transportation management since we entered the era of airline deregulation in 1979. . . . [Yield management] creates a pricing structure which responds to demand on a flight-by-flight basis. As a result, we can more effectively match our demand to supply. . . . We estimate that yield management has generated $1.4 billion in the last three years alone [and we] expect yield management to generate at least $500 million annually for the foreseeable future. (Smith et al. 1992, pp. 30–31)

Here is another interesting example of yield management:

[G]rants no longer are based overwhelmingly on a student's demonstrated financial need, but also on his or her "price sensitivity" to college costs, calculated from dozens of factors that all add up to one thing: how anxious the student is to attend. The more eager the student . . . the less aid they can expect to get. Although students and families awaiting word of college admissions this week aren't being told, these colleges are employing some of the same "yield management" techniques used to price and fill airline seats and hotel rooms.

The statistical models, which have become widespread only in the past few years, go by innocuous names like "financial aid leveraging." But they are quietly transforming the size and shape of student bodies in all sorts of ways, some of which are alarming educators. A sampling:

- The Johns Hopkins model—which the school isn't currently using but may try again in the future—suggested slashing aid to some prospects who came for on-campus interviews. The reason: Those students are statistically more likely to enroll, so need less aid to entice them. A school official now denies putting that part of the model into practice.
- At Pittsburgh's Carnegie Mellon University and other schools, eager freshmen accepted through the early-admissions program can end up with less financial aid than comparable students who apply later. "If finances are a concern, you shouldn't be applying any place early decision," says William F. Elliott, vice president for enrollment management.
- For the current school year, St. Bonaventure University in Bonaventure, N.Y., gave the poorest of its top-ranked prospects just over half the grants they needed—but gave more-affluent prospects more than three times their need. The result: A more affluent student body, since 75% of the wealthier students decided to enroll, while only one in 11 of the neediest did so. (*Wall Street Journal*, April 1, 1996, p. 1)

The Forte Hotel yield-management exercise implements a simple yield-management procedure in the hotel industry, illustrating the application of these concepts.

Nonlinear pricing or quantity discounts

Quantity discounts are a common form of price discrimination: high-volume buyers get lower prices than small-volume buyers. The correlation being exploited here is between purchase quantity and reservation price. People who avail themselves of the discounts have lower reservation prices for the later units (of a large order) than those who do not. There are various ways of implementing quantity discounts that differ in how finely they discriminate among consumers, including two-part tariffs and block tariffs (Monroe 1990):

Two-part tariff: In a two-part tariff the seller charges a fixed up-front payment F and then a per-unit charge p. For example, membership clubs (like Sam's Club) charge a membership fee and offer discounted merchandise. The pricing of a durable good such as instant cameras that require specialized film or razors with specialized blades can also be thought of as two-part tariffs. Here the price of the durable good is the fixed fee, and the unit price of supplies is the per-unit charge of using the durable good.

A two-part tariff is similar to a simple linear price in that the marginal price charged and paid is constant in quantity. Everyone who buys pays the same marginal price regardless of quantity. A two-part tariff is a quantity discount scheme only because the "average price" paid—$(F/Q) + p$—decreases with the quantity Q purchased. In a linear pricing scheme, on the other hand, both marginal and average prices are constant for any quantity purchased. The presence of a fixed fee in a two-part tariff allows the seller to extract more consumer surplus than a simple linear pricing scheme.

Block tariffs: Block tariffs are the most widely used form of quantity discounts. A block tariff has at least two marginal prices; it may or may not have a fixed fee. For example, local telephone company tariffs typically have a fixed "subscription fee" as well as several price breaks built into the schedule. In Exhibit 10.9 we show a three-block pricing scheme with no fixed fee. The customer pays P_1 per unit if she purchases Q_1 or less; she pays P_1 for each of the first Q_1 units and P_2 ($< P_1$) for each unit between Q_1 and Q_2 if she purchases between Q_1 and Q_2 units; and for purchase quantities greater than Q_2, she pays P_1 per unit for the first Q_1 units, P_2 per unit for the next $Q_2 - Q_1$ units, and P_3 per unit ($P_3 < P_2$) for any units beyond Q_2.

The larger the number of price blocks, the finer the price discrimination possible, but also the greater the difficulty of administering and explaining the tariff to consumers. A quantity discount schedule in which each additional unit is priced differently and a simple linear schedule in which each unit is priced the same no matter how great the quantity purchased represent opposite sides of this spectrum.

Other forms of price discrimination

Promotions and coupons are another means of price discrimination. The idea is that coupon users are more price sensitive than nonusers. The manufacturer sets a price that is higher than

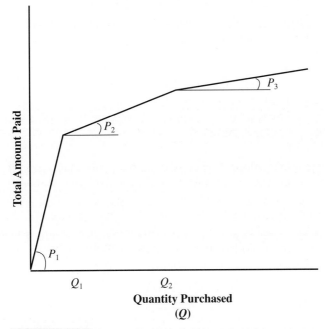

EXHIBIT 10.9
In this three-block tariff, marginal prices decrease when prices increase past points Q_1 and Q_2.

the optimal price for the price-sensitive segment and uses coupons to promote sales to this segment. Thus the manufacturer can realize optimal prices for both the price-sensitive segment and the segment in which customers are willing to pay more.

Customer characteristics are also used for price discrimination, especially for services. The most common such characteristics are

- Age—special prices for children, senior citizens
- Income/education status—student prices for movies, subscriptions, and the like; income-linked membership fees in organizations
- Profession—government employee discounts, teacher discounts
- Membership—AAA discounts on auto rentals, employee discounts, Sam's Club

The distribution outlet can be used as a mechanism for price discrimination. For example, specialty stores charge higher prices than supermarkets.

Products themselves can be differentiated. Software companies often sell "student versions" of software packages that include all but one or two features of the $300 version (or limit spreadsheet size) for 10 percent or less of the price of the unrestricted software.

Companies also use brand differentiation as a price discrimination mechanism, particularly by selling generics at a lower (unbranded) price than their branded counterparts.

PRICING PRODUCT LINES

Most firms market more than a single product. If these products are not related, either through shared costs or through interdependent demand, then the price discrimination approaches we have outlined may be appropriate. Monroe (1990, p. 464) cites several reasons that the prescriptions arising from an analysis of single-product pricing may not be appropriate:

- Products in a line may be related to one another on the demand side, either as substitutes or as complements.
- There may be cost interdependencies such as shared production, distribution, or marketing expenditures.
- Some products may be sold as a bundle (stereo system vs. components), thereby creating complementarity.
- The price of one product in a line may influence the buyer's subjective evaluation of other products in the line.

In addition to the information on demand (i.e., price elasticities) that the firm needs for pricing a single product, it needs some knowledge of cross-price elasticities to price product lines.

Under conditions like those that lead to Eq. (10.7) (average costs are fairly constant for any level of demand and costs are constant over time), when a firm sells multiple products Reibstein and Gatignon (1984) show that the optimal price of product i in a two-product $(i + j)$ line is

$$P_i^* = \frac{\varepsilon_i}{1 + \varepsilon_i} \text{MC}_i - \frac{\varepsilon_{ij}}{1 + \varepsilon_i} \frac{Q_j}{Q_i} \left(P_j - \text{MC}_j\right). \tag{10.21}$$

What Eq. (10.21) shows is that the optimal price for a product in a demand-interdependent line is the single-product optimal price (the first term in Eq. (10.21) modified by the second term in that equation—which is a function of the product's own price and cross-price elasticity, the demand for both products, and the price and marginal production cost of the other product. If the demand-price relationship is stochastic, the function is further modified to include the effect of uncertainty in demand.

In general there will be n equations like (10.21) that the firm would have to solve simultaneously to determine optimal product-line prices for n products.

For this model and others it is often difficult to obtain key pieces of information—the self- and cross-price elasticity.

SALES PROMOTIONS: TYPES AND EFFECTS

Sales promotion comprises a wide variety of tactical promotion tools in the form of short-term incentives designed to stimulate earlier or stronger response from customers in a target market. Most promotions can be viewed as temporary, advertised price reductions, although promotions can take many other forms. Among the more popular forms are coupons, premiums, and contests for consumer markets; buying allowances, cooperative-advertising allowances, and free goods for distributors and dealers; discounts, gifts, and extras for industrial users; and sales contests and special bonuses for members of the salesforce.

A key factor in most types of promotions is that, properly applied, they *complement* other elements of the marketing mix and therefore require a coordinated effort among retailers, wholesalers, salespersons, advertising, and (often) manufacturing and distribution. Exhibit 10.10 shows the types and the flow of promotions and suggests the importance of understanding and modeling the individual and combined effects of promotional activity at several levels.

Thus to model promotional effects we must determine (1) the objectives of the promotion, (2) the characteristics of different promotion types and their purported effects on

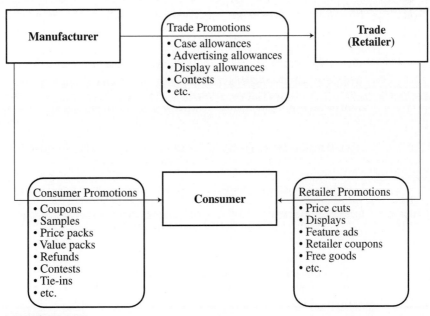

EXHIBIT 10.10
Promotion types vary widely and can be directed at either the trade (retailer) or the consumer.

the objectives, (3) the effectiveness of different promotions, and (4) the range of promotion decisions.

Objectives of promotions

Because sales-promotion tools are so varied in form, no single purpose can be advanced for them. For example, a free sample stimulates consumer trial, while a free management-advisory service may cement a long-term relationship with a customer. Sales-promotion techniques make three contributions:

1. Communication: They gain attention and usually provide information that may lead the consumer to the product.
2. Incentive: They incorporate some concession, inducement, or contribution designed to represent value to the receiver.
3. Invitation: Most include a distinct invitation to engage in the transaction now.

Exhibit 10.11 is a partial list of specific marketing objectives and the promotions that can be used to meet them.

Objective	Promotional Type
Increase repeat buying	In-pack coupons, continuity programs (e.g., frequent flyer, "*N* for" retail promotions)
Increase market share among brand switchers	FSI coupons, coupons targeted to users of other brands, retail promotions
Increase retailer's promotion frequency	Trade deals, combination of consumer promotions and trade deals (big-bang theory)
Enhance the product's image	Coop image advertising with image-oriented retailers
Increase category switching	Retail promotions, FSI coupons, large rebates
Target deal-sensitive consumers	Coupons, "*N* for" retail promotions
Increase category consumption	Retailer promotions, promotions tied to events (e.g., back to school)
Increase trial among nonusers	Cross-couponing, free samples, trial packs, direct-mail coupons
Liquidate short-term inventories	Trade deals, rebates, inventory financing
Increase distribution	FSI coupons, (increase demand), trade deals (increase DPP)

"*N* for" = multiple unit promotion (e.g., 6 for 99¢)
FSI = free standing insert in newspapers and magazines
DPP = dealer price promotion

EXHIBIT 10.11
A range of marketing objectives and the promotions firms can use to meet those objectives.
Source: Blattberg and Neslin 1990, p. 464.

The range of possible objectives is broad and the effects are numerous (and possibly confounding). For example, while a seller's primary purpose in a promotion may be to attract nonbrand purchasers to the brand, sellers may also want to reward brand-loyal users for their loyalty. Because both types of buyers buy during the promotion period, the seller accomplishes both purposes. Thus it is important to set objectives and measure the effect for the particular promotion, whether the objectives concern the level of retail inventory, increased retail distribution, coupon-redemption rates, or sales effects.

Characteristics of promotions

Marketing managers choose promotions for their cost-effectiveness in accomplishing their objectives. Some of the key considerations vary with promotional type.

For *sampling*, implementation can be door to door, by mail, or free with the purchase of another product. Furthermore, the size of the sample can vary. (The promotion for the introduction of Gainesburgers by General Foods, which included, in a sample pack, *half* the recommended size of a dog's meal, had less than ideal results.)

For a *manufacturer-price-off offer*, the seller must determine the total quantity of the promotion, which partly depends on the amount the retailer will accept—too small a quantity may not motivate the retailer to feature the item. The seller must carefully determine the percentage of the price off and the frequency of such offers: a too-frequent price-off offer may lead buyers to expect the discount to continue or to perceive the regular price as an increase.

For *couponing*, the redemption rate is important (and easy to measure), and it depends on the value of the coupon (Reibstein and Traver 1982). However, as Lodish (1986) points out, most promotions are not profitable for the manufacturer and the manufacturer might more appropriately focus on the more difficult-to-measure effects of the coupons on long-term sales and profitability. As with sampling, the manufacturer has partial control of the type of household it reaches with coupons.

For premium offers included *in-* or *on-pack* (i.e., with a packaged consumer good), the selection of the premium type and the duration of the offer is important. The premium should be consistent with the quality image of the brand and if appropriate should be in place long enough so that a regular buyer can obtain a set (as with glassware).

In-store displays are effective means of moving merchandise, but display space is limited and the display must pay for itself according to the retailer's criteria for such programs.

Each promotion type has dimensions that make it unique and that affect its cost and its impact on short- and long-term brand sales.

Marketers disagree about what promotions do and how they should be viewed; however, they seem to concur that promotions (in contrast to advertising) do *not* build up long-term brand customer loyalty. Blattberg, Briesch, and Fox (1995, pp. G123–G125) provide some useful generalizations about promotional effects:

1. *Temporary reductions in retail price increase sales substantially*: Researchers have found that temporary retail-price promotions (promoted through supermarket flyers, for example) cause short-term sales to spike. In contrast, it is rare to see such a response for most consumer advertising on television or in other media.
2. *Brands that have higher shares of the market are less deal elastic*: That is, higher-share brands show less sales response to deals, even though they may capture a large proportion of switchers.
3. *The frequency of deals changes the consumer's reference price*: This finding is important. It explains why brands that are heavily promoted lose equity (i.e., consumers

think they are less valuable). A lower consumer reference price reduces the premium the firm can charge for a brand in the marketplace.

4. *The greater the frequency of deals, the lower the height of the sales spike in response to a deal*: This result is likely to be caused by (1) consumer expectations about the frequency of deals, (2) changes in the consumer's reference price, and (3) stockpiling effects from previous deals.

5. *Cross-promotional effects are asymmetric, and promoting higher-quality brands affects weaker brands (and private label products) disproportionately*: Promoting Coke causes customers to switch from a store brand in greater numbers than promoting that store brand will cause them to switch from Coke. One possible explanation for this asymmetry in switching is differences in brand equity. An extension of this finding focuses on asymmetries in brands' perceived type. Promoting higher-tier brands generates more switching than does promoting lower-tier brands.

6. *Retailers pass through to consumers less than 100 percent of trade deals*: Because retailers are the vehicles for passing trade promotional money on to consumers, sellers should recognize that most brands receive far less than 100 percent pass-through. (*Pass-through* is the percentage of the funds a manufacturer offers to a retailer that are reflected in promotional discounts to the consumer. Greater than 100 percent pass-through means the retailer offers discounts to the end user in excess of the compensating funds received from the manufacturer.)

7. *Display and feature advertising have strong effects on item sales*: In addition, feature advertising and display interact synergistically.

8. *Advertising promotions can result in increased store traffic*: The weight of evidence is that advertised promotions of some products and categories do have an impact on store traffic. (With increased store traffic may come store switching or consumers visiting multiple stores.)

9. *Promotions affect sales in complementary and competitive categories*: Practitioners understand this effect but not its magnitude. The impact of promoting one category on the sales of a complementary or competing category is very likely a function of the type and characteristics of the categories themselves.

These general findings and those of Blattberg and Neslin (1990) lead to the following observations for modeling and evaluating promotional results:

- Brand loyalty may (or may not) be affected.
- New triers may (or may not) be attracted.
- Promotions interact with other elements of the marketing mix (advertising, in particular).
- Promotional results interact with production and distribution, affecting inventory levels rapidly and dramatically.
- Promotional frequency influences promotional effects and is linked to the average length of the product's purchase cycle (how often the consumer purchases the product).
- The type of promotion selected may have differential effects on brand loyalty and promotional attractiveness.
- Promotion size may have threshold and saturation effects, suggesting an S-shaped sales-response relationship.
- Finally, firms may experience different levels of success in implementing different promotions; a failure may be due to poor implementation, a poor promotion design, or both.

Historically, the most common technique for evaluating consumer promotions has been to compare sales or market share before, during, and after a promotion. Researchers then attribute increased sales to the impact of the sales-promotion program, all other things being equal. Exhibit 10.12 portrays results that manufacturers would like to see. In the promotion period the company's brand share rose to 10 percent. This gain in share of 4 percent is made up of (1) deal-prone consumers, who switched to this brand to take advantage of the deal, and (2) brand-loyal customers, who increased their purchases in response to the price incentive. Immediately after the promotion ended the brand share fell to 5 percent because consumers were overstocked and they were working down their inventory. After this stock adjustment brand share went up to 7 percent, showing a one-percentage-point increase in the number of loyal customers. This pattern is likely to occur when the brand has good qualities that many nonbrand users did not know about.

If we assume that the effects of a promotion are short-lived, then use of this method for analyzing promotional effects seems sound. However, even with the increased availability and use of retail-scanner data, the problem of determining the effects of a promotion is quite challenging: to get accurate measures of incremental sales, we need accurate estimates of baseline sales—*sales for the brand that would have occurred if the promotion had not taken place*. If we use sales in a nonpromotional period (prior to the promotion) (as in Exhibit 10.12) as a base and if sales accelerate strongly, then our estimate of the baseline will be biased *downward*, and we will overstate the effect and profitability of the promotion: note that the sales rate immediately following the promotion is much lower than the long-run postpromotional sales rate.

In addition, to calculate the profitability of a trade promotion we must evaluate how much of the promotional effect is passed on to the consumer and how much is simply excess buying by the retailer to stockpile for future use. As Blattberg and Levin (1987) point out, forward buying is so extensive that it may be impossible to infer a baseline from whole-

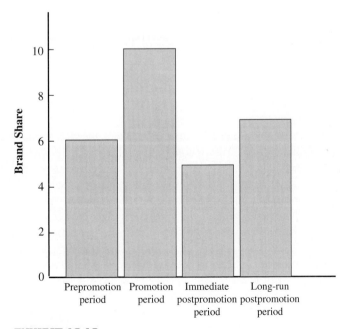

EXHIBIT 10.12
Expected effect of a consumer deal on brand share: Share increases during the promotion period, drops afterward (due to stockpiling), and returns to (perhaps) a different level in the long run.

sale sales data, and therefore manufacturers need good models of both consumer response to retailer promotions and retailer response to trade promotions to evaluate the profitability of trade promotions.

AGGREGATE MODELS TO ANALYZE PROMOTIONAL EFFECTS

Most of the operational models in use today, even those based on scanner data, develop some form of aggregate regression-based analysis. These response models generally focus on the level and allocation of promotional spending across different market areas.

EXAMPLE

Shapiro (1976) describes a series of studies of promotional effectiveness at H. J. Heinz company. Initial work indicated that promotional effectiveness in terms of effect on market share differed by package size within district (or market area) and differed widely across markets. The analysts captured these effects in a series of individual-market regression models, linking share of features and promotions (by size) to market-share variation in that district. They incorporated these response models into a model designed to determine the optimal level and allocation of effort, which demonstrated that Heinz could make significant improvements that would lead to the dual benefits of higher market share *and* lower cost. By implementing the model recommendations in 1973–74, Heinz reduced its promotional expenditures by 40 percent from what they had been the previous year. In addition, by concentrating its promotional efforts on the more responsive markets Heinz increased its national market share by over three share points!

The Conglomerate, Inc., promotional analysis exercise (Chapter 2) illustrates the allocation process that Shapiro employed.

As another example, consider Blattberg and Levin's (1987) model:

EXAMPLE

Blattberg and Levin developed a model to evaluate the effectiveness of trade promotions (Exhibit 10.13). They model both effects of a trade deal: (1) The trade promotion encourages the retailer to run a consumer promotion (the outcome the manufacturer desires), and (2) the promotion may also encourage the retailer to buy more during the trade period (forward buying), resulting in increased shipments during the trade period and decreased shipments afterward.

Exhibit 10.14 shows the net effect of this activity: while consumer sales (adjusted unit sales) vary very little, shipments (to retailers) show large jumps during each promotional period, followed by troughs afterward. To understand the effectiveness of a trade promotion we must analyze all of the stages of the process; indeed each equation that follows represents the flow in and out of a box in Exhibit 10.13:

Manufacturer's shipment model:

$$\text{Shipments}_t = f_1(\text{Inventory}_{t-1}, \text{Trade promotions}_t, \text{Other factors}_t). \qquad (10.22a)$$

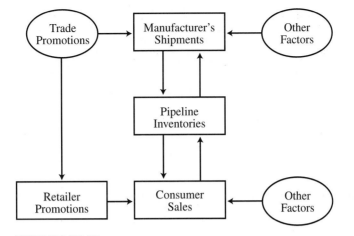

EXHIBIT 10.13

How a trade promotion influences shipments and sales: Trade promotions affect both retailer orders and the promotions that retailers run that are aimed at consumers, affecting both shipments and pipeline inventories in turn. *Source*: Blattberg and Levin 1987, p. 127.

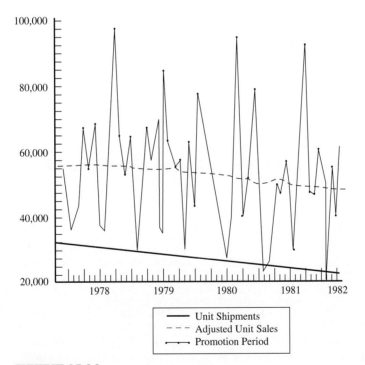

EXHIBIT 10.14

A plot of consumer sales and shipments shows major promotional peaks and troughs for shipments to the trade but less apparent effects at the consumer level. *Source*: Blattberg and Levin 1987, p. 128.

Retail promotions model:

$$\text{Retail promotions}_t = f_2(\text{Trade promotions}_t, \text{Trade promotions}_{t-1}, \text{Inventories}_{t-1}).$$

(10.22b)

Consumer sales model:

Consumer sales$_t$ = f_3(Retailer promotions$_t$, Other factors$_t$). (10.22c)

Inventory model:

Inventory$_t$ = f_4(Inventory$_{t-1}$, Shipments$_t$, Consumer sales$_t$). (10.22d)

Note that Eq. (10.22d) is simply an accounting equation, as

Inventory$_t$ = Inventory$_{t-1}$ + Shipments$_t$ − Consumer sales$_t$. (10.22e)

Thus in general we will have three equations for which we must specify and estimate parameters.

Assuming that consumer sales revert to their baseline level at some time after retail promotions cease, we can assess the profitability of the promotion as the gain in gross margin associated with incremental consumer sales less the loss in gross margin associated with sales to the trade resulting from the promotion. Formally

Promotion profitability = $I \times$ MARGIN − $P \times$ DISC, (10.23)

where

I = incremental sales to the consumer;

P = total sales to the trade during the promotional period;

DISC = average discount per unit given to the trade during the promotional period; and

MARGIN = gross margin per unit sold.

Exhibit 10.15 shows what is happening: since shipments during the trade deal are partially "stolen" from future periods and sales during that period are at a discount, these stolen shipments decrease the profitability of the promotion. In general we have

$F = P - N - I$, (10.24)

where

F = forward buying; and

N = "normal" (baseline) sales of the product.

As F increases relative to I, the profitability of the promotion becomes lower.

Blattberg and Levin used this approach to analyze a manufacturer's trade promotions of 10 products in six markets. The data that they had were

- Factory shipments
- Bimonthly sales data from retail audits
- Manufacturer's prices
- Trade promotions
- Advertising expenditures

The manufacturer did not have data on the promotion activity of retailers (although such data are routinely available commercially), and so the researchers dropped Eq. (10.22b) and eliminated the retailer-promotions variable from Eq. (10.22c).

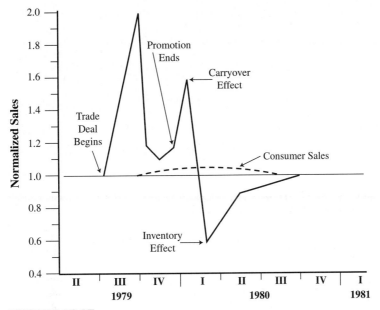

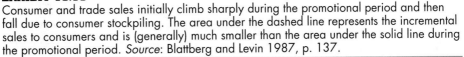

EXHIBIT 10.15
Consumer and trade sales initially climb sharply during the promotional period and then fall due to consumer stockpiling. The area under the dashed line represents the incremental sales to consumers and is (generally) much smaller than the area under the solid line during the promotional period. *Source*: Blattberg and Levin 1987, p. 137.

The remaining models (in log-linear form) incorporated "other factors" to account for different promotional types, for the difference between retail orders and shipments, and for trends, seasonality, and the like. Blattberg and Levin estimated 60 separate cases of the shipment and consumer equations, with mean adjusted R^2's of 0.66 and 0.57, respectively. They found that

1. Trade deals significantly increase shipments.

2. Forward buying is significant, leading to significant decreases in sales after the promotional period.

3. Consumer sales increase during the promotion, but to a significantly lower degree than shipments.

Blattberg and Levin also performed the type of profitability analysis outlined above and concluded that most deals lost money.

Many regression-type models have become increasingly useful in practice because of the availability of scanner data, which reveal consumer response precisely at the retail level. The value of Blattberg and Levin's work was limited in 1987, when they did their work, because such data were not available at the time. Blattberg and Neslin (1990) describe a number of promotional models that can be used to determine the size, timing, and allocation of promotional resources.

One of the biggest challenges in analyzing the results of a promotion is to develop an appropriate baseline (i.e., an estimate of what sales would have been without a promotion). As Abraham and Lodish (1987, 1989) note in describing their PROMOTER and PROMOTION-

SCAN models, this is far from a trivial task, and their models incorporate trends, seasonality, exception indices (for special factors), and promotional types in a combined multiplicative-additive model form. Neslin and Stone (1996) also discuss the difficulty of estimating a baseline.

ANALYZING INDIVIDUALS' RESPONSES TO PROMOTIONS

The increasing availability of scanner data linked to individual characteristics (a scanner panel) has given a large boost to modeling individual choice behavior, including the effect of promotions. Because technical and methodological issues abound, building these models requires expertise, but many of the models share the following goal: to estimate the likelihood of an individual choosing a brand as a function of the following categories of variables (Blattberg and Neslin, 1990, p. 220):

1. Brand dummies (to represent the intrinsic value of brands)
2. Promotion occurrences
3. Last purchase effect on loyalty
4. Last purchase effect on promotion responsiveness
5. Personal and demographic characteristics

The most frequently cited (and criticized) approach in this area is the Guadagni and Little (1983) logit model (Chapter 3):

$$P_k = \frac{e^{V_k}}{\displaystyle\sum_{j=1}^{J} e^{V_j}}, \; j = 1, \cdots, J \, (\text{number of brand sizes}), \tag{10.25}$$

where

brand size is a particular size of a particular brand like "2-liter coke";

$P_k =$ the probability of buying brand-size k; and

$V_k =$ the deterministic component of utility of brand-size k at time t, where the t subscript is suppressed.

V_k is defined as

$$V_k = \sum_{l=1}^{7} \beta_l X(l, k) \, , \tag{10.26}$$

and where

$$X(1, k) = \text{brand-size constant} = \begin{cases} 0, & \text{not brand-size } k, \\ 1, & \text{brand-size } k; \end{cases}$$

$$X(2, k) = \text{promotion indicator} = \begin{cases} 0, & \text{not on promotion,} \\ 1, & \text{on promotion;} \end{cases}$$

$$X(3, k) = \text{regular price in dollars per ounce;}$$

$$X(4, k) = \text{prior promotional purchase} = \begin{cases} 0, \text{ if the previous purchase was not} \\ \text{brand-size } k \text{ on promotion} \\ \\ 1, \text{ if the previous purchase was} \\ \text{brand-size } k \text{ on promotion;} \end{cases}$$

$$X(5, k) = \text{second prior promotional purchase} = \begin{cases} 0, \text{ if the second previous purchase} \\ \text{was not brand-size } k \text{ on promotion} \\ \\ 1, \text{ if the second previous purchase} \\ \text{was not brand-size } k \text{ on promotion} \end{cases}$$

$X(6, k, t) = \alpha X(6, k, t-1) + (1-\alpha)\delta_1(t);$

$\delta_1(t) \quad = 0$ if brand k was not bought on purchase $t-1$,

$\quad\quad\quad = 1$ if brand k was bought on purchase $t-1$;

$X(7, k, t) = \gamma X(7, k, t-1) + (1-\gamma)\delta_2(t);$

$\delta_2(t) \quad = 0$ if size k was not bought on purchase $t-1$,

$\quad\quad\quad = 1$ if size k was bought on purchase $t-1$;

$\alpha, \gamma \quad\quad =$ carryover effect of previous brand (and size) purchases, respectively.

Note that the model deals with the probability of an individual's buying a specific brand-size combination. This model is based on the following stylized behavioral assumption: The customer will compute his or her utility for each brand and pick the one that has the highest utility at a particular time. At any time, the utility of brand k (U_k) is the sum of the deterministic component (V_k) and a random component (ε_k). The specific form of the foregoing model measures brand loyalty in variable $X(6)$ as an exponentially decaying measure of past purchases of this brand, and it measures size loyalty similarly in $X(7)$. Variables $X(4)$ and $X(5)$ measure the effects of previous purchases on the sensitivity of the current response.

Several researchers have criticized this model for the way it handles loyalty—it assumes a homogeneous market with customers differing only in their level of loyalty, *not* in their receptivity to promotions—and for the way it deals with the effect of past purchases on customer response to current promotions. In addition, critics often think that the nature of the market and competition might better be addressed through more general models (e.g., the nested logit model in Chapter 3).

Blattberg and Neslin (1990) discuss the use of individual choice models to predict customer response to promotions and thus to guide firms' decisions about promotions. Other researchers have developed some very elaborate models to decide which brands a retailer should promote, what the level of promotion should be, what its timing should be, and the like and have obtained some very encouraging results, as the following example illustrates.

EXAMPLE

Tellis and Zufryden (1995) developed a model to help the retailer to maximize cumulative profits over a planning period. The retailer can determine which brands to discount, by how much, and when (and the model even incorporates the cost of retagging the shelves when prices change).

At the heart of this retailer model is a customer response model:

$$E(S_{ijt}) = E(Q_{ijt} \mid B, C, V) \, P_{ijt}(B \mid C, V) \, P_{it}(C \mid V), \tag{10.27}$$

where

i = customer;

j = brand;

t = time period;

S = sales;

V = store visit;

C = category purchased;

B = brand choice;

Q = quantity purchases;

E = expectation; and

P = purchase probability.

Their model has three submodels: a purchase-incidence model, a brand-choice model, and a purchase-quantity model.

They model the customer's decision process as a (nested) logit model where the purchase incidence is a binary logit model (purchase or not) and the brand choice is a multinomial logit model. The probability that customer i will purchase in the product category during period t *given* a store visit is

$$P_{it}(C \mid V) = \frac{1}{1 + \exp\left[-\left(b_0 + b_1 \mathrm{CatPur}_i + b_2 \mathrm{Inv}_{it} + b_3 \mathrm{Inc}_{it}\right)\right]}, \tag{10.28}$$

where

CatPur_i = mean long-term probability that the customer purchases in the product category;

Inc_{it} = category attractiveness or inclusive value (log of denominator of Eq. (10.29));

Inv_{it} = number of units of inventory the customer held at the start of period t; and

$b_0, \ldots, b_3$ = model coefficients to be estimated.

They model brand choice as a multinomial logit model (conditional on category purchase in a period) as

$$P_{ijt}(B \mid C) = \frac{\exp\left(\beta X_{ijt} + \gamma_j \, \mathrm{Disc}_{ijt}\right)}{\sum_k \exp\left(\beta X_{ikt} + \gamma_k \, \mathrm{Disc}_{ikt}\right)}, \tag{10.29}$$

where

Disc_{ijt} = discount level available to customer i for brand j in period t;

X_{ijt} = vector of causal variables, including brand loyalty, indicator of previous brand chosen, list price, feature indicator, and display indicator;

γ_j = parameter for discount for brand j, to be estimated;

β = vector of causal parameters (= β_0, β_1, . . ., β_v where γ is the number of casual variables); to be estimated and

k = index for brands in the choice set.

Finally, they model the expected quantity of brand j purchased by customer i during time period t *given* that the customer chooses brand j as

$$E(Q_{ijt} \mid B) = \exp(a_0 + a_1 \text{Price}_{ijt} + a_{2j} \text{Disc}_{ijt} + a_3 \text{Inv}_{it} + a_4 H_{ijt}), \qquad (10.30)$$

where

Price = list price;

Disc = discount for the specific brand;

Inv = inventory of that category of household product at beginning of the period; and

H = brand attractiveness (derived from Eq. (10.29)).

$a_0, \ldots a_4$ = model coefficient to be estimated.

H accounts for why customers buy different quantities of different brands—for example, a customer might buy a small amount of (expensive) premium coffee for guests and a larger quantity of less expensive coffee for everyday use.

Tellis and Zufryden apply the model to the saltine cracker category. Their results show that the optimal timing and level of a promotion vary with the degree of customer loyalty, with the way customers respond to changes in the marketing mix, with retail margins, and with retagging costs. Their results also suggest that retailers should give higher discounts as retail margins, customer response to discounts, and category attractiveness increase, and lower discounts as customer response to their product inventory and customer loyalty increase.

They implemented the model on a PC and optimized it in Excel, using Excel's Solver tool.

The Promotional spending analysis software and the MassMart case illustrate how this model works and how it can be used.

As the quantity and quality of data on response to promotions grow and as instant promotions (via on-line sales) become more common, we expect that marketers will understand promotional effects better and be able to create better models of those effects.

SUMMARY

While nonprice elements of the marketing mix grow in importance, price and the short-term promotional variations in price will continue to hold the central position in the marketing mix. Setting price requires knowledge of the consumer's willingness to pay for the product, the cost of producing the product, the probable reactions of competitors, and how these factors change over time. Most pricing decisions are fundamentally based on costs, on demand, or on the nature of competition, and we have described marketing engineering methods based on each of these factors. One demand-based approach to pricing relies on price discrimination and takes advantage of the different levels of need that different customers have for the product. Yield management is an effective way to implement price discrimination.

Because most firms price multiple products that interact with one another, the problem of pricing products in product lines is important. The firm must understand those interactions.

Promotions are most often short-term reductions in price. Knowledge about the effects of promotions is growing, and manufacturers and retailers are using many effective models to design and implement promotions.

With the widespread availability of scanner data and procedures to analyze the data, we are better able to understand the effect of promotions at the customer level and to use that understanding to guide firms in their promotional decisions. With these rich data sources, supplemented by measurements of consumer response to promotions in interactive Internet environments, researchers will be able to develop better operational models and make more precise empirical generalizations in the years to come.

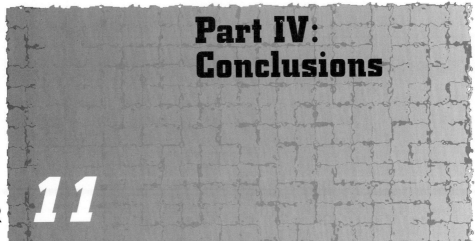

**Part IV:
Conclusions**

CHAPTER **11**

Marketing Engineering:
A Look Back and a Look Ahead

In this chapter we

- Summarize the main lessons that we have learned in teaching marketing engineering and that we hope you have learned from your experience with the material
- Provide tips to help you use marketing engineering successfully within an organization
- Highlight trends that we think will shape the development of marketing engineering during the next decade

MARKETING ENGINEERING: A LOOK BACK

Marketing models have become much more usable since Kotler (1971) summarized in his pioneering book what we then knew about marketing models and their value in decision making. Developments in modeling and personal computing over the past decade have given us the know-how and ability to use decision models in decision making and to do so effectively. In this book we bring together many of the new concepts, tools, and insights useful in making marketing decisions under the name *marketing engineering*. We hope you have found that marketing engineering is a practical, accessible approach, not an arcane, theoretical topic.

In developing and teaching this material we have learned several things, some of which surprised us:

Marketing engineering is marketing: We started off thinking we would be teaching marketing models and modeling in a more user-friendly way. While we did teach modeling (especially early on), we found that we were really teaching marketing in a different way. All students did not find this new way comfortable, but many now have the tools and the confidence to address marketing questions in more precise and, often, in broader terms than before. The approach and the associated tools can help you to expand your ways of thinking about marketing.

Marketing engineering is a means to an end: Marketing engineering allows marketers to take advantage of data, information, and computer models in making important marketing decisions. However, marketing engineering is not just about data, information, or analyses. It is a systematic process to help people improve decisions, and the outputs of that process are better decisions. Your experience with the decision models in this book should help you to articulate how and why you make decisions and encourage you to use these models when making those decisions.

Models require judgment: This book contains models that are relevant to both operational and strategic decisions. But models are simplified and incomplete representations of reality. Models developed to support strategic decisions (e.g., positioning) usually provide insights concerning the directions of actions but often no specific guidelines; while models developed to support operational decisions are both narrow and specific (how many sales calls should a salesperson make to a given account in the next quarter?). In using both types of models managers must temper the model results by using their own judgment. For strategic decisions managers must use judgment to translate broad guidelines into specific actions. For operational decisions managers must use their judgment to fine-tune specific recommendations to fit with the overall strategy of the firm. Decision models are very useful, but they are too simple to be trusted entirely.

The whole is greater than the sum of its parts: When you need to explore an entire business problem you have a full marketing engineering toolkit to support you—for example, you have tools to segment a market, to select a segment to serve, to customize a product offering for that segment, to target and position that product, and to develop promotional plans and ad copy. The value of the concepts and of the associated software multiplies as the business problem broadens. The material allows you to go farther and deeper in solving marketing problems, often well beyond what individual models would permit. Ideally every tool should raise questions beyond its limits and expose unexplored areas of the total marketing system.

More information can obscure rather than enlighten: We are near the end of the era when firms could gain competitive advantage merely by having market information. Today large firms have access to more market and customer information than they can use. To gain the most value from information, firms are trying new approaches: (1) They are using computer and communication technologies to make relevant information available in a timely manner to their entire workforce. (2) They are developing new ways to help employees use specialized knowledge (e.g., marketing decision models) to convert information into more effective decisions and actions. For example, if a firm has a superior process for developing new products, it should make sure that market information feeds that process, so that it can develop new products better tuned to customer needs and introduce them sooner than its competitors. Marketing engineering approaches that include firm-specific knowledge (e.g., a customized conjoint analysis model) can help firms to transform market information into superior products. Such uses of information are not transparent to competitors and are not likely to be replicated by them, leading to competitive advantage. Information has value only if you use it to drive decisions and actions. As Barabba and Zaltman (1991, p. 3) put it, "competitive advantage resides increasingly in how information is used rather than in who has information."

The software allows rapid prototyping: Markets are changing so quickly that decisions must reflect quick adaptation rather than careful optimization. Thus to be useful decision aids must be capable of rapid prototyping. The software accompanying the book enables you to quickly explore the potential value of a model in a particular decision context before you decide either to invest more effort in developing customized models or to use more traditional approaches. Even when a full-blown marketing engineering project is not feasible, trying out a model on a smaller, related problem can provide you with useful insights and document the potential opportunity cost of not doing a full-scale study.

Software empowers: In years past we have taught managers many of the concepts and cases described in this book, but without using the software. When managers evaluate case situations supported by the software, they often see things differently. An interesting example is the Syntex case (Chapter 9). In traditional case discussions most managers recommend allocations of sales resources that are fairly close to those the company explores (i.e., increase salesforce size substantially and devote more resources to Naprosyn). However, managers who use the software more often make unconventional recommendations (e.g., reduce the size of the salesforce; focus all effort on a few successful products such as Naprosyn, and use outside reps for selling other products). We surmise that those who use the software are more likely to determine that the potential profit associated with increasing the salesforce is not substantial, and that Syntex can get close to its current profits by reducing the size of the salesforce and at the same time reallocating the sales effort. The software enables managers to explore more options (quickly)—options that are not "anchored" only to those included in the case report. Using an experimental study, van Bruggen, Smidts, and Wierenga (1997) compared the relative performance of managers using a decision support system to make decisions in a simulated environment with that of managers who did not use the system. They report that managers using the system are less susceptible to anchoring current decisions to prior decisions (anchoring typically leads to poorer performance in less predictable environments). The authors also report that the superior performance is more pronounced in earlier stages of the multiperiod simulation when the managers have not yet fully understood the important drivers of market behavior.

Empowerment has its downside: The deceptive simplicity of using the software and the presumed scientific credibility of the underlying models gives users a false sense of security. We have observed two interesting situations: Students with strong quantitative backgrounds are often drawn to the technical aspects of the results and sometimes miss the big picture. Students with weak analytical skills either ignore model results and go with their intuition or accept the results uncritically. For example, we saw one group inadvertently reverse the scale (changing it from low to high to high to low) on some critical data but accept the model results anyway. The best outcomes we have seen come from groups that include people with different levels of analytical abilities who pool their efforts while questioning and supporting one another. These groups use the model results as one input into a decision process that also includes common sense and subjective judgment.

Lifelong learning: No book or course can communicate all the richness of marketing problems or all the opportunities and challenges associated with marketing engineering. Some of you may recall watching "slicer-dicer" demonstrations on TV: the demonstrator shows how the slicer can slice tomatoes perfectly in 15 different ways. When you try it, you get less than perfect results—learning to use the device takes time. In a similar vein, after studying marketing engineering and using the software you may underestimate the difficulties in applying this approach to new decision situations. Successful application requires a blend of modeling knowledge, common sense, educated judgment, good communication skills, patience, practice, and most important, a willingness to learn through experimentation.

Instructors should be coaches more than teachers: The pedagogic focus should be on learning by students rather than teaching by instructors. Marketing engineering cannot be taught through lectures alone. You cannot learn how to ride a bicycle by listening to a lecture, but you can learn both quickly and well under the direction of a guide or coach. The same holds for marketing engineering. The more we acted as guides, critics, and facilitators, the more students learned and the more they liked it. This is obvious in hindsight, but it was not so clear when we began. Leidner and Jarvenpaa (1995) suggest that teacher-centered methods (e.g., lectures) are efficient for imparting factual or procedural knowledge.

However, learner-centered methods (e.g., hands-on cases and exercises completed with peers under the guidance of a coach) are appropriate for helping students to develop their own abilities to solve problems. Because the marketing engineering software is powerful and fairly easy to use, students can see their skills (and thinking) developing rapidly.

Marketing engineering should link academics and practitioners: In marketing, practice without theory teaches little while theory without practice means even less. Decision makers pressured to understand and operate in complex and risky markets increasingly depend on the concepts and tools of marketing engineering. For example, the executives we teach invariably try our software using some of their own data and immediately see the relevance and the benefit of the marketing engineering approach. The pressure on academics to show greater relevance for their work is increasing academic interest in marketing engineering as well. These two pressures point to an exciting marriage of convenience that should lead to improved tools for practitioners and interesting problems for academics to work on. As with all successful partnerships, both stand to gain.

USING MARKETING ENGINEERING WITHIN FIRMS

Marketing engineering succeeds because of sophisticated managers, not because of sophisticated models. Such managers recognize that decisions affect many stakeholders and that people resist change and will not embrace decision processes they do not understand or decisions not favorable to their interests. Therefore making good decisions is only half the challenge. It is just as important to make those decisions acceptable to stakeholders within a firm. Models can also help people understand and accept decisions: models improve communications among the stakeholders. By clearly stating model assumptions and understanding the results, managers can replace positions with principles: Instead of saying "Let's do X," one might say "I believe that our objective should be A, and based on the model, X is a good way to achieve that objective." In addition, a model provides an explicit mechanism for including stakeholders in the decision process. For example, at Syntex Labs (Chapter 9) the stakeholders participated by providing inputs to the model and by helping implement model results. Managers are more likely to accept decisions resulting from a model if they know their inputs and judgments are part of the process.

The following tips and suggestions should help you to increase the likelihood of your achieving success with marketing engineering:

Be opportunistic: Select problems or issues that have a good chance of rapid and demonstrable success. A successful application of a model that favors a negative decision (e.g., do not introduce the new product) is likely to have less impact than an application of a model that favors a positive decision (e.g., introduce the new product). When managers within the firm agree that it needs drastic improvements in a particular area, you have an opportunity to prove the value of marketing engineering. Managers are open to new approaches in such situations, and noticeable improvements are possible.

Start simple, and keep it simple: It is best to start with problems that are understandable and familiar to the stakeholders. For example, if the firm has a large customer database and is trying to figure out how to identify and target its efforts to the most profitable accounts, choice-segmentation software might offer a quick solution. It is easy to explain: "We will target customers who, based on their previous purchase behavior, are more likely to respond favorably to our future selling efforts." The software could be programmed to tag promising accounts and update predictions regularly. Everybody wins. The salesforce is likely to increase its sales per salesperson and thus increase its commission income. Managers will be happy about the more effective use of the firm's resources. Finally, the less responsive accounts can be turned over to a newly created telemarketing salesforce, which can provide new sources of revenue.

Even if a model simply points out a new option, the model may be a success. Marketing engineering should help us to use our imagination and expand our decision options, even if we are not able to use the model to make a decision.

Work backward—begin with an end in mind: Start with an understanding of the goal of the modeling effort. Is it to provide justification for a course of action? Is it to resolve an issue for which judgment seems to be inadequate? Is it to facilitate a group decision? Is it for forecasting (what will happen) or for explaining something (why did it happen)? It is also useful to undertake the marketing engineering effort with target dates for meetings and presentations in mind. This will force discipline in completing the modeling effort, and the meetings will provide a forum for discussing modeling results and facilitating follow-through.

Score inexpensive victories: Look for areas in which the costs of model development are low compared with potential benefits. For example, the salesforce-allocation model is fairly inexpensive to implement. It can be used successfully with just judgmental data. And it offers the potential of increasing current sales revenues by 5 to 10 percent by reallocating effort.

Develop a program, not just projects: We described marketing engineering applications at Syntex Labs and at ABB Electric that were both successful. But there was one important difference between them: the Syntex application was a project, and turnover in the original team, and in management more generally, prevented Syntex from getting the most out of this effort. The firm claimed that it could have increased its profit from the project by more than 10 percent (at no additional cost) by properly monitoring and adapting the implementation of the recommendations.

At ABB in contrast, marketing engineering has been an integral part of the organization for over two decades, affecting the allocation of sales and promotional efforts, the development of new products and advertising copy, the positioning of products, and decisions in manufacturing. Its marketing engineering program saved ABB and helped it to survive; ABB's president, Daniel Elwing, puts it this way: "It had to be a program; it could not be a project."

MARKETING ENGINEERING: A LOOK AHEAD

To improve their performance and future prospects, firms are investing heavily in information technology infrastructures linked to communication networks. The marketing function is also undergoing fundamental transformations because of these technologies: the marketing operations of direct mail firms depend on toll-free telephone systems; salespeople keep in touch with customers and headquarters using laptop computers; large retailers cannot survive without on-line price-lookup systems. Firms today install computers and software everywhere, not just in their back offices. Yet many marketing managers continue to make decisions in the traditional old-fashioned way, without using the information and decision-aiding technologies that are already available.

Some firms have recognized that one of their most important assets is relevant information whose business implications decision makers can interpret in a timely manner. To take advantage of the information available to them, firms are integrating decision-aiding technologies into the fabric of their day-to-day operations and decisions. Consider the following examples:

- American Express is a leading-edge user of information technologies. It developed the Authorizer's Assistant, a rule-based expert system with more than 1000 rules, to automate the credit-approval process for purchases based on the past spending patterns of the credit card holder (this is an important function because the AmEx card does not impose a credit limit). Another model American Express is using is a complex neural network to analyze the hundreds of millions of entries in its database that include how and where its cardholders spend their money. This analysis recognizes patterns and allows the company to send cardholders special customized offers with their bills.

  In another successful effort American Express uses customer records to identify stores that do not carry the card but are located in areas where there are many card members. This type of analysis, combined with a minimum sales guarantee, convinced Wal-Mart to accept the American Express card. Other information systems in the company support analyses of customer records to summarize the profile of American Express card members who use a particular establishment versus profiles of customers using competing establishments. For example, this type of analyses can be used to see if the Marriott located in downtown Philadelphia attracts more women customers than the Four Seasons Hotel located a mile away.

- Frito-Lay, a leading producer of snack foods, has introduced a number of successful information-technology innovations to enhance its marketing efforts. For example, its Zone Workbench System puts timely information into the hands of front-line managers. The system grew out of the company's decentralization in 1990, when it reduced the number of management levels and broadened employee responsibilities. Frito-Lay's headquarters began to manage its 10,000-person salesforce through new zone offices. The Workbench provided zone managers, each responsible for about 100 salespersons, with information they use daily in managing key accounts, overseeing the placement of promotion displays, planning sales routes, and managing expenses associated with selling. In 1991 Frito-Lay won the prestigious Computer World–Smithsonian Award for using information technology to make a positive impact on society.

- Sensormatic is a large electronic security firm that markets surveillance and theft-prevention equipment to businesses. It uses an information system to develop strategic plans by segments instead of treating all customers as one homogeneous group. The company has developed a large database that contains detailed customer and market information, some of which was previously unavailable to the marketing managers. This information has been the basis for improved segment-level forecasts. One of Sensormatic's executives commented that they once viewed their customers as homogeneous, but they now use information technologies to anticipate evolving customer needs and to understand the differences among customers, and they now exploit these differences to generate growth.

- The Franklin Mint, a worldwide direct response marketer of quality collectibles and luxury and home-decor products, has developed a system called AMOS (automatic model specification) that is a leading-edge application of database marketing. As Zahavi (1995) explains, "The most challenging part of the system was the specification problem—the process of selecting the subset of predictors that 'best' explain, in a statistical sense, the customer's choice decisions, from among a much larger set of potential predictors." For the Franklin Mint that means choosing from among more than 800 predictor variables. Its choice model incorporates past purchase history, demographic variables (often data acquired from outside vendors and appended to its database), and product attributes (theme, artist, material, etc.).

The choice model drives the Franklin Mint's entire planning and decision process, which includes such problems as

■ Targeting the right audience for each promotion
■ Determining how many mailings to send each customer
■ Predicting the number of orders the promotion will generate
■ Determining how many units of a promoted item to manufacture or procure

AMOS has resulted in increases in profitability of nearly 10 percent for the Franklin Mint over previous approaches (including a judgmental procedure and one using more standard segmentation methods like the cluster and discriminant analysis approaches we described in Chapter 3). It is now being used to support operations in Europe and Asia as well as in North America.

We expect that during the next decade the major developments in technologies to support marketing decisions will be geared to helping managers process the information that is already available to them: to filter the relevant from the irrelevant and to draw out insights from information. Many large firms are putting together a new corporate activity called Marketing Information Systems (MKIS) to support and enhance enterprise-wide performance using marketing information. Although the concept of MKIS has existed for a number of years (see, for example, Kotler 1966), the scope and potential value of the present-day MKIS is far greater than was envisioned in those early days.

MKIS, typically located within the marketing department, is charged with harnessing marketing-related information and distributing and facilitating its use within the firm. Even as the marketing function seems to be in decline, the marketing concept itself appears to be gaining wider acceptance in firms (Doyle 1995). Marketing is becoming an enterprise-wide activity rather than the exclusive domain of a specific department. Firms see MKIS as a way to use marketing information to make everyone in the firm realize that they must be more responsive to customer needs and wants and to the competitive environment.

Historically, a major function of information systems has been to provide timely access to information. MKIS can now integrate end-user decision models with traditional information systems to enhance the firm's ability to use marketing engineering. At least six current trends favor this integration of information. Firms are

1. Investing in the infrastructure they need to develop and maintain extensive corporate databases (also called data warehouses)
2. Using On-Line Analytical Processing (OLAP) to integrate modeling capabilities with databases
3. Deploying intelligent systems to automate some modeling tasks
4. Developing computer simulations for decision training and for exploring multiple options
5. Installing groupware systems, such as Lotus Notes, to support group decision making
6. Enhancing user interfaces to make it easier to deploy even complex models more widely

We describe these trends next:

Data warehouses: The transaction databases typically maintained by information systems departments are restricted to information on order processing and inventory control. A data warehouse contains information collected and organized specifically to support decision making. A transaction database supports such operational tasks as looking up the price of a product or the location of the nearest dealer. On the other hand, a data warehouse is useful for managing a business, and it can be designed to answer such questions as, "How does the response to our sales promotion in Philadelphia compare with the response in New York?" A data warehouse supports decisions in many different areas (e.g., yield management, promotions management), and it is designed to take advantage of the various transaction databases already being used by the firm. A customer-support data warehouse could be structured around several databases:

- Bank of America maintains a data warehouse that contains 1.2 million gigabytes of data and is a composite of 30 different databases containing 35 million records of checking, savings, and other transactions (*Business Week*, July 31, 1995; *Wall Street Journal*, November 18, 1996). One use of this database is to support the firm's phone reps who field about 100,000 calls each day from customers regarding credit balances, loan rates, and the like. They use the database to translate customer calls into business opportunities by offering other products or services tailored to the specific needs of the persons calling. For example, if a customer has more than 20 percent of his or her savings in a passbook account, a model could recognize that such a customer is likely to buy a higher-interest product. Another use of the database is to support ad hoc planning. For example, the bank found out that it was losing checking-account customers who were unhappy with the bank's fees. Using the database and some modeling efforts, the bank developed a lower-cost checking plan targeted to those customers and was able to reverse the trend.
- US West, a major telecommunications company, designed a data warehouse to improve its customer service by measuring the quality of all customer interactions. This warehouse, which the firm called the Performance Analysis System, automatically summarizes transactions data on all interactions with customers and provides decision-aiding information to managers within 24 hours. They can then filter this information through an integrated high-end statistical software package to interpret it and to visualize the information.

Firms can support other decision areas using different data warehouses, although they may build all the data warehouses on the same few transaction databases. To get the most value from such large databases, firms need mass-produced marketing models (Blattberg, Kim, and Ye 1994). This need is driving the development of On-Line Analytical Processing, described next.

On-Line Analytical Processing (OLAP): The analytical tool most widely used by corporations is the spreadsheet. The typical spreadsheet is limited to analyzing small databases, and it provides primarily a two-dimensional view of the data. Decision makers often want to cut data along several dimensions: across time (How are we doing compared with last year?), and across products and geography (Which of our products are prescribed by family practitioners in rural communities?). Database vendors such as Oracle and Sybase offer multidimensional analytical tools for use with their database-management systems. These tools provide on-line decision support for managers without requiring them to learn complex database query languages. For example, Wal-Mart is using sophisticated decision support systems to help its store managers identify the top 10 to 20 products in each store on each day of the week; they then alter shelf displays and end-of-aisle displays to take advantage of the changing mix of top products by day of week. If the Wal-Mart managers in the Wheat Ridge, Colorado, store find that it sells more diapers on a given Thursday, they will then plan special displays of diapers for the following Thursday!

Currently OLAP tools are stronger in on-line data retrieval than in analytic capabilities. However, as firms integrate more marketing engineering models into OLAPs, these tools will gain the ability to support complex decisions on-line. For example, corporations could integrate a library of models into their corporate data warehouses. Managers could then get on-line support to help them answer such questions as, "Why is the promotion more profitable in New York than in Philadelphia?" and to help them decide whether to cut back on promotions in Philadelphia. For some decision areas the data warehouse would need to include enterprise-wide models rather than just end-user models. For example, yield management requires the execution of complex optimization procedures on large dynamic databases. However, end-user models are still useful for many small, localized applications.

Intelligent marketing systems: Currently most managers use marketing engineering in a reactive mode after they have identified decision problems. This limits the usefulness of marketing engineering. Simon (1977) suggested that problem solving consists of three phases: intelligence, design, and choice. In the intelligence phase the decision maker identifies problems and situations that call for decisions. In the design phase the decision maker generates many potential solutions to the problem, and in the choice phase he or she selects specific solution(s). Historically, decision models have emphasized the design and choice phases. However, information-intensive environments call for decision support systems that can also be used in the intelligence phase.

Many marketing organizations generate millions of pieces of data a day. For example, a firm might distribute 20 products to 10 accounts in each of 300 markets and employ 300 salespeople. The only way it can interpret and use the large amounts of data it accumulates is by deploying intelligent models that automate the process of interpreting the data. Several firms are experimenting with an emerging technology called *data mining*, a process that relies on automated analysis agents to sift through the data looking for nuggets of insight. Neural networks (Chapter 5) and several other new modeling approaches can help with data mining. Data mining is useful for identifying patterns in the data that indicate problems that require managers' attention and decisions.

Another approach to dealing with such large amounts of data is automated intelligence that links models and databases directly to customer communications. Such systems help managers automate both the modeling process and the implementation of some of the modeling results. For example, an automated segmentation and targeting system can identify attractive segments and then arrange to send segment members an electronic message or piece of mail or arrange for a sales call.

Expert systems (also called knowledge-based systems) are a third way to automate the filtering of large amounts of data and the subsequent modeling. They are particularly useful for repetitive decision problems that have highly varying input conditions (e.g., credit authorization, automated analysis, and report writing). In such situations we can specify the structure of the problem and the range of variation in inputs reasonably well in advance, but we cannot anticipate what to do under every combination of input conditions that we might encounter. For example, Mrs. Fields Cookies, Inc., has developed an expert system to cut down on errors in signing store leases. With 800 stores, the company is trying to ensure that idiosyncratic local conditions are properly incorporated into the contract along with appropriate overall terms. "The expert system can check each lease," says Fields (Light 1992).

Another important application for expert systems is in automatically generating top-line management reports based on statistical analyses of frequently collected marketing data. Two such systems that analyze scanner data are CoverStory (Schmitz, Armstrong, and Little 1990) and INFER (Rangaswamy, Harlam, and Lodish 1991). Exhibit 11.1 shows a sample report that CoverStory generated automatically after extensive data analysis. A related system called Salespartner (Schmitz 1994) tunes its report to the needs of the sales representative for consumer packaged goods rather than to the needs of managers.

To: Sizzle Brand Manager
From: CoverStory
Date: 07/05/89
Subject: Sizzle Brand Summary for Twelve Weeks Ending May 21, 1989

Sizzle's share of type in total United States was 8.3 in the C&B Juice/Drink category for the twelve weeks ending 5/21/98. This is an increase of 0.2 points from a year earlier, but down .3 from last period. This reflects volume sales of 8.2 million gallons. Category volume (currently 99.9 million gallons) declined 1.3% from a year earlier.

Sizzle's share of type is 8.3—up 0.2 from the same period last year.

Display activity and unsupported price cuts rose over the past year—unsupported price cuts from 38 points to 46. Featuring and price remained at about the same level as a year earlier.

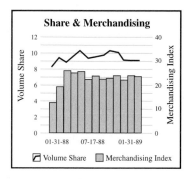

Share & Merchandising

Volume Share / Merchandising Index

01-31-88   07-17-88   01-31-89

▨ Volume Share   ▢ Merchandising Index

Components of Sizzle Share

Among components of Sizzle, the principal gainer is:
  Sizzle 64 oz: up 0.5 points from last year to 3.7

and losers:
  Sizzle 48 oz: down 0.2 to 1.9
  Sizzle 32 oz: down 0.1 to 0.7

Sizzle 64 oz's share of type increase is partly due to 11.3 points ride in % ACV with Display vs. year ago.

Competitor Summary

Among Sizzle's major competitors, the principal gainers are:
  Shakey: up 2.5 points from last year to 32.6
  Private Label: +.5 to 19.9 (but down .3 since last period)

and loser:
  Generic Seltzer: -.7 to 3.5

Shakey's share of type increase is...

EXHIBIT 11.1
The first page of a CoverStory memorandum shows how an expert system can generate a coherent management report with no human intervention. *Source*: Schmitz, Armstrong, and Little 1990, p. 38.

Its report focuses on customer-specific programs and events that the salesperson can talk about during customer visits.

Customer service employees in many firms have diagnostic tools at their disposal to help solve customer problems. These tools—and the entire service encounter—represent other promising areas for commercial applications of expert systems. Firms can use these systems to increase their profitability by improving customer service, helping customers use products and solve problems. For example, a customer service representative at a help desk supported by expert systems can find out if a customer is a candidate for other programs, update information about the customer's new needs (product design feedback), and provide early warning about major problems.

Expert systems are most useful when we need models that (1) explain their behavior or recommendations (e.g., why they came to a specific conclusion in a report) or (2) simulate the recommendations of expert decision makers in well-specified decision areas. Many early expert systems failed because they were expensive to develop and maintain and because they operated on specialized hardware not linked to other systems within the firm. However, the new generation of "embeddable expert systems" that are linked to conventional systems have gained wider acceptance, use, and a secure role in industry (Hayes-Roth and Jacobstein 1994). In the next decade we expect to see many more embedded expert systems that support marketing managers, a clear marketing engineering trend.

Simulations: Managers use market simulations to learn marketing concepts (business simulations such as MarkStrat and InduStrat are widely used in MBA and executive programs) and to explore and understand the possible outcomes of potential decision options.

EXAMPLE

(Adapted from Whitaker 1995.) Lufthansa's consulting group developed an eight-period (each period corresponds to six months) simulation to train its managers to prepare for privatization and deregulation of the airline industry in Europe. In the simulation three airlines start out with identical resources and market positions, and they have complete freedom to decide their frequencies of flights, fares, marketing policies, and purchases of fleet after the airlines are deregulated. The simulation covers most day-to-day activities of running an airline and embodies relationships that reflect real market data. However, it ignores some complex issues, such as traffic feeding across the hub, code-sharing alliances with other carriers, and negotiations with labor unions.

Managers participating in these simulations learn by making errors, which Lufthansa hopes they will avoid on the job. For example, they may order aircraft in anticipation of demand that does not materialize. This error will teach them to use modeling approaches to more carefully consider the costs (e.g., higher debt and loan payments) and benefits (e.g., improved punctuality, lower fuel and maintenance costs) in uncertain situations before ordering new aircraft. Likewise, when competition intensifies managers might start investing large amounts of money in marketing without seeing adequate returns. This error will teach them to use modeling approaches to more carefully evaluate where, how, and why they should increase their marketing dollars before making such an investment.

In addition to their use in training, computer simulations are increasingly being used in actual decision making. For example, surgeons can first practice a complex surgical procedure on a computer-generated replica of their patient before carrying out the actual surgery. This process is called anticipatory learning. Marketing managers can do the same—make decisions in a simulated marketplace before committing to a course of action. For example, conjoint analysis reports often include a market simulator that managers can use to explore options that they were not considering when they commissioned the conjoint study. Firms use simulations (like our simplified bidding-analysis software) in competitive bidding situations for oil leases and for broadcast spectrum rights.

With simulation, marketing managers can experiment on a simulated representation of the marketplace and see the likely result of their actions. And they can do so at low cost and more rapidly than any real market experiment would allow. Organizations can also use simulations effectively to spread learning and new thinking among their employees (Senge and Lannon 1990).

Groupware for decision support: *Groupware* is a general term that describes a variety of computer- and communications-based systems that enhance the efficiency and effectiveness with which a group of people make decisions. Using groupware, project teams can share information (e.g., reports and presentations) as well as make and record decisions (e.g., on-line voting). Such systems can circumvent temporal, geographic, and organizational barriers in supporting collaborative work:

- Price-Waterhouse, a leading accounting firm, has one of the world's largest installed bases of Lotus Notes to support collaborative decision making. About 40,000 of its employees (consultants) each have a Lotus Notes program with which they access corporate-wide Lotus Notes databases, as well as databases specific to individual projects. With the systems Price-Waterhouse can make specialized expertise widely available within the company and quickly put together and support ad hoc teams that make decisions to take advantage of emerging opportunities.

- Computer Language Research (CLR) is the leading firm in the tax software business, designing and marketing hundreds of different software packages for managing audits and taxes for such customers as banks, accounting firms, and corporate tax departments. Because of changing tax laws, the firm must be able to modify and enhance existing products quickly and develop new products for new customers in other industries. CLR has used Lotus Notes to improve both the speed and quality of its new products. For example, team members make many decisions on-line without having to arrange face-to-face meetings, which helps compress product-development time. Also, project teams have improved access to expertise available within the company and improved coordination in reporting and fixing problems before the new product is shipped, both of which improve product quality.

In the future we expect firms to use the marketing engineering approach to enhance groupware, incorporating further decision-aiding components. As a step in this direction Ventana Corporation has developed a software package called GroupSystems that organizations can use to set up electronic brainstorming with a number of participants. The system can be used to create agendas (e.g., problems to be resolved), to record ideas generated simultaneously and anonymously by participants, to obtain votes on action items, to produce reports summarizing discussions, and to maintain records for future use. Participants may gather in the same room or log in from remote locations. Such systems can also be used to collect the judgmental inputs many marketing engineering models require.

Improving the user interface: As end-user computing increases within firms, the need for user interfaces that operate in an intuitive manner becomes critical. To be successful, decision models have to serve users who have poor computer skills. Many decision models have failed to attract users because they are incorporated in systems that are difficult to use. For example, several systems for automating the activities of the salesforce are not meeting their performance goals because they require salespeople to adapt to a nonintuitive software design. The software developer should have designed the software around familiar, existing sales processes rather than around an imagined notion of how salespeople work.

People are becoming accustomed to better designed software packages and are coming to expect ease of use from every software package they encounter. The best software hides what the novice does not need (covering the engine with a streamlined hood) and highlights those inputs and outputs that are most important to that user at that time. To assure that increasing numbers of people use their products, software vendors must provide increasingly user-friendly packages. We have tried to make our software very easy to use.

Other trends: Glazer (1991) has tried to predict what might occur in the next decade or so because of the increasing availability of information and the decreasing cost of processing that information; he expects

> shorter and less predictable product life cycles,
>
> a shift in power from sellers to buyers,
>
> more focus on product profitability and less on share,
>
> more (and less formal) alliances,
>
> more focus on cooperation and less on competition, and
>
> greater reliance on decision teams whose members simultaneously process shared information.

All of these changes demand rapid and coherent marketing decisions, supported by the marketing engineering approach. Shorter product life cycles mean that analysis has to be both quick and sound. Increased buyer power means that companies must better understand buyer values to succeed in the market. An emphasis on profitability means that marketers must focus on setting objectives. Alliances and cooperation mean that we need newer models to support these multiple decision makers. And the increase in team decisions means that groupware will increase in importance.

In Exhibit 11.2 we summarize our vision of the evolution of marketing engineering along three dimensions: (1) the type of user who uses models, (2) the type of decision tasks supported, and (3) the modeling technologies that enhance marketing engineering. Until the mid-1980s marketing engineering was carried out primarily by analysts who submitted reports to managers. Those analysts used general-purpose analysis programs running on mainframe computers (e.g., such statistical packages as SPSS and linear-programming packages) to generate forecasts and develop plans for optimally deploying organizational resources. The growth of personal computers has put managers in direct control (e.g., through spreadsheet models focused on specific decision areas), permitting richer manager-model interactions (e.g., simulations based on what-if analyses). In the future, marketing engineering will support a broadening range of users (e.g., customer service representatives) using a wider range of technologies (e.g., OLAP, intelligent systems, groupware systems) to enhance decision making by richer means (e.g., using simulation to explain market events).

While the marketing function in companies may decline in importance in the years to come, marketing can only increase in importance. Years ago Peter Drucker pointed out that marketing is too important to be left to marketers; that statement is even more true today. Marketing engineering, a bridge between conceptual and disciplined, systematic marketing, is poised to take its place among the critical management tools for the successful twenty-first-century firm.

POSTSCRIPT

Writing this book has been the most rewarding work we have undertaken. We hope that we have brought many previously abstract academic concepts and ideas to life and shown you how to apply them in business as well as in the classroom. There is nothing as rewarding as

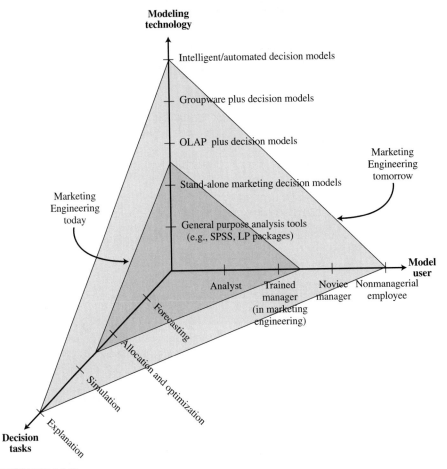

EXHIBIT 11.2
An overview of the evolution of marketing engineering to support a wider range of users and decision tasks using emerging technologies.

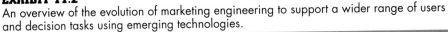

seeing good ideas used. We hope that you have found some good marketing engineering ideas and made them your own. Use them well.

We conclude with a request. We would like to hear from you about your own experiences with successful (and unsuccessful) applications of these decision models. Let us hear from you!

References

Aaker, David A., and Carman, James M., 1982, "Are you overadvertising?" *Journal of Advertising Research*, Vol. 22, No. 4 (August–September), pp. 57–70.

Aaker, David A., and Day, George S., 1990, *Marketing Research*, fourth edition, John Wiley and Sons, New York, p. 574.

Aaker, David A., and Myers, John G., 1987, *Advertising Management*, third edition, Prentice Hall, Englewood Cliffs, New Jersey.

Abell, Derek F., and Hammond, J. S., 1979, *Strategic Marketing Planning*, Prentice Hall, Englewood Cliffs, New Jersey.

Abraham, Magid M., and Lodish, Leonard M., 1987, "PROMOTER: An automated promotion evaluation system," *Marketing Science*, Vol. 6, No. 2 (Spring), pp. 101–123.

Abraham, Magid M., and Lodish, Leonard M., 1989, "PROMOTIONSCAN: A system for improving promotion productivity for retailers and manufacturers using scanner store and household panel data," working paper #89-007 (February), Marketing Department, The Wharton School of the University of Pennsylvania.

Agostini, Jean-Michel, 1961, "How to estimate unduplicated audiences," *Journal of Advertising Research*, Vol. 1, No. 3 (March), pp. 11–14.

Alberts, William W., 1989, "The experience curve doctrine reconsidered," *Journal of Marketing*, Vol. 53, No. 3 (July), pp. 36–49.

Albion, Mark S., 1984a, "Suave (C)," *HBS Case 9-585-019*, Harvard Business School, Boston.

Albion, Mark S., 1984b, "Suave (D)," *HBS Case 9-585-020*, Harvard Business School, Boston.

American Salesman, 1995, "It takes 3.9 calls to close a sale," Vol. 40, No. 8 (August), pp. 8–9.

Anderson, Erin, 1985, "Salesperson as outside agent or employee—a transaction cost analysis," *Marketing Science*, Vol. 4. No. 3 (Summer), pp. 234–254.

Anderson, James; Jain, Dipak C.; and Chintagunta, Pradeep K., 1993, "Customer value assessment in business markets: A state-of-practice study," *Journal of Business-to-Business Marketing*, Vol. 1, No. 1, pp. 3–29.

Anderson, Paul F., 1979, "The marketing management/ finance interface," in *1979 Educator Conference Proceedings*, eds. N. Beckwith, M. Houston, R. Mittelstaedt, K. B. Monroe, and S. Ward, American Marketing Association, Chicago, pp. 325–329.

Anderson, Paul F., 1981, "Marketing investment analysis," in *Research in Marketing*, Vol. 4, ed. J. N. Sheth, JAI Press, Greenwich, Connecticut, pp. 1–38.

Anterasian, Cathy; Grahame, John L.; and Money, R. Bruce, 1996, "Are U.S. managers superstitious about market share?" *Sloan Management Review*, Vol. 37, No. 4, p. 67.

Appel, Valentine, 1971, "On advertising wear-out," *Journal of Advertising Research*, Vol. 11 (February), pp. 11–14.

Armstrong, J. Scott, 1985, "The ombudsman: Research on forecasting: A quarter century review, 1960–1984," *Interfaces*, Vol. 16, No. 1 (January–February), pp. 89–109.

Assael, Henry, and Day, George S., 1968, "Attitudes and awareness as predictors of market share," *Journal of Advertising Research*, Vol. 8, No. 4 (December), pp. 3–10.

Assael, Henry, and Roscoe, A. Marvin, Jr., 1976, "Approaches to market segmentation analysis," *Journal of Marketing*, Vol. 40, No. 4 (October), pp. 67–76.

Aumann, R., 1987, "What is game theory trying to accomplish?" in *Frontiers of Economics*, eds. K. J. Arrow and S. Honkapohja, Blackwell, Oxford, England.

Axelrod, Joel N., 1968, "Attitude measures that predict purchase," *Journal of Advertising Research*, Vol. 8, No. 1 (March), pp. 3–17.

Barabba, Vincent P., and Zaltman, Gerald, 1991, *Hearing the Voice of the Market: Competitive Advantage Through Creative Use of Market Information*, Harvard Business School Press, Boston.

Bass, Frank M., 1969, "A new product growth model for consumer durables," *Management Science*, Vol. 15, No. 4 (January), pp. 216–227.

Bass, Frank M.; Krishnan, Trichy V.; and Jain, Dipak C., 1994, "Why the Bass model fits without decision variables," *Marketing Science*, Vol. 13, No. 3 (Summer), pp. 204–223.

Baumol, William J., 1972, *Economic Theory and Operations Analysis*, Prentice Hall, Englewood Cliffs, New Jersey.

Bensoussan, Alain; Bultez, Alain; and Naert, Philippe, 1978, "Leader's dynamic marketing behavior in oligopoly," *TIMS Studies in the Management Sciences*, Vol. 9, pp. 123–145.

Bettman, James R., 1971, "The structure of consumer choice processes," *Journal of Marketing Research*, Vol. 8 (November), pp. 465–471.

Bettman, James R., 1979, "Memory factors in consumer choice: A review," *Journal of Marketing,* Vol. 43, No. 2 (Spring), pp. 37–53.

Blasko, Vincent J., and Patti, Charles H., 1984, "The advertising budgeting practices of industrial marketers," *Journal of Marketing*, Vol. 48, No. 4 (Fall), pp. 104–110.

Blattberg, Robert C.; Briesch, Richard; and Fox, Edward J., 1995, "How promotions work," *Marketing Science*, Vol. 14, No. 3, Part 2, pp. G122–G125.

Blattberg, Robert C., and Hoch, Stephen J., 1990, "Database models and managerial intuition: 50 percent model and 50 percent manager," *Management Science*, Vol. 36, No. 8 (August), pp. 887–899.

Blattberg, Robert C.; Kim, Bong-Do; and Ye, Jianming, 1994, "Large scale data bases: The new marketing challenge," in *The Marketing Information Revolution*, eds., Robert C. Blattberg, Rashi Glazer, and John D. C. Little, Harvard Business School Press, Boston, pp. 173–203.

Blattberg, Robert C., and Levin, Alan, 1987, "Modelling the effectiveness and profitability of trade promotions," *Marketing Science*, Vol. 6, No. 2 (Spring), pp. 124–146.

Blattberg, Robert C., and Neslin, Scott A., 1990, *Sales Promotion: Concepts, Methods, and Strategies*, Prentice Hall, Englewood Cliffs, New Jersey.

Boeing Commercial Airplane Group 1988, "B727 rejuvenation," *World Jet Airplane Inventory*, The Boeing Company, p. 7.

Boston Consulting Group 1970, *Perspectives on Experience*, Boston.

Bower, John, 1963, "Net audiences of US and Canadian magazines: Seven tests of Agostini's formula," *Journal of Advertising Research*, Vol. 3 (March), pp. 13–21.

Boyd, Harper W., Jr., and Ray, Michael L., 1971, "What big agency men in Europe think of copy testing methods," *Journal of Marketing Research*, Vol. 8, No. 2 (May), pp. 219–223.

Brock, Timothy C., 1965, "Communicator-recipient similarity and decision change," *Journal of Personality and Social Psychology,* Vol. 1, No. 10, pp. 650–654.

Brown, Rex V.; Lilien, Gary L.; and Ulvila, Jacob W., 1993, "New methods for estimating business markets," *Journal of Business-to-Business Marketing*, Vol. 1, No. 2, pp. 33–65.

Business Week, July 31, 1995.

Buzzell, Robert D., 1966, "Competitive behavior and product life cycles," in *New Ideas for Successful Marketing*, eds. J. S. Wright and J. L. Goldstucker, American Marketing Association, Chicago.

Buzzell, Robert D., and Gale, Bradley T., 1987, *The PIMS Principles, Linking Strategy to Performance*, The Free Press, New York.

Camerer, Colin, 1981, "General conditions for the success of bootstrapping models," *Organizational Behavior and Human Performance*, Vol. 27, No. 3, pp. 411–422.

Camparelli, Melissa, 1994, "Reshuffling the deck: Sales territory realignment," *Sales and Marketing Management*, Vol. 146, No. 6, Part 1, pp. 83–90.

Cannon, Hugh, 1987, "A theory-based approach to optimal frequency," *Journal of Media Planning*, Vol. 2, No. 2 (Fall) pp. 33–44.

Cannon, Hugh, and Goldring, Norman, 1986, "Another look at effective frequency," *Journal of Media Planning*, Vol. 1, No. 2 (Fall), pp. 29–36.

Cardozo, Richard, and Wind, Yoram, 1980, "Portfolio analysis for strategic product market planning," working paper, Wharton School, University of Pennsylvania, Philadelphia.

Carpenter, Gregory S.; Cooper, Lee G.; Hanssens, Dominique M.; and Midgley, David F., 1988, "Modeling asymmetric competition," *Marketing Science*, Vol. 7, No. 4 (Fall), pp. 393–412.

Carroll, J. Douglas, 1972, "Individual differences and multidimensional scaling," in *Multidimensional Scaling: Theory and Applications in the Behavioral Sciences, Vol. 2, Applications*, eds. A. K. Romney, R. N. Shepard, and S. B. Nerlove, Seminar Press, New York.

Carroll, Vincent P.; Rao, Ambar G.; Lee, H. L., Shapin, A.; and Bayus, Barry L., 1985, "The Navy enlistment marketing experiment," *Marketing Science*, Vol. 4, No. 4 (Fall), pp. 352–374.

Choffray, Jean-Marie, and Lilien, Gary L., 1978, "Assessing response to industrial marketing strategy," *Journal of Marketing*, Vol. 42, No. 2 (April), pp. 20–31.

Choffray, Jean-Marie, and Lilien, Gary L., 1980, *Market Planning for New Industrial Products*, John Wiley and Sons, New York.

Clarke, Darral G., 1976, "Econometric measurement of the duration of advertising effects on sales," *Journal of Marketing Research*, Vol. 13, No. 4, pp. 345–357.

Claycamp, Henry J., and McClelland, Charles W., 1968, "Estimating reach and the magic of K," *Journal of Advertising Research*, Vol. 8 (June), pp. 44–51.

Cocks, Douglas L., and Virts, John R., 1975, "Market diffusion and concentration in the ethical pharmaceutical industry," internal memorandum, Eli Lilly and Company, Indianapolis, Indiana.

Cole, Bradley, and Swire, Donald, 1980, "The limited information report," in *Marketing Strategy*, ed. D. Sudharshan, Prentice Hall, Englewood Cliffs, New Jersey p. 292.

Colley, Russel H., 1961, *Defining Advertising Goals for Measured Advertising Results*, Association of National Advertisers, New York.

Cooper, Lee G., 1983, "A review of multidimensional scaling in marketing research," *Applied Psychological Measurement*, Vol. 7, No. 4 (Fall), pp. 427–450.

Cooper, Lee G., 1993, "Market share models," in *Handbooks in Operations Research and Management Science, Vol. 5, Marketing*, eds. Jehoshua Eliashberg and Gary L. Lilien, Elsevier Science Publishers B.V., North Holland, New York, pp. 259–314.

Cooper, Lee G., and Nakanishi, Masao, 1988, *Market-Share Analysis*, Kluwer, Norwell, Massachusetts.

Cooper, Robert G., 1986, "An investigation into the new product process: Steps, deficiencies, and impact," *Journal of Product Innovation Management*, Vol. 3, No. 2 (June), pp. 71–85.

Cooper, Robert G., 1992, "The newprod system: Industry experience," *Journal of Product Innovation Management*, Vol. 9, No. 2 (June), pp. 113–127.

Cort, Stanton G.; Lambert, David R.; and Garret, Paula L., 1982, "Frequency in business-to-business advertising: A state-of-the-art review," *4th Annual Business Advertising Research Conference Proceedings*, Advertising Research Foundation, New York.

Cox, William, Jr., 1967, "Product life cycles as marketing models," *Journal of Business*, Vol. 40, No. 4 (October), pp. 375–384.

Cravens, David W., 1995, "The changing role of the sales force," *Marketing Management*, Vol. 4, No. 2 (Fall), pp. 49–57.

Daganzo, Carlos, 1979, *Multinomial Probit*, Academic Press, New York.

Danaher, Peter, 1989, "A log linear model for predicting magazine audiences," *Journal of Marketing Research*, Vol. 26, No. 4, pp. 473–479.

Day, George S., 1981, "The product life cycle: Analysis and applications issues," *Journal of Marketing*, Vol. 45, No. 4 (Fall), pp. 60–67.

Day, George S., 1986, *Analysis for Strategic Market Decisions*, West Publishing, St. Paul, Minnesota.

Day, George S., and Montgomery, D. B., 1983, "Diagnosing the experience curve," *Journal of Marketing*, Vol. 47, No. 2 (Spring), pp. 44–58.

Day, George S., Shocker, Allan D., and Srivastava, Rajendra K., 1979, "Consumer-oriented approaches to identifying product markets," *Journal of Marketing*, Vol. 43, No. 4 (Fall), pp. 8–19.

Deming, W. Edwards, 1987, in Hogarth, Robin Miles, *Judgment and Choice*, second edition, John Wiley and Sons, New York, p. 199.

DeVincentis, John R., and Kotcher, Lauri Kien, 1995, "Packaged goods sales force—beyond efficiency," *McKinsey Quarterly*, No. 1 pp. 72–85.

Diamond, Daniel S., 1968, "A quantitative approach to magazine advertisement format selection," *Journal of Marketing Research*, Vol. 5, No. 4 (November), pp. 376–386.

Dillon, William R., and Goldstein, Matthew, 1984, *Multivariate Analysis: Methods and Applications*, John Wiley and Sons, New York, pp. 173–174

Dolan, Robert J., 1981, "Models of competition: A review of theory and empirical evidence," in *Review of Marketing*, eds. B. Enis and K. Roering, American Marketing Association, Chicago, pp. 224–234.

Dolan, Robert J., 1993, *Managing the New Product Development Process*, Addison-Wesley Publishing Company, Reading, Massachusetts.

Dowling, Grahame R., and Midgley, David F., 1988, "Identifying the coarse and fine structures of market segments," *Decision Sciences*, Vol. 19, No. 4 (Fall), pp. 830–847.

Doyle, Peter, 1995, "Marketing in the new millennium," *European Journal of Marketing*, Vol. 29, No. 13, p. 23–41.

Eastlack, Joseph O., and Rao, Ambar G., 1986, "Modelling response to advertising and price changes for 'V-8' cocktail vegetable juice," *Marketing Science*, Vol. 5, No. 3 (Summer), pp. 245–259.

Eastlack, Joseph O., and Rao, Ambar G., 1989, "Advertising experiment at the Campbell Soup Company," *Marketing Science*, Vol. 8, No. 1 (Winter), pp. 57–71.

Eliashberg, Jehoshua; LaTour, Stephen A.; Rangaswamy, Arvind; and Stern, Louis W., 1986, *Journal of Marketing Research*, Vol. 23, No. 2 (May), pp. 101–110.

Eskin, Gerald J., 1985, "Tracking advertising and promotion performance with single source data," *Journal of Advertising Research*, Vol. 25, No. 1, pp. 31–39.

Frey, Albert Wesley, 1955, *How Many Dollars for Advertising?* Ronald Press, New York.

Fudge, William K., and Lodish, Leonard M., 1977, "Evaluation of the effectiveness of a model based salesman's planning system by field experimentation," *Interfaces*, Vol. 8, No. 1, Part 2 (November), pp. 97–106.

Fulgoni, Gian M., 1987, "The role of advertising: Is there one?" *33rd Annual Conference Proceedings*, Advertising Research Foundation, New York, pp. 153–163.

Funk, Thomas F., and Phillips, Willard, 1990, "Segmentation of the Market for Table Eggs in Ontario," *Agribusiness*, Vol. 6, No. 4 (July), pp. 309–327.

Gardner, Yehudi A., and Cohen, Burleigh B., 1966, "ROP color and its effect on newspaper advertising," *Journal of Marketing Research*, Vol. 3, No. 4 (November), pp. 365–371.

Garry, Michael, 1996, "GIS: Finding opportunity in data," *Progressive Grocer*, Vol. 75, No. 6 (June), pp. 61–69.

Garvin, David A., 1987, "Competing on the eight dimensions of quality," *Harvard Business Review,* Vol. 65, No. 6 (November–December), pp. 101–109.

Gensch, Dennis H.; Aversa, Nicola; and Moore, Steven P., 1990, "A choice-modeling market information system that enabled ABB Electric to expand its market share," *Interfaces*, Vol. 20, No. 1 (January–February), pp. 6–25.

Glazer, Rashi, 1991, "Marketing in an information intensive environment: Strategic implications of knowledge as an asset," *Journal of Marketing*, Vol. 55 (October), pp. 1–19.

Goldberg, Lewis R., 1970, "Man versus model of man: A rationale, plus some evidence for a method of improving on clinical inferences," *Psychological Bulletin*, Vol. 73, No. 6, pp. 422–432.

Goodwin, Stephen, and Etgar, Michael, 1980, "An experimental investigation of comparative advertising: Impact of message appeal, information load and utility of product class," *Journal of Marketing Research*, Vol. 17, No. 2 (May), pp. 187–202.

Grapentine, Terry H., 1995, "Dimensions of an attribute; summated scales measure the relationship between product attributes and their perceptual dimensions," *Marketing Research*, Vol. 7, No. 3 (Summer), pp. 18–27.

Grass, Robert C., 1968, "Satiation effects of advertising," *14th Annual Conference Proceedings*, Advertising Research Foundation, New York.

Green, Paul E., 1974, "On the design of choice experiments involving multifactor alternatives," *Journal of Consumer Research*, Vol. 1, No. 2 (September), pp. 61–68.

Green, Paul E., 1975, "Marketing applications of MDS: Assessment and outlook," *Journal of Marketing,* Vol. 39, No. 1 (January), pp. 24–31.

Green, Paul E., 1984, "Hybrid conjoint analysis: An expository review," *Journal of Marketing Research*, Vol. 21, No. 2 (May), pp. 155–169.

Green, Paul E.; Carmone, Frank J., Jr.; and Smith, Scott M., 1989, *Multidimensional Scaling: Concepts and Application*, Allyn and Bacon, Boston.

Green, Paul E., and Kim, Jonathan S., 1991, "Beyond the quadrant chart: Designing effective benefit bundle strategies," *Journal of Advertising Research*, Vol. 31, No. 6 (December), pp. 56–63.

Green, Paul E., and Krieger, Abba M., 1991, "Modeling competitive pricing and market share: Anatomy of a decision support system," *Journal of the European Operational Research Society*, Vol. 60, No. 1 (July), pp. 31–44.

Green, Paul E., and Srinivasan, V., 1978, "Conjoint analysis in consumer research: Issues and outlook," *Journal of Consumer Research*, Vol. 5, No. 2 (September), pp. 103–123.

Green, Paul E., and Srinivasan, V., 1990, "Conjoint analysis in marketing: New developments with implications for research and practice," *Journal of Marketing*, Vol. 54, No. 4 (October), pp. 3–19.

Green, Paul E., and Wind, Yoram J., 1973, *Multiattribute Decisions in Marketing,* The Dryden Press, Hinsdale, Illinois.

Griffin, Abbie, 1993, "Metrics for measuring product development cycle time," *Journal of Product Innovation Management*, Vol. 10, No. 2 (March), pp. 112–125.

Gross, Irwin, 1972, "The creative aspects of advertising," *Sloan Management Review*, Vol. 14 (Fall), pp. 83–109.

Guadagni, Peter M., and Little, John D. C., 1983, "A logit model of brand choice calibrated on scanner data," *Marketing Science*, Vol. 2, No. 3 (Summer), pp. 203–238.

Gupta, Sunil, 1990, "Testing the emergence and effect of the reference outcome in an integrative bargaining situation," *Marketing Letters*, Vol. 1, No. 2, pp. 103–112.

Gupta, Sunil, and Livne, Z. A., 1988, "Resolving conflict situations with a reference outcome: An axiomatic model," *Management Science*, Vol. 34, No. 11, pp. 1303–1314.

Haley, Russell L., and Case, Peter B., 1979, "Testing thirteen attitude scales for agreement and brand discrimination," *Journal of Marketing*, Vol. 43, No. 4 (Fall), pp. 20–32.

Hanssens, Dominique M., 1980, "Marketing response, competitive behavior, and time series analysis," *Journal of Marketing Research,* Vol. 17, No. 4 (November), pp. 470–485.

Hanssens, Dominique M.; Parsons, Leonard J.; and Schultz, Randall L., 1990, *Market Response Models: Econometric and Time Series Analysis*, Kluwer Academic Publishers, Boston.

Hanssens, Dominique M., and Weitz, Barton A., 1980, "The effectiveness of industrial print advertisements across product categories," *Journal of Marketing Research*, Vol. 17, No. 3 (August), pp. 294–306.

Harrell, Stephen G., and Taylor, Elrner D., 1981, "Modeling the product life cycle for consumer durables," *Journal of Marketing*, Vol. 45, No. 4 (Fall), pp. 68–75.

Hauser, John R., and Koppelman, Frank S., 1979, "Alternative perceptual mapping techniques: Relative accuracy and usefulness," *Journal of Marketing Research*, Vol. 16, No. 3 (November), pp. 495–506.

Hauser, John R., and Shugan, Steven M., 1980, "Intensity measures of consumer preference," *Operations Research*, Vol. 28, No. 2 (March–April), pp. 278–320.

Hax, Arnoldo C., and Majluf, Nicolas S., 1982, "Competitive cost dynamics: The experience curve," *Interfaces*, Vol. 12, No. 5 (October), pp. 50–61.

Hayes-Roth, Frederick, and Jacobstein, Neil, 1994, "The state of knowledge-based systems," *Communications of the ACM*, Vol. 37, No. 3 (March), pp. 27–39.

Hendon, Donald W., 1973, "How mechanical factors affect ad perception," *Journal of Advertising Research*, Vol. 13, No. 4, pp. 39–46.

Hess, Sidney W., and Samuels, Stuart A., 1971, "Experiences with a sales districting model: Criteria and implementation," *Management Science*, Vol. 18, No. 4, Part II (December), pp. 41–54.

Hill, Tim; O'Connor, Marcus; and Remus, William, 1996, "Neural network models for time series forecasts," *Management Science*, Vol. 42, No. 7 (July), pp. 1082–1092.

Hise, Richard T.; O'Neil, Larry; McNeal, James U.; and Parasuraman, A., 1989, "The effect of product design activities on commercial success levels of new industrial products," *Journal of Product Innovation Management*, Vol. 6, No. 1 (March), pp. 43–50.

Hise, Richard T., and Reid, Edward L., 1994, "Improving the performance of the industrial sales force in the 1990's," *Industrial Marketing Management*, Vol. 23, No. 4, pp. 273–279.

Hoch, Stephen J., and Schkade, David A., 1996, "A psychological approach to decision support systems," *Management Science*, Vol. 42, No. 1 (January), pp. 51–64.

Hofmans, Pierre, 1966, "Measuring the cumulative net coverage of any combination of media," *Journal of Marketing Research*, Vol. 3, No. 3 (August), pp. 269–278.

Hogarth, Robin Miles, 1987, *Judgment and Choice*, second edition, John Wiley and Sons, New York.

Holbrook, Morris B., and Lehmann, Donald R., 1980, "Form versus content in predicting Starch scores," *Journal of Advertising Research*, Vol. 20, No. 4 (August), pp. 53–62.

Huber, Joel, 1993, *CBC Manual*, Sawtooth Software, 502 South Still Road, Sequim, Washington 98382.

Huff, David L., 1964, "Defining and estimating a trading area," *Journal of Marketing*, Vol. 28, No. 3 (July), pp. 34–38.

Hunt, Morton, 1982, *The Universe Within: A New Science Explores the Human Mind*, The Harvester Press Limited, Brighton, Sussex, England, p. 72.

Jedidi, Kamel; Kohli, Rajeev; and DeSarbo, Wayne S., 1996, "Consideration sets in conjoint analysis," *Journal of Marketing Research*, Vol. 33, No. 3 (August), pp. 364–372.

Johnson, Richard M., 1987, "Adaptive conjoint analysis," *Sawtooth Software Conference on Perceptual Mapping, Conjoint Analysis, and Computer Interviewing*, Sawtooth Software, Ketchum, Idaho.

Johnson, Walter E., 1994, "Special report on forecasting consumer attitudes," *National Retail Hardware Association, Do-It-Yourself Retailing*, Vol. 167, No. 1 (July), pp. 57–66.

Jolson, Marvin A., and Rossow, Gerald L., 1971, "The Delphi process in marketing decision making," *Journal of Marketing Research*, Vol. 8, No. 4 (November), pp. 443–448.

Jones, J. Philip, 1986, *What's in a Name*, Lexington Books, Lexington, Massachusetts, p. 268.

Kalish, Shlomo, and Lilien, Gary L., 1986, "A market entry timing model for new technologies," *Management Science*, Vol. 32, No. 2 (February), pp. 194–205.

Kalyanaram, G.; Robinson, W. T.; and Urban, Glen L., 1995, "Order of market entry: Established empirical generalizations, emerging empirical generalizations, and future research," *Marketing Science*, Vol. 14, No. 3, Part 2, pp. G212–G221.

Kamin, Howard, 1988, "Why not use single source measurements now?" *Journal of Media Planning*, Vol. 3, No. 1 (Spring), pp. 27–31.

Kaul, Anil, and Wittink, Dick R., 1995, "Empirical generalizations about the impact of advertising on price sensitivity and price," *Marketing Science*, Vol. 14, No. 2, Part 2, pp. G151–G160.

Keeney, Ralph L., and Raiffa, Howard, 1976, *Decisions with Multiple Objectives: Preferences and Value Tradeoffs*, John Wiley and Sons, New York.

Kotler, Philip, 1966, "A design for the firm's marketing nerve center," *Business Horizons*, Vol. 9, No. 3 (Fall), pp. 63–74.

Kotler, Philip, 1971, *Marketing Decision Making: A Model Building Approach*, Rinehart and Winston, New York.

Kotler, Philip, 1991, *Marketing Management: Analysis, Planning, Implementation, and Control*, seventh edition, Prentice Hall, Englewood Cliffs, New Jersey.

Kotler, Philip, 1994, *Marketing Management: Analysis, Planning, Implementation, and Control*, eighth edition, Prentice Hall, Englewood Cliffs, New Jersey, p. 424.

Kotler, Philip, 1997, *Marketing Management: Analysis, Planning, Implementation, and Control*, ninth edition, Prentice Hall, Englewood Cliffs, New Jersey, p. 284.

Krugman, Herbert E., 1972, "Why three exposures may be enough," *Journal of Advertising Research*, Vol. 12 (December), pp. 11–14.

Kuritsky, A. P.; Little, J. D. C.; Silk, A. J.; and Bassman, E. S., 1982, "The development, testing and execution of a new marketing strategy at AT&T long lines," *Interfaces*, Vol. 12, No. 6 (December), pp. 22–37.

Lambin, Jean-Jacques, 1976, *Advertising, Competition and Market Conduct in Oligopoly Over Time,* North Holland, Amsterdam.

Lambin, Jean-Jacques; Naert, Philippe; and Bultez, Alain, 1975, "Optimal marketing behavior in oligopoly," *European Economic Review*, Vol. 6, No. 2, pp. 105–128.

Lambkin, Mary V., and Day, George S., 1989, "Evolutionary processes in competitive markets: Beyond the product life cycle," *Journal of Marketing*, Vol. 53, No. 3 (July), pp. 4–20.

Lancaster, Kent M., and Martin, Thomas C., 1988, "Estimating audience duplication among consumer magazines," *Journal of Media Planning*, Vol. 3, No. 2 (Fall), pp. 22–28.

Larréché, Jean-Claude, and Montgomery, David B., 1977, " A framework for the comparison of marketing models: A Delphi study," *Journal of Marketing Research*, Vol. 14, No. 4 (November), pp. 487–498.

Lavidge, Robert J., and Steiner, Gary A., 1961, "A model for predictive measurement of advertising effectiveness," *Journal of Marketing*, Vol. 25, No. 6 (October), pp. 59–67.

Leavitt, Clark, 1962, "The application of perception psychology to marketing," in *Marketing Precision and Executive Action*, ed. Charles H. Hindersman, American Marketing Association, Chicago, pp. 430–437.

Leckenby, John D., and Ju, K-H., 1989, "Advances in media decision models," in *Current Issues and Research in Advertising*, Issue 2, eds. J. Leigh and C. Martin, University of Michigan, Division of Research, Ann Arbor, Michigan.

Lee, Donald D., 1978, *Industrial Marketing Research*, The Chemical Marketing Research Association, Technomic Publishing Co., Westport, Connecticut.

Leidner, Dorothy E., and Jarvenpaa, Sirkka L., 1995, "The use of information technology to enhance management school education: A theoretical view," *MIS Quarterly*, Vol. 19, No. 3, pp. 265–291.

Leone, Robert P., 1995, "Generalizing what is known about temporal aggregation and advertising carryover," *Marketing Science*, Vol. 14, No. 2, Part 2, pp. G141–G150.

Levitt, Theodore, 1960, "Marketing myopia," *Harvard Business Review*, Vol. 38, No. 4 (July–August), pp. 45–56.

Lieberman, Marvin B., and Montgomery, David B., 1980, "First mover advantages," *Strategic Management Journal*, Vol. 9, pp. 41–48.

Light, Larry, 1992, "Software even a CFO could love," *Business Week*, November 22, p. 132.

Lilien, Gary L., 1979, "ADVISOR 2: Modeling the marketing mix decision for industrial products," *Management Science*, Vol. 25, No. 2 (February), pp. 191–204.

Lilien, Gary L., 1993, *Marketing Management; Analytic Exercises for Spreadsheets*, Boyd and Fraser Publishing Company, Danvers, Massachusetts.

Lilien, Gary L., and Kotler, Philip, 1983, *Marketing Decision Making: A Model-Building Approach*, Harper and Row, New York.

Lilien, Gary L.; Kotler, Philip; and Moorthy, K. Sridhar, 1992, *Marketing Models*, Prentice Hall, Englewood Cliffs, New Jersey.

Lilien, Gary L., and Weinstein, David, 1984, "An international comparison of the determinants of industrial marketing expenditures," *Journal of Marketing*, Vol. 48 (Winter), pp. 46–53.

Lilien, Gary L., and Yoon, Eunsang, 1990, "The timing of competitive market entry: An exploratory study of new industrial products," *Management Science*, Vol. 36, No. 5 (May), pp. 568–585.

Little, John D. C., 1970, "Models and managers: The concept of a decision calculus," *Management Science*, Vol. 16, No. 8 (April), pp. B466–B485.

Little, John D. C., 1979, "Aggregate advertising models: The state of the art," *Operations Research*, Vol. 27, No. 4 (July–August), pp. 629–667.

Little, John D. C., and Lodish, Leonard M., 1966, "A media selection model and its optimization by dynamic programming," *Industrial Management Review*, Vol. 8 (Fall), pp. 15–23.

Lodish, Leonard M., 1971, "CALLPLAN: An interactive salesman's call planning system," *Management Science*, Vol. 18, No. 4, Part 2 (December), pp. 25–40.

Lodish, Leonard M., 1974, "'Vaguely right' approach to sales force allocations," *Harvard Business Review*, Vol. 52, No. 1 (January–February), pp. 119–124.

Lodish, Leonard M., 1986, *The Advertising and Promotion Challenge*, Oxford University Press, New York, p. 73.

Lodish, Leonard M.; Abraham, Magid; Kamenson, Stuard; Livelsberger, Jeanne; Lubetkin, Beth; Richardson, Bruce; and Stevens, Mary Ellen, 1995a, "How TV advertising works: A meta analysis of 389 real world split cable TV advertising experiments," *Journal of Marketing Research*, Vol. 32 (May), pp. 125–139.

Lodish, Leonard M.; Abraham, Magid; Livelsberger, Jeanne; Lubetkin, Beth; Richardson, Bruce; and Stevens, Mary Ellen, 1995b, "A summary of fifty five in-market estimates of the long term effect of advertising," *Marketing Science*, Vol. 14, No. 2, Part 2, pp. G133–G140.

Lodish, Leonard M.; Curtis, Ellen; Ness, Michael; and Simpson, M. Kerry, 1988, "Sales force sizing and deployment using a decision calculus model at Syntex Laboratories," *Interfaces*, Vol. 18, No. 1 (January–February), pp. 5–20.

Longman, Kenneth A., 1968, "Remarks on Gross' paper," *13th Annual Conference Proceedings*, Advertising Research Foundation, New York.

Luce, R. Duncan, 1959, *Individual Choice Behavior*, John Wiley and Sons, New York.

MacKay, David B., and Zinnes, Joseph L., 1996, "A probabilistic model for the multidimensional scaling of proximity and preference data," *Marketing Science*, Vol. 5, No. 4 (Fall), pp. 325–344.

Mahajan, Vijay; Muller, Eitan; and Bass, Frank M., 1993, "New-product diffusion models," in *Handbooks in Operations Research and Management Science, Vol. 5, Marketing*, eds. Jehoshua Eliashberg and Gary L. Lilien, Elsevier Science Publishers B.V., North Holland, New York, pp. 349–408.

Malhotra, Naresh K., 1993, *Marketing Research: An Applied Orientation*, Prentice Hall, Englewood Cliffs, New Jersey.

Maloney, John C., 1962, "Curiosity versus disbelief in advertising," *Journal of Advertising Research*, Vol. 23 (January), pp. 51–59.

Maloney, John C., 1963, "Copy testing: What course is it taking?" *9th Annual Conference Proceedings*, Advertising Research Foundation, New York.

Mansfield, Edwin, 1979, *Microeconomics: Theory and Applications*, Norton, New York.

Mantrala, Murali; Sinha, Prabhakant; and Zoltners, Andris, 1994, "Structuring a multiproduct sales quota-bonus plan," *Marketing Science*, Vol. 13, No. 2 (Spring), pp. 121–144.

Martino, Joseph P., 1983, *Technological Forecasting for Decision Making*, Elsevier, New York.

McCann, John M., 1974, "Market segment response to the marketing decision variables," *Journal of Marketing Research*, Vol. 11, No. 4 (November), pp. 399–412.

McCann, John M., and Gallagher, John P., 1990, *Expert Systems for Scanner Data Environments*, Elsevier Science Publishers B.V., North Holland, New York, p. 168.

McDonald, Colin, 1971, "What is the short term effect of advertising?" Special Report No. 71-142 (February), Marketing Science Institute, Cambridge, Massachusetts.

Mehrabian, Albert, 1982, *General Dimensions for a General Psychological Theory*, Oelgeschlager, Gunn and Hain, Cambridge, Massachusetts.

Meulman, J.; Heiser, Wilhelm; and Carroll, J. Douglas, 1986, *PREFMAP-3 User's Guide*, Bell Laboratories, Murray Hill, New Jersey 07974.

Milligan, Glenn W., and Cooper, Martha C., 1987, "Methodology review's clustering methods," *Applied Psychological Measurement*, Vol. 11, No. 4 (December), pp. 329–354.

Monroe, Kent B., 1990, *Pricing, Making Profitable Decisions*, second edition, McGraw-Hill, New York, p. 464.

Moore, William L., and Pessemier, Edgar A., 1993, *Product Planning and Management*, McGraw Hill, New York.

Morrison, Donald G., 1979, "Purchase intentions and purchase behavior," *Journal of Marketing*, Vol. 43, No. 2 (Spring), pp. 65–74.

Naples, M. J., 1979, *Effective Frequency*, Association of National Advertisers, New York.

Nash, John F., 1950, "The bargaining problem," *Econometrica*, Vol. 18 (April), pp. 155–162.

Nemhauser, G. L.; Kan, A. G. Rinooy; and Todd, M. J., eds., 1989, *Optimization*, North Holland, New York.

Neslin, Scott A., and Greenhalgh, Leonard, 1983, "Nash's theory of cooperative games as a predictor of the outcomes of buyer-seller negotiations: An experiment in media purchasing," *Journal of Marketing Research*, Vol. 30 (November), pp. 368–379.

Neslin, Scott A., and Greenhalgh, Leonard, 1986, "The ability of Nash's theory of cooperative games to predict the outcomes of buyer-seller negotiations: A dyad-level test," *Management Science*, Vol. 32, No. 4 (April), pp. 480–498.

Neslin, Scott A., and Stone, Linda G., 1996, "Consumer inventory sensitivity and the postpromotion dip," *Marketing Letters*, Vol. 7, No. 1 (January), pp. 77–94.

Ogilvy and Mather Research Department 1965, "An experimental study of the relative effectiveness of three television day parts," Authors, New York.

Parry, Mark E., and Bass, Frank M., 1990, "When to lead or to follow? It depends," *Marketing Letters*, Vol. 1, No. 3 (November), pp. 187–198.

Patti, Charles H., and Blasko, Vincent J., 1981, "Budgeting practices of big advertisers," *Journal of Advertising Research*, Vol. 21 (December), pp. 23–29.

Peppers, Don, and Rogers, Martha, 1993, *The One to One Future, Building Relationships One Customer at a Time*, Currency Doubleday, New York.

Petty, Richard E.; Cacioppo, John T.; and Schumann, David, 1983, "Central and peripheral routes to persuasion: The moderating role of involvement," *Journal of Consumer Research*, Vol. 10, No. 2, pp. 135–146.

Porter, Michael E., 1980, *Competitive Strategy: Techniques for Analyzing Industries and Competitors*, Macmillan, New York.

Powell, Stephen G., 1996, "From intelligent consumer to active modeler: Two MBA success stories," working paper, Amos Tuck School of Business Administration, Dartmouth College, Hanover, Vermont.

Ragsdale, Cliff T., 1995, *Spreadsheet Modeling and Decision Analysis*, Course Technology, New York.

Raiffa, Howard, 1968, *Decision Analysis, Introductory Lectures on Choices Under Uncertainty*, Addison-Wesley, Reading, Massachusetts.

Ramond, Charles, 1976, *Advertising Research: The State of the Art*, Association of National Advertisers, New York.

Rangaswamy, Arvind, 1993, "Marketing decision models: From linear programs to knowledge-based systems," *Handbooks in Operations Research and Management Science, Vol. 5, Marketing*, eds. Jehoshua Eliashberg and Gary L. Lilien, Elsevier Science Publishers B.V., North Holland, New York, pp. 733–771.

Rangaswamy, Arvind; Harlam, Bari A.; and Lodish, Leonard M., 1991, "INFER: An expert system for automatic analysis of scanner data," *International Journal of Research in Marketing*, Vol. 8, No. 1 (April), pp. 29–40.

Rangaswamy, Arvind, and Lilien, Gary L., 1997, "Software tools for new product development," *Journal of Marketing Research*, Vol. 34, No. 1 (February), pp. 177–184.

Rangaswamy, Arvind; Sinha, Prabhakant; and Zoltners, Andris, 1990, "An integrated model based approach for sales force restructuring," *Marketing Science*, Vol. 9, No. 4 (Fall), pp. 279–298.

Rao, Ambar G., 1978, "Productivity of the marketing mix: Measuring the impact of advertising and consumer and trade promotions on sales," paper presented at ANA Advertising Research Workshop, New York.

Rao, Ambar G., and Miller, P. B., 1975, "Advertising/sales response functions," *Journal of Advertising Research*, Vol. 15, No. 2 (April), pp. 7–15.

Rapoport, Anatol, 1966, *Two-Person Game Theory*, University of Michigan Press, Ann Arbor, Michigan.

Reibstein, David J., and Gatignon, Hubert, 1984, "Optimal product line pricing: the influence of elasticities and cross elasticities," *Journal of Marketing Research*, Vol. 21, No. 3 (August), pp. 259–267.

Reibstein, David J., and Traver, Phillis A., 1982, "Factors affecting coupon redemption rates," *Journal of Marketing*, Vol. 46 (Fall), pp. 102–113.

Reis, Al, and Trout, Jack, 1981, *Positioning: The Battle for Your Mind*, McGraw Hill, New York.

Rice, Marshall D., 1988, "Estimating the reach and frequency of mixed media advertising schedules," *Journal of the Market Research Society*, Vol. 30, No. 4 (October), pp. 439–451.

Rink, David R., and Swan, John E., 1979, "Product life cycle research: A literature review," *Journal of Business Research*, Vol. 7, No. 3 (September), pp. 219–242.

Roberts, John H., and Lilien, Gary L., 1993, "Explanatory and predictive models of consumer behavior," in *Handbooks in Operations Research and Management Science, Vol. 5, Marketing*, eds. Jehoshua Eliashberg and Gary L. Lilien, Elsevier Science Publishers B.V., North Holland, New York, pp. 27–82.

Robertson, Tom S., and Barich, Howard, 1992, "A successful approach to segmenting industrial markets," *Planning Review*, Vol. 20, No. 6 (November–December), pp. 4–11, 48.

Robinson, William T., and Fornell, Claes, 1985, "The sources of market pioneer advantages in consumer goods industries," *Journal of Marketing Research*, Vol. 22, No. 3 (August), pp. 305–317.

Rossiter, John R., 1982, "Visual imagery: Applications to advertising," in *Advances in Consumer Research*, Vol. 9, ed. Andrew A. Mitchell, Association for Consumer Research, Provo, Utah, pp. 101–106.

Rossiter, John R., and Percy, Larry, 1987, *Advertising and Promotion Management*, McGraw-Hill, New York.

Roth, Alvin E., 1979, "Axiomatic models of bargaining," *Lecture Notes in Economics and Mathematical Systems*, 170, Springer-Verlag, New York.

Rubinstein, Ariel, 1991, "Comments on the interpretation of game theory," *Econometrica*, Vol. 59, No. 4 (July), pp. 909–924.

Runyon, Kenneth E., 1984, *Advertising*, second edition, Charles E. Merrill Publishing, Columbus, Ohio.

Russo, J. Edward, and Schoemaker, Paul J. H., 1989, *Decision Traps*, Doubleday and Company, New York.

Rust, Roland T., 1986, *Advertising Media Models: A Practical Guide*, Lexington Books, Lexington, Massachusetts.

Rust, Roland T.; Zimmer, Mary R.; and Leone, Robert P., 1986, "Estimating the duplicated audiences of media vehicles in national advertising schedules," *Journal of Advertising*, Vol. 15, No. 3, pp. 30–37.

Saaty, Thomas L., and Vargas, Luis G., 1994, *Decision Making in Economic, Political, Social and Technological Environments with the Analytical Hierarchy Process*, RWS Publications, Pittsburgh, Pennsylvania.

Saunders, John, 1987, "The specification of aggregate market models," *European Journal of Marketing*, Vol. 21, No. 2, pp. 1–47.

Scherer, Frederic M., 1980, *Industrial Market Structure and Economic Performance*, second edition, Rand McNally, Skokie, Illinois.

Schmitz, John, 1994, "Expert systems for scanner data in practice," in *The Marketing Information Revolution*, eds. Robert C. Blattberg, Rashi Glazer, and John D. C. Little, Harvard Business School Press, Boston, pp. 102–119.

Schmitz, John D.; Armstrong, Gordon D.; and Little, John D. C., 1990, "CoverStory: Automated news finding in marketing," in *DSS Transactions*, ed. Linda Bolino, TIMS College on Information Systems, Providence, Rhode Island, pp. 46–54.

Seligman, Daniel, 1956, "How much for advertising?" *Fortune* (December), pp. 120–126.

Senge, Peter M., and Lannon, Colleen, 1990, "Managerial microworlds; computer simulation to facilitate decision making," *Massachusetts Institute of Technology Alumni Association Technology Review*, Vol. 93, No. 5 (July), pp. 62–68.

Sewall, Murphy A., and Sarel, Dan, 1986, "Characteristics of radio commercials and their recall effectiveness," *Journal of Marketing*, Vol. 50, No. 1 (January), pp. 52–60.

Shapiro, Arthur, 1976, "Promotional effectiveness at H. J. Heinz," *Interfaces*, Vol. 6, No. 2 (February 1976), pp. 84–86.

Shocker, Allan D., and Hall, William G., 1986, "Pretest market-models: A critical evaluation," *Journal of Product Innovation*, Vol. 3, No. 2 (June), pp. 86–107.

Siemer, R. H., 1989, "Using perceptual mapping for market-entry decisions," *3rd Proceedings of the Sawtooth Software Conference on Gaining a Competitive Advantage Through PC-Based Interviewing and Analysis*, Sawtooth Software, Sun Valley, Idaho, pp. 107–114.

Silk, Alvin J., and Urban, Glen L., 1978, "Pre-test market evaluation of new packaged goods: A model and measurement methodology," *Journal of Marketing Research*, Vol. 15, No. 2 (May), pp. 171–191.

Simon, Herbert A., 1977, *The New Science of Management Decision*, Prentice Hall, Englewood Cliffs, New Jersey.

Simon, Hermann, 1989, *Price Management*, North Holland, New York.

Simon, Hermann, and Thiel, Michael H., 1980, "Hits and flops among German media models," *Journal of Advertising Research*, Vol. 20, No. 6, pp. 25–29.

Singer, Eugene M., 1968, *Antitrust Economics: Selected Legal Cases and Economic Models*, Prentice Hall, Englewood Cliffs, New Jersey.

Smith, Barry C.; Leimkuhler, John F.; and Darrow, Ross M., 1992, "Yield management at American Airlines," *Interfaces*, Vol. 22, No. 1 (January–February), pp. 8–31.

Starch, Daniel, 1966, *Measuring Advertising Readership and Results,* McGraw-Hill, New York.

Stern, Louis; El-Ansary, Adel; and Coughlan, Anne, 1996, *Marketing Channels*, fourth edition, Prentice Hall, Englewood Cliffs, New Jersey.

Stewart, David W., and Furse, David H., 1986, *Effective Television Advertising: A Study of 1000 Commercials*, Lexington Books, Lexington, Massachusetts.

Stewart, M., 1990, "Was STAT scan really an advance on AMTES?" *ADMAP*, Vol. 26 (April), pp. 32–35.

Sudharshan, Devanathan, 1995, *Marketing Strategy: Relationships, Offerings, Timing and Resource Allocation*, Prentice Hall, Englewood Cliffs, New Jersey.

Sultan, Fareena; Farley, John U.; and Lehmann, Donald R., 1990, "A meta-analysis of applications of diffusion models," *Journal of Marketing Research*, Vol. 27, No. 1 (February), pp. 70–77.

Tayman, Jeff, and Pol, Louis, 1995, "Retail site selection and geographic information systems," *Journal of Applied Business Research*, Vol. 11, No. 2 (Spring), pp. 46–54.

Tellis, Gerard J., and Zufryden, Fred S., 1995, "Tackling the retailer decision maze: Which brands to discount, how much, when and why?" *Marketing Science*, Vol. 14, No. 3, Part 1, pp. 271–299.

Thietart, R. A., and Vivas, R., 1984, "An empirical investigation of success strategies for businesses along the product life cycle," *Management Science*, Vol. 32, No. 6 (June), pp. 645–659.

Thomas, Charles M., and Keebler, Jack, 1994, "Focus shifts from electric to hybrid," *Automotive News* (January 17), pp. 3, 41.

Thomas, Robert J., 1985, "Estimating market growth for new products: An analogical diffusion model approach," *Journal of Product Innovation Management*, Vol. 2, No. 1 (March), pp. 45–55.

Thorelli, Hand, and Burnett, Stephen C., 1981, "The nature of product life cycles for industrial goods businesses," *Journal of Marketing*, Vol. 45, No. 4 (Fall), pp. 97–108.

Trodahl, Verling C., and Jones, Robert L., 1965, "Prediction of newspaper advertisement readership," *Journal of Advertising Research*, Vol. 5 (March), pp. 23–27.

Twedt, Dik W., 1952, "A multiple factor analysis of advertising readership," *Journal of Applied Psychology*, Vol. 36, No. 3 (June), pp. 207–215.

Ulvila, Jacob W., and Brown, Rex V., 1982, "Decision analysis comes of age," *Harvard Business Review*, Vol. 60 (September–October), pp. 130–141.

Urban, Glen L., 1993, "Pretest market forecasting," in *Handbooks in Operations Research and Management Science, Vol. 5, Marketing*, eds. Jehoshua Eliashberg and Gary L. Lilien, Elsevier Science Publishers B.V., North Holland, New York, pp. 315–348.

Urban, Glen L.; Carter, Theresa; Gaskin, Steve; and Mucha, Zofia, 1986, "Market share rewards to pioneering brands: An empirical analysis and strategic implications," *Management Science*, Vol. 32, No. 6, pp. 645–659.

Urban, Glen L., and Hauser, John R., 1980, *Design and Marketing of New Products*, Prentice Hall, Englewood Cliffs, New Jersey.

Urban, Glen L., and Hauser, John R., 1993, *Design and Marketing of New Products*, second edition, Prentice Hall, Englewood Cliffs, New Jersey.

Urban, Glen L., and Katz, Gerald M., 1983, "Pre-test market models: Validation and managerial implications," *Journal of Marketing Research*, Vol. 20, No. 3 (August), pp. 221–234.

Urban, Glen L., and Star, Steven H., 1991, *Advanced Marketing Strategy: Phenomena, Analysis, and Decisions*, Prentice Hall, Englewood Cliffs, New Jersey.

van Bruggen, Gerrit H.; Smidts, Ale; and Wierenga, Berend, 1997, "Improving decision making by means of a marketing decision support system," working paper, Erasmus University, Rotterdam, The Netherlands. (Forthcoming: *Management Science*.)

Vandenbosch, Mark B., and Weinberg, Charles B., 1993, "Salesforce operations," in *Handbooks in Operations Research and Management Science, Vol. 5, Marketing*, eds. Jehoshua Eliashberg and Gary Lilien, Elsevier Science Publishers B.V., North Holland, New York, pp. 653–694

Vidale, H. L., and Wolfe, H. B., 1957, "An operations research study of sales response to advertising," *Operational Research Quarterly*, Vol. 5, pp. 370–381.

Wall Street Journal, April 1, 1996, p. 1.

Wall Street Journal, November 18, 1996.

Ward, J., 1963, "Hierarchical grouping to optimize an objective function," *Journal of the American Statistical Association*, Vol. 58, pp. 236–244.

Wells, William D., 1981, "How advertising works," working paper, Needham, Harper and Steers Advertising, Chicago.

Wells, William D.; Leavitt, Clark; and McConnell, Maureen, 1971, "A reaction profile for TV commercials," *Journal of Advertising Research*, Vol. 11, No. 2 (December), pp. 11–17.

Wenzel, Wilfred, and Speetzen, Rolf, 1987, "How much frequency is enough?" *Journal of Media Planning*, Vol. 2, No. 1, pp. 5–16.

Whitaker, Richard, 1995, "Make believe airline," *Airline Business*, Vol. 11, No. 4 (April), pp. 46–49.

Wierenga, Berend, and van Bruggen, Gerrit H., 1997, "Integration of marketing problem-solving modes and marketing management support systems," *Journal of Marketing*, Vol. 6, No. 3 (July).

Wilson, Elizabeth. J.; Lilien, Gary L.; and Wilson, David T., 1991, "Developing and testing a contingency paradigm of group choice in organizational buying," *Journal of Marketing Research*, Vol. 28, No. 4 (November), pp. 39–48.

Wind, Jerry; Green, Paul E.; Shifflet, Douglas; and Scarbrough, Marsha, 1989, "Courtyard by Marriott: Designing a hotel facility with consumer-based marketing models," *Interfaces*, Vol. 19, No. 1 (January–February), pp. 25–47.

Wind, Yoram J., 1978, "Issues and advances in segmentation research," *Journal of Marketing Research*, Vol. 15, No. 3 (August), pp. 317–337.

Wind, Yoram J., 1981, "Marketing-oriented strategic planning models," in *Marketing Decision Models*, eds. R. Schultz and A. Zoltners, North Holland, New York, pp. 207–250.

Wind, Yoram J., 1982, *Product Policy: Concepts, Methods, and Strategy*, Addison-Wesley Publishing Company, Reading, Massachusetts.

Wind, Yoram J., and Claycamp, Henry, 1976, "Planning product line strategy: A matrix approach," *Journal of Marketing*, Vol. 40, No. 1 (January), pp. 2–9.

Wind, Yoram J., and Lilien, Gary L., 1993, "Interaction, strategy and synergy", in *Handbooks in Operations Research and Management Science, Vol. 5, Marketing*, eds. Jehoshua Eliashberg and Gary L. Lilien, Elsevier Science Publishers B.V., North Holland, New York, pp. 773–820.

Wind, Yoram J., and Robertson, Thomas S., 1983, "Marketing strategy: New directions for theory and research," *Journal of Marketing*, Vol. 47, No. 2 (Spring), pp. 12–25.

Wittink, Dick R., and Cattin, Philippe, 1989, "Commercial use of conjoint analysis: An update," *Journal of Marketing*, Vol. 53, No. 3 (July), pp. 91–106.

Wittink, Dick R.; Krishnamurthi, Lakshman; and Nutter, Julia B., 1982, "Comparing derived importance weights across attributes," *Journal of Consumer Research*, Vol. 8, No. 4 (March), pp. 471–474.

Wolfe, H. B.; Brown, Joel. R.; and Thompson, G. C., 1962, "Measuring advertising results, studies in business policy," The Conference Board, New York, No. 102, pp. 62–68.

Wyner, Gordon A., and Owen, Hilary, 1994, "What's your position?" *Marketing Research*, Vol. 6, No. 1 (Winter), pp. 54–56.

Yamanaka, Jiro, 1962, "The prediction of ad readership scores," *Journal of Advertising Research*, Vol. 2, No. 1 (March), pp. 18–23.

Yelle, Louis E., 1979, "The learning curve: Historic review and comprehensive survey," *Decision Sciences*, Vol. 10, No. 2 (April), pp. 302–327.

Yoon, Eunsang, and Lilien, Gary L., 1985, "New industrial product performance: The impact of market characteristics and strategy," *Product Innovation Management*, Vol. 2 (September), pp. 134–144.

Young, Jeffrey, 1995, "Can computers really boost sales?" *Forbes* (August 28), pp. 84–98.

Young and Rubicam 1988, *Non Verbal Communication in Advertising*, eds. Sidney Hecker and David W. Stewart, Lexington Books, Lexington, Massachusetts.

Yurkiewicz, Jack, 1996, "Forecasting software survey," *OR/MS Today* (December), pp. 70–75.

Zahavi, Jacob, 1995, "Franklin Mint's famous AMOS," *OR/MS Today*, Vol. 22, No. 5 (October), pp. 18–23.

Zangwill, Willard I., 1993, *Lightning Strategies for Innovation*, Lexington Books, New York.

Zielski, Hubert A., 1959, "The remembering and forgetting of advertising," *Journal of Marketing*, Vol. 23, No. 3 (January), pp. 239–243.

Zoltners, Andris A., and Sinha, Prabhakant, 1983, "Sales territory alignment: A review and model," *Management Science*, Vol. 29, No. 11 (November), pp. 1237–1256.

Index

Name Index